Gilbert Elliott of Elizabeth City, N.C.,
circa 1860-1861

IRONCLAD OF THE ROANOKE
Gilbert Elliott's *Albemarle*

by

Robert G. Elliott

White Mane Publishing Co., Inc.

This White Mane Publishing Company, Inc. publication
was printed by
Beidel Printing House, Inc.
63 West Burd Street
Shippensburg, PA 17257

In respect for the scholarship contained herein, the acid-free paper used in this book meets the guidelines for permanence and durability of the Committee on Production Guidelines for Book Longevity of the Council on Library Resources.

For a complete listing of available publications please write

White Mane Publishing Company, Inc.
P.O. Box 152
Shippensburg, PA 17257

Library of Congress Cataloging-in-Publication Data

Elliott, Robert Garrison.
    Ironclad of the Roanoke : Gilbert Elliott's Albemarle / by Robert
G. Elliott.
        p.   cm.
    Includes bibliographical references (p.) and index.
    ISBN 0-942597-63-X : $29.95
    1. Albemarle (Confederate Ironclad) 2. Albemarle Sound (N.C.)-
-History, Naval. I. Title.
    E599.A4E45 1994
    973.7'57--dc20
                                                        94-11747
                                                        CIP

CONTENTS

LIST OF ILLUSTRATIONS

PREFACE

How many of those who have known that Gilbert Elliott built the *Albemarle* have known of his background? Few have been certain where his birth place was, and even fewer have been aware of his shipbuilding activities prior to the prominence he attained from building the *Albemarle*.

The *Albemarle* was not his first shipbuilding venture, nor was she his last. Historians credit Gilbert Elliott for the *Albemarle* achievement, but is it generally known his shipbuilding career lasted only from mid-1861 until April 1865?

He was born in Elizabeth City, North Carolina, about seventeen years before the War Between the States began. As was true of so many other young men in waterfront towns throughout the land, North and South, his ancestors were shipbuilders. From Colonial days shipbuilders had launched vessels for trade, pleasure, sport and warfare. Elliott's early experience in ship construction was with trading vessels, but in the fall of 1861 necessity channelled his talents towards the building of defensive naval craft.

Gilbert Elliott's genealogical background was relatively easy to document (See Appendix I). Scattered pieces of correspondence originating in 1861 were sufficient to establish the birth of his teenage shipbuilding career. It lasted three years and eight months.

With the Atlantic Blockading Squadron stationed at strategic locations along the Confederate States shores, the Confederate Navy Department directed great attention to harbor and river defenses. Unlike today, when charted river and coastal water ways are considered navigable, successful river travel then was directly related to the absence of exposed sand bars created by seasonal low water levels.

The Confederate Navy revealed its defensive policy when construction plans for a large fleet of shallow-draft gunboats and ironclads were approved. Elliott has been remembered for having been the builder of a shallow-draft ironclad on the upper Roanoke River.

General features of the *Albemarle* have long been known. Basic information was made public by Elliott himself in July 1888, when the Century Magazine published his brief sketch describing her construction as well as her first battle when he served as volunteer assistant to Commander Cooke.

In this book I have endeavored to identify Gilbert Elliott, while providing substantive reasons why the Confederate Navy Department contracted for his shipbuilding talents. A natural progression of events led to his *Albemarle* contract. Borrowing Elliott's early quotation, "No vessel was ever constructed under more adverse circumstances."

From letters, reports, materiel vouchers, official Navy and Army correspondence, family histories, newspapers, public records, etc., have been chronologically assembled events relating to the *Albemarle's* construction, launch, completion, and subsequent battles. It is the true story of her birth, life, and death.

Extracted from the medley of documentation, an incomplete 1864 second quarter crew roster has been developed. No doubt other crewmen will become identified as additional records are brought to public view (See Appendix II). A crew roster for the third quarter 1864 was published in the Official Records of the Union and Confederate Navies in the War of the Rebellion (See Appendix III).

It seemed appropriate to compose a roll of craftsmen and general workers. Their identities have been tabulated according to skills. By no means complete, the roll provides insight as to the diversity of talent assembled to build the vessel (See Appendix IV). In time, perhaps other names may be added to this recognition roster.

An effort was made to obtain given names of all individuals. In several instances where credible reference was unavailable, given names have been expressed by initial only. In several cases only surnames were found.

This book was written to honor the thousands of boatmen who labored under severe odds to construct, sail, and fight their ships in defense of their cause. Their zeal was sustained by devotion to their families, homes, and soil, and to the principles of freedom.

Built under trying circumstances, the *Albemarle* steamed into battle under Commander James W. Cooke's canny skill. Her first engagement with the *Southfield* and *Miami* at Plymouth was an uncontested victory. After Cooke encountered the Union flotilla on May 5, 1864, he discovered he was outnumbered seven to one.

Many have expressed opinions that he emerged victorious because his vessel was still afloat and under her own power, as she steamed towards the Roanoke's safe haven. She performed as Cooke expected, and despite deficiences known only to those on board she was ready for further engagement, when her severely injured opponents disengaged and ceased firing. *R.G.E.*

ACKNOWLEDGEMENTS

The name C.S. ram *Albemarle* has been recognized by students of Confederate Naval History, in particular by residents of eastern North Carolina, as having brought honor to her builder; to her captain and crew; to the State of North Carolina; and to the Confederate Navy Department. She wreaked such havoc upon the U.S. Naval forces in Albemarle Sound that the Atlantic Blockading Squadron literally concentrated all efforts towards her destruction.

When I began to research the *Albemarle* and her builder Gilbert Elliott, it quickly became apparent that everyone I talked with could offer a piece of information. Some proved to be fact, and some remained fancy. It was soon clear that the abundance of clues would require exploration. Individuals offering information were encouraged to recall where and when he or she first learned of it. And yet, there emerged no complete story of the *Albemarle* ... anywhere!

Were it not for the following team of gracious, generous, and willing contributors it would have been impossible to create the *Albemarle* story: a story which may change tomorrow as new information is discovered. I respectfully say Thank You to all who have so generously contributed pieces of the puzzle. Because of information diversity from various sources, I have elected to categorize the credits. Though all contributors' records have been diligently reviewed, I offer apologies to anyone I have inadvertently omitted.

Development of Gilbert Elliott's pre-*Albemarle* shipbuilding career was vital. My deepest gratitude is extended to Dr. Charles V. Peery, of Charleston, South Carolina, for generously offering access to his 1861-1862 correspondence collection to and from Gilbert Elliott and his shipbuilding associates.

My profound thanks are offered to the Confederate Naval Museum Director Robert "Bob" Holcombe, at Columbus, Georgia, for always being "aboard ship." Repeated requests for information, definitions, and suggestions were always met with a cheery and rapid response.

To a North Carolina friend, Whitmel Joyner of New Hill, I offer my sincere thanks. Whit responded willingly to various questions from time to time, and often supplemented his enclosures with additional data and advice he knew I could use.

The stalwart support extended by these gentlemen, and their belief in the project, provided the zest to pursue searching for the puzzle pieces. Because all information sources were equally important in completing the manuscript, their order of presentation does not diminish their degree of value. To each of the following contributors I extend my sincere thanks.

Mary Burton Anderson, family records, St. Louis, Mo.; Kurt W. Annaheim, computer services, Daytona Beach, Fl.; Vernon T. Bradley, permission to inspect Halifax Yard property, Halifax, N.C.; Peggy Jo Braswell, local historian, Halifax, N.C.; Donald L. Canney, naval researcher, Bowie, Md.; George G. Carey, IV, diary and photograph, Cincinnati, Oh.; Shelby A. Daniels, local history, Charlotte, N.C.; Gilbert Elliott, VI, photograph, Bloomfield, N.J.; John Page Elliott, family history, Charlottesville, Va.; Jim Enos, photographic service, Carlisle, Pa.; Allan Flanders, recommendations, Newport News, Va.; Shelby Foote, use permission, Memphis, Tn.; William W. Forehand, county historian, Shiloh, N.C.; David B. Gammon, family history, Raleigh, N.C.; Dorothy (Mrs. Lewis) Gregory, family history, Winterville, N.C.; William A. Griffin, Elizabeth City history, Elizabeth City, N.C.; Dr. Carolyn Hampton, recommendations, Greenville, N.C.; Mrs. Frances D. Harding, family history, Alexandria, Va.; John M. Hilliard, photographs, Bronx, N.Y.; Chuck Israel, researcher, Carrboro, N.C.; Marine Lt. Col. Donald Jilliskey, photo escort, Norfolk Naval Base, Va.; John M. Kelley, local history, Weldon, N.C.; Joseph C. Leary, micro reel research, Washington, N.C.; William R. McGrath, dust jacket artwork, Cleveland, Oh.; Maurice Melton, recommendations, La Grange, Ga.; Jaquelin D. (Mrs. Pembrooke) Nash, history of select Calvary Church furniture, Tarboro, N.C.; Mrs. Coralee Paull, genealogical research, St. Louis, Mo.; Sally (Mrs. Mark) Pemberton, computer tutoring, Deland, Fl.; James E. Poole, dust jacket artwork, Ormond Beach, Fl.; Claiborne T. Smith, Jr., M.D., family history, Ardmore, Pa.; Dr. William N. Still, project support, East Carolina University, Greenville, N.C.; Harry Thompson, local history, Windsor, N.C.; Dr. William K. Wassink, owner/resident of Milford, Camden, N.C.; Mrs. William B. Wingo, genealogist, Norfolk, Va.

Those at Historical Societies

Brooklyn Historical Society, Brooklyn, N.Y.; Confederate Naval Historical Society, John Townley, Director, White Stone, Va.; Martin County Historical Society, Doris L. Wilson, Williamston, N.C.; Missouri Historical Society, St Louis, Mo.; New York Historical Society,Diana Arecco, New York, N.Y.; Staten Island Historical Society, Staten Island, N.Y.

Those at Museums and Archives

American Museum-Hayden Planetarium, Suzanne Chippindale, Astronomical Writer/Producer, New York, N.Y.; G.A.R., Post 10, Memorial Hall, Mrs. Jean Bonnin, City Hall, Worcester, Ma.; Hampton Roads Naval Museum, Joseph M. Judge, Curator, Norfolk Naval Base, Va.; Mariner's Museum Library, Tom Crew, Archivist, Newport News, Va.; Museum of the Albemarle, Raymond Sheely, Elizabeth City, N.C.; Museum of the Confederacy, Corrine P. Hudgins, photographs, Richmond, Va.; North Carolina Division of Archives & History: Jesse R. Lankford, Jr., Ass't State Archivist; Stephen E. Massengill, Iconographic Archivist; James O. Sorrell, Registrar, Raleigh, N.C.; Port O'Plymouth Roanoke River Museum, Patricia Monte, Director, Plymouth, N.C.; Portsmouth Naval Shipyard Museum, Alice Haines, Director, Portsmouth, Va.

Those at Libraries

Halifax County Library, Martha Holloman, former Librarian, and Betsy H. Hudgins, researcher, Halifax, N.C.; Joyner Library, Mary Boccaccio, Curator, Archives & Manuscript Collection, East Carolina University, Greenville, N.C.; Manhattan Hall of Records, New York, N.Y.; New York City Public Library, Research Section, New York, N.Y.; Pasquotank-Camden Library, Becky Callison, Librarian, Elizabeth City, N.C.; Sargeant Memorial Room, Peggy A. Haile, Norfolk Public Library, Norfolk, Va.; Scotland Neck Library, Martha Leach, Librarian, Scotland Neck, N.C.; Southern Historical Collection, University of North Carolina, Chapel Hill, N.C.; Stetson University Library, Deland. Fl.; Wilson Library, John White, University of North Carolina, Chapel Hill, N.C.

Those with Publishers

Historical Publications Section, Division of N.C. Archives & History, Jeffrey L. Crow, Administrator, Raleigh, N.C.; Stackpole Books, Judith M. Schnell, Harrisburg, Pa.; University of North Carolina Press, Kathy Shaer, Chapel Hill, N.C.; University of Virginia Press, Carol M. Rossi, Charlottesville, Va.

Those with Government Agencies

National Archives, Robert Richardson, Cartographic & Architectural Branch; National Archives, Milton Gustafson, Head, Civil Reference Branch; National Archives, Barry Zerby, Military References Branch; National Archives, Dale Connally & Gary Stern, Still Pictures Branch; Norfolk Navy Yard, Joseph Law, P.A.O., Portsmouth, Va.; Smithsonian Institution, Harold D. Langley, Curator of Naval History, Division of Armed Forces History, National Museum of American History; Suitland Federal Records Center, Greg Dradsher, Suitland, Md.; U.S. Army Military History Institute, Michael Winey, Carlisle, Pa.; U.S. Coast Guard, Kevin Foster, Washington, D.C.; U.S. Naval Institute, Linda Cullen, Annapolis, Md.; U.S. Navy Memorial Museum, Dr. William S. Dudley, Senior Historian, Charles Haberlein, Ed Finney, Washington, D.C.; Washington Navy Yard, Mrs. Margaret B. Wadsworth, Historian, Ship's History Branch, Washington, D.C.

CHAPTER 1

BAPTISM OF FIRE

The thunderous blast of a 100-pounder Parrott in Fort Grey at Warren's Neck broke the pre-dawn silence as it belched forth solid shot on Tuesday morning April 19, 1864. On the south side of the Roanoke River opposite Tabor Island about $1^1/2$ miles above Plymouth, North Carolina, the fort guarded upriver approaches to Plymouth. When the reverberations and echoes faded, they were replaced with a staccato 'snapping and crackling' of small arms fire, until the illusionary target disappeared in the mists.

An observer about three-thirty that morning would have been left with an impression the gunners at Fort Grey were practicing their craft by firing into the swirls of fog rising from deep shadows beneath trees bordering the Roanoke's north bank. Their real target though was a ghostly apparition of dark iron floating down river with the current.

River obstructions in the form of sunken hulls, torpedoes, and piles blocked the channel from a point above Fort Grey to another location about a mile downstream. Lt. Commander Charles W. Flusser, Senior U.S. Naval Officer at Plymouth, had ordered the obstructions placed. He believed they would impede or prevent passage of the long awaited iron monster, but he failed to recognize that recent spring freshets had raised the river's level.

Commander James W. Cooke, C.S.N., and his crew aboard the vessel had avoided disaster by floating safely over obstructions upriver from Fort Grey, and had sustained no damage from the fort's battery. Wisps of steam and smoke puffed from the vessel's tall funnel, but not a light was visible. Smoke alone disclosed that men were inside. Through the swirls of fog obscuring the ship, one could have caught glimpses of the Confederate States' Second National Flag, known as the 'Stainless Banner'. It waved from the peak of a staff atop the casemate, aft of the funnel. The gunners were firing at the Confederate ironclad *Albemarle*, but their shot and shell were ineffective.

Recalling the occasion in later life, Gilbert Elliott had observed,

> Protected by the ironclad shield, to those on board[,]
> the noise made by the shot and shell as they struck the
> boat sounded no louder than pebbles thrown against an
> empty barrel.[1]

Without answering fire from Fort Grey, the *Albemarle* continued to drift slowly with the current, though minimum speed was
maintained to provide steerageway. At the east end of Tallow (or
Tabor) Island, nearly midway between Fort Grey and Welch's Creek,
there was another barricade across the Roanoke constructed of debris similar to that used above Fort Grey. About a mile further
downriver was Battery Worth. The battery was adjacent to an entrenched Union camp situated on the river bank at Plymouth's western boundary. A 200-pounder Parrott was mounted there. Perhaps
because the *Albemarle* had not been detected the battery did not
open fire as she steamed by, though Cooke said later in his report
"the river is only 200 yards wide at that point."[2]

From his forward vantage point beside the helmsman's elevated
cupola, Cooke navigated the silent-running *Albemarle* down the
Roanoke with the tender *Cotton Plant* close behind. Obviously
though, when passing the shore batteries, Cooke went below to safety
within the ironclad's casemate.

Once past Battery Worth, Plymouth lay before him on the starboard. Lookouts were promptly posted, one topside the casemate, and
another forward on the main deck. In the East the sky's color announced
a hint of dawn as the *Albemarle* steamed slowly and quietly ahead,
holding to the river's north side and taking advantage of the shadows.

Ever aware of the *Albemarle's* stealthy approach, Flusser developed his defensive strategy. The *Albemarle's* anticipated arrival time
had been forecast since Sunday, April 17, when Flusser ordered early
warning lookouts posted upriver. Accordingly, the U.S.S. *Whitehead* was
assigned guard duty just below the uppermost obstructions. At 2:00
P.M. on the seventeenth Acting Ensign George W. Barrett, commanding the *Whitehead*, accepted Flusser's orders to relieve the U.S.S. *Ceres,*
which had been temporarily on station for brief periods. As the
Whitehead anchored in a strategic position at Hyman's Ferry, with an
unchallenged view upriver as far as the next bend, the *Ceres* retrieved
her anchor and headed downstream. By 6:10 P.M. the *Ceres* had returned bearing the message from Flusser that "sharp lookouts be detailed." The *Ceres* had departed again for Plymouth by 8:00 P.M. on
April 17.

At 8:10 P.M. on the eighteenth, lights of two steamers were sighted moving slowly around the river's bend above the barricade. Barrett immediately issued orders to slip the cable, the boatswain piped "to quarters," and the *Whitehead* crossed to the river's north side and steamed downstream.

Complying with orders, Barrett had a rocket fired to warn Flusser's observers of the approaching enemy. Moments later it flared across the dark sky. Cooke mistakenly thought the rocket was from Brig. General Robert F. Hoke's Confederate pickets upriver from Fort Grey, so he ordered a responding flare to be fired. Alerted by Cooke's flare, a Confederate battery commanding the river just west of Fort Grey interrupted the *Whitehead's* safe passage downriver.

Barrett's only chance to escape being fired upon by the approaching enemy, and of avoiding an exchange of fire with the Confederate battery, was to pass through a very narrow and crooked natural sluice connecting the Roanoke and Cashie rivers. On maps of the Roanoke it was called Ryan's Thoroughfare, but locals knew it as Upper Thoroughfare.

About eight that same evening Flusser wrote two reports while aboard his flagship *Miami*. The first was to Commander Henry K. Davenport, Senior Officer, Sounds of North Carolina.

> The ram will be down tonight or tomorrow. She was, just after daylight this morning, foul of a tree 6 miles above Williamston. I think, if she does not stay under cover of their battery established above Fort Grey, that we shall whip her. I had to destroy the obstruction in the Thoroughfare, as the *Whitehead* was above and could not run by the battery placed below her on the Roanoke.[3]

Rear Admiral Samuel P. Lee, Commanding the North Atlantic Blockading Squadron off Newport News, Virginia, received a variation of the first message. Repeating only his estimate of when the *Albemarle* would arrive, Flusser expressed concern for the town's protection and that his former plan of fighting the ram with his ship lashed to the *Southfield* was abandonded. He closed by saying that he had given 100 projectiles to Fort Grey that day for their Parrott 100-pounder rifle.[4]

Later in the night of April 18, strong currents swept the *Whitehead* against the bank where she grounded. Barrett ordered a bow line fastened to the opposite bank, and by winching slowly the bow swung into the channel, but her stern was still mired. Tension was great for both Barrett and his crew. The approaching enemy vessels were very close, and unless his ship could break free of the bank the *Whitehead* could be subjected to heavy fire from the ironclad. With engines "All ahead, full," she finally moved off the bank and surged ahead towards a pile blockade some fifty yards further. It was Barrett's intention to force his way through the piles to evade discovery by the ironclad, but when he tried to do so the *Whitehead* stuck fast.

All engines were immediately stopped. Perfect silence was ordered as the *Albemarle* steamed past the sluice without seeing the enemy gunboat. With the ironclad below the sluice, Barrett forced the *Whitehead* through the piles, but in so doing wrenched off the shoe which kept the rudder's heel and iron sternpost in place. By 12:30 A.M. on the nineteenth, he was anchored at Plymouth reporting to Flusser.

About 3:15 A.M. on the nineteenth the *Ceres,* which had been coaling alongside the Plymouth wharf, arrived with news that the enemy was coming. Aboard the *Miami,* Flusser signalled the *Southfield* to again be lashed to the *Miami.* Both ships were then at the picket station below Plymouth. Before all hawsers were secured, Flusser signalled an order to steam towards the ironclad. The point of their encounter would be about one mile below Plymouth off the Roanoke's south bank. About 3:35 A.M. an almost full moon was setting.[5]

When Cooke realized he was abreast of Plymouth where the river ran straight for a short distance, he ordered all gun-port shutters opened. A levered exterior-mounted chain device, operated from inside the casemate, allowed gun crews to swing the iron-covered shutters down to one side.

Forward and stern roller-mounted 6.4-inch Brooke rifle carriages were fastened upon center-pivoted carriages, which allowed gun muzzles to be rotated through 180° to any one of their three ports without undue delay and effort. Rollers of the pivot carriage were mounted so that they would traverse the circumference of a circle, the center of which was the carriage pivot.

When in the withdrawn position, gun muzzles could swing either way without interfering with the casemate's structure, but when rolled forward on their tracks the muzzles protruded outside the casemate. Twin sets of heavy blocks and falls, attached either side of the guns to ring-mounted bolts through the casemate, absorbed the explosive recoil.

When the *Albemarle* was opposite Plymouth, Cooke's lookouts could see running lights of two ships ahead. The gun crews were ordered to load solid shot and stand by for orders. Most likely the smaller wooden steam tender *Cotton Plant* lingered behind to avoid involvement in the battle. The *Albemarle* was on her own.

Although nautical twilight began at 4:07 A.M.,[6] Cooke did not immediately see the hawsers and chains linking the two approaching vessels, but when he realized the implications of such a tactic he lost no time in signaling "All ahead, full." His position to their starboard and across the river was ideal. Cooke probably feinted avoidance of the linked ships, but at the opportune moment he ordered the helm "Hard-a-starboard." At full speed, though only of about five knots, the 376-ton *Albemarle* headed straight for the space between the bows of both vessels. The angle of approach was about 30° off their starboard bows.

In seconds the *Albemarle* had traversed the river's width. Heavy guns of the *Southfield* and *Miami* began firing. Closest to the *Albemarle's* course was the *Miami*. She lay slightly to port between the *Albemarle* and the *Southfield* dead ahead. The curved section of the *Albemarle's* port knuckle rammed the *Miami* at her port bow. For about ten feet along the hull at the waterline, two planks were nearly gouged through by the impact. At practically the same instant the *Albemarle's* ram penetrated the *Southfield's* starboard bow, crashed through her forward store room, and came to rest in the fire room ten feet inside the hull.

The *Southfield* began sinking at once. Depth of penetration, and the *Southfield's* sudden list to starboard, caused the *Albemarle's* bow to become jammed in the wreckage. Cooke ordered all engines stopped at the moment of impact.

With his propellers briefly motionless, momentum allowed the ram to penetrate the *Southfield's* wooden hull. Calling for "All astern, full" as momentum ceased, Cooke depended on full reverse thrust to release his bow. For what seemed an eternity, his judgement appeared to have failed. Gradually the *Albemarle's* bow began to sink with the *Southfield*. In his later report of the battle, Cooke said of the occurrence

I immediately commenced backing the *Albemarle,* but was unable to extricate her from the sinking vessel for some time. In the meantime the weight of the vessel so depressed the forward deck of the *Albemarle* as to cause the water to run into the forward port.[7]

The *Southfield's* uninjured crewmen below decks scrambled topside, hastily lowering small boats in which to escape. Others leapt into the water. Some tried to throw debris overboard to which they could cling. When their forward lashings parted, the *Miami's* stern swung towards the *Southfield's* starboard aft rail, enabling other surviving officers and men to climb aboard. Blended with the turmoil of commands, shouts, curses and screams of wounded sailors, was the screeching of escaping steam. The crescendo of sound was enhanced by the creaking and groaning of ships timbers that strained to resist such overwhelming forces.

During the brief moments after the *Albemarle* had struck the *Miami,* and while she was trying to extricate herself from being pressed under the water by the sinking *Southfield,* Flusser ordered several broadsides fired at the *Albemarle's* port casemate. Over all the *Miami* carried eight guns.

The *Miami's* forward gun was an IX-inch Dahlgren. About eighteen hours earlier the *Miami* had been shelling Plymouth with Dahlgren shells employing 10-second fuses. Perhaps during the *Miami's* barrage against the *Albemarle's* port casemate, as she lay jammed within the *Southfield,* Flusser's zeal led him to fire shots with his bow mounted Dahlgren.

At point blank range of probably thirty feet, Flusser fired his third shot. It was his last moment alive. The shell ricocheted back from the *Albemarle's* casemate. Directly over Flusser's gun it exploded in the air, instantly killing him, and wounding several of his gun crew.

With his vessel stuck inside the *Southfield,* Cooke was unable to use his great guns. Rising to the challenge, he ordered all idle crewmen to be armed and clamber to the casemate's top, where they were to engage the *Miami's* crew in a brisk small arms skirmish.

When the *Southfield* touched the river's bottom her hull rolled slightly, thus freeing the *Albemarle's* ram. She had sunk in three to five minutes from the time the *Albemarle* had crashed against the *Miami,* until the ram's release from the sunken *Southfield.* Only her superstructure remained visible above water.

Cooke intended to maneuver the *Albemarle* rapidly for an attack on the *Miami.* William N. Welles, the *Miami's* Acting Master and Executive Officer, had a similar intention, but before he could bring his bow gun to bear on the *Albemarle,* he had to reverse his engines to prevent grounding on the river's bank.

During the time of straightening the *Miami,* the *Albemarle* had righted herself, turned towards the *Miami,* and was steaming at "All ahead, full." Though some distance away, Cooke's gunners were firing the forward Brooke rifle loaded with solid shot.

Welles had second thoughts about risking the *Miami* in light of the *Southfield's* fate, so he turned away and steamed downstream towards the Sound's friendly waters. As the encounter was ending the *Whitehead* and *Ceres* arrived from downriver, but were of no assistance to the *Miami.* They did, however, escort her eastward to safer waters, while firing a few shots at the *Albemarle* to cover their retreat. At 5:11 A.M.,[8] the sunrise cast a brassy glow over the embattled waters of the Roanoke River at Plymouth.

Satisfied that his enemies had retired, Cooke ordered the *Albemarle* anchored about one mile below Plymouth to await further orders from General Hoke. Taking advantage of the enemy's departure he ordered a damage report, and found that only nine iron plates had been fractured. The small boat which had been used to rescue eight crewmen from the sunken *Southfield* was still intact. Those prisoners were later turned over to Hoke.

The *Albemarle's* baptism of fire produced only one casualty, and that because of curiosity. At the height of the exchange with the *Miami* a crewman, later identified only as Harris, sought a quick glimpse of the noisy clash. Someone at the *Miami's* rail saw Harris peek from a gun port and dispatched him with a pistol shot.

One notable crewman of the *Albemarle* welcomed the opportunity to ascend from below and savor the day's beginning. When Cooke was signing his crew a twelve-year-old black youth, Benjamin H. Gray, enlisted as powder boy on the *Albemarle.* For the six months while the *Albemarle* was at war, his major duty was to carry bags of powder from the magazine below to the gun deck above, though he also may have occasionally served as cabin boy.[9]

CHAPTER 2

GILBERT ELLIOTT, THE YOUNG MAN

At daybreak in the spring, a crimson angry sun can cast a brassy glow upon the waterfront, as it pierces a slowly rising haze over the Pasquotank River at Elizabeth City, North Carolina. "Red sun in the morning, a sailor's warning," was the old adage. Elizabeth City lay along the 'Narrows,'[1] the river turning there in an ox-bow bend as it flows from northeast to southeast. Out of sight downriver beyond Cobb's Point, the river merged into Albemarle Sound. There Gilbert Elliott was born and reared.

In Gilbert's day the river banks were grassy places on which he could have stretched his lanky length, with head propped against a tree or stump, while watching the haze slowly dissipate on a humid May morning. At the 'Narrows' the river bottom dropped sharply from the bank to great depths.[2] That natural feature had led to the establishment of shipbuilding interests as early as 1795, which lasted for more than a century.

Attraction to water, as it related to commerce and shipbuilding, was common on both sides of Elliott's family. His father's father, Peter Elliott (1754-1821), once owned a portion of that riverbank in 1817.[3] Ownership had been brief, yet the place became known as 'Elliott's Wharf.'

Gilbert's mother's father, Charles Grice (1763-1833), was a

CHARLES GRICE
maternal grandfather of Gilbert Elliott
courtesy of George Gibson Carey, IV, Cincinnati, Ohio

son of Francis Grice, a Philadelphia shipbuilder during the Revolutionary War. Charles' older brother, Joseph, had actually served in the Colonial Navy.[4] Charles arrived in North Carolina at the town of Reding before 1795,[5] bringing his family's shipbuilding reputation with him. (Members of the General Assembly meeting in Fayetteville in 1793 passed an Act to establish "A town at the 'Narrows'...on the Pasquotank," to be known as Reding. By 1794, the Assembly voted to change the name of Reding to Elizabeth.)[6]

Grice had acquired sixty acres of land in and around Elizabeth by 1795, as well as over 1,500 acres in Camden County just across the river. He also purchased town properties, including Lot #4 on the riverfront, which became the Grice shipyard.[7] It was profitable during the first decade of the nineteenth century.[8] That lot was just down river from the site of 'Elliott's Wharf' on Lot #6.[9] The locations of Elliott's grandfather's properties appear on the 1832 town plat.[10]

In 1801 the Legislature again voted community name changes. Since the Tyrrell County seat was also named Elizabeth, the name Columbia was substituted there, and the Pasquotank County seat became Elizabeth City.[11]

Gilbert's grandfather Peter, a Virginia resident as a young man, was said to have migrated from Scotland.[12] While a resident and property owner in Norfolk, Peter married Tamar Burgess, daughter of George Wright Burgess of Camden County, North Carolina, on October 8, 1790.[13] Even though they lived in Norfolk for about twenty-two years, Tamar never became acclimated to a municipality environment. She dreamed of returning to her ancestral home in rural Camden County, so in accommodation of his wife's wishes, Peter closed his business and sold their new home on November 2, 1812.[14]

With his wife and two sons, Peter Elliott set forth on the nearly fifty-mile journey to Camden. Their probable route was the crude roadway being built alongside the newly dug Dismal Swamp canal.[15] Within a few days the little family had arrived at their new home next to the Float Bridge, over the Pasquotank, near the village of Camden.[16] Their older son Peter[17] and his brother William were born in Norfolk. Six months after arriving at Float Bridge, their third son and last child, Gilbert, was born on May 20, 1813.[18]

To clarify identities of persons with similar names in different generations, the grandfather will be cited where necessary as Peter(1), his eldest son as Peter(2), his youngest son as Gilbert(1) and his grandson (this book's subject) as Gilbert(2).

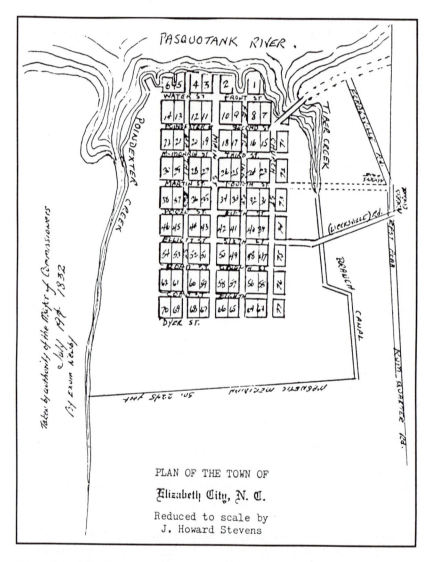

Town plan of Elizabeth City, N.C., July 19, 1832. Riverfront lots 4 and 6 were once owned by Gilbert Elliott's maternal and paternal grandfathers respectively.

Map courtesy of William A. Griffin, Elizabeth City N.C.

About eight years later, Peter Elliott(1) died in Elizabeth City of unknown causes. His obituary simply said, "Peter Elliott died on Sunday last (April 1, 1821) in Elizabeth City, North Carolina. He was formerly of this Borough."[19]

Gilbert(1) was then only seven years and eleven months old. He acquired his preliminary education in the local schools of Elizabeth City. The youth then received his secondary education while beginning his career as a clerk in John Williams' mercantile establishment in Elizabeth City. Mr. Williams became so impressed with the young man's ability, that he persuaded Charles Kinney, Esq., to invite Elliott into his law office to read law. In a short time Elliott received a license to practice, which led to a partnership with Mr. Kinney. Their clients were scattered throughout several neighboring counties. David L. Swain, for many years President of the University at Chapel Hill, once said that "Gilbert Elliott had the finest legal mind of any man he had ever known."[20]

In 1833 when Gilbert(1) was age twenty, Charles Grice died in Elizabeth City at age sixty-nine.[21]

When he was twenty-six years old in 1839, Gilbert(1) married Sarah Ann Grice of Elizabeth City. Sarah Ann, the daughter of shipbuilder Charles Grice and Mary Grandy Grice, was born in Camden County on June 1, 1819, at an estate called 'Milford.'[22]

The marriage of Gilbert and Sarah Ann was blessed with five children,[23] all born in Elizabeth City. Their third child, Gilbert Elliott(2), was born on December 10, 1843. Later he achieved acclaim for being the builder of the Confederate ironclad *Albemarle*. When young Elliott was about seven and one half years old, his father died on May 20, 1851 his thirty-eighth birthday.[24] He was buried in the Elizabeth City Episcopal Church cemetery, and his grave covered with a large white marble slab.

As children have been known to do, Gilbert likely played along the river bank with his brothers and sister. Their play area could very well have encompassed the old Lots #4 & #6 that had once belonged to both grandfathers. During the next nine years the youth Gilbert lived at home with his mother, sister Susan Elizabeth and brothers Charles Grice and Warren. He was educated in the local schools. It appears he had developed an interest in law, since he was listed in the 1860 Pasquotank County Census as a 'lawyer's clerk.'

The Honorable William Francis Martin, a prominent Elizabeth City lawyer, was his friend and employer.[25] It was Mr. Martin who encouraged Elliott to choose the law profession. It proved a good decision, as the practice of law sustained Elliott all his life. He was to become the third generation of land dealers in his family.

With the clouds of war looming ever closer, Elliott's future appeared in doubt. In all likelihood he sought a morning's quiet solitude along the river bank. The thin veil that separated his reverie from reality rose as slowly as the sun. With the gradual awakening and emergence of hustling pedestrians, he knew another day had begun. Walking along Water Street, he turned west on Main and headed home. It was only five blocks to the southeast corner of Main and Elliott Streets.[26] There that morning he shared breakfast with his mother and younger brother Warren. The three remained at home during the first months of the war, but when Elizabeth City was occupied by the enemy in February 1862, Gilbert's mother and fourteen year old brother Warren moved to Oxford, North Carolina. Gilbert remained since he was responsible for attending business affairs of the captured Colonel William F. Martin who had commanded the 17th Regiment, North Carolina Troops at Hatteras.[27]

Before long those inland waters of eastern North Carolina dramatically altered his life. He may already have envisioned a turbulent and uncertain future. One morning that spring in 1861 North Carolina, the tenth state to secede, was at war with the Union.

CHAPTER 3

A FLEDGLING SHIPBUILDER EMERGES

On July 21, 1861, an overconfident Union Army was routed at First Manassas by the audaciously effective Confederate Army. As a result, Union forces spent nearly nine months in rehabilitation.

That was not so, however, for the Union Navy. At war's onset, a blockading plan was implemented. It would soon prove to be a growing threat to Confederate sea lanes as Union blockading squadrons threatened Confederate traffic in the Atlantic Ocean and the Gulf of Mexico.

By the end of August, Union Flag Officer Silas H. Stringham and General Benjamin F. Butler had captured Forts Hatteras and Clark at Hatteras Inlet off the shores of North Carolina. It was even planned to sink an assembled stone fleet (disused hulls filled with stones) in hopes of blocking inlets to the North Carolina Sounds.

STEPHEN R. MALLORY
Secretary of the Confederate Navy
Library of Congress

The emerging Confederate government had begun to form their Navy in February 1861. Early on, it appeared that a prudent defensive policy would be effective. However, that would leave only the blockade runners to maintain a tenuous life line for the Confederacy.

An early order of business confronting the infant Confederate government's President, Jefferson Davis, was to establish a Navy Department. Though Davis faced an enormous array of executive decisions in those beginning days of the Confederacy, he was aware of the urgency to provide for the protection of Confederate waters.

By Act of Congress on Wednesday, February 20, 1861, the Confederate Navy Department was formally established. On the following day, President Davis appointed Stephen Russell Mallory of Florida to be Secretary of the Confederate States Navy Department.[1]

Though born in British Trinidad circa 1813, young Mallory and his widowed mother soon moved to Key West, Florida, where she operated a boarding house. The youth was often called upon to help his mother with the usual boarding house chores. As he grew older he began the reading of law, and at age nineteen he became a Key West Customs Inspector. His law studies continued and by 1840 he was admitted to the bar. In 1851 after having seen service in the Seminole War and served as a judge in Key West, Mallory was elected U.S. Senator from Florida. An early Senatorial Committee assignment was the Committee on Naval Affairs, of which he became Chairman in 1853. At the time of the secession of Florida on January 10, 1861, Mallory had served as Florida's senator for about ten years.

As Secretary of the Confederate Navy, Mallory was a forceful advocate of a powerful navy. He dispatched officials to the Northern states, across the borders to Canada, and to Europe in search of vessels equipped for military use or for conversion to such use.[2] In his report of Friday, April 26, 1861, Mallory said,

> I propose to adopt a class of vessels hitherto unknown to Naval services...Rifled cannon...having attained a range and accuracy beyond any other form of ordnance...I propose to introduce them into the Navy.[3]

Mallory declared to the Congressional Committee on Naval Affairs two weeks later on May 10 that,

> I regard the possession of an iron-armored ship as a matter of the first necessity...Naval engagements between wooden frigates, as they are now built and armed, will prove to be the forlorn hopes of the sea, simply contests in which the question, not of victory, but of who shall go to the bottom first, is to be solved.[4]

When the war began, both France and England had ironclads. The United States had recognized the importance of ironclads when

Congress appropriated funds for an armored steam vessel in 1842. A vessel, the *Stevens Battery*, was built at Hoboken, N.J. by Robert L. Stevens. After several modifications the project was abandoned, though it was still on the stocks when the war began.[5]

John A. Stevenson, of New Orleans, met with Secretary Mallory on May 21, 1861, to discuss and formulate plans to counteract efffects of the Union blockade. A summary of ideas and proposals was sent by Stevenson to President Davis, in which he elaborated on specific plans to alter and adapt..."powerful tow-boats on the Mississippi...by preparing their bow in a peculiar manner, as my plans and model will show, render them capable of sinking by collision the heaviest vessels ever built..."[6]

With the burning and scuttling of the U.S.S. *Merrimack* at the Norfolk Navy Yard by the departing Union forces, and the subsequent raising of the hull by Confederate Navy personnel on May 30, 1861,[7] another page was written in the scenario of decisions and events which would eventually influence Elliott's career.

Brig. General Robert E. Lee wrote Virginia Governor John Fletcher on June 15, 1861, informing him that the frigate *Merrimack* had been raised and was in dry dock.[8] At Gosport Navy Yard, by Sunday the twenty-third, the Confederate Navy had begun to reconstruct the former U.S.S. *Merrimack* as ironclad C.S.S. *Virginia*.[9]

In his report to Congress on July 18, Secretary Mallory stated the *Merrimack* had been raised and docked at an expense of $6,000. Necessary repairs to hull and machinery, were estimated to cost about $450,000. She was to be shielded completely with 3-inch iron (though 4-inch armor was used), and the armor to be placed at such angles as to render her ball-proof.[10] The vessel was also to be equipped with an armored ram at the bow.

Mallory strongly embraced three additional innovative decisions that were to become standard specifications for Confederate ironclad gunboats. Those were the use of rifled cannon; solidly reenforced ship's bows, ironclad for ramming; and exposed surfaces above water to be covered with armor plates.

Three prominent C.S.N. authorities, John L. Porter, Chief Naval Constructor; William P. Williamson, Chief Naval Engineer; and Commander John Mercer Brooke, Office of Ordnance and Hydrography, followed and enforced Mallory's policy.

Responding to orders from Mallory, Porter collaborated with Williamson and Brooke in designing an acceptable ironclad ship.

Though Brooke enjoyed Mallory's support for his contribution to the *Virginia's* design,[11] it was Porter who became supervisor of the Confederate shipbuilding programs. From Porter's desk flowed a variety of ship 'Types,' one to be known as 'Albemarle.'

John Luke Porter was born in Portsmouth, Virginia, on September 19, 1813, where he later learned the craft of shipbuilding in his father's shipyard. By 1857 Porter had passed a Navy Department exam for Naval Constructor. He was a Naval Constructor at Pensacola, Florida, when Virginia seceded. Resigning his U.S. Navy commission, he subsequently was appointed by Stephen R. Mallory to the post of Naval Constructor. By spring 1863, he was Chief Naval Constructor, an office he held until war's end.[12]

JOHN LUKE PORTER
Chief Naval Constructor, C.S. Navy
Naval Shipyard Museum, Portsmouth, Virginia

William P. Williamson was born in Norfolk, Virginia, circa 1810. A student of mechanical engineering in New York City as a youth, he gained employment at Gosport Navy Yard. By 1842 he supervised the yard's machine works. He was appointed Chief Engineer in the U.S. Navy on October 10, 1842. Refusing the oath of allegiance in 1861, he was imprisoned, then dismissed from service. He joined the Confederate Navy on June 11, 1861 as Senior Engineer, and was on duty in North Carolina waters as early as October 10. By October 17, 1862, he had become Engineer-in-Chief.[13]

Near Tampa, Florida, on December 18, 1826, John Mercer Brooke was born. In 1847 he graduated from the U.S. Naval Academy. Upon resignation of his commission on April 20, 1861, he accepted appointment as lieutenant in the Confederate Navy. Two months later he discussed ironclads with Secretary Mallory, and was given responsibility for armor and guns. Commander Brooke's research confirmed a general belief that an ironclad's casemate armor, placed from 35° to 38°

from the verticle, would best deflect enemy projectiles. His famous Brooke Rifle, in various calibers, became the favored heavy gun of the Confederacy.[14]

In the drama of Elliott's unfolding Confederate naval experience there were three additional players. They would greatly influence Elliott's daily activities for nearly four years. The North Carolina Legislature met May 1, 1861, and authorized Governor John W. Ellis to raise ten regiments of state troops for the War, before the State Convention met. An Adjutant General and other staff officers were also authorized. Major James G. Martin, arriving in Raleigh after his resignation from the U.S. Army, was appointed Adjutant General by the Governor.[15]

When his shipbuilding career began in the fall of 1861, Elliott met the first additional player, James Green Martin, Adjutant General, North Carolina Troops. James Martin became Gilbert Elliott's friend and mentor. He was the older brother of William F. Martin, Elliott's employer. A native of Elizabeth City, Martin graduated from West Point in 1840 at age twenty-one. He was a veteran of the Mexican War in 1849, participating in the Battles of Monterey, Vera Cruz, Cerro Gordo, Contreras and Churubusco. In the latter engagement he lost an arm.[16]

As the bright green days of spring changed to the days of summer in 1861, James G. Martin, found himself buried in duties as Adjutant General, North Carolina State Troops. Among his numerous responsibilities was one of great urgency, that of recruiting troops. Martin produced a series of General Orders from Headquarters, N.C. State Troops in Raleigh. These were published in all newspapers, large and small, throughout the State.

The Southerner, published at Tarboro in Edgecomb County, published an 'Order' on July 19, in which the Adjutant General set forth rules pertaining to the organization of companies of seventy-four men plus officers; limits to further enlistments in such companies; methods of payment; restrictions upon Commissioned Officers receiving bounties; and directions that all communications to the Governor must pass through the office of Adjutant General.[17]

Adjutant General Martin's office also handled requisitions for materials and the payment of all bills thereof. This was the channel through which Gilbert Elliott received directives pertaining to his role in the defense of eastern North Carolina. In fact, as he gradually found himself embroiled in the shipbuilding business, he was recognized as agent for James G. Martin,[18] while he managed Colonel Martin's shipyard at Elizabeth City.

Not everyone knew of Colonel William Martin's military commitment. Such was the case of sawmill operator James N. Perry at Columbia, the Tyrrell County seat, directly south of Elizabeth City on the south side of Albemarle Sound. Columbia also was a waterside town situated on the east bank of Bull Bay.

Sawmill owner Perry was a frequent supplier of ship's timber for William Martin's shipyard. He wrote Martin in care of Elliott on Sunday, September 8, 1861, informing him that,

> The bill of ship timber ordered by you is ready and has been for several days. When you send for it pleas send me 10 or 15 bushels salt and oblige.[19]

Further evidence of Elliott's growing prominence as a shipbuilder at the 'Narrows,' was contained in a letter he received from recently promoted Major General of Militia, James G. Martin. From Raleigh on Saturday, September 14, Martin wrote a cordial letter to Elliott.

> My dear Gil, I received today your two letters of the 10th and 12th with their enclosures, except the blank note. I do not understand the charge of $39 for damages on the draft of $1300. I shall sign the note for $3000 and send it to mother and ask her to sign it and send it to you. I should not have objected to putting the $1300 in the note had it not been for the charge for damages. As soon as I understand that, I am willing to give the note, but would like to know why you advise to leave it as it is...

The reference to Martin's mother is convincing evidence that she and her son James were actively engaged in maintaining the Martin shipyard under Gilbert Elliott's supervision. Elliott's involvement in preparations for the imminent defense of Elizabeth City was revealed when Martin continued,

> When you get through working on the battery at Cobb's Point, make out your bill, get it certified (in duplicate) by the person who has charge of the battery and send it to me. Send me at once the dimensions of the vessel you have on the stocks & when she could be launched & how much she is worth the day you launch her. The Confederate States want some gun boats built. Could you build one or more, how soon & at what price per ton or other measure?[20]

The Cobb's Point fort on the west bank of the Pasquotank River below Elizabeth City, referred to by Martin, was armed with four smooth bore thirty-two pounders and twenty-eight rounds of ammunition. It was in charge of a civilian, known only as Mr. Hinrick, who had militiamen to supplement his few volunteers.[21]

The vessel "on the stocks" could very well have been the one waiting for timber from James Perry. If this was the case she was either under contract, or being built on speculation by William Martin. And the keel must have been laid before he changed his identity from that of attorney to C.S.A. officer. At any rate, it was Elliott's obligation to build and sell sufficient vessels to make the shipyard profitable.

Again on Sunday, September 22, Martin wrote a short note to Elliott. It may be that weekends were the best times for him to write, since his Raleigh office would likely not be busy. With his message to Elliott, he enclosed letter copies from Navy Secretary Mallory to Military Secretary Colonel Warren Winslow, and one from himself to Commodore William F. Lynch. He directed Elliott to read them and forward Lynch's to Roanoke Island. That implied there were behind-the-scenes inquiries, whether or not Martin knew of shipbuilding interests in northeastern North Carolina. In a more personal vein, Martin concluded by acknowledging receipt of the preceding Wednesday's letter which included a list of servants, and a note which he would delay signing.[22]

The servants mentioned could well have been those of Sophia Martin, the mother of James G. and William F. Martin. In the absence of Colonel Martin, Sophia left the family home in Elizabeth City and moved to Raleigh near her older son James. Evidently Elliott had an additional duty as custodian of the Martin home.

The first naval victory of Flag Officer William F. Lynch, C.S.N., on October 1 in North Carolina waters no doubt stimulated the Confederate Navy Department's interest in launching warships locally. That decision naturally enhanced Elliott's prospects as fledgling shipbuilder of eastern North Carolina.

Lynch's flotilla, the C.S.S. *Curlew, Raleigh,* and *Junaluska,* was supplemented when the U.S.S. steamer *Fanny* was captured in Pamlico Sound on October 1, 1861. The latter had been loaded with Union troops. Two rifled guns and large amounts of army stores were also captured, all highly prized and much needed.[23]

Martin was becoming somewhat anxious about Elliott's inability to interest parties in purchasing a partially completed hull on the stocks. The matter was of great concern, since no funds were being returned to William Martin's shipyard account. Expenses continued unabated. With that disturbing thought in mind, James Martin wrote Elliott on October 3 acknowledging his letter of September 30. He called attention to an enclosed check for $200 and suggested that Elliott go to Portsmouth, Virginia, and do everything possible to contract for a gun boat. Failing this, Elliott was to offer his men for hire to the Confederate States shipyard known as Gosport (formerly known as the Norfolk Navy Yard).

In the specialized venture of shipbuilding, talented craftsmen were never easily located. When work was plentiful, one enjoyed a continuous procession of ships down the ways, but without contracts in hand many experienced workmen were known to drift away. The system of hiring out one's men assured their return, after temporary employment elsewhere.

Without Elliott's knowledge, General Martin had written Commander Arthur Sinclair, Sr., headquartered in the Gosport Navy Yard contract department across the Elizabeth River from Norfolk. He hoped to drum up a contract. More subtly, Martin was making it known that shipbuilding capabilities existed in Elizabeth City.

Continuing his instructions to Elliott, Martin suggested a visit to Commander Sinclair emphasizing the hull on the stocks. Martin further speculated the Confederate States might require many such vessels.

Following further remarks about cash reimbursements being sent to Elliott he inquired about the exact sum he owed Mr. Starke, and asked whether Starke would take North Carolina bonds payable the following June. Martin mentioned he had no means of copying letters so he cautioned Elliott to keep them. In closing he said, "If you cannot get work in the yard, close it and hire out the hands on the best terms you can."[24]

Cdr. Arthur Sinclair, to whom General Martin wrote, was headquartered in the contracts department at Gosport Navy Yard across the Elizabeth River from Norfolk. Martin's inquiry generated a positive response. Though Sinclair had received only a verbal briefing of Martin's letter, his response on October 9 was typically direct and brief. He called Elliott's attention to enclosed specifications, while recommending proposals be submitted in duplicate for the building of a steam gunboat at Elizabeth City. Plans were available from the Naval Constructor at Gosport. Sinclair advised dispatch was important.[25]

Elliott reacted immediately to Martin's suggestion to visit Sinclair. He must have impressed the commander, who then prepared a letter of introduction to Secretary Mallory. Martin's letter of the tenth to Elliott acknowledged receipt of Elliott's communication from Richmond where he had visited with Mallory. He further indicated a preference for building a hull alone as proposed by Commander Sinclair, with the government furnishing engines and related equipment.

Martin's following remarks were cautious in nature, since he was not proficient in the art of shipbuilding. Additionally, he harbored a concern about whether Elliott and his craftsmen were qualified to engage in a government contract. He desired assurance that if it were necessary to fulfill all of Mallory's wishes by furnishing a boat ready to use, then Martin's yard must be protected against subcontractor's failure to supply engines and support machinery. Further, he stipulated someone should be on duty to supervise all work and alert Elliott to discrepancies. He also called attention to the fact that at any moment the vessels risked falling into enemy hands.

Martin was asking for on-site quality control by a government inspector. In addition he was requesting a contractual indemnification against possible loss to the enemy. As an afterthought he added, "The government also to pay at intervals as you say Mr. Mallory was willing to do, as the work progresses."

Since there would be no prepayment on the contract, with only assurances of payment upon launching and acceptance, progress payments were a strict necessity. Ever aware of his limited financial resources, Martin recommended that Elliott arrange a credit purchasing plan for lumber, to be paid later as increment payments were received. He also asked for a start-up estimate so he could commence acquiring the funds. Elliott was to keep him constantly informed of all events.

Somewhat timorously, his final paragraph reflected his inexperience in such a new venture and his doubts about Elliott's ability to carry out the project.

> I feel some hesitation to undertake a regular contract not knowing anything about the business & suggest that you be very careful in your calculations & allow for contingencies. I am inclined to think it would be safer to rent the yard & hire the hands to the government.[26]

Martin's reference to Mr. Starke may have been due to the fact that in August 1861, a Colonel Lucian D. Starke had been court appointed to take charge of the Cobb's Point battery construction. Supplies and labor charges were the responsibility of the state, to be paid by the Adjutant General.

Along with the latest mail from Martin, Elliott received another letter of inquiry about constructing steam powered vessels. Thomas M. Crop[s]on at Raleigh wished to know,

> What will you construct a gun boat of Porters model, also of Graves, [probably William A., a Norfolk shipbuilder] and any model of your own[,] of similar dimensions[,] for completion so far as the wood work is involved and if you are inclined to contract for the engines and boilers you may propose[,] ... address me at your earliest convenience at Raleigh.[27]

Authorities at Gosport Navy Yard appear to have been formulating plans that included Elliott and the Martin shipyard as supplementary shipbuilding facilities. William P. Williamson, Chief Engineer, C.S.N., set forth preliminary machinery requirements to be incorporated in any naval vessel to be constructed at Elizabeth City. The specifications were to be compatible with gunboat plans proposed by Chief Naval Constructor Porter. Williamson's October tenth memo specified standards which applied to the engines, boilers, and propellors for the gunboats proposed by Porter. Each would be fitted with two non-condensing engines having 16-inch diameter cylinders, and 20-inch piston strokes. There would be two boilers with 800 feet of fire surface within, and two return flues. Two 3-bladed screw propellors of seven feet diameter and twelve feet pitch would be mounted on wrought iron shafts, with journals $5\frac{1}{2}$ inches in diameter. The engines were to produce one hundred revolutions per minute, and the builder was to guarantee successful performance for six months.[28]

Definitions of 'pitch' and 'journals' will make those specifications clear.

> Pitch of the screw: The distance a given point in a screw propellor would move in the direction of its axis if turned through one complete revolution in a solid, fixed medium.

A journal was the part of a rotating shaft that turned in a bearing within an exterior mounted journal box attached to the hull below water line at the stern.[29]

On Friday, October 11, Porter wrote a short letter to Mallory within which he included drawings and specifications for a proposed Elizabeth City gunboat. He assured the Secretary she would be of light draft and great speed. She would be armed with two broadside carriage-mounted rifled guns of four-inch bore. Porter believed that experienced crews could roll one gun to the stern port to oppose enemy fire. He preferred a larger gun of six-inch bore be bow-mounted.[30]

Within a remarkably brief time, Martin's earlier letter to Commander Sinclair at Gosport had ignited intense interest in Confederate Navy circles. Just before October 13, Elliott had written Sinclair proposing the building of hulls only. As agent of James G. Martin he may have agreed to move slowly in this new shipbuilding venture. Sinclair's response from Norfolk on October 15 served official notice that C.S.N. Department policy was now changed.

> I have just received yours of the 13th inst. The Secretary of the Navy has instructed me to make no more contracts for gunboats without machinery. They must be complete, so your offer must be for all. My plan of boat was furnished by Mr. Porter & doubtless the same will be given you by him. Please let me hear from you as early as practicable.[31]

The policy of accepting only complete vessels, ready to sail away, was very much to the benefit of the Confederate Navy. Had they continued to accept 'hulls only' from various contractors, their problems of fitting the vessels elsewhere would have been overwhelming.

At Columbia, meanwhile, timbering was underway. Lumberman Perry notified Elliott, on the sixteenth, that for the moment he might be forced to delay filling his timber order because he was awaiting word from Norfolk to cut 100,000 feet of timber, provided the price was right. If the deal failed, Perry would be able to furnish Elliott with all the pine lumber he needed, and would probably have decking timbers as well. He was out of oak, and promised to notify Elliott when word was received from Norfolk.[32]

Knowing of Elliott's plan to continue purchasing timber, James Martin hastily reminded him on the seventeenth that Perry had purchased the sawmill from William F. Martin. A percentage of each sale to the state was to be withheld in escrow for return to William Martin. In this instance the amount was $314.39. For the record, James Martin wished Perry to prepare a bill against the state for their recent acquisition, from which this amount would be withheld.[33]

The next day Martin again wrote Elliott. He had waited for his mother, Sophia, to sign two notes pertaining to financing William Martin's shipyard operation. It appears she continued to be an active financial backer of the Martin shipyard's daily expenses.

One note for $1300 was to a Mr. Welsh, while the second was for $280 in favor of Norfolk iron vendor George Reid. Included with those notes was a $200 check for Elliott. Martin said he had approved a bill for the schooner *Calhoun's* services. She was sometimes leased for transporting materials to the shipyard. He assured Elliott that the money would be delivered by Mr. M. O. Jordan (A Lt. M. O. Jordan was variously connected with the State or Navy Finance Department at Roanoke Island).

Martin offered an admonition to Elliott when he continued,

I will attend to the Life Insurance note and the money due also. I hope you have something in writing to show you were authorized to go on hiring hands and buying timber to build the gunboats before any contract was made. The contract when made must be signed by me.

Then in a lighter mood, Martin wrote,

I trust you will succeed in selling the boat you have ready to launch[,] to be fitted up by the Confederates with all the old machinery of the *Raleigh* (I think you said). If it will answer that purpose and you can get any judge to say so in writing[,] you had better inform Commander Lynch at once. If you get the money from Mr. Jordan let me know, the two will be something over $500.[34]

Disposal of this completed hull had caused a continual worry with Martin, and Elliott as well.

James Perry, from across Albemarle Sound, wrote Elliott on the nineteenth with news that he could furnish timber. He requested Elliott submit an order specifying beams 3" x 10" x 29', though he asked if planks 3" x 6" x 29' would not be adequate for decking. He also had a quantity of ¼" and ½" planking on hand, all of which was 12" wide. He remarked that, "Mr. Martin [W. F.] and Mr. Hinton [James W.] have been paying me for that kind of lumber, say 15 at Elizabeth City or 13 at the mill."[35]

Feeling secure with the knowledge that timber was available for a price, Elliott was pleasantly surprised when summoned by Flag Officer William F. Lynch to his flagship *Sea Bird* off Roanoke Island. He was being invited to discuss an agreement, whereby he could be awarded a shipbuilding contract. Lynch was the second of the three additional players mentioned earlier in the drama of Elliott's unfolding Confederate Naval experience.

William F. Lynch, C.S.N., had attained captain's rank in the U.S. Navy, before resigning his commission in 1861. Six months later in October, he was commanding a small flotilla in Pamlico Sound. On the first of the month he had celebrated the first Confederate naval success in North Carolina waters.[36]

After a discussion of Elliott's qualifications and the Martin shipyard facilities, an agreement was signed on Tuesday, October 22, 1861, between Gilbert Elliott, Agent for James G. Martin, and Flag Officer William F. Lynch, C.S.N. Mr. William B. Selden was witness to the signing of Elliott's first Confederate Naval contract which stipulated only general specifications.

> Agreement made and entered into between Flag Officer William F. Lynch, C.S.N., on the part of the Confederate States Government and Gilbert Elliott, Agent for J.G. Martin, on the day and date aforesaid.
>
> It is agreed by said Elliott that he will construct for said Government, the hull of a gun boat to be fitted to the machinery of the Steamer *Empire*, which steamer *Empire* is to be purchased by the said Government. The specifications, plans and details are to be furnished by Constructor John L. Porter, C.S.N.
>
> In consideration of the construction of said gun boat the said Elliott[,] agent as aforesaid[,] is to be paid by the said Government the sum of fifty dollars per ton of Carpenters Measurement.

The length of keel of said boat is to be one hundred and thirty feet, the breadth twenty-five feet, the depth of hold seven feet provided they be not changed by the said Constructor John L. Porter.

It is agreed that when the frame of the vessel is in place twenty-five percent of the whole amount of construction is to be paid, and the remainder when the vessel is completed.

In the event of the work at any stage of its construction falling into the hands of the enemy[,] the Contractor shall not be required to reimburse any amount which may be advanced by the Government.

In witness of the foregoing the said parties have hereunto set their hands and seals.[37]

The vessel thus contracted was of the *Chattahoochee* Class with twin screws, and mounting five to six guns.[38]

When Elliott returned to Elizabeth City after his initial meeting with Lynch on the *Sea Bird* off Roanoke Island, he received a letter written on the twenty-fourth from Lieutenant M. O. Jordan at Roanoke Island. Jordan acknowledged the receipt of Perry's bill for lumber, and that Adjutant General Martin had requested him to resolve the matter. He wished Elliott to visit Perry at Columbia, unless he was in Elizabeth City, and have him receipt duplicate bills, all the while maintaining confidentiality that Jordan had the money. He further noted he was in possession of certified bills for the schooner *Calhoun* as well as a quartermaster order for the Cobb's Point construction expenditures.[39]

Elliott was reminded by General Martin's letter on September 14 that,

> when you get through working on the battery at Cobb's Point, make out your bill, get it certified (in duplicate) by the person who has charge of the battery and send it to me.

The endorsed quartermaster order represented payment for the Cobb's Point battery.[40] Business transactions were often delayed, as shown by the interwoven intricacies of simply paying a debt.

In a letter on October 25 to Elliott, Martin first called attention to Colonel Martin's affairs when he reminded Elliott please, "Don't forget if there is any danger of the negroes falling into the hands of the enemy to bring them away in time." Those individuals probably were the property of Colonel Martin, and might have worked before the war in either Mr. Martin's sawmills, or the shipyard. At that time they were the responsibility of Elliott who served the private interests of William Martin with intermittent counsel from James G. Martin.

In reading on, Elliott noted Martin's rising spirits when he expressed his pleasure at learning a shipyard engineer was engaged. Martin also favored the concept of contracting directly with the government, or Secretary Mallory, if the furnishing of ship's machinery became necessary.

In conclusion, Martin warned of the risk of losing all to enemy action, or the consequences of financial loss due to last minute unplanned alterations. He decided that both he and Elliott should number their letters for easier recall. In his postscript he said, "Have heard nothing from brother William who was last heard of at Fort Hatteras." [41]

By then, Martin knew that a majority of the 17th Regiment had been captured at Fort Hatteras, but he did not necessarily know of his brother's immediate whereabouts. When Fort Hatteras fell to the Union invaders on August 29, 1861, Companies A,C,D,F,G, and H of the 17th Regiment were captured, including a majority of the regimental officer staff. Transported north, they were first confined at Fort Hamilton, New York Harbor, and later at Fort Warren, Boston Harbor.[42]

James F. Snell, then of Elizabeth City, was boss carpenter. For services to date on October 26, he submitted his bill for $620.00.[43] Elliott took advantage of Mr. Snell's expertise throughout his career in shipbuilding. Again acting as Martin's agent, on the twenty-sixth Elliott paid six dollars and seventy-five cents for the hire of boys George and David for four days [work].[44]

While the confidential negotiations were being finalized with the Confederate Navy, from which Elliott anticipated a contract award for the building of gunboats, he began to receive requests for employment. The first inquiry was dated October 28, 1861. A North Carolina soldier, J. N. Gilbert of Company A, 1st Regiment, North Carolina State Troops, wrote to Elliott while on duty at Brooks' Station, Stafford County, Virginia. (This was near the mouth of Acquia Creek which emptied into the Potomac River).[45] Soldier Gilbert came right to the point in his opening statement by saying he would come to work in the yard, if the Adjutant General would grant him discharge from the state troops. He suspected that if Elliott were indeed in a hurry, he could encourage the Adjutant General to release him. Gilbert alleged there were no other ship carpenters in the regiment though an excellent workman, by the name of Patrick P. Monroe, would render efficient service doing joiner's work.[46]

Despite an effort by government officials to restrict the revelation of its shipbuilding plans, plugging information leaks was no more successful in 1861 than today. Gilbert wished to work in the shipyard, but perhaps was using an excuse to gain discharge from the army.

On the heels of receiving Gilbert's letter, another reached Elliott from the same location. It was dated a day earlier, and signed by P. F. Kenedy whose initial request was identical to that of Gilbert. He also belonged to Company A, as did Gilbert, but alleged that Gilbert didn't know he was also a carpenter.[47]

By October 31, Elliott received a long letter from Martin covering a wide range of subjects.

> I received tonight your letter of the 26th and its enclosure. I have signed and herewith return. I had previously received yours of the 24th endorsing copy of contract or agreement ... with Commodore Lynch. You should have put the whole loss of lumber gathered for this boat on the government in case the enemy destroyed it. I see no other objection if you could not get any further advance as the work progressed. You say the boat is to be 230 tons at $50 = $13,500. I make it $11,500. Keep trying to sell the boat you have on hand. If necessary to sell her you had better contract in Richmond with the parties you saw for the machinery. They[,] binding themselves to satisfy the government and the government taking the risk of the boat at once & paying something on her. This will require time but is better than not selling. If you think you can build two boats[,] it is better in my judgement to undertake both as soon as you can. If you hear any news from Roanoke send it to me at once. I have also received your letter of the 25th and was sorry to hear Lt. Jordan did not get the $200. You did right about Perry. Continue to give money in lieu of pork as long as the hands prefer it and the price is as high as now. I send you a check for

$1000 on the Exchange Bank, Norfolk. Make it go as far as you can and send me a monthly statement soon after the end of the month. Until Mother returns and directs otherwise you will have the control of her servants[,] but you will have to give Dock and Enoch the money for their meat[,] or make some other better arrangement to feed them. I see none. I received the list of servants and approved all your suggestions. Enoch it seems to me ought to be fed by Mr. Davis. Mother will probably be home next week.

About Col. Martin's houses, you must do the best you can to collect the rent and change tenants next year if that will help. You cannot get any [gun] powder here. I think Commander Lynch would let you have it. I approve of your mode of paying Hodges and Baker.

As Col. Martin always kept his accounts with them as bankers, you had better continue. <u>Dont talk much about your business</u>. It is [a] very bad plan, especially to persons with whom you are doing no business. In anything that is done about the Wadsworth servants let the circumstances of the case[,] as far as the children are concerned[,] be distinctly set forth. I believe I have answered everything requiring answers in your letters. We are all well.[48]

With Martin's endorsement of the agreement signed on the *Sea Bird,* confirmation of a contract with the Navy Department seemed imminent. He remained concerned, however, that in the event of disaster the Martin shipyard interests be protected from financial loss not of their causing. Emphasis was again placed upon selling the 'hull on the stocks.' By now Martin had modified his views, and was willing to install machinery in hopes of generating buyer interest. Since a government contract seemed possible, he perceived the business wisdom of building two vessels simultaneously, a cost effective arrangement for vendor and customer.

The custom "give money in lieu of pork" was a reversal of an occasional payment practice exercised between employer and employee. A type of barter system in lieu of cash, it was used to satisfy needs of the moment. The check for $1000 drawn on the Exchange Bank of Norfolk assured that additional shipyard expenses were covered. Possibly Elliott required powder for blasting stumps while cutting timber, or for future use in the battery then building at Cobb's Point. Martin strongly cautioned Elliott to remain silent on matters of business.

October was ending with a positive development from the Navy Secretary. Since the October 22 'agreement,' Elliott's activites had pivoted around locating materiel vendors, hiring hands to complete the "hull on the stocks," and tending daily needs of Colonel Martin's affairs.

CHAPTER 4

THE JUNIOR NAVAL CONTRACTOR

A slight misunderstanding about payment policy on the new contract had bothered Elliott, prompting him to address the question to Secretary Mallory on October 25. Elliott received Mallory's letter of October 30 sometime during the first week in November.

> ...Your letter of the 25th instant has been received. The Department prefers, if no stipulations as to payments have been made, that they should be provided for by distinct agreement, say when the frame is up, one fifth of the price agreed upon for the vessel, when planked one fifth, when decked one fifth, when ceiled and all wood work done, one fifth, and when completed one fifth. Or, one eighth of price agreed upon when each one sixth of the work shall be completed. The remaining two eights to be paid when the vessel is completed and delivered. Flag Officer Lynch has been instructed to confer with you on the subject and agree upon the terms of payment.[1]

Elliott's question concerning frequency of payment was answered. When Flag Officer Lynch mentioned the machinery of the *Empire* in the October 22 agreement, it became a signal for Chief Engineer William P. Williamson to initiate a survey of her engines.

Chief Constructor John L. Porter received the report, then conferred with Secretary Mallory, whose opinion was expressed in Porter's November first letter to Elliott, in which he related that Mr. Williamson had reported against using the *Empire's* machinery for a gun boat and the Secretary of the Navy didn't want it. He granted permission to continue with the boat that was planned and Mr. Williamson would search for her machinery. He closed by saying the plans went to Captain Sinclair at Washington, N.C."[2]

In the William F. Martin Collection, at Chapel Hill, what may be specifications for a *Chattahoochee* Type vessel were found. Since the October 22 agreement called for a vessel resembling this type, by reading these specifications one will appreciate the age-old talents of those who built the wooden ships.

Specifications for a steam gun boat, 130 feet long, 30 feet beam moulded and 10 feet depth from the lower edge of the rabbet on the keel to the top of the deck beam at the side of the vessel. Spring of beams, three inches. Draft of water when loaded for sea, six feet.

KEEL [Main & lowest timber of ship's hull, formed of several pieces scarfed together, extending from stem to stern posts]. The keel wideside 10 inches and mould 10 inches, the floors jogging one inch into it, and projecting six inches below the planking to be of white oak.

STEM [Main timber of hull's forepart, erected vertically to accept bow planks ends]. The stem, stern post, deadwood, apron, etc., will side 9 inches and the keel tapered on each end to suit them. The whole to be fastened through with iron bolts $7/8$ inches in diameter, and not over 18 inches asunder. The stemson and stern post to be of white oak.

FRAME [Bends of timber forming ship's body, composed of floor timber, two or three futtocks, and top timbers each side of keel]. The frames will be placed 2 feet apart from centre to centre, fastened through the keel and keelson with two $7/8$ bolts in each the futtocks, all siding 7 inches and when framed together will show a space of 10 inches between the frames, to be bolted together with three $3/4$-inch iron bolts in each scarf.

The floor timbers and the crooked futtocks in the ledge, of white oak to be of natural growth. The first futtocks and top timbers may be of heart yellow pine. The frame will be double to the port sill line and oak stancheons from thence to the rail, one on every other frame with plank sheer three inches thick [all] over. The main rail will be 4 inches thick to be cut off in the rake of the pivot guns with a hammock rail and nettings on top.

BEAMS [Timbers placed horizontally across ship's hull, on which decks are laid]. Of yellow pine sided 10 inches and moulded 7 inches, spring three inches, to be placed five feet apart with fore and aft stubb and two ledges between each.

CLAMPS, KNEES [Timber piece with natural or artificial crook, used to support deck beams ends]. To have a thick pine clamp and a hanging knee under the end of each beam sided 5 inches and bolted through with $3/4$-inch iron bolts and rivetted on rings on the knees.

KEELSON [Long timber sections exactly fitted over the hull to bind and strengthen lower hull]. Of yellow pine sided 10 inches, moulded 12 inches to be planked with $1^1/2$-inch pine plank tongued and grooved.

PLANKING [Broad timbers covering deck beams, sides and hull bottom]. The bottom plank to be of white oak 3 inches thick fastened with two spikes and two locust or white oak tree nails in each frame and to be bolted with $3/4$-inch iron bolts driven through and rivetted on rings.

BENDS [Extra thick & strong planks over bottom planks]. May be of yellow pine or oak 5 inches thick fastened with two spikes and two through bolts of $5/8$-inch diameter in each frame. The bolts to be driven through and rivetted on rings.

WATERWAYS [Groove at edge of ship's deck for draining]. Of yellow pine.

CEILING [Inside planking of ship]. Of yellow pine $1^1/2$ inches thick spiked on.

LIMBERS [Space along keelson sides, including floor timberholes at lower edge, allowing accumulated bilge water to flow to pump well]. To be cut over each garboard strake for water courses and boards fitted over them.

SPIRKETING [First strake of inside planking next to waterways, above beams, reaching to gun-port sills]. Of pine or oak 3 inches thick fastened with spikes.

GUN DECK Of yellow pine 3 inches thick fastened with iron spikes and plugged over the heads.

BERTH DECK To be laid in hatches (so as to get in barrels, etc.) of $1^1/2$-inch yellow pine and fastened to the carlings with wrought nails.

BOATS Two good boats complete 16 feet long and two sets of iron boat davits, with boat tackle of blocks and falls complete for hoisting, etc., all to be fitted.

[Vessel] to be fitted with rudder, stem plates, hawser pipes, chain nippers, cat heads, airports, cable bitts, etc. Two good pumps, one head pump, two anchors and chain cables and the necessary eye and ring bolts for gun tackle. The joiners work according to the drawing and such cabin ward rooms, shell room, shot and chain, lockers, hatches, windlass, etc.

The outside work all to be planed off, the nail and bolt holes filled up with putty and to have two good coats of paint as desired. The inside work to have two good coats of paint as desired. All the work between decks to be planed. The whole to be done in a workmanshiplike manner and of good materials to the satisfaction of the Department.

It is expressly understood that the Department desires to get a vessel complete and any little thing which may have been omitted are to be furnished without cost to the Government. The furniture is not included, nor is the armament.[3]

Additional terms commonly used in wooden ship construction were:

APRON [Timber attached to aft side of stem sloping from head downward].

CARLINGS [Timber or heavy plating placed fore & aft between two deck beams at ends of hatch or other deck opening, to which intervening beams were butted].

DEADWOOD [Solid timbers fore & aft built up on vessel's keel].

FUTTOCKS [Frame timbers between top timbers and floor].

GARBOARD STRAKE [Line of planking next to keel].

JOGGING [Notching clinker-planked boats frames in a fashion to present a full laying surface to planking, for added rigidity].

MOULDED [Light pieces of board as templates for cutting ship's hull timbers].

RABBET [Groove or channel joint in timber, to accept or secure edge or ends of planks to keel, stem & stern posts].

SCARF [Two timbers joined by fashioning one end into another, making one solid even surface. Obvious in the keel].

STERN POST [Main vertical timber at vessel's stern, accepting ends of stern planks. Rudder was mounted aft of this on sailing ships].

George Reid, a Norfolk iron vendor, responded on the second of November to Elliott's inquiry about iron.

> I have been greatly disappointed in receiving some iron from Richmond, from which I would have been enabled to fill your order of the 28th ulto for ⅝ and ¾ rod. It is not yet received and the uncertainty of getting it renders it impossible to say when I can furnish you. I have made every possible effort but cannot procure it in the city.
>
> The bank here requires the power of attorney for Mr. Martin to be lodged with them, otherwise they will receive any curtail or payment and credit the note with the same. Therefore if it is not convenient to you to send and lodge with them your power of attorney, I will pay the interest on old note and let it remain as it now stands and return you the note you recently sent me.[4]

The increasingly frequent shortages of iron posed frustrating problems, and certainly were a portent of the future. Lack of iron prevented the launching of a superior Confederate ironclad fleet.

Elliott was beginning to establish a vendor supply network from which he could acquire shipbuilding materials. Most frequently he dealt directly with sawmill owners and iron merchants, but sometimes he chose agents who had better connections than he.

Such was the case when, on Sunday November 3, he wrote H. L. Hinds who was representing him just across the Pasquotank in Camden County. Hinds, a field agent for Elliott, was hiring sawmill hands and supervising their work. Elliott set forth wide ranging instructions.

I am sorry to hear that there are not as many trees as Snell counted. However one must be satisfied. I am trying to hire Frank Duke from Isaac Pritchard and William Berry from Thomas Berry. They are both good sawyers. You can put them to doing anything which you please. Horatio Dozier, who is hired by Thos Roton, will see you tomorrow. Put him to work. You are authorized to make any bargain with him which suits you. When he is done work[,] give him an order on me for the amount which you owe him. In the same way you can hire other hands[,] if any come to you.

Continue to board with Mr. Gregory as long as you like and when you want money send to me for it. I will send you hands next week if I can hire any over here. If your son has any powder, use it and charge it to me. If I can get powder I shall do so. Let me hear from you whenever convenient. If I can find time I will come over some day.[5]

It was a custom of timbermen to use blasting powder when removing stumps, or in providing access to the curved root systems of oak trees as they spread out from the trunk. In his response to Elliott, Hinds noted that paper "is scarse here." In tabulating the work times he remarked,

The E. City hands did not get here until 12 oclock Monday. I give you the time they have been at work with me.

Then he listed the workers and their times.

Nixon Morser	4½ days	Heith	3½ days
Denny Morser	4½ days	Phillop	4½ days
John Baley	3½ days	Mill	5 days
Charles Harvey	4½ days	Frank	5 days
Bill Moss	4½ days	Bill	5 days
John Sawyer	4½ days	Alan Dozier	5 days

In a lighter vein Hinds concluded,

I hav had [Margry] Gregory stews 3 days this weak. We have got along first rate...this weak. We hav got a new road thru the field...you will let me hear from you.[6]

By November 4, Elliott received a response to his October 20 letter of inquiry to Richmond steam engine broker Talbott & Brother, requesting availability of gunboat marine engines. Every large engine in their inventory "had been sold to the Confederate States, however, two 9-inch cylinder engines are in New Orleans that could be shipped to Richmond for alterations."

The brokerage firm estimated $6,000 would cover all costs, making them satisfactory for use on gunboats with 6 or 7-foot propellors. In conclusion, they advised haste since marine engines were becoming scarce.[7]

On Thursday the seventh, Elliott dashed off a short inquiry to Constructor Porter, at Gosport Navy Yard, requesting clarification of certain ambiguous plan measurements. He asked for dimension clarification of depth of floor timbers specified in gunboat plans Porter had sent him. Not clearly understood was whether or not nine inches was the depth of floor timbers. Porter verified that nine inches was correct by jotting brief remarks on the bottom of Elliott's letter.[8]

By Saturday November 9, Chief Engineer Williamson responded to Elliott's inquiry of the sixth to Mallory. Elliott was seeking the Navy Department's decision whether or not they would purchase his 'hull on the stocks' for conversion to a gunboat. Williamson provided an unfavorable reply when he wrote,

> The very extensive alterations and additions to the hull and the small engine of 9 cylinders which you propose, render it inexpedient to adopt your suggestion at this time. I shall however probably be in Elizabeth City in the course of a week, when some other arrangement may be made.
>
> Having now the sole duty of providing machinery for the numerous gun boats now being built in various parts of the South, I have purchased from Talbot and Brothers, of this city [Richmond] all the portable engines (8 inches)[cylinders] which are large enough for the small class of gunboats...and have contracts for the engines (6 inches) for the three gunboats building in Washington, N.C. under a contract with Commander Sinclair. I am looking for suitable engines now for the boat you are building under specifications made by Constructor Porter.
>
> My greatest difficulty is in furnishing boilers and the principal object of my visit to E. City is to examine the boilers and engine of the *Leonora,* which has been offered me and which vessel (now sunk at Roanoke Island) is to

be immediately raised and brought up there [Elizabeth City].[9]

Hopes for a quick sale of the 'hull on the stocks' to the Confederate Government were dashed. An alternate customer might be the State of North Carolina, and Elliott certainly pursued any opportunity.

Shortly after the twelfth, Tredegar Iron Works responded in the affirmative that iron was available. A brief note signed by Joseph R. Anderson advised that they could supply ship spikes for eight cents a pound. Larger spikes, of ³/₄ & ⁷/₈ inches round, would cost nine cents cash per pound. Rail shipment to Norfolk was presumed to be $6 per ton.[10]

The good news of an iron materials source was tempered when Perry reported that no timber was forthcoming from him because an individual who earlier claimed a supply had vanished. He also noted the militia had gone to Hyde County, and he was burdened with the responsibility for their families.[11]

On Saturday the sixteenth of November, Norfolk iron vendor George Reid adjusted his charges for an iron shipment leaving that day by Steamer *Flying Cloud*. A drayage charge of $.15 per pound was applied to the shipment of nine bars, ³/₄-inch anvil iron and two bundles of ⁵/₈-inch anvil iron. Upon the invoice for $31.09 he suggested,

> You may add to your remittance the interest on Mr. Martins note, $4.93 up to the 20th proximo if you please, and you will find the note signed as atty, returned as suggested. The Bank preferring to let the old note remain and receiving the interest as I before stated.[12]

It appears that Elliott's power of attorney for Colonel Martin, as requested on November 2 by George Reid, was permitting business as usual.

From South Mills about fourteen miles north of Elizabeth City, William R. Abbott, another of Colonel Martin's sawmill debtors, wrote Elliott on the eighteenth acknowledging receipt of his agreement, but would delay signing it until he was sure Elliott understood the terms. Indeed, he could furnish cut timbers in excess of twenty-four feet long, and heart lumber clear of knots, but the latter would be more costly. Abbott then concluded,

I will pay one half of my indebtedness to Mr. Martin, and balance must be <u>cash</u>. If this arrangement will suit you, you can draw agreements according[,] and send them up and I will sign them. You will please make the time of delivery longer if you can and I will deliver it as soon as possible anyhow.[13]

Abbott spoke plainly. He had the timber, he would cut it to order, and he would repay half his proceeds to Mr. Martin on account, if the whole deal could be for cash. His letter was written on the eighteenth. Elliott received and endorsed it the same day.

Friday, November 22 brought a letter written three days earlier by Martin in Raleigh. Financial matters were first to be dispatched. Colonel Martin's note to George Reid had been retired. Several bills against the state, representing shipyard expenses amounting to $1,990.60, were paid by Lieutenant M. O. Jordan by means of three checks. Then Martin announced,

...This is all the money I have & when you want more you will have to give me longer notice[,] as I shall have to borrow. I hope you will so manage as to get the 1st payment, from the Confederate States, before this gives out. You should push enemy threat for this object. When you get that first payment pay the taxes[,] if [it] is to save anything by doing so. I hope you will sell the vessel you have already to launch. If you cannot sell her to the Confederate States[,] you may perhaps do so to Captain Crosson for the State. (This was Thomas M. Cropson who had made inquiry on October 10, requesting a vessel construction proposal). He will probably be in E. City the first of next week and I have asked him to look at her. If you cannot get another boat to build for the C.S.[,] you might for the State, as that is what Captain Crosson is after. He should be charged the same rate as the C.S. & try to make the payments more frequent. As the work progresses [have them] furnish engines.

I had an official letter last night from Col. Martin of the 8th inst. He says all the officers are well. Says nothing of moving to Sandusky (Ohio).

Push your work for the first payment. I have received Colonel Martins pay (all that is due him) to the end of October amounting to $970.60...[14]

The unsold hull constantly drained Elliott's account. Costs of labor, timber, iron, shipping, and managing the personal affairs of the Colonel while a prisoner of war were becoming insurmountable. Over and above the extraordinary expenses was the burden of financing construction of a government boat between increment payments. Though no document has been located other than the October 22 agreement between Elliott and Flag Officer Lynch, most likely the government vessel under construction in Martin's shipyard was indeed the ship to be built by that 'agreement.' Word of Colonel Martin's safety and health boosted both their spirits.

A commodity of which the Confederacy experienced serious shortage was the mineral iron. It was of critical necessity for the Confederate ironclad fleet envisioned by Mallory. The dearth of iron could in fact delay, or prevent, the launching of essential Confederate naval vessels. Two events on Monday, the twenty-fifth of November, exemplified the ever present concern.

Of primary consolation to Secretary Mallory was the Department's acceptance of the first armor plate shipment for the C.S.S. *Virginia* (former U.S.S. *Merrimack*).[15]

Elliott received disappointing news in George Reid's letter from Norfolk, in which Reid acknowledged satisfaction of Colonel Martin's note with Farmers Bank. Reid protested the increasing scarcity of iron supplies, as well as sharply rising prices. Of the three types of iron available, American, English and Swedish, the latter two were, in his opinion, extremely difficult to procure in quantities of any consequence. An assortment of American iron was very incomplete and hard to obtain. In closing, he assured Elliott he would continue the quest for iron and would charge the lowest market rates.[16] Nothing could more clearly state the facts. Iron and time were the keys to Elliott's shipbuilding success.

From his office at Gosport, Porter sent a memo to William P. Williamson on November 26. It provided a glimpse of Porter's harmony with Elliott.

I send you a draft of the Washington [N.C.] gun boats [under contract for Cdr. A. Sinclair] for Mr. Elliott. Let him use the same specifications. He will have to increase his length to suit or he can make her the same length by cutting 20 feet out of the middle[,] say from 'E' in the fore body to 5 in the after body[,] which will make her 130 feet long, 25 [feet] beam and 10 feet depth. If they had rather have the whole length which I think best, no changes will be necessary. I want to see you. PS Tell Elliott to send the other plans back to me.[17]

Aside from a brief mention in Williamson's November 9 letter to Elliott advising of the three gunboats building at Washington, specific plans for those vessels may be nonexistent.

As Porter was writing to Williamson, Williamson was visiting Elliott in Elizabeth City. No doubt he shared with Elliott numerous demonstrations of 'how to do' in the business of shipbuilding. When Williamson was ready to return to Norfolk, Elliott sent him down the road with his own driver, horse, and buggy. After a safe, but rough, journey along the Dismal Swamp Canal road Williamson wrote Elliott on the twenty-sixth, advising,

> I have arrived here last evening and have been in bed with my broken back (cushioned). I however wrote to Porter this morning and obtained from him the enclosed, so you can go on with the Washington gunboats[,] and I think [you] may afford to sharpen her up at both ends.

Then below 'CONFIDENTIAL' he continued,

> We are about to build a <u>large number</u> of gun boats to carry 2 guns each, and shall probably get you to build several. Dont speak of this to anybody, not even your foremen, as it is only known at this time to the Secy and myself. They will be about 100 or 120 ft long and 18 or 20 ft beam. I am in pain writing in bed and I hope your man, horse and buggy got back in [time for] Sunday safely.[18]

Williamson was referring to Elliott's recently received specifications, which may have been similar to those used at Washington, N.C.

Also written on the twenty-sixth was a letter from sawmill operator J. J. Jordan at Winton, N.C. (Winton was situated on the west bank of the Chowan River, about fifty miles west of Elizabeth City as the crow flies. Straight north of Winton, about ten miles or so, was the Virginia state line). Jordan remarked that he had searched throughout the neighborhood for white oak plank, and could find only one man who had a supply. Although he wasn't home, Jordan said he would continue the search. The cutting of pine lumber could start any time. Jordan asked Elliott what he considered a fair price for oak so he could dicker with his neighbor at the first opportunity. He closed by requesting information if a vessel was leaving Elizabeth City for Norfolk, since he had two loads of lumber for transport.[19]

This was a straightforward letter setting forth a willingness to acquire scarce timber, a request for specific dimensions of sawed timber, a question of what would be paid for the white oak, and the need to engage an Elizabeth City cargo vessel bound for Norfolk.

Also on the twenty-sixth Phillips & Co., of Norfolk, wrote Elliott acknowledging his inquiry for iron products. They had no iron spikes suitable for gunboats, no supply was promised, nor was the cost known. On hand, however, were $3\frac{1}{2}$ tons of $\frac{3}{4}$-inch round, and one ton of $\frac{7}{8}$-inch round for $7\frac{1}{2}$ cents per pound.

Offered for cash sale were $\frac{1}{2}$-ton of $\frac{1}{2}$-inch round, and $\frac{1}{2}$-ton of $\frac{5}{8}$-inch round at eight cents per pound. In addition they had about fifteen pounds of 10-inch spikes and two kegs of 4-inch boat nails, all for ten cents per pound.[20] Since ready made spikes were not always available, there's little doubt that blacksmiths could fashion long spikes from the round iron.

On Friday the twenty-ninth came a disturbing note from E. L. Dozier, another sawmill operator, about four miles away in Camden across the Pasquotank to the east. Dozier bemoaned the fact that as he had commenced sawing Elliott's dry oak logs his saw broke. Without a saw, Dozier was essentially out of business. He recommended that Elliott send over a boat with lots of strong rope with which to tow the logs to the shipyard. All but three or four were still floating in his ditch.[21]

Elliott's options were few. Cancellation would not be in his best interest. He could contract with another sawmill nearby, or haul the rough timber to one of Colonel Martin's tenant sawmills. Either way, a delay was costly.

In his never ending quest for iron, Elliott again turned to George Reid in Norfolk. Though Reid could not satisfy the actual requirement, he did offer substitutes in his response of November 29. Reid said he had thoroughly searched the market for spikes of 10, 7, and 6 inches. None were to be had. He did have, however, five bundles of assorted round iron, some $\frac{1}{2}$-inch, and some $\frac{3}{8}$-inch. In all there were about 1,200 pounds at eight cents per pound. He also had 3 and 4-inch spikes which could be shipped by steamer. All sales were for cash.[22] Those limitations furnished work for the blacksmiths in the forging of spikes from round iron rods.

After Chief Engineer Williamson had conferred with Elliott, and returned to Norfolk in Elliott's borrowed carriage on the twenty-fifth, he had then traveled on to confer with Mallory in Richmond. Upon his return to Norfolk, Williamson discovered Elliott's letters of the twenty-eighth and twenty-ninth. In a letter to Elliott on December 4, Williamson defended his views exchanged with the youthful contractor during their November visit. He also described the inner workings of Constructor Porter's department.

I am sorry to hear that you find the last drafts as objectionable as the first. The beam being 25 ft instead of 30 ft[,] on the same draft, certainly makes the midshipsection $\frac{1}{5}$ less, consequently the resistance is decreased in that ratio. The lines are also finer and as the engines are the same in both[,] the last model must be the most speedy. As I am already in a scrape by objecting to Mr. Porter's plans and have really no right to interfere with them, I cannot do so again. My object before was to reconcile the difficulty you labored under, between Mr. Porter's model and Capt. Lynch's contract. The Secretary gives Mr. Porter whole control in the designs of the hulls and unless you can exhibit to him (the Secy) a better model and gain his approval thereto, the whole control rests with Mr. Porter.
In regard to the 50 gun boats now wanted[,] Mr. Porter made the drawings. They are 106 ft long, 21 ft beam and 8 ft deep. These designs have [been] accepted by the Navy. The engines are all to be alike size and design and I am now hunting up the various engine builders in the Confederacy to undertake the work. Mr. Porter will[,] I presume[,] have the same authority with regard to the hulls, so if you desire to building of them, you had better communicate with him on the subject. I leave in a day or two again to be absent some time on my various duties and have to go to Augusta, Ga. and other cities of Ga. and S.C. Should I again visit Elizabeth City, I will avail myself of your kind offer.[23]

Without Elliott's letter of the twenty-eighth in which he must have expressed apprehension about the specifications, one can assume Williamson successfully addressed the problem by his reasoning for the beam's reduction. His further comments reveal that on too many past occasions he had objected to Mr. Porter's designs. His occasional objections were prompted by his engineering background, although Mr. Porter was the C.S.N. Chief Constructor. Williamson continued with explanatory remarks about the proposed fifty gunboats to be constructed, with a veiled recommendation that Elliott contact Mr. Porter if he wished consideration as a contractor. Judging from his brief description of the proposed specifications, a uniformity of engine design might allow more rapid manufacture. His impending journey through several states spoke loudly of the Secretary's policy to build gunboats for coastal defense. Elliott's 'kind offer' was probably an invitation for Williamson to enjoy his hospitality upon a return visit to Elizabeth City.

H. L. Hinds, one of Elliott's timber agents in Camden, sent his monthly report on December 14. His homely revelations said it all.

> We have got along vary well this weak sawing and carrying out the plank and timber and also hewing with the exception of an accident of my son. Cut his foot last evening wich will confin him for som tim. I think I have hiard the boy Edmund of Mrs. Williams for 75c per day and he finds himself he is quite good hand he has work 1½ days this weak all the trees are down but 4 and 2 of them are to [be] dug up. Frank and Bill dug 4 large trees the last two weak and Manuell & Terry has dug one wich you will pay them for[.] You can have Mr. Tillett Sawyer and son if you want them at one dollar a day and he will find then you will lend more. Mr. G. Parker wishes me to say that he has not quite got his job done and cannot come west.[24]

There was a good reason why timber cutters were digging up trees. In the days of wooden ship construction it was necessary to fashion a naturally curved piece of timber, to be placed beneath the deck beam at the point it attached to the vertical hull surface. This curved member was known as a 'knee'.[25] Oak trees were the source of those 'knees.' They were the curved root portions that immediately became the base of the trunk. Naturally curved, they provided immense strength and desired reinforcement.

The digging out of a stump was to be preferred in order to retain the natural integrity of the 'knee'. There were times though when timber cutters resorted to using blasting powder to sever outer root members, thus allowing the removal of the stump portion.

On December 23, Lieutenant T. M. R. Talcott, C.S.A., whose offices were at the Engineer Headquarters in Norfolk, responded to Elliott's letter of solicitation of the twenty-second. Elliott received Talcott's response on December 30, and learned that the engineers desired information relative to the costs and descriptions of vessel's at his yard.

Talcott envisioned a schooner from 30 to 40 tons not to draw over $4^1/_2$ to 5 feet when loaded, and be a good sailer with accommodations for crew on board. She would be used for transporting bricks, lumber and other materials to batteries, with an occasional gun weighing from 3 to 6 tons each.[26]

Here was another opportunity to sell the hull on the stocks. Although there seems to be no hull description, one can only imagine the amount of alterations required to satisfy this inquiry.

From Richmond came news that the Navy Department would soon be making the first increment payment of $5,000 for Flag Officer Lynch's vessel. That was in accordance with Secretary Mallory's letter to Elliott on the thirtieth. Long awaited, it was a very welcome Christmas gift to allay the worries of Martin, Elliott, the creditors and workers. Secretary Mallory's notification the day after Christmas was succinct.

> Commander A. Sinclair having reported that the gun boat being constructed by you will be framed in a few days, a requisition has this day been drawn in favor of Paymaster George H. Ritchie, C.S. Navy at Norfolk[,] to make the first payment about $5000 and as soon as he receives the money he will proceed to Elizabeth City and pay you that amount. The Department has no copy of the specifications furnished you by Constructor Porter and will you please forward a copy.[27]

The prolonged series of iron delivery delays was briefly broken with a shipment from Richmond. From Tredegar Iron Works came a December 27 payment receipt for six casks of ship spikes, totaling $72.00 for 900 spikes. Drayage to depot was thirty cents.[28]

Within one day Mallory's letter of the twenty-eighth to Elliott had arrived. He acknowledged Elliott's proposal to construct three gunboats according to plans and specifications already delivered. Individually, they would each cost $10,000 with no construction time limit.

Mallory emphasized that the Department could entertain no proposition which did not embrace the time within which the vessels were to be constructed. To that end Mallory advised, "...You will therefore please state immediately within what time you will build and deliver the vessels in question, time being more important than price."[29]

The pressure on Elliott was beginning to mount. Those gunboats may have been the ones alluded to by Mr. Williamson on November 9, and once again on the twenty-sixth. John L. Porter's communication to Williamson on the twenty-sixth also lends credence to this belief.

The year 1861 ended in a rather grand manner. Elliott had one hull for sale ready to launch; one framed gunboat, its first payment soon to come; and the probability of a multi-hull contract. Elliott's shipbuilding activities were indeed expanding.

CHAPTER 5

1862, THE SOLDIER SHIPBUILDER

Dawn on New Years Day 1862, was ushered in by a "red sun in the morning, a sailor's warning." As the New Year of 1862 began, Elliott's shipbuilding career appeared to have been launched. With receipt of the first increment payment, settlement of outstanding obligations would be assured. He was expecting that any day.

Secretary Mallory wrote positively on January 4.

> Your letter of the 1st instant offering to build three gun boats according to the specifications furnished you[,] in four months[,] for the sum of $10,000 each has been received. You can proceed at once with the work under your offer and the contract will be drawn and sent to you[,] the four months to begin from the day you receive this letter. The Department further offers you a bonus of one thousand ($1000) dollars on each boat if completed within three months and of five hundred ($500) dollars if delivered within three and a half months. A copy of the specifications is herewith enclosed. The drawing will be sent with the contract.[1]

A letter of transmittal dated January 6 arrived from Mallory, and in the same package was the contract dated January 13, 1862. The secretary noted that the contract for construction of three gun boats was in duplicate, and he requested that both copies be signed in presence of two witnesses and returned to the Department immediately. One signed copy would be returned to contractor.[2]

Drawings and specifications have not been identified and preserved. Extracts from the contract required the builder,

> ...to construct and deliver to the said party of the second part, or to the authorized agent of the Navy Depart-

ment, at the town of Elizabeth City, the hulls of three gun
boats, of the character and description provided in the
plans and descriptions, together with the outfits therein
named, and which are made part and parcel of this contract. The boats to be delivered within four months from
the sixth day of January, 1862...to pay or cause to be paid
to the party of the first part, his authorized agents or as-
signs, the sum of ten thousand dollars for each gunboat...payment in the manner and form following, when
one-sixth part of the work upon each vessel shall be completed, one-eighth of the sum agreed upon for each vessel
will be paid, and so on until the vessel shall be completed
and delivered, when the remaining two-eights will be paid.

GILBERT ELLIOTT, Agent for J. G. Martin
S. R. MALLORY, Secretary of the Navy
Local witnesses: Joseph E. Ferebee and William E.Mann[3]

The three hulls to be completed within four months at Elizabeth City made an obvious statement about the Martin shipyard
facilities. Space permitted their being built simultaneously, and sufficient craftsmen were available although procurement of adequate
supplies presented daily problems. Two ships ways were then occupied, one for the unsold 'hull on the stocks', and one for the
Chattahooche Type gunboat under contract.[4]

Flag Officer Lynch on C.S.S. *Sea Bird,* with C.S.S. *Raleigh* in company, reconnoitered the Hatteras Inlet on January 20 and 21, and
"there saw a large fleet of steamers and transports." In a letter to
Secretary Mallory, Lynch emphasized how important was the area
which Roanoke Island controlled.

Here is the great thoroughfare from Albemarle Sound
and its tributaries, and if the enemy obtain lodgements or
succeed in passing here[,] he will cut off a very rich country from [the] Norfolk market.[5]

The approaching fleet was that of Maj. General Ambrose E.
Burnside, who would in time wrest Confederate control of North
Carolina's sea approaches. If Elliott had known of Flag Officer Lynch's
sighting off Roanoke Island, his enthusiasm for shipbuilding might
have been diminished.

**MAP OF NORTH CAROLINA,
SHOWING FORT HATTERAS AND THE SOUNDS IT COMMANDS**

On that same day Elliott placed an order with the Tredegar Iron Works in Richmond. Joseph R. Anderson acknowledged Elliott's order on the twenty-fifth by stating they were expending every effort to furnish the iron within a few days. In conclusion Anderson said, "The Government pressed us hard, but we will try to work [it] out after a while."[6]

Elliott had written Adjutant General Martin on the twenty-first of January asking about the powder he had ordered a day or two after November 3. Martin received the letter in Raleigh on the twenty-fourth and responded on the twenty-sixth.

> I received two nights since your letter of the 21st and was very sorry to hear you had not received the $5000 nor the powder. I hope ere this reaches you[,] both will have come safely to hand. I suppose your difficulty about your lumber man Williams is over before now. If it is not[,] I will have him excused as being employed in getting lumber for gunboats for the Confederate States.... I was sorry Colonel Starke made such a mistake about the order calling for one third of Militia. I thought it very plain and still think so, but suppose I must be wrong as there have been so many difficulties. You must excuse my paper as I am writing at home and have no other near. The governor was not willing to buy the boat [on the stocks] as I wished[,] thinking the Confederate States should fix all the batteries required. I think now about the only chance to sell her will be to Genl Wise[,] to be made into a floating battery and placed in a canal in the swamp, opposite one of the batteries on the island or some similar place. This it seems to me would strengthen the defense of Roanoke very much. I am sorry your boat progresses so slowly[,] but hope you will get along better now. I write tonight to Col. Martin in Norfolk.[7]

One month had passed since Secretary Mallory wrote that the first increment payment would be forthcoming. It hadn't arrived, and Elliott's purse strings were too tight for comfort. He wondered what had happened to the powder he had ordered a few days after November 3. Norfolk was only one day away by horse, three days by freight wagon, and several days by rail.

Though the nature of Elliott's complaint about timber agent Williams is not known, it must have been severe enough to risk eliminating a timber source while ship's hulls were on the ways.

Col. Lucian D. Starke had been a close personal friend of Elliott's father. At the end of August 1861, the colonel had been court appointed to be officer in charge of building a battery at Cobb's Point. Later in September he was authorized by the court to muster the militia. They were to man the newly built battery. As news of impending disaster at Roanoke Island reached the court, Colonel Starke was again ordered to "muster the militia." Martin might have been referring to that series of delays in his remarks to Elliott. After having been apprised of the meager defense perimeter for Elizabeth City, the governor no doubt thought it more prudent to pay for fortifications than to buy a ship's hull.[8]

Though some imprisoned men of the 17th Regiment at Fort Warren in Boston harbor were paroled on December 17, 1861, the rest of the troops were paroled on January 25, 1862.[9] Colonel Martin, one of the fortunate early parolees, had reached Norfolk before January 26, since Adjutant General Martin ended his remarks by saying he intended writing the colonel in Norfolk that night.

Powder was on the way. It was being shipped via the Raleigh and Gaston Railroad to Gilbert Elliott, care of W. T. Baker at Norfolk. On January 16 the Raleigh Ordnance Office had signed over to Captain A. W. Lawrence one barrel containing 125 pounds of blasting powder, and he had promptly sent it on to Baker the same day to be forwarded to Elliott. In his letter of transmittal to Elliott, Captain Lawrence had requested that enclosed duplicate receipts be signed, with one being returned to the Raleigh Ordnance Department. Elliott's dismay at the delay in receiving his powder was alleviated with the knowledge that Raleigh, rather than Norfolk, was the point of the powder's origination.[10]

Secretary Mallory owed Elliott an explanation for the first increment payment's delay, and was prompted to respond on the twenty-ninth to Elliott's inquiry of the twenty-sixth.

Paymaster Ritchie has been delayed in making the payment of $5000[,] to which you refer and which he has been authorized to make[,] by not receiving the funds from the Treasury Department under this requisition made in his favor[,] and the delay is caused by the want of the Treasury notes which cannot be printed and signed fast enough to meet the demands upon the Treasury. He has, by this time received the amount of the draft and has doubtless made arrangements to pay you.

The second payment upon the large gun boat building by you will[,] I presume[,] soon be due and no delay will occur in making payments hereafter as Paymaster Ritchie will be supplied with funds in advance.

The Department cannot advance the first payment upon the three small boats as you request[,] as no progress has been made with them, but will take care that no delay shall occur in making the payments as they come due.

If delays occur from any failure of the Department to meet the payments as they become due or from other unavoidable and unreasonable causes[,] the Department will make due allowance for your failure to comply with the contract within the time specified.[11]

The Confederate Treasury had engaged scores of women for the purpose of signing freshly printed notes. As the war progressed their numbers grew, though the speed by which notes reached the public diminished. An advance payment on the three gun boats could prepare for their construction, or could pay current expenses of the *Chattahoochee* Type on the ways. Thus January 1862 ended with high hopes but little progress.

Dulton Wheeler of the J. A. Saunders Company, a Norfolk anchors and chains vendor, cast gloom on Elliott's hopes with a brief note on the first of February announcing all his anchors and chains were sold, with the exception of two chains retained for the Confederacy. Wheeler assured Elliott he would write if a source was located.[12]

No definite records of events during the final days of the Martin shipyard remain. For the vessels of the Confederate Navy, assigned to the Sounds of North Carolina, they were final days also. During the second week of February 1862, a Union flotilla steamed up the Pasquotank River to be greeted by clouds of black smoke rising from the court house, a few homes and business buildings, and shipyards as some citizens torched their properties.

By the tenth a sizeable number of vessels vainly defending the Pasquotank River and those in construction at Elizabeth City were captured, blown up, sunk or burned. The nine vessels were:

Appomattox/Empire, burned near South Mills.[13]
Black Warrior, burned near Elizabeth City.[14]
Ellis, captured near Elizabeth City. [15]
Fanny, grounded & blown up in Pasquotank River.[16]
Forrest, damaged, burned on ways at Elizabeth City.[17]
M. C. Etheridge, burned near Elizabeth City.[18]
Sea Bird, sunk near Elizabeth City.[19]

In the Martin Shipyard:

'Hull on Stocks,' for sale.
Chattahoochee Type, on ways being planked.

There was better news from Virginia. On February 17 ironclad C.S.S. *Virginia* (former U.S.S. *Merrimack*) was commissioned. Captain Franklin Buchanan, C.S.N., was her commander. Here for all the Confederacy to see was proof of Secretary Mallory's resolve to have an ironclad fleet.[20] Eight days later in New York Harbor the U.S.S. *Monitor* was commissioned. Her commander was Lieutenant John L. Worden, U.S.N.[21]

The dark clouds of impending disaster looming over city and harbor interests brought more anger than panic to the citizens. Many decided to remain, while some left for destinations further west. Among those who remained was Gilbert Elliott. He did what he could to secure the business and personal affairs of Colonel Martin since he managed Martin's various rental properties. Moreover, he supervised events in the lives of Martin's slaves, and was rapidly becoming a recognized and respected shipbuilder. And above all, he had the responsibility of his mother and younger brother. When it became evident that hostilities would erupt in Elizabeth City, he moved his mother and 14 year-old brother Warren to Oxford, N.C., where the youth was enrolled in Horner's Military School.[22]

The family of Richard Benbury Creecy who resided on their farm near the Pasquotank, about nine miles south of Elizabeth City, hastily rode their horses into town when, from an upstairs window, they had seen the Federal fleet steaming up the river. Many residents were fleeing along the country roads carrying the few personal belongings they had grabbed in their haste. Friends who had not yet departed said they had seen the "Elliotts starting out on foot for Oxford, and the Martins had passed them in their buggy."[23]

The hurried conclusion of business matters at Elizabeth City included not only his own, but also those of his family and of Colonel Martin. When he again read the contents of Adjutant General Martin's October the twenty-fifth letter, he was reminded, "don't forget[,] if there is any danger of the negroes *(sic)* falling into the hands of the enemy[,] to bring them away in time."

With the exception of several domestic servants, they were experienced workers in Martin's shipyard. A new location was urgently needed if he was to continue the Confederate Navy contract. Within a matter of days, Elliott and his workers had gathered together all tools and materials salvaged from Martin's shipyard before it was burned on February 10, 1862. They then moved everyone and everything to a suitable location near Norfolk.[24]

In Richmond on March 4, Secretary Mallory summarized his navy's needs to President Davis.

> [We will need] fifty light draft and powerful steam propellers, plated with 5-inch hard iron, armed and equipped for service in our own waters, four iron or steel-clad single deck, ten gun frigates of about 2000 tons, and ten clipper propellers[,] with superior marine engines, both classes of ships designed for deep-sea cruising, 3000 tons of first-class boiler-plate iron, and 1000 tons of rod, bolt, and bar iron are means which this Department could immediately employ. We could use [to] equal advantage 3000 instructed seamen, and 4000 ordinary seamen and landsmen, and 2000 first rate mechanics.[25]

The Secretary could as well have wished for the moon. He would soon learn of a major impediment that would hinder complete success: the lack of iron. Other factors with negative impact were the shortage of competent seamen and insufficiently protected construction facilities.

Elizabeth City's prominence was best described by <u>Harper's Weekly</u> in their Saturday edition of March 15, 1862.

> Elizabeth City, where General Burnside has exchanged prisoners with the rebels is the Capital of Pasquotank County, North Carolina, on the right bank of the Pasquotank River, about 20 miles from its mouth. It is

225 miles from Raleigh, and 50 miles south of Norfolk, Va. It is one of the most considerable towns in the northeastern part of the State. The population was about 3000, and it contained two banks, two or three printing offices, and several churches. There was a large amount of Government stores in the place, which were destroyed by the rebels on the appearance of our gunboats. It was at Elizabeth City that Commander [Stephen C.] Rowan met and destroyed the enemy's fleet in Albemarle Sound.[26]

The location of Elizabeth City on the "right bank of the Pasquotank River," was directly related to whether one was traveling up or down the river. To be specific, Elizabeth City was situated on the river's west bank where it changed direction at the 'Narrows.'

And it was on the Pasquotank River, between Elizabeth City and the river's mouth at Albemarle Sound, that Cdr. Stephen C. Rowan's U.S. naval flotilla rapidly overtook and vanquished Flag Officer Lynch's retiring Confederate naval defenders.

Charles Grice Elliott was correct when, in an article to the <u>Richmond Dispatch</u>, he said Gilbert moved his shipbuilding enterprise to the vicinity of Norfolk after Elizabeth City fell.[27]

Secretary Mallory's order entitled 'Dismal Swamp Ironclads' dated April 3, 1862, was addressed to Lt. George W. Harrison in Richmond. Harrison's orders directed him to Norfolk for duty under Captain Sidney Smith Lee. He was to superintend construction of gunboats by Gilbert Elliott and R. L. Myers, agents for the Department. Captain Lee fully briefed Harrison of construction details, and assigned him for duty on April 22, 1862.[28]

Two months to the day after Elizabeth City fell victim of Federal strength, the U.S.S. *Whitehead* returned to the Pasquotank. Encountering the schooner *J. J. Crittenden* and capturing her, the *Whitehead* towed her to the mouth of New Begun Creek[29] about eight miles south of Elizabeth City, where the Federals sunk her as an obstruction.[30]

The third contract issued by Secretary Mallory to Elliott on April 16, 1862 was concise.

One ironclad gunboat...of character and description provided in the specifications hereto annexed...part and parcel of this contract...party of the first part, is to construct and deliver the boat complete in all its parts, ready to receive the engine, machinery, and iron plating, which are to be placed on the boat by the party of the second part, the boat to be delivered in three months from the date hereof. And the party of the second part, undertakes...to pay said party of the first part, the sum of twenty-three thousand dollars in the manner following...five thousand in advance upon contract execution, with bond of indemnity satisfactory to party of the second part...4500 dollars when two-fifths are completed...4500 dollars when three-fifths are completed...4500 dollars when four-fifths are completed...4500 dollars when completed and delivered. It is understood party of the first part will make alterations or additions to the specifications, which party of the second part may require...for which he is to receive additional compensation, with additional time to perform the work if so required. If work is interrupted by the enemy, party of the first part is to receive compensation for work done upon the boat to the time of interruption...also party of the second part is to furnish any iron fastening, which cannot be obtained by party of the first part, cost of which to be deducted from the contract price.

Signatories were S. R. Mallory and Gilbert Elliott. Witnesses for Elliott were Ed. M. Price and William P. Young, Jr.[31]

The absence of 'Agent for J. G. Martin' after Elliott's signature is significant, because Elliott was considered an independent contractor working in the state of Virginia.

Departure from Mallory's policy which required machinery be installed in all vessels under contract appeared to have been eased. Commander Sinclair had stated the policy in his letter to Elliott on October 15, 1861. A modification pertaining to delivery of a complete vessel was being offered, since construction was to be in close proximity to Gosport Navy Yard where materials from ships stores were readily available.

On Wednesday and Thursday, the twenty-third and twenty-fourth of April, Lt. Charles W. Flusser, U.S.N., returned to the Pasquotank with a flotilla including the U.S.S. *Lockwood, Whitehead,* and *Putnam.* Their purpose was to block the mouth of the Albemarle and Chesapeake Canal near Elizabeth City by sinking a schooner and other obstacles in the canal. That canal, running somewhat parallel to the old Dismal Swamp Canal, was a rather direct inland water link between Norfolk and the North Carolina sound.[32]

By the spring of 1862, the Confederacy was becoming well aware that they could lose both the Norfolk area, and Gosport Navy Yard to the advancing Federals. Secretary Mallory had dispatched a confidential memo to yard commander Capt. Sidney Smith Lee, urging immediate packing for transportation of all fine machinery and tools not then required for current workshop operation. Under the guise of 'security measures' workers removed the machinery to equip an additional workshop.[33]

Captain Lee received a further dispatch on April 30, repeating the first order with a supplemental request to prepare the most valuable of naval stores for shipment.[34]

The next day another confidential dispatch notified Captain Lee that "all valuable machinery not really needed for service...be boxed or secured and sent away from Norfolk at once." Mallory assured Lee the destination would be named within a day, and further ordered all public property be destroyed to prevent falling into enemy's hands.[35]

Detailed withdrawal instructions for Gosport Navy Yard arrived on May 3. Shipping destinations were Richmond and Charlotte, N.C. Navy Yard workers and their families followed the army to Richmond, where some were retained to work in the naval facility there. The remainder were sent to Charlotte.[36]

When the Confederate forces completed their evacuation of Norfolk and Gosport Navy Yard on May 9 they applied the torch. Major General John Ellis Wood's Union troops arrived at Norfolk late in the afternoon on May 10.[37] They had been ordered ashore by President Lincoln, on board the command ship U.S.S. *Miami.*

Mustering sufficient troop strength to repulse the enemy in eastern North Carolina was fast becoming a serious matter. Union forces were gradually penetrating overland, and by water in their quest for domination. Such an event occured on May 14, when Lt. Charles W. Flusser, aboard the U.S.S. *Perry,* captured the *Alice* in the Roanoke River. She was loaded with bacon for the Confederate Army. Other cargo was that of church bells from Plymouth, N.C., to have been cast into cannon.[38]

The next day on May 15, General Robert E. Lee appointed Maj. Gen. James Green Martin, N.C. Militia, to the rank of Brigadier General, C.S.A. Elliott's friend would soon command the Martin Brigade.[39]

From the day his latest naval contract was awarded until the ninth of May, Elliott could have accomplished nothing more than preliminary planning for his latest shipbuilding venture. Because he was so close to Naval Headquarters he would have been well aware of impending plans to withdraw. He prepared for the worst by disbanding his workmen, and then returned to North Carolina.

Col. William F. Martin, after having been exchanged, lost no time in resuming active status. He made rapid progress in reorganizing the 7th Volunteers to become the 17th Regiment (2nd Organization). That was accomplished during early May at Camp Mangum near Raleigh. After mustering to serve for three years or the duration, the regiment was ordered to Camp Johnson. [40]

Since Elliott and Colonel Martin were friends with a former employer/employee relationship, Elliott most likely enlisted on May 16, 1862, at Camp Mangum. On the following day he was appointed 1st Lieutenant with duties as Regimental Adjutant. By June 1862, the 17th Regiment began training at Camp Johnson near Kinston, N.C.[41]

At month's end the Martin Brigade, to which the 17th was attached, was ordered to Camp Campbell near Petersburg, Virginia. Their destination was Drewry's Bluff, where they arrived about July 14.[42] They were to reinforce the engaged Confederate troops during the Seven Days Campaign (June 25 to July

LT. GILBERT ELLIOTT, ADJUTANT
17th Regiment, N.C. Infantry
Clark, N.C. Regiments, 1861-1865, Vol. II

1), but arrived too late. The 17th was joined by others in camp near Proctor's Station midway between Petersburg and Richmond. While there, General Martin was recalled to North Carolina, and he brought the 17th back with him.[43]

According to the 17th Regiment's July 1862 muster, Lieutenant Elliott was present at Camp Campbell, Virginia. There were no further entries.[44] For the period from May 19 to July 31, 1862, Lieutenant Elliott was paid ninety dollars per month, with a supplemental twenty dollars as Adjutant. His total pay was $240.00.[45]

In some manner it became known to Secretary Mallory that Lieutenant Elliott was nearby. Elliott's older brother Captain Charles Grice Elliott, Assistant Adjutant General of the Martin-Kirkland Brigade, authored a newspaper article in which he sketched Gilbert's life while he was rising to fame as a Confederate Navy shipbuilder.

> ...But he had not long been in camp at Petersburg when he was urgently solicited by Secretary Mallory, of the Confederate Navy Department, who had formed a very high opinion of Elliott's business capacity and energy, to undertake the building of another gunboat, this time to be an ironclad ram, as the career of the *Virginia* has revolutionized naval warfare.
>
> Upon Mr. Mallory's request the Confederate States War Department granted Lieutenant Elliott two years' furlough, and he was relieved of the duties of Adjutant, returned to North Carolina, gathered up the tools and carpenters, and began his new venture at Tarboro on the Tar River.[46]

Mallory's opinion of Elliott had been formed by young Elliott's Elizabeth City performance, as well as his brief effort near Norfolk.

Two officers were detailed as substitute adjutant during his absence. For a temporary period which lasted until early 1864, duties of Regimental Adjutant were performed by 2nd Lieutenants Wilson G. Lamb and M. S. Cotten. The former had been promoted from Sergeant Major to 2nd Lieutenant for the purpose.[47]

CHAPTER 6

THE ADJUTANT WHO WASN'T

Gilbert Elliott had substantial unsolicited support from fellow North Carolinians. The brothers Martin, General James Green and Colonel William Francis, favorably endorsed the continuance of Elliott's shipbuilding career. In the military, Elliott was recognized as someone capable of accepting assignments not common to infantry soldiers. As an infantry officer and regimental adjutant, he built ironclad vessels for the Confederate Navy as a bonafide naval contractor.

Just before June 10 Lt. Charles W. Flusser, U.S.N., led an expedition to the Pasquotank and North Rivers bordering Camden County. His flotilla included the U.S.S. *Commodore Perry, Putnam,* and *Hunchback.* He wished to "capture a prominent rebel," but the man had left his residence weeks earlier. The raid's secondary purpose was to find a rumored supply of oak timber destined for the construction of "a rebel war steamer at Deep Creek." He found the schooner *Scuppernong* (hidden behind sunken obstructions) partly loaded with timber. Those had been placed earlier by Brig. Gen. Henry A. Wise, C.S.A., as a delaying action to avoid attack from the rear while he occupied a position at the canal bridge.

Flusser decided that removing the obstructions would require too much time and effort, so the *Scuppernong* with the timber on board was burned.[1] It was possible that Flusser burned timber from one of Elliott's Camden County sawmill operators that could have been used on the contracted vessel he was to have built at Norfolk [Deep Creek].

During July others in eastern North Carolina were also reporting intrusions by Federal forces upon their properties. Catherine Ann Edmondston wrote in her 'Journal' that three Federal gunboats were at Hamilton, and had commenced indiscriminate shelling.[2]

Flusser advanced upon Hamilton on the ninth with a small flotilla from Plymouth. The expedition's purpose was interdiction and reconnaissance. Flusser's action report pointed out that they had fired only into the wooded river banks, though they landed one hundred men and one field piece at Hamilton.[3] As time passed, residents as well as the Confederate military in eastern North Carolina began noticing an acceleration of Union probes throughout the eastern counties.

Governor Henry T. Clark at Raleigh received a letter from Jones W. J. Muse of Wilmington who wrote on July 26 that he had,

> ...been on the eve of suggesting...the building of an ironclad gun boat on the Roanoke for the purpose of ridding our waters of the Yankees...I think it is worth the effort.

Muse called the Governor's attention to a sketch of the boat drawn by Mr. Scott of Louisiana, and asked that receipt of the plan be acknowledged because Scott wished it not to fall into other hands. It was alleged the vessel would draw eight feet of water, have great strength, and be capable of good speed.[4] No sketch or plan of that vessel seems to have survived, but how encouraging it must have been that there were those, other than the Confederate Navy Department, who were thinking of similar defensive projects.

Special Order #192, originating from Ass't Adj. Gen. John Withers in Richmond on August 18, 1862, was sent to General Daniel H. Hill, Petersburg, Virginia, stating that,

> A leave of absence for thirty days is granted Lieutenant Gilbert Elliott, Adjutant, 17th Regiment North Carolina Infantry, by Command of the Secretary of War.[5]

That special order showed that Elliott was still involved in some way with activities at Drewry's Bluff. The level of government within which Special Order #192 originated, indicated that he was on special assignment because it required the Secretary of War to grant him leave.

Pay vouchers were again due by August 30. Voucher #532 authorized payment of $100.00 to Lt. Gilbert Elliott on September 2. The itemization was ninety dollars for the month as lieutenant and ten dollars for adjutant.[6]

In due course a long awaited fourth contract reached Martin & Elliott of Elizabeth City. Dated September 17, 1862, performance obligations for the party of the first part (Martin & Elliott) were stipulated.

> The party of the first part agrees to deliver to the C.S.N. on or before March 1st, 1863, at Tarboro, North Carolina, the hull of one ironclad according to specifications hereto annexed as part and parcel to this contract...to deliver the vessel complete...ready to receive the engine and machinery, and to put in place and fasten the iron plating on said vessel...iron plates and bolts for fastening to be furnished by C.S.N...party of first part to employ all mechanical skill, labor, industry and energy to complete and deliver said vessel in shortest possible time, and omit no effort to attain this end...party of first part to receive the sum of forty thousand dollars in manner following; five thousand dollars on signing of contract, with bond of indemnity of ten thousand dollars...when one sixth part of work completed, one eighth of the sum agreed to be paid, and so on until the vessel shall be completed to satisfaction of the Navy Department, and when delivered the remaining one eighth shall be paid. Contractor shall make alterations or additions to specifications which Department shall require, and for which they are to receive additional compensation with additional time to perform the work if such alterations are required. If interrupted by the enemy, party of the first part is to receive compensation for work done to the time of interruption, and customer is to furnish any iron fastenings which cannot be obtained by contractor, cost of same to be deducted from price of boat. It is further understood that one or more vessels will be built under terms of this contract at option of the second party.
>
> Witness day and date first herein written by Martin
> & Elliott and S. R. Mallory, Secretary of the Navy.[7]

The phrase "of the town of Elizabeth City" indicated that Secretary Mallory was again dealing with Col. William F. Martin's shipbuilding operation formerly located at Elizabeth City. Routine continued, and Special Order #218 was posted on September 17 granting Lt. Gilbert Elliott a continuation of his leave.[8]

Others in eastern North Carolina envisioned any tactical defense only as strong as the number of ironclad vessels afloat. Chief Constructor John L. Porter had received a request for a contract from Messrs. Thomas S. Howard and Ellijah W. Ellis, natives of Carteret County.[9] In Porter's letter to Secretary Mallory on October 3, he wrote they proposed to build a light draft gunboat on the Neuse River between Kinston and Vanceboro. It was to cost about forty thousand dollars, "...like the one contracted for by Mr. Elliott. They are practical men and I have no doubt [they] could execute the contract."[10]

Lieutenant Elliott had probably returned to North Carolina well before the first of September in order to make his successful proposal for the Tarboro ironclad, and to prepare a followup proposal then being packaged. By the tenth, Martin & Elliott had forwarded their second proposal to Secretary Mallory. They were taking advantage of a clause in the Tarboro ironclad contract which allowed for the construction of other vessels. Elliott stated,

> We have the honor to propose to construct for your Department one ironclad gunboat and ram at Tillerys Farm on the Roanoke River in North Carolina, seven miles below the town of Halifax, upon the same terms and conditions as are expressed and stated in the contract under which we are now working. Said boat and ram to be of the same plans and dimensions as the one we are now building at Tarboro, N.C.
>
> It is conceded by everyone that the defense of Tarboro involves as a necessity the defense of the Roanoke River at or below the town of Hamilton. By the defense of this place, which is but 18 miles from Tarboro[,] the double purpose will be answered of defending Tarboro and Tillerys farm on the Roanoke River. We will deliver the boat on the 1st of April next.[11]

Following an endorsement by Mallory from his Richmond office on October 10 to Cdr. James W. Cooke, calling his attention to the clause permitting construction of several vessels on the current Tarboro contract, Cooke formally authorized Martin & Elliott to proceed with the second vessel according to terms of the contract, said vessel to be delivered by April 1, 1863.[12]

With the appearance of Commander James W. Cooke upon the scene, Elliott became acquainted with the third influential person who would enhance his career.

Upon receipt of Martin & Elliott's latest proposal, Cooke was introduced to the unfolding naval drama upon the rivers of eastern North Carolina. On October 17 Mallory addressed a letter to Cooke at Warrenton, N.C. He advised Cooke that his attention was directed to a proposal by John H. Leary to board and carry enemy gunboats on the Roanoke and Chowan rivers. Such plans, in Leary's opinion, seemed not only justified, but worthy of an attempt. Mallory was referred to Messrs. H. A. Gillian at Scotland Neck and James Mysell of Coleraine for further information. His final remarks to Cooke were, "...I refer the subject to you as a North Carolinian and a Naval Officer, and if you shall deem it practicable I will offer you all means in my power to carry out your plans."[13]

COMMANDER JAMES W. COOKE , C.S.N.
represented the Navy Department as site superintendent, and later commanded the *Albermarle* during the Plymouth battle, and in the engagement with seven Union gunboats in Albemarle Sound.

Century Magazine, July, 1888

Cooke's decision in that matter remained unknown. It could very well have required the use of sunken obstructions to hamper the passage of enemy vessels, combined with overwhelming land forces to board them. No such forces were available to Cooke or any army command in the area.

Commander James Wallace Cooke, son of Thomas and Esther Cooke, was a native North Carolinian, born in Beaufort in 1812. By the age of four he and a sister Harriet were orphans living with Colonel Henry M. Cooke, an uncle. When he was sixteen, James received an appointment to the U.S. Navy and thereafter was placed in training as midshipman on the U.S.S. *Guerierre* in 1828. By February 25, 1841, he was promoted to lieutenant. Twenty years thereafter Lieutenant Cooke resigned his commission on May 2, 1861. Two days later he received the same rank in the State Navy of Virginia. On June 11, his appointment as lieutenant in the C.S. Navy was approved.[14]

No reference has been found as to where Lieutenant Elliott was headquartered during that transitional period. He could have been staying at Halifax, or with a friend at Scotland Neck. The latter seemed logical, since he and Peter Evans Smith were friends. Because of Smith's inventive genius and mechanical prowess, Elliott could very well have been recruiting Smith as his associate while the shipbuilding venture gained momentum.

Elliott did not, however, forget his friend Colonel Martin who was at Oxford, probably visiting his family on brief leave. While at Tarboro on the twentieth of October 1862, Elliott wrote the colonel.

> The case of yellow fever has been removed from town. It may spread but trust not. I met Captain Cooke at Rocky Mount and delivered him our bond. He had been here to see me. General Gwynn has been ordered to report what fortifications are necessary for the protection of the Roanoke River.[15] I am told that the Secretary of War promises to keep all the troops now in North Carolina within the State. If old Gwynn dont take too much "new dip" he may do something yet.
>
> I wrote Mallory tonight and offered to build the battery for $30,000. General Martin asked me to do it. If the Secretary does not accept[,] the State will.[16]

James W. Cooke was the official liaison between North Carolina contractors and the Navy Department. He was acting in much the same capacity as had Maj. Gen. James G. Martin during the fall of 1861, when Elliott was building vessels at Elizabeth City.

Elliott also revealed an unsolicited proposal to build an armored floating battery on the Roanoke River, this to be the third unit generally authorized within the Tarboro contract. It's obvious that General Martin considered an armored floating battery a unique means of defending the upper reaches of the Roanoke River.

The Navy Department's ever growing concerns about the scarcity of iron were declared by Secretary Mallory in his October 31 letter to Commander Cooke.

...I learn from Mr. Elliott that railroad iron has been collected at Kinston by Messrs. Jno. and Nickolas Long, who live near Weldon, and that several miles of railroad iron may be secured from the tracks between Kinston and New Bern without detriment to the public interest. See to this at once as iron to roll into plate is greatly wanted....

Mallory went on to say that all iron had be be sent to Tredegar [Iron] works to be rolled into plate, then returned to North Carolina for placement upon boats and batteries for defense of her waters. He then became quite specific.

...Those roads which are required for the military defenses of the country must not be interferred with, but short roads that are not thus used or required[,] and which may be taken [may be seized] for Naval use with advantage to the public interests. You will endeavor to get the iron at a fair price, informing the parties that it is required for the defense of North Carolina. If they refuse to sell at any price[,] you will notify them that you will take the iron for the public service, have it appraised and paid for, in which [case] you will call upon the District Attorney or Judge and request the iron and state it's price. Should they prefer it you can agree to repay the iron pound for pound in kind, within six months after the declaration of peace, allowing them seven percent interest in the meantime. You are required to act promptly.[17]

As contractor, Elliott deserved credit for requesting early action to locate iron sources. He had already experienced that dilemma preceding the fall of Elizabeth City. It was beginning to appear that Commander Cooke would, as some have said, become the "Ironmonger Captain."[18] As time passed, his job became doubly frustrating.

And as this was happening, muster time was again upon the 17th Regiment. From a camp near Plymouth, the muster for September-October, 1862, declared Lieutenant Elliott was "absent, on detached service."[19]

Residents of Hamilton were becoming increasingly apprehensive over rumors of an impending Federal naval expedition to their town. They had every reason to worry. Cdr. Henry K. Davenport,

U.S.N., in collaboration with Maj. Gen. John G. Foster, U.S.A., conferred on November 3 to plan a joint advance upon Hamilton. Davenport reported that by 11 A.M. on November 4 he had failed to receive a prearranged signal from the Army, so he decided to "get underway and proceed up the river."

Davenport's flotilla included the U.S.S. *Hetzel, Commodore Perry, Hunchback,* and *Valley City,* as well as the *Seymour* which had arrived earlier that morning. Hamilton had been evacuated when the Union forces arrived and took possession of the town. Then Davenport's gunboats

> ...proceeded a few miles farther up the river to divert the attention of the enemy, while the army continued its march to Tarboro. On the 5th the *Seymour* was sent down river to destroy the works at Rainbow Bluff.

By the seventh Union troops, having failed to reach Tarboro, returned to Hamilton where 300 sick and wounded were placed on board the gunboats for transportation downriver to Williamston.[20]

After the letter to Commander Cooke about the acquisition of iron from the railroad companies, Secretary Mallory composed another to Governor Zebulon B. Vance on November 4.

> Sir: Commander Cooke, sent by me to North Carolina to obtain iron for plating the gunboats being built for the defense of the State, has returned without having accomplished this object. He reports that you have the control of a quantity of railroad iron, and I therefore address myself to you upon the subject. To enable the boats to resist the guns of the enemy[,] their armor must be at least 4 inches thick, placed at an angle of at least 36 degrees. This armor, from the limited power of our mills, we are compelled to roll into plate 2 by 7 inches and 10 feet long, and to put them upon the vessels in two courses. If you will let the Department have the rails and facilitate its [their] transportation to Richmond[,] they will be immediately rolled into plates for the vessels in question and for such other defenses as we may build in the waters of your State.

Commander Cooke will remove the iron if you consent to its transportation and will arrange the compensation according to his instructions. Please telegraph your
reply.[21]

That was the first direct appeal to the Governor. Mallory had,
perhaps unwittingly, revealed confidential construction information
in his letter when he mentioned the armor plate thickness and angle
of casemate slope. Those ordnance details were the result of testing
by Lt. John Mercer Brooke during earlier construction of the C.S.S.
Virginia. The Secretary waited a few days for the Governor's reply.

Commander Cooke was in Whitehall, N.C.,[22] when he received
a letter from Col. Jeremy F. Gilmer, Chief of Engineer Bureau, as well
as a response to his earlier inquiry to Col. Walter Gwynn. Cooke was
questioning the probability of protective forces being stationed in
the vicinity of Whitehall, where he was arranging for the construction of an ironclad on the Neuse River. Writing from Richmond on
November 4, 1862, Colonel Gilmer repeated Cooke's question about
whether or not the river could be defended to protect the vessel.
Cooke had requested a response through Colonel Gilmer or Secretary Mallory. Colonel Gwynn's response was optimistic. He judged
that,"...land defenses would be completed within six weeks." But if
the south side of the Neuse was not occupied, he considered "...it
probable that the Union would make every effort to reach that site
and destroy the vessel at Whitehall."[23]

Mrs. Edmondston wrote in her diary on Sunday, November 9,
relating detailed events of the preceding week during which soldiers
of Maj. Gen. John G. Foster unleashed their depredations against
the populace. Shortly after retiring on the evening of the fifth, her
household was awakened with news that Hamilton was occupied
and 12,000 troops with 1,200 cavalry were advancing on Tarboro.
Winter weather had arrived by Friday the seventh. 'Hascosea,'
their plantation about half a mile west of Hill's crossroads, was blan-
keted with a heavy snow fall creating an "unusual & brilliant spectacle of the autumn leaves, crimson, yellow & orange[,] covered with
a fleecy veil."[24]
After breakfast a day or so later Mr. Leary, a refugee from Chowan
[County] arrived with unusual news of General [James G.] Martin.

When regret was expressed of the enemy's having escaped, Mr. Leary remarked,

> Well sir, as to that, from what I can learn, if the General in command, Martin, was in heaven the rest of mankind would be no worse off for anything he can do.

Mrs. Edmondston explained that,

> Martin was on his way to his own house in Chowan, intending to make his way through enemy lines in order to bring off his carpets which he secreted when he left, to cut up for blankets for the soldiers, and he being an old man near seventy.[25]

Meanwhile, Secretary Mallory's November 4 letter to Governor Vance was answered by his Aide-de-Camp David A. Barnes on the fifteenth of November, 1862. He acknowledged,

> His Excellency Governor Vance has received your letter stating that he had control of the quantity of railroad iron and asking his consent to have the same rolled into plate to be used upon boats now being built in this State. His Excellency presumes that your informant, Commander Cooke, alludes to the iron of the Atlantic road. The State is but a stockholder in the road, a large portion belonging to private individuals. A meeting of the directors of the company has been called and your proposition will be submitted to them. Their decision will be made known to you.[26]

The Governor's response, while not in the negative, typified what was to become a repetitious series of reserved decisions from various railroad executives when they were approached to contribute iron for the Cause.

True to his word, Governor Vance made his reply to Secretary Mallory on November twenty-first.

> Upon consultation with the directors of the Atlantic and North Carolina Railroad Company, I have concluded to let you have the iron for the gunboat building on the

Neuse River if you will get it from the torn-up portion of the road nearest the enemy. In consideration of the alarming condition of our main roads (the iron giving way, etc.), it is deemed advisable that the iron taken from the Atlantic road, which is nearly new, be exchanged with the other roads for their damaged rails, which I am told will answer for rolling as well as the others. The bolt iron of the destroyed bridges across the Neuse you can also have. In regard to the other boat in the Tar or Roanoke [rivers], I think you ought to furnish with iron from the Seaboard and Roanoke Road, which is close on hand and is principally the property, as I am informed, of an alien enemy. Please let me know if these propositions meet your approval. The railroad company, of course, expects to accept your proposition for providing for a return of the iron.[27]

Evidently Governor Vance found the A & N C Railroad Co. staunch supporters of Mallory's plan. And with the prospect of newer replacement iron being received from the Government some day, the deal was to their advantage.

Two days later on November 23, the Union Navy struck Jacksonville on the New River, some eighteen miles inland from the sea coast. A landing party from the U.S.S. *Ellis*, under command of Lieutenant William B. Cushing, confiscated arms, mail and two schooners. The next day while under Confederate artillery fire the *Ellis* grounded. Unable to refloat her, Cushing burned the *Ellis* on November 25, 1862, to prevent her recapture by Confederate forces. Reporting later Cushing stated,

I fired the *Ellis* in five places and having seen the battle flag was still flying, trained the gun on the enemy so that the vessel might fight herself after we had left her.[28]

While Cushing was vainly trying to float the *Ellis* on November 24, Lieutenant Elliott's hired hands at Tarboro began cutting timber for his ironclad under contract. The timbering site was east of town across the Tar River.[29]

Within two years Cushing would be known in Northern communities as a naval hero, while in the South he would be sadly remembered as one who had shattered the Confederacy's plans of controlling the Carolina Sounds.

Elliott's circle of activity was defined by December 1. His ironclad construction site at Tarboro was about thirty miles south of Tillery's downriver from Halifax. His proposal to build a floating battery at Tillery's had become a contractual reality.

The contract of December 1, 1862, was between Martin & Elliott of Elizabeth City as parties of the first part, and Cdr. James W. Cooke, C.S.N., acting as authority of Secretary of the Navy, party of the second part.

> The party of the first part is to deliver to party of the second part, or it's agent on or before February 1st, 1863, the hull of one stationary, floating, four gun ironclad battery according to plans and specifications attached hereto.... Further it is understood party of the first part is to deliver the vessel complete in all respects[,]...ready to receive the armament[,] and to put in place and fasten the iron plating.... The iron plates with punched holes and bolts for fastening same to be furnished by party of the second part.... Party of the second part to cause to be paid to party of the first part the sum of twenty-six thousand six hundred and fifty-four dollars, in the manner following;...When one-fifth of work completed, five thousand dollars will be paid,...two-fifths of work, five thousand dollars,"...(and so on until completed, when the) "...remaining six thousand fifty-four dollars will be paid."
>
> Further it is understood that party of first part will make alterations in, or additions to specifications, which party of the second part may require,...for which party of the first part will receive additional compensation, and additional time.... If the work is interrupted by the enemy, party of the first part will receive compensation for work done.... Finally, party of the second part is to furnish any iron fastenings which cannot be obtained by party of first part,...and cost of which to be deducted from contract price of the battery.
>
> Signatories were Martin & Elliott and James W. Cooke, C.S.N.[30]

There is a similarity between Elliott's former contract and this, with the exception that no advance payment is offered, and that a bond of indemnity in the amount of ten thousand dollars was not required. Elliott was distinctly relieved to know that the procurement of iron plates would not be his responsibility, though as the weeks passed the shortage of iron caused more delays.

Word of Commander Cooke's supervisory authority over construction of vessels became known to Flag Officer Lynch in Wilmington. Although Cooke had been assigned to the iron gathering project by Secretary Mallory, the chain of command dictated that he also report his activities to Lynch. Thus it was that Flag Officer Lynch, on December 7, wrote Commander Cooke at Warrenton.

> Your communication of the 4th instant is received. You will be pleased to report to me upon the receipt of this letter, with whom you have contracted for building gunboats, and what location they are to be constructed, and what preparatory measures have been taken. Send to me for approval timely requisitions for money, which, when approved will be paid by the Assn't Paymaster here.[31]

Three days later on December 10, 1862, Gilbert Elliott became nineteen years old. Perhaps his friends wished him many happy returns. Though his superiors like Seddon, Porter, and Lynch may not have known his age, his youth could have been a factor when he first met Mallory.

Elliott prepared a transmittal memo to accompany the contract he would send to Commander Cooke who was at Warrenton. His transmittal memo simply stated,

> We enclose our contracts for the battery. Please sign them and return one to us, Halifax, care of Jno. R. Tillery. We go to Richmond tomorrow. Return Sunday [the fourteenth].[32]

On Monday the fifteenth Elliott had returned from Richmond and was back at Tillery's farm on the Roanoke. While there he gathered contract copies, and specifications with instructions requesting Cooke sign them and return one to himself. The other copy with endorsed specifications was to be forwarded to Mallory.[33]

The 17th Regiment's November-December 1862 muster placed it at Camp Vance. Although several camps were named Vance in North Carolina, the nearest within the 17th's area of activity was two miles east of Goldsboro. For that period, Lieutenant Gilbert Elliott was said to be 'absent, on detached service.'[34]

Elliott could have little doubt that his shipbuilding career had really begun. He was an officer in the Confederate Army. Two important naval contracts were securely in his possession, with the full cooperation and backing of the C.S. Navy Department. Confederate land forces, later to be assigned, would provide much desired security. He would soon be surrounded by capable and talented workmen. And best of all he had loyal friends and associates who provided support in darker moments as the months slipped by.

CHAPTER 7

ANVILS, HAMMERS & SAWS

New Year's Day fell on Thursday in 1863. Considering Elliott's recent floating battery contract award one month earlier, Gilbert was probably headquartered in Halifax on that holiday. Tillery's farm, where the battery would be built, was about seven miles down the Roanoke from Halifax, where the Confederate Navy Department had a small yard.

Thankfully, Catherine Edmondston's Journal provided a private glimpse of how landed gentry welcomed the New Year. At Looking Glass, her plantation home, she and Susan Harrison Devereux, her step sister, began the day with a quiet chat while glove knitting. Catherine, in promising Susan a goose, recalled it was

> ...her favourite dish,...today I had one which had hung to a turn...with wild ducks...and a pudding for which sugar [cost] $87^1/₂ to $100 a pound,...a dinner of four courses, or as Sue reminded, 'a rarity now-a-days, but New Years must have a new face to welcome it.'[1]

With the December contract in hand, Elliott also acquired a security problem. Although Col. Walter Gwynn was responsible for obstructing the enemy's passage up the Roanoke, Tar, Neuse and Chowan rivers, in Elliott's view priority protection ought to be granted to the Roanoke between Hamilton and Halifax. His apprehension was expressed on January 2, 1863, in a letter to Secretary of War James A. Seddon.[2] He reviewed how hazardous was the intended gunboat construction in wide open spaces along the river, far from friendly troop concentrations of any note. The selected site could be attacked from land or water.

Commander Cooke's double assignment was more physically taxing than productive. Detailed originally by Mallory to procure

iron, he was then ordered by Flag Officer Lynch to supervise construction of the ironclad at Whitehall on the Neuse, and submit
reports to Lynch's Wilmington Headquarters. Cooke had written
Lynch on December 29, joining with Mr. J. J. Roberson in a damage
report about the gunboat on the Neuse. Though details of the reported damage are unknown, the letter triggered a quick response
from Lynch who wrote to Commander Cooke at Warrenton on January 3.

> I have to acknowledge the receipt of your communi-
> cation of the 29th ultimo, enclosing report of Mr. Roberson
> relative to the partial destruction of the gunboat on the
> Neuse River. Until further orders, you will discontinue the
> construction of boats and bridges on or near the Neuse
> River and will give your continued personal
> superintendence to the building of the boat near Halifax,
> N.C.[3]

Three days later Secretary Mallory pressed Cooke on the matter
of iron. Perhaps he did not know how Cooke was otherwise involved
with Lynch. A sharply worded telegram keyed over the Southern
Telegraph Companies' wire was received at Weldon, N.C., on January 6. Addressed to Commander Cooke at Warrenton, nearly thirty-
five miles west of Weldon, it may have required a rider to deliver.
Mallory's impatience was evident.

> The Department has heard nothing from you rela-
> tive to iron for completing the battery and boats. No time
> is to be lost[.] If the iron can be obtained at all it must be
> sent here to be rolled out, at the earliest moment[.] You
> are requested to keep yourself in communication by tele-
> graph with the Department and to keep it advised of your
> progress in getting iron.[4]

Elliott had not been idle since New Year's Day. In his own quest
for iron he had boarded a train for Richmond sometime during the
weekend, arriving there on the fourth. What he thought would be
no more than a day or two endeavour to procure a rail car of iron
plates, was stretching into a week. By Thursday the eighth he wrote
Cooke.

> Please find enclosed bills in triplicate acccording to
> direction of Paymaster [Adam] Tredwell, [C.S.N.] for the

iron. Please approve them and return to me at Halifax at once as we expect to leave for Wilmington very shortly after our arrival there [Halifax].

We are here after a car load of iron and have been ever since last Sunday. We hope to get through with it by Sunday [the eleventh]. We telegraphed Mr. Roberson to meet us at Halifax after making an examination of the work at Tarboro. I will write you more fully after seeing Mr. Roberson.[5]

Mr. J. J. Roberson was an inspector with the C.S.N. Engineering Department at Wilmington. He approved an increment payment after an inspection of certain work phases. And then it was Commander Cooke's responsibility to endorse Robertson's approval before Elliott could receive a payment. Cooke was anxious not to appear resistant to Lynch's authority, while at the same time placating the Secretary by submitting timely 'Ironmonger' reports.

Elliott's train arrived in Halifax on Sunday, January 11. A letter from Colonel Martin was waiting to which he responded without delay.

Upon my arrival here today from Petersburg, I found your favour of the 6th. My man Tillery[,] after consulting his lawyer[,] came to terms and [ever] since I have had very little trouble with him about timber. He bothers us terribly about other things, such as corn, fodder, meat, meal, etc. You know what the law is, of course, but I think it strange that offering a bonus for the delivery of a part of the timber, in a certain time, would invalidate the contract for the remainder. However, I did not offer him a bonus, but contested the matter very warmly.

The power of attorney and official letter came safely to hand. I am exceedingly indebted for your very kind and elaborate statement of the Dan's matter. Without the information which you gave me I should have made a false settlement. I have not yet received any money in addition to the $3000 paid me by [Adam] Tredwell in Tarboro. I shall go to Wilmington tomorrow or the next day after $5000 [on] which I have had an order for some time. Cooke is a decided humbug. I was delaying my visit to Wilmington expecting to receive an order, as I wrote you, for the additional $5000 on the Tarboro boat when lo and behold here came a letter from Cooke stating that he had ordered Mr. Roberson to report upon it.

Such a time as I have had for the last seven days. I went to Richmond last Sunday after one car load of iron, thinking that I would get back in a day or so. I have just gotten here [Halifax], and have had the hardest week's work it has been my fortune to be charged with. For want of this iron our work has been going backward and for the last week our expenses will be sure to overreach the income.... I enclose the power of attorney and also a certificate of Col. Stark's. Please acknowledge the power of attorney before a JP [Justice of the Peace] and send both papers to William Stin for the County Clerk's certificate under seal. I use the auditors words, viz: 'Let the signatures be proved by the affidavit of some witness who is acquainted with the signatures taken before a notary public or some judicial officer with seal of court attached[,] showing the character of the Judicial Officer before whom certificate is given.'

Please attend to the matter at once and send the papers to me. I have proved Lynch's and Hunter's signatures and sent Colonel Shaw's to him for acknowledgement. It will be necessary for me to make an affidavit showing that you owned no other schooners which were sunk and armed with those papers, I think I shall soon have the money. The Yankee Captain Sanders lately commanding at Elizabeth City and Joe McCabe who was with him, were shot dead near the Leigh home a short time ago by some of our people. A just fate for a wretch who deserts his country and leagues himself with a miserable Yankee.

Rosanna's husband [Andrew], has been returned by the Yankees. Fred Cartwright paid Dr. Piemont $100 and swore that he would not take Andrew out of the county. You can have Julian, Alphius and Charles brought back on the same terms. I enclose your statement of our account to January 1st, 1863.[6]

With reference to the power of attorney, gathering of signatures, and mention of sunken vessels, possibly Elliott was attempting to recover from the State, and/or the Confederate Navy Department, some or all costs of Martin's ships which were burned when his shipyard was destroyed by the enemy in February, 1862. On the stocks had been the unsold hull and the *Chattahoochee* type gunboat. Since preceding letters discussing that subject are missing, it can only be surmised that these had been Elliott's intentions.

Captain E. C. Sanders, U.S.A., had led expeditions into Pasquotank County from Plymouth during the months of April and May, 1863. His excursions were primarily to locate Union sympathizers, and to capture partisan troops whenever possible. The four men mentioned might have been Southern sympathizers who had been detained by the Union, or slaves considered to be contraband by the Federals.

True to his expectations, Elliott traveled to Wilmington on the thirteenth. He was presented Voucher #8 by Assistant Paymaster Adam Tredwell, which was an 'Appropriation for purchase and building of Gun Boats.' It provided an advance payment of $5,000 against the Roanoke gunboat contract.[7]

One week later Elliott received Secretary of War Seddon's response to his inquiry of January 2. The Secretary's message was brief.

> Gilbert Elliott, Esq., Halifax, N.C. Your letter of the 2nd instant relative to the defenses of Roanoke River was referred to the Chief of Engineers, who replies that every exertion has been made to procure guns for the defense of that river. Four guns have been ordered to be sent, one of which is a rifled, banded 32-pounder.[8]

Elliott had to wait a while longer before protective forces were assigned.

After having been satisfied with Mr. Roberson's quality examinations of the work at Tarboro and on the floating battery at Tillery's farm, Commander Cooke wrote Secretary Mallory on the twenty-first.

> I have the honor to report that after careful inspection of the work being done by Messrs. Martin & Elliott, I find the following payments to be due them, viz., the third payment upon the Tarboro boat, of which I have previously reported, also the fourth payment of the five thousand dollars upon the Tarboro boat. And upon the Floating Battery two payments of five thousand each, making

it all the sum of twenty thousand dollars due Messrs. Martin & Elliott.[9]

Simultaneously with Cooke's endorsement of payment to Martin & Elliott, Flag Officer Lynch was preparing a letter for Governor Vance to be personally delivered by Lt. Carter B. Poindexter, C.S.N. Again he called attention to the urgent need of iron for naval defense of North Carolina waters, and urged the Governor to read the attachments. The first was received from Commander Cooke who was charged with supervising construction of the floating battery and gunboat on the Roanoke.[10]

As all the force is now concentrated on the Roanoke River on the battery, this work could soon be completed. All of the timber could be transported by rail to Halifax and floated down to where we are now building, but if no iron can be obtained to clad these boats, I think the entire work ought to be abandonded.

I have stated to you in a former letter that I think it is impossible to procure any railroad iron unless it is seized. The Petersburg Railroad agent says that he must have the old iron on the Petersburg road to replace the worn out rails on that road. The Kinston and Raleigh road requires the iron taken below Kinston to replace the iron on the Charlotte and N.C. road, and these roads are considered a military necessity[.]

The whole subject of R.R. iron was laid before the North Carolina Legislature and I am unable to obtain any iron for these boats and battery.[11]

The second enclosure, a letter from Mallory to Lynch dated the twenty-third of January, was very direct.

Enclosed you have a letter from Commander Cooke who has been attending to the construction of vessels in North Carolina. These vessels would not have been undertaken[,] had the Department not had good reason to believe the railroad iron could be obtained in North Carolina to form the plate armour.

Convinced that they would clean the waters of that State of the enemy's vessels I have felt great anxiety to complete them. All the efforts of Commander Cooke however, to obtain iron have failed and I commit the subject again to you.

The Tredegar Mills are proposing to roll thirty (30) tons per day and if we can obtain eight or ten miles of rail, we can send them here and roll them into plates for these vessels. The importance of the subject prompts me to urge you to leave no means untried to obtain it.

Railroad iron, as you have doubtless learned from our private experiments with inclined surfaces covered with it here[,] and from the vessels of the *Arkansas*[,] affords but little protection against heavy shot. Whereas rolled into plate[,] we can produce vessels that will run every gun boat out of North Carolina. The engines of these boats are ready and are delayed for iron alone.[12]

There it was, the gauntlet had been thrown down. Time and circumstances would decide whether the vessels would be completed.

Before January 23 had passed, Elliott enlightened Secretary Mallory by relating recent events which, if allowed to continue, would jeopardize the launching of his vessel under contract.

You will recollect having received a few days since, a telegram from us announcing that we had secured the iron for our floating battery. We were supported in making that assertion by the messages of Governor Vance, which we can produce at any time. When the agent of the Department applied for transportation for this iron, the Quartermaster of the post at Goldsboro referred him to Mr. Jno. D. Whitford, President of the A & NC railroad. Governor Vance happened to be at Goldsboro at the time. Mr. Whitford became alarmed about his iron and induced Governor Vance to countermand the order which he had given us.

Immediately upon becoming apprised of this unfortunate circumstance our Mr. Elliott came to Raleigh and called upon the Governor. Enclosed you will please find a letter from Governor Vance to yourself which will explain itself. We are sure that the iron cannot be obtained from the south side of the Neuse River in time for the battery which is even now, ready for the iron which is put on under water.

While it is true that our contract provides that the iron for covering this battery is to be furnished by the Navy Department, we, nevertheless do you the justice to say, that by means of our own exertions the state has pledged for the iron. If the Department can furnish us forty tons of iron at once the work can go on. If you are unable to do this we respectfully ask for instructions in regard to the construction of the Battery. Vance says in his letter that the work must be stopped. Please address us at Halifax, whither we go immediately.[13]

The question of iron was becoming an aggravation for Elliott and Cooke. Surprisingly the North Carolina Legislature did not support the shipbuilding venture, which would benefit the State if it were successful. As Mallory had written to Vance on the twenty-third of January, Elliott did likewise when he as much as said to Mallory, "What next.?"

Governor Vance had been in contact with Maj. Gen. Gustavus W. Smith at Goldsboro on the matter of securing rail transportation for iron. He gained small success when he read General Smith's message of January 26, 1863.

Your letter calling attention to the impressment of transportation by Brig. Gen. W. H. C. Whiting was received yesterday and copy at once forwarded to Gen. Whiting requesting that he would[,] except in expectation of immediate attack[,] not hold the transportation.[14]

Two days later on the twenty-eighth, the Governor sent a letter to Lynch at Wilmington.

Yours by Lt. Cdr. Poindexter, C.S.N., has been received in regards to iron for the completion of the gunboats on the Roanoke. The question is an interesting one to me indeed. I have offered the whole of the iron of the Atlantic & North Carolina roads within our lines below Kinston, save fifteen miles, but this you say cannot be got for want of transportation. The small amount at Besse's Station, not enough for your purposes[,] is held by Col. Whitford, the President, for the repairs of his own and our other roads who have no reserved iron, and our roads as you are aware are fast wearing down under the great amount of running they are compelled to do.

Such being the case you may perceive my embarrassment. I am of course exceedingly anxious for the completion of the boats and [to] the railroad we say, to give up the iron would soon render it impossible for them to repair and in case of such accident (by no means unusual) as the burning of a bridge, they would be powerless to rebuild.

I have referred Lt. Poindexter to Col. Whitford again instructing him to give up the iron if in his opinion it can be safely done, otherwise to retain it. I am still confident in the opinion that [with] proper application to Gen. [G. W.] Smith the iron below Kinston could be secured and if so the whole difficulty would be solved.[15]

Negotiations between Lieutenant Poindexter and Colonel Whitford for the Besse's Station iron remained deadlocked. With that setback Lynch returned Commander Cooke to the disputed scene. Cooke's orders arrived in Lynch's February the second letter.

All my efforts to procure the iron lying at Besse's Station have proved unsuccessful. You will, therefore, proceed without delay to Kingston and make the best arrangement you can, for the speedy transportation of railroad iron below that point, using your best judgement in determining whether it shall be brought across the Neuse or conveyed by wagons to the Wilmington and Weldon railroad.

Present the enclosed letter to General Smith or the Military Commandant and spare neither labor or expense in having the iron conveyed to the floating battery near Halifax, employing Mr. Roberson in anyway wherein he can assist you.[16]

That resolute reaction on Lynch's part raised the spirits of both Cooke and Elliott. Though they would be required to transship the iron to Tredegar, each would rest in the assurance that delivery of iron plates was imminent. Severe winter weather and a heavy snow fall in Tarboro brought the ironclad construction work to a stand-still.[17]

By virtue of his authority as Assistant Paymaster, Adam Tredwell obtained Elliott's signature for 'Martin & Elliott' on Voucher #23 in the amount of ten thousand dollars. This represented the first and second payments for the floating battery. The receipt bore a Wilmington date of February 4.[18]

On Friday the sixth of February, 1863, Elliott wrote Cooke at Warrenton reminding him that the third and fourth payments on the Tarboro boat were delinquent.

> The matter of the Tarboro boat has not yet been settled and we have not received our money. We sent you from Raleigh[,] Mr. Robersons certificate as to the fourth payment, but we have heard nothing either from you or the Secretary. Howard & Ellis [at Whitehall] received their money upon Mr. Robersons certificate. Commodore Lynch writes us that he has nothing to do with the matter until he receives a report from you. Please fix the papers so that we can get the third and fourth payments on the Tarboro boat and we will waive the question of damages. The third payment is due upon our battery. Please order a survey.[19]

Either Cooke might have personally visited the Tarboro construction site, or he was reacting to Mr. Roberson's proposed solution to a problem there, when he recommended to Secretary Mallory that the vessel might be moved to the Roanoke for completion. Mallory responded on February 11.

> Proceed at once to Wilmington and confer with Flag Officer Lynch as to the expediency of removing the gun boat under construction at Tarboro to the Roanoke River for completion[,] as recommended in your letter of the 10th ultimo, copy of which was sent to Flag Officer Lynch, and report at once to the Department the result of the conference.
>
> Messrs. Martin & Elliott desire to be paid for the work done on the vessel and the Department has delayed payment until your report is received. You will report also what

progress has been made towards obtaining the iron for the boats and battery under construction.[20]

Other than increment payment requests, no records have been found indicating to what degree construction of the Tarboro ironclad had progressed. Possibly the 'move' referred to transporting overland to the Halifax Navy yard the partially completed hull, all building materials, supplies, and personnel. (Such an undertaking would even be a supreme challenge for present-day heavy equipment movers.)

Secretary Mallory informed Governor Vance of an iron supply in his letter of February 13.

> I am informed by Flag Officer Lynch that there are at Lawrenceburg, N.C., 4,224 bars, or about 707 tons of railroad iron, and that all operations upon the extension of the railroad beyond that point have been suspended and will not be renewed during the war. I have the honor to request that this iron may be turned over to this Department to be rolled into plates for protecting the gunboat and battery under construction on the Roanoke River.
>
> The iron will be paid for at its market value, or the Department will agree to return it six months after a declaration of peace. All efforts to obtain iron in North Carolina and elsewhere have failed, and I beg leave to urge upon your consideration the expediency of turning over the lot of iron referred to, with the understanding that it will be used exclusively for plating gunboats and batteries now nearly ready for it in your State.[21]

Less than a week earlier President Jefferson Davis had dispatched naval officer Lt. John Taylor Wood to Wilmington on a survey mission. He would report to President Davis the status of ironclad construction, and make recommendations how best to defend bays and rivers in the Wilmington area. An excerpt from Lieutenant Wood's report of February 14, 1863, confirmed what Davis may have heard from Mallory that, "two others of lighter draft were commenced some time ago; one on the Roanoke at Halifax, the other on the Tar at Tarboro, but owing to the want of iron the work on them is partially suspended."[22]

Catherine Edmondston's diary entry on February 16, emphasized how poorly protected the Roanoke River valley was against the enemy's incursions.

> The Abolitionists came up last week on Friday [the 13th] to Hamilton in three gunboats, landed and burned the Hotel & retired without doing further damage. This is supposed to be a piece of petty personal spite, unworthy the arms of a great nation. The building in question is the 'private' property of Lieut. Col. [John C.] Lamb who commanded the expedition which some weeks ago attacked Plymouth battering down the Custom House, retaking many negroes, & disabling one of their gunboats.
> So like cowards they wreak their vengeance on Col. Lamb instead of the country which directs him.[23]

The fact that Federal troops could so freely descend upon Hamilton probably caused many to ask, "Where were the defenses to have been built by Colonel Gwynn?"

Flag Officer Lynch had been attempting to locate carpenters and ships craftsmen through the Army. He considered it possible that many in that branch of service might be experienced in shipbuilding. Soon he received the February seventeenth report from Maj. Gen. Samuel G. French at Goldsboro.

> I caused an inquiry to be made to ascertain the number of carpenters there were in Col. Poole's Battalion. There are nine good workmen, but they are all busy in building a pontoon train,... I think the gunboats of more importance than the pontoon train, but as it will soon be finished perhaps these men had better remain for a while. From out [of] the forces now enroute for Wilmington, I hope you will be able to get a number of carpenters and I did not make the examination on account of their leaving. I presume of course Gen. Whiting will make the detail. Gen. [Daniel H.] Hill has relieved me in command here and I will refer the detail for mechanics here to him.[24]

When Elliott experienced another cash flow pinch, he apprised Secretary Mallory of the problem. On February 23, Mallory sent a two-sentence note to Cooke at Warrenton.

> Messrs. Martin & Elliott represent to the Department that the third payment is due upon the battery being constructed by them on the Roanoke River. You will proceed without delay...and report upon it.

A routine entry in the 17th Regiment's muster for January-February, 1863, noted Lieutenant Gilbert Elliott, "absent, detailed to build gunboat for Confederate Government at Halifax, N.C."[25]

When Maj. Gen. Daniel H. Hill had settled into command at Goldsboro, Flag Officer Lynch began briefing the General about his ever present iron acquisition problem. On March 9 he wrote a long letter to General Hill no doubt hoping to gain Hill's support.

> Enclosed herewith please find the letter of Col. Fremont which you have referred to me. My greatest difficulty is the opposition, not always defensible, of railroad officials.
> There was a quantity of railroad iron at Besse's Station near Goldsboro, [for] which I obtained the consent of Gov. Vance to have rolled into plates for the gunboats building in this state, but His Excellency subsequently withdrew his consent upon the representation of the President of the North Carolina Railroad, who thus did all he could to frustrate the hope of recovering New Bern. There is a short railroad track of about two miles running from the terminus at Tarboro to the Tar River, the absolute distance from the terminus of the former to the point on the latter, to which the boats can come, being half a mile.
> I applied to the President of the Wilmington & Weldon railroad for the iron upon that short road, stating that what little freight was brought up the Tar River could certainly be transported half a mile by wagons, and represented how sorely the Government stood in need of iron for gunboats. I also offered to purchase for the same purpose a quantity of old railroad iron lying at this depot of the Wil. & Weld. R.R., which the President took me to see, stating that 'it was registered as unfit to repair,' and expressed a readiness to let me have it and promised to submit my applications to the Board of Directors. The result was a refusal to let me have either.

　　　Ascertaining that there was a quantity of railroad iron near Laurensburg [Laurinburg], on [the] Wilmington, Charlotte & Rutherford R.R. for the completion of the road, which design cannot be carried into execution during the war, I applied, as you are aware, for that iron to plate gunboats with, pledging in the name of the Government, as I had done in the former case, that every pound of iron as taken should be used solely for the defense of North Carolina and that at the close of the war every rail would be replaced. Old iron will answer my purpose as well as new, and I shall readily exchange bar for bar at this place, but iron must be had or the further construction of the gunboats discontinued. I have only enough iron for one of the two gunboats building here, that [iron] designed for one of them having been diverted to Charleston. The rails sent on can be rolled in Richmond, at the rate of thirty tons per day, and if expeditious, we may yet be prepared to close the Cape Fear against invasion. It is time that we should all work together, and I am well aware as any one of the importance of our railroads, but how diminished in usefulness would the Wil. & Weld. R.R. be were this place to fall into the hands of the enemy. And to what avail would the iron at Laurensburg then be.?[26]

　　　These issues had been addressed before. Citing Laurinburg as a possible source of iron was, however, a new revelation. His plea that all parties should work together for their mutual interest was well made, though it would not be readily heeded.

CHAPTER 8

THE EDWARDS FERRY SHIPYARD

During the month of March, 1863, Elliott moved from Halifax. He was establishing his shipyard in a corn field down river at Edwards Ferry. Though Halifax enjoyed the benefit of being on the rail line, and a Navy Yard had been built with an assortment of service buildings consisting of a hospital, drug store, ships stores, commissary, forges, etc.[1], it probably suffered from limited space on which to build an ironclad vessel of the magnitude contracted for.

Elliott's Tarboro contract provided for other vessels to be built. For this newest venture additional space would be required with immediate access to raw materials, and suitable opportunity for a resident security force to guard the project.

No doubt Elliott had been planning for that relocation from the time the Tarboro contract was amended. He had become acquainted with William Ruffin Smith, Jr., a vigorous supporter of the Confederate cause, and his son Peter Evans Smith. Both owned extensive property along the Roanoke. Peter E. Smith, a large plantation owner in his own right as well as a mechanical wizard, owned property surrounded by the lands of others of his family. And those lands bordered the south banks of the Roanoke River just north of Scotland Neck, N.C.[2]

PETER EVANS SMITH
circa 1880

As superintendent of construction, he coordinated all work in building the *Albemarle*.

Port O'Plymouth Roanoke River Museum,
Plymouth, N.C.

Elliott and Smith rode their horses over those fields along the river searching for a place that would, in their collective opinion, make a suitable shipyard. The spot they chose was a field gently sloping north towards the river while nestled between slightly higher banks. It was near the river crossing called Edwards Ferry.[3] About thirty-two miles downriver was Hamilton and about twenty two miles upriver was Halifax. The community of Clarksville (now Scotland Neck) was about five miles south of Edwards Ferry.

The horseman stands on the site where *Albemarle's* keel was laid at the Edward's Ferry shipyard along the Roanoke River. Peter Evans Smith arranged for the photograph to be made.

Southern Historical Collection, University of North Carolina, Chapel Hill

The Edwards Ferry shipyard was created in the middle of a freshly planted corn field owned by William Ruffin Smith, Jr. His consolidated plantation of about 15,000 acres bordered the Roanoke's south banks from Edwards' to Norfleet's Ferrys. To facilitate preparation of various size ship's timbers a portable steam sawmill was assembled on the farm of his son, Benjamin Gordon Smith, since his stand of oak and yellow pine was of the choice quality required for wooden hulled vessels. While the shipyard was being built and materials collected, Benjamin was serving as a Captain in the Scotland Neck Mounted Riflemen. Probably his brother Peter chose to tap Benjamin's abundant source of yellow pine and oak situated not far from the shipyard.[4]

Peter Smith possessed an elaborate forge on his plantation, from which could be fashioned tools and equipment of all descriptions. Gilbert Elliott charged Peter with the duties of Chief of Construction, a responsibility for which he was well qualified. Labor was also plentiful, since Smith made available many of his plantation workers. Most appealing to Elliott was the remoteness of the site since there would be little time to entertain visitors.[5]

The question of accommodations never became a factor. In keeping with rural customs, Peter and Rebecca Smith opened their home to Elliott, extending homespun hospitality for as long as the project lasted. Until the ironclad construction project ended Elliott was a permanent guest, while his mother and younger brother Warren were frequent guests. Cdr. James W. Cooke, Mrs. Cooke, and their ten year old son also lived with the Smiths in their plantation known as 'Sunnyside.'[6] Theirs was literally an open house for Confederate Navy personnel.

Charles Stuart Smith, a younger brother of Peter, was also assigned duties at Edwards Ferry. He was the official courier when he reached age 16 in 1863. A cousin, Francis [Frank] Johnston Smith, assumed the duties of courier when Charles reached the age for army service.[7] William Henry Smith, Peter's next younger brother, for a time served as Captain of the Scotland Neck Mounted Riflemen, but when construction began at Edwards Ferry he was placed in charge of the supply department.[8]

During March 1863 wood work on the floating battery at Tillery's was nearing completion. An informant of questionable integrity visited Lt. Cdr. Charles W. Flusser, at his Plymouth headquarters, offering construction information of the floating battery being fabricated on the Roanoke. Although no plans have survived, the informant's description revealed some clues to the battery's appearance.

> The battery is built of pine sills, 14 inches square, and is to be plated with railroad iron.... The battery carries two guns on each of two opposite faces, and one on

each of the two remaining sides.... The roof [slanting] of the battery and all parts exposed are to be covered with 5 inches of pine, 5 inches of oak, and then plated with railroad iron,...so say the workmen.[9]

Flusser included a cross section sketch of the battery in his report to Rear Adm. Samuel P. Lee, U.S.N., Commanding, North Atlantic Blockading Squadron, Hampton Roads, Virginia.

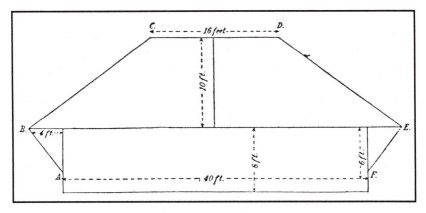

On June 8, 1863, Lt. Charles W. Flusser, U.S.N., submitted to Acting R. Adm. Samuel P. Lee this rough mid-section elevation of Elliott's floating battery. Said to have been under construction on the Roanoke River above Hamilton, informers stated it was of wooden construction with iron plates to cover surfaces A to B, C, D, E, & F. A hatch was planned for placement between C & D.

Official Records of the Union and Confederate Navies in the War of the Rebellion, Ser. I, Vol. IX

Catherine Edmondston's observation in her Journal on April 1, 1863, shed light of an accident that could have ended in complete disaster for Elliott's floating battery.

> Last week the Battery constructed above us [at Tillery's] was taken in tow by a steamer to be carried down to a landing below us [Edwards Ferry] to be ironed. From some mismanagement they allowed her to drag the boat then underway of steam past the landing & attempting to turn she ran afoul of the boat[,] crashing her wheel and damaging her greatly.
> Shameful conduct somewhere & conduct which will be felt in the Army, for this is one of the two Steamers upon which we depend to carry our supplies to Weldon.

One boat was lost from the drunkenness of the person in charge last summer...now this from incapacity.[10]

As the steamer approached the landing the helmsman reduced speed but failed to consider the fact that the battery was being propelled by the river's current. Mrs. Edmondston's candid observations have added a personal view seldom found in formal governmental correspondence.

Flag Officer Lynch wrote a lengthy letter to Senator George Davis in Richmond on April 6. Lynch hoped to solicit Senator Davis' support in lobbying for Navy improvements, such as recruiting Army personnel for Naval training, and the organization of Marine artillery. He also included a status report about ironclads then building in North Carolina. The brief mention of Elliott's two ironclads and floating battery was of signal importance.

> At Whitehall upon the Neuse, we have a gunboat in nearly the same state of forwardness as the *Raleigh*. At Tarboro we have one with the frame up, and the keel of one is laid near Scotland Neck, where we have a floating battery with its woodwork complete. For all these demands I have about 60 men, and the Navy Department, to which I have applied, is unable to assist me.[11]

For some time Lynch had been contacting Army units requesting that men who desired to serve the Confederate Navy be transferred. Lynch's letter to Senator Davis continued,

> There are many men in the Army who, from having been fishermen, pilots, and navigators of sounds and rivers, are admirably adapted to our purpose, and many such have applied to me for transfer to the Navy; but General Order #77, of the War Department, requires the commanding officer in all cases of transfer to certify whether the applicant is, or is not, a "seafaring person," which term precludes them, as their voyages have been mostly limited to inland navigation.[12]

On April 13, Lynch again wrote Cooke.

You are authorized to agree to the proposition of Messrs. Martin & Elliott respecting the *Cora,* and also the one respecting transportation of iron, with the exception of the conditions that what may be transported by Messrs. M. & E. shall be applied exclusively to any particular boat. The Navy Department cannot part with the right to control the use of the iron, saving the pledge to Gov. Vance that all it may obtain from the railroads in N.C. shall be applied exclusively to the defense of the State.

From what I understand of the progress of the work under Messrs. M. & E. there is little doubt that the boat under their construction will first require the iron, and I am willing to stipulate that other things being equal and no emergency interfering on the Roanoke [they] shall have the preference. Should Messrs. M. & E. refuse to enter into the agreement without the above named conditions and you cannot between the Roanoke and the Neuse obtain means of transportation for the iron, you are authorized & enjoined to seize their teams and proceed with all expedition to have the R. R. iron conveyed to the rail road and thence to Richmond. Use every argument before proceeding to extremity and if compelled to do so, appoint assessors to estimate a fair remuneration for the wagons and horses seized.[13]

Somehow Lynch had transferred the C.S. Navy Department authority to his Wilmington Command. After all, Secretary Mallory had first ordered Cooke to seek iron for the Department, but now Lynch wanted to dictate a priority plan for its use. The seizure of Elliott's wagons and teams was a serious step. Unfortunately no further information of the *Cora* proposition is known, though she operated on the Roanoke in a commercial capacity.

On April 16, 1863, Assistant Paymaster Tredwell accepted Elliott's signature for Voucher #10 authorizing ten thousand dollars which was the third and fourth floating battery payment.[14]

For some months Secretary Mallory and lower echelon officers had complained about the shortage of navy recruits. Most eligible men were in the army and were prevented transfer to the navy because of General Order #77, and its narrow definition of eligibility, allowing any commander to reject applicants if they were not "seafaring persons."

Finally the Confederate Congress, upon Mallory's request, enacted legislation "to create a Provisional Navy of the Confederate States." Captain Raphael Semmes explained that the object of the legislative act was to select,

> Without interferring with the rank of Regular Navy Officers, to cull from the navy-list, younger and more active men by placing them in the Provisional Navy with increased rank. Thus the Regular Navy became a kind of retired list, allowing the Secretary of the Navy to accomplish his objective of bringing forward younger officers for active service, without wounding the feelings of older officers who might have objected to younger men being promoted over their heads.

The Congress also provided that,

> All persons serving in the Confederate States land forces who shall desire to be transferred to naval service, and whose transfer as seamen or ordinary seamen shall be applied for by the Secretary of the Navy, shall be transferred from land to naval service.

Mallory complained that the law was not complied with.[15]

A short time after Elliott became Peter E. Smith's house guest, he was introduced to the Smiths' circle of friends and relatives. One notable plantation couple (Patrick and Catherine Edmondston) were almost next door neighbors to the shipyard. Looking Glass, their nearest plantation, was upriver from the shipyard. The Edmondstons lived there during the colder months. Spring, summer, and fall were spent on higher ground at Hascosea, just west of Hills Crossroads about two miles from the shipyard.

On Thursday, May 14 Catherine Edmondston invited Elliott for dinner. Since Hascosea was a commodious residence, the Edmondstons entertained Lieutenant Elliott there. She later wrote that "he feels uneasy for want of a guard. A bold Yankee commander could make a dash & burn it [the ironclad] without meeting the slightest opposition, so denuded is our country of both men and arms."[16]

For months Elliott had been listed as adjutant on the 17th Regiment's roster. And always the bimonthly musters accounted for Lieutenant Elliott as being "on detached service, building ironclads." On May 16, 1863, he submitted an unsolicited letter of resignation for obvious reasons. Colonel Martin chose to take no action.[17]

The second and third payments for Elliott's ironclad on the Roanoke, totaling $10,000, were incorporated out of sequence in Voucher #33, and delivered on May 20 by Paymaster Tredwell.[18]

Work on the ironclad was progressing slowly. One of the first duties had been to prepare the site upon which the stocks would be placed. Slope was important. Too much, and the vessels weight might create an unstable condition. Too little, and her weight might be greater than could be moved by man and beast.

Chief Constructor Porter's plan called for a hull length of 152 feet between perpendiculars, with an extreme beam of thirty-four feet at knuckle above water. Her depth from the gun deck to the keel was nine feet, and when launched she was to draw $6\frac{1}{2}$ feet of water, but after being ironed and completed her draught [draft] was about eight feet. Her tonnage on Porter's plan was calculated at 376.[19]

Artist's version of how an ironclad's frame members were placed upon the keel. Constructed of timbers 8 inches by 10 inches, morticed at the joints, they were bolted to each other upon the keel.

From C.S.S. Neuse, A Question of Time, N.C. Division of Archives & History

There was only one eyewitness to the vessel's construction who later told the story in print. Twenty-five years after the keel was laid at Edwards Ferry, Gilbert Elliott wrote the *Albemarle* story which was published in the Century Magazine of July 1888. Over the succeeding years his original text was to become the basis for all stories which often quoted his words, "No vessel was ever constructed under more adverse circumstances."

He described the awesome labor and logistical problems he encountered and solved, while building a 376 ton vessel from scratch in a corn field.

The keel was laid and construction was commenced by bolting down across the center a piece of frame timber, which was of yellow pine eight by ten inches. Another frame of the same size was then dovetailed into this, extending outwardly at an angle of 45 degrees, forming the side, and at the outer end of this the frame for the shield was also dovetailed, the angle being 35 degrees, and then the top deck was added, and so on around to the other end of the bottom beam. Other beams were then bolted down to the keel, and to the one first fastened, and so on, working fore and aft, the main-deck beams being interposed from stem to stern. The shield was 60 feet in length and octagonal in form.

When this part of the work was completed she was a solid boat, built of pine frames, and if calked would have floated in that condition, but she was afterwards covered with 4-inch planking, laid on longitudinally, as ships are usually planked, and this was properly calked and pitched, cotton being used for calking instead of oakum, the latter being very scarce and the former almost the only article to be had in adundance. Much of the timber was hauled long distances. Three portable sawmills were obtained, one of which was located at the yard, the others being moved about from time to time to such growing timber as could be procured.[20]

That introductory description in Elliott's hand, gave a sense of the enormity of the project he had undertaken. The technique of bolting frame to frame assured a hull of massive strength capable, he observed, "of floating if calked." Perhaps that frame method was his idea, or adapted from specifications of Constructor Porter, or was a recommendation of Peter Evans Smith.

Catherine Edmondston mentioned an event in her May 23 entry, which would cause Gilbert some concern in the future.

> To our pleasure we hear that the Abolitionists are blockading the River just above Plymouth in order to keep the Gun Boat which we are building at Edwards Ferry from attacking them. I hope that their barricade will be effectual against themselves also. Yesterday a company of Infantry passed here on their way to the Ferry, with orders to guard it and to picket the River from Norfleet's to Pollock's Ferry.[21]

Over a period of months the Union Navy was known to have been placing barricades and torpedoes in the Roanoke to thwart passage of Confederate shipping. They discovered, however, that to be effective the torpedoes required personnel on the river banks to detonate them manually by pulling lanyards. Because of that inconvenience and great concern for their own vessels' safety, the Union removed many torpedoes from strategic locations to avoid blowing up their own ships.[22]

Once again Catherine Edmondston recorded an incident of slight aggravation when she wrote on the twenty-fourth,

> Lt. W. C. Orrell [Co. E, 22nd N.C. Regiment] in command of the picket station at Edwards Ferry order[ed] the removal of all canoes from the River...a wise precaution but one which I doubt me originated with Lt. Col. [Patrick] Edmondston, for those young inexperienced [boys] never thought of it. Lt. O's order proved him both young and ignorant for he 'assumes the command of the River from Pollock's to Norfleet's Ferry,' and does not tell us by whose orders or by what authority.[23]

There can be little doubt that Elliott found the presence of troops welcome, although Lieutenant Orrell's picket force was far less than he had been led to expect, when Secretary of War Seddon had responded on January 20, 1863, to Elliott's request for protection.

Seddon had assured Elliott that "every exertion has been made to procure guns for the defense of that river. Four guns have been ordered...one of which is a rifled, banded 32-pounder."[24] After four months Edwards Ferry shipyard was still unprotected.

Construction of the ironclad continued at a steady pace. As rough timbers were cut, they were hauled to the shipyard where carpenters began the task of measuring and cutting each piece to a prescribed length. When cut to length, the ends of each piece were notched to assure firm connection to the next piece. Adopting the technique of fashioning complete frames to be bolted together required boring holes through very thick timbers. The tedium of drilling by hand was magnified by the fact that all the timbers were freshly cut and green. As timbers were cut it was imperative that they be fashioned readily, and bolted to their companion sections to reduce warping as the wood dried.

In anticipation of overcoming the drilling problem, Elliott had ordered a drilling machine from Lynch on May 31. Lynch responded on June the fourth.

> By Assistant Engineer Roberts I send you a drilling machine, and also, if it can be procured, the cast steel you require. The grate bars will be made and forwarded and the hawser pipes, when the moulds are received.
>
> If Commander Cooke be with you, ask him why he sent Hickason back. He is a first class ship carpenter and could have worked as such under your superintendence. A lot of railroad iron will soon be at Halifax. An effort is being made to bring the 'armor' round by railroad.[25]

By definition, 'grate bars' could have been iron bars on which fuel was supported while burning in a furnace, or they also may have been iron bars to form the lattice-like casemate top. In addition to the pilot house, Constructor Porter's plan required the casemate to be open on top, not only to illuminate the gun deck but also for ventilation. Cooke's return of Hickason remains a matter of conjecture.

Elliott's personal, though superficial, observations of how the ironclad was constructed made it possible to assess the work accomplished by Peter Evans Smith, Chief of Construction.

When the hull was ready for completion, but before main deck beams were fitted, the engine keelson was to be attached. Those were

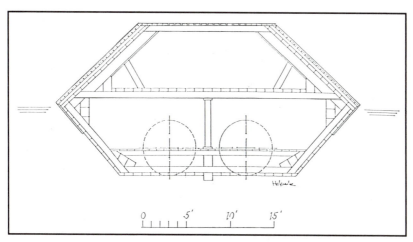

Midsection Elevation of *Albemarle* Showing Arc of Propeller Blades
Courtesy of Robert Holcombe, Director, Confederate Naval Musuem

the fore and aft timbers, or iron framework, made fast to the ship's bottom. To this the engine bedplate would be secured. The bedplate was a foundation piece on which the engine would be erected.

From the bedplate to the stern were built two shaft alleys. Those were passageways from the engine to the stern through which the propellor shafts passed. At the stern the hull had to be drilled to allow passage of the propeller shafts, then to be supported on the exterior surface by cast iron shaft housings. Within the housings were shaft bearings and packing to prevent leakage. The shafts, with heavy propellors attached, extended beyond the hull surface and required suitable iron bracing.

Forging each of two propellors, shafts, and casting both shaft housings was accomplished at the Charlotte Navy Yard. When it had become apparent the Union would take Gosport Navy Yard in early 1862, hasty preparations had been made to move all materiel, personnel and essential machinery to the newly established yard at Charlotte, N.C.[26] That quietly planned move from Gosport had been the reason for those confidential dispatches which ordered "all valuable machinery not really needed for service...be boxed or secured and sent away from Norfolk at once."

Simultaneously with the hull's construction, engines and boilers were being sought. A serious shortage of such machinery existed in the Confederate Navy. Thus Elliott's plans for installation probably were delayed. To facilitate construction while awaiting the machinery, a sizeable opening was left in the main deck to allow lowering the engines and boilers into position.

The months of April, May and June 1863, were adequate to build the hull and frame the casemate. In the meantime other happenings diverted Elliott's attention.

The Federal Navy Command at Plymouth was always receiving rumors pertaining to the ironclad being constructed on the Roanoke, but those tales were usually short on facts. The Union Navy's strength inspired bravado, aptly displayed by Lieutenant Commander Flusser in his June 8, 1863, report to Acting Rear Admiral Samuel P. Lee at Hampton Roads. Flusser included a description and a sketch of the floating battery he supposed to be building up the river. In a terse conclusion Flusser bragged, "We are driving piles in the river and preparing to receive them. I do not doubt we shall whip them if they venture down."[27]

Had the Edwards Ferry workmen known of Flusser's rash boast, wagers would have probably been placed in favor of the ironclad.

The summer heat at Wilmington could not have been worse than at Edwards Ferry, especially since Wilmington could enjoy the ocean breezes. It was, however, too much for Flag Officer Lynch. On June 25 he wrote Cooke at Scotland Neck.

> The awnings taken from the prize steamers on the Black-water were sent by mistake to Edwards Ferry. Be pleased to have them at once returned to M. McMahon at Halifax, with instructions for him to send them to this place as soon as possible. I am about [to] sending you two rifled 32's which will leave in a day or two.

Lynch's post script must have triggered incredulity, then scorn, and then laughter as news of his request spread about the yard.

> The awnings are indispensable for comfort [in] North Carolina even if they have been taken apart, send the pieces.[28]

Lynch was devasted by the heat while working in his office, but the workmen laboring on a vessel in the heat of an open field, where there was no natural shade, felt it even worse.

Several days later Cooke read Lynch's letter of June 26, in which he admonished Cooke.

> Your letter of the 25th instant, received. It was wrong in you to leave your station without permission. I do not visit Richmond until the Secy of the Navy has sanctioned it.
>
> The Department directed me, by telegram, to send the iron to Atlanta to be rolled and the agent there promised to have 300 tons of plates within 30 days. Sixteen thousand pounds of plates have been sent to Halifax. About one hundred and fifty thousand pounds are now at the Depot, awaiting transportation, and I have this morning received invoices for one hundred and seventy six thousand pounds, now on the way, so that you will not be in need of plates. The load now enroute from Goldsboro will continue on to Atlanta but Mr. Roberson will be directed to send the next load to Richmond.[29]

Cooke's letter of the twenty-fifth was probably a report made in good faith for it related his recent activities. Since Cooke was also under orders from Secretary Mallory, there was little reason for rebuke from Lynch.

The eight tons of iron in transit to Halifax were ferried by steamer down the Roanoke to Edwards Ferry, and rapidly applied to the floating battery. Delivery date of the remaining 163 tons of rolled plates was not firm. Lynch's decision allowing the Goldsboro shipment to proceed to the newly built Gate City rolling mill at Atlanta may have been a mistake.[30] He had no guarantee that the iron might not disappear. And "the next load to Richmond" might never have arrived in time for mounting on the battery.

In little less than one year Gilbert Elliott's vision of building an ironclad gunboat was becoming reality.[31] Work had been progressing on the ironclad's casemate framing. That structure was most likely to receive direct impacts from the enemy's cannonading, and therefore required walls of great strength. Three layers of wooden underlayment were fashioned, to which the iron plates would be bolted on the outside. To the vertically placed 12-by-13-in. frame members were horizontally attached 5-in. thick yellow pine planks, and these were covered with vertically placed 4-in. thick oak planks.

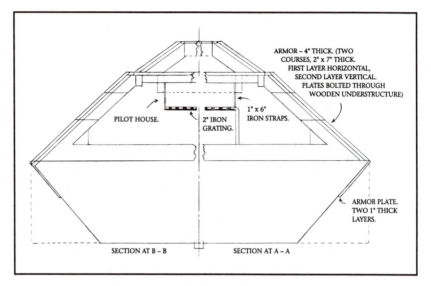

The helmsman's platform within his cupola above the gun deck, forward of the *Albemarle's* funnel, is shown in this cross section elevation.

Drawing by W. E. Geohegan - Record Group #19 - National Archives

The vertical frames had been bolted to each other, and the planks could have been attached with both iron spikes and treenails. (Treenails were wooden pegs often used in place of metal spikes or bolts.) Since the iron plates would require a relatively smooth surface upon which to be bolted, the 5-in. thick yellow pine planks were horizontally attached on the casemate's exterior.[32] The yellow pine beams forming the main deck were about 12-by-12-in.[33]

At that stage of the casement's construction, openings for the six gun ports were made. There were to be two on each side and one on each end. Breadth of each hole was to be twenty-two inches, with a height of 2 ft. 6 in. The vertical slant was a ratio of 1 to 4.[34]

Though Constructor Porter's plan had not so specified, at some point in the ironclad's construction it was decided to transform the bow into a ram. Elliott's personal description of its design was brief.

> The prow was built of solid oak, running 18 feet back, on center keelson, and solidly bolted, and it was covered on the outside with iron plating, 2 inches thick and, tapering off to a 4 inch edge, formed the ram.[35]

The vessel's first enemy engagement would prove the value of that alteration.

On Friday, July 3 Cooke and Elliott left the construction site and rode over to neighboring Hascosea to visit Patrick Edmondston and his father-in-law Thomas Pollock Devereux, but found them both away. Catherine Edmondston graciously invited both friends "to remain for dinner, so they might not be disappointed on the object of their visit."[36]

Mr. Devereux arrived at the shipyard on July 5, creating a welcome interval in Cooke's daily routine. Devereux, in his courtesy call, expressed regrets for being absent two days earlier when Cooke and Elliott had arrived unannounced. He succeeded in encouraging Cooke to accompany him to Hascosea, for Mrs. Edmondston wrote, "father brought Capt. Cook[e] home with him."[37] Cooke might have been invited for a few days rest and relaxation.

On July 7 the Edmondstons welcomed to the hospitality of their home Elliott, and his guest Adam Tredwell from Wilmington. Mrs. Edmondston seemed to have been well impressed with Commander Cooke during his visit for she wrote,

> Capt Cook[e] still with us, a gentlemanly, well informed, & eminently practical man. I hope he will construct such a boat as will deter the Yankees from an advance up our river.[38]

The purpose of Tredwell's visit had been to deliver the fourth payment of $5000.00 due on the Roanoke ironclad contract.[39]

In her journal on July 8, Mrs. Edmondston mentioned that,

> Colonel Martin holds Rainbow Banks where he is strongly entrenched. Brisk firing has been heard there today. The Yankees may intend only a diversion or they may be coming up to destroy the gunboat now building.[40]

Rainbow Banks, about two miles down river from Hamilton, was about thirty-two miles downriver from Edwards Ferry, certainly close enough to be a threat to the yard's security.

As work on the hull framework neared completion, Smith's sawyers were cutting straight, and very tall yellow pines of large diameter. Those logs would then have been transported to the shipyard where they were to be cut into planks 4 inches thick and probably about 8 or 10 inches wide. Those uncured planks were used to cover the hull's exterior.

The planks were attached in the strake fashion, that is, fastened in a continuous line fitted end to end from stem to stern. Since oakum was unavailable, the only alternate material was cotton, of which there was an abundant supply. After twisting the cotton strands into long lengths, and dipping them in hot tar, workers then tamped the sticky strands into the seams. Hot tar was then brushed over the filled seams, thus making the hull acceptably leakproof.[41]

Since Cooke's assignment as superintendent of the ironclad's construction, in addition to his other duties, he began to experience not only an increase in the number of required reports but also in the frequency. Flag Officer Lynch addressed a directive to Cooke on July 13, requesting that Cooke submit weekly reports to him at his Wilmington office, all of which would then be forwarded to the Navy Department in Richmond. Those were to contain information on all vessels under Cooke's supervision, and would state all work done the preceding week, as well as condition of the vessel or vessels being built. The first report was to have been submitted to Lynch's office at Wilson, N.C.[42]

Cooke immediately complied with Lynch's wishes by his response on the eighteenth, and included a copy of a recently received communication from Brig. Gen. James G. Martin. Cooke was advised by General Martin that his Command would be unable to provide troops in sufficient numbers to protect Edwards Ferry. Cooke's letter to Lynch inquired about the fortifications and security forces so often promised for the shipyard site.[43]

The same day that Cooke had most recently written Lynch, he had made his way to Hascosea for a visit with the Edmondstons. He brought only belated news of the war, though ever present in their minds was the knowledge that Federal troops were steadily working their way inland.[44] At that time a six-day invasion was underway.

Federal forces from New Bern were raiding Greenville, Tarboro, and Rocky Mount, in an orgy of burning and pillaging private and commercial property. At Greenville they fired the Tar River bridge. Among the properties destroyed by their burning frenzy at Rocky Mount were the railroad bridge, and 'Battles,'a six-story cotton mill. At Tarboro they destroyed the Naval works, railroad cars, supplies, and Elliott's ironclad on the stocks, along with the huge supply of timber prepared for the vessel. A well organized Confederate resistance assaulted the Federals at Old Sparta causing their precipitate retreat back toward New Bern. Confederate losses other than property and lives, amounted to 100 prisoners, 300 slaves, and about 300 horses and mules.[45]

Mrs. Edmondston's entry on July 21, 1863, alleged,

> The other column threatens us, their object being, it
> is said, to destroy the gunboat and battery now being built
> at Edwards Ferry...the men [civilian workers] from the
> gunboat with a single field piece which they have there
> now, are to join the raw troops & if Lt. Col. [John C.]
> Lamb be forced to retire [they] would form a corps of re-
> serves upon which he can fall back. We are entirely
> defenseless.
>
> The handfull of elderly men left to us are unable to
> do much towards protecting their homes & want of orga-
> nization tells sadly against them.[46]

Flag Officer Lynch and Lieutenant Kerr made a strong statement supporting the general belief that little was being done to protect the populace by either state troops, or the regular Confederate
Army.

Her entry of Thursday the twenty-third was a revelation of deser-
tions, sabotage, incompetence and deception, all key factors in unfolding events at the shipyard.

> Yesterday came Lt. Elliott and Mr. Peter Smith with
> bad news for our future comfort. Two Yankees, originally
> deserters from them to us, have redeserted and returned
> to their former friends. One was a workman, the other an
> enlisted soldier employed at Edwards Ferry; one to con-
> struct, the other to guard the boat and battery now in
> process of building there.
>
> The soldier gained the confidence of his officers by
> shooting a Yankee prisoner who attempted to escape from
> the prison at Salisbury, he being on guard at the time.
> The workman came with papers from the Secy. of War
> and General [John H.] Winder [Confederate Provost Mar-
> shal Department] & was accordingly put to work on his
> fiat.
>
> They surveyed all the approaches to the boat, we
> now find some days since, & were noted amongst their
> companions as being remarkably inquisitive. They left in
> a canoe under the pretense of getting chickens. On their
> absence being known an express was sent to Rainbow

[Banks] with orders to have them arrested as they passed. The sentries were doubled & the river picketed on both sides by Col. Martin [of the 17th Reg.] & yet his sentinel allowed them to pass even after hailing & making them come ashore! The dunderhead allowed himself to be deceived into the belief that they were neighborhood people!

My mind misgives me that they will yet work us mischief as they are remarkably intelligent & are possessed of full information as to the forces available for the protection of the boat, the roads leading to [it] & the work done upon it...they destroyed every vestige of a gunboat being built at Tarboro, even burning a quantity of timber in the ship yard there. They set the county bridge over the Tar [river] on fire in five places, but our troops were fortunately in time to extinguish it before much damage was done. The rail road bridge over the Tar at Rocky Mount was entirely consumed.[47]

On July 25 Flag Officer Lynch responded to Cooke's letter of the eighteenth, and offered an explanation to Cooke's question of security. He stated that Lieutenant Kerr had been meaning to visit Edwards Ferry for some time, but had been unable to acquire transportation for gun carriages, their destination being Edwards Ferry. Lynch then added,

> I did not wish the ammunition to leave Halifax until he took it in charge. Now that you have it[,] it is advisable to construct a proper magazine with all expedition. As Lt. Kerr is officially charged with Ordnance duty, I did not mean to disrupt you in your superintendence of the gun boat.

With unfavorable news from General Martin, Lynch hesitated to remove guns already at Halifax, since they might be lost to the enemy as result of an unexpected assault. Lynch further remarked that he had instructed Lieutenant Kerr to "keep them at Halifax until General Whiting, the military department commander, had replied" to Lynch's appeal. There had been recent work upon a [gun] battery at Edwards Ferry, but without guidance little had been accomplished, but Lynch cautioned,

> In the meantime have the battery in readiness to re-
> ceive the guns at any time. We had to buy such ammuni-
> tion as we could just for the 6 pieces. Can you not have
> the charges altered?[48]

Lynch's mention of "6 pieces," provided a specific clue as to
where the guns were to be used. Further corroboration of this belief
is found in Lieutenant Commander Flusser's analysis of the floating
battery's armament, which was expressed in his letter to Admiral
Lee on June 8, 1863. Flusser had written that an informant told him
the floating battery would have two guns on each of two opposite
faces, and one on each of the two remaining sides.[49]

Possibly ordnance personnel with the experience to alter ammunition charges were then at Edwards Ferry, though perhaps someone in the temporary guard unit might have been capable of this
task. Lynch closed his letter to Cooke with another rebuke.

> I do not approve of your applying for troops except-
> ing through me. Your application was anticipated by one
> from me some time ago with the same result, but I hope
> to succeed through General [D. H.] Hill now transferred
> elsewhere. But for sickness, I would before this have been
> at Edwards Ferry.

Lynch asked Commander Cooke to assure Mr. Elliott that his
order for 3/4-inch bolt iron, as well as 8 and 9-inch spikes had been
requisitioned, and that Lynch's Richmond agent had been directed
to acquire sufficient quantity for distribution to all gunboats under
construction within his [Lynch's] jurisdiction.

He expressed some distress that Mr. Elliott had applied simultaneously to himself and Mr. Anderson for a bending machine, and
that this would lead to confusion. He would, however, write Mr.
Anderson requesting immediate shipment with assurances of the
Secretary's authorization. Lynch then added he would prefer Cooke
initiate all future requisitions. His closing comment eased Cooke's
concerns about the vessel's crew.

> My efforts will now be directed to processing a crew
> for the boat you are superintending[,] upon which we must
> also man the battery [floating] for her defense while un-
> der construction. The prospect is far from a bright one
> but we must not the less persevere.[50]

The ³/₄-inch bolt iron mentioned above was to have been used by Peter E. Smith, who, with his portable forge was making the long bolts used to attach framing and timbers. (He later hand forged bolts 1¹/₄ inches in diameter by about 24 inches in length.)

Lynch displayed an obvious disregard for priorities. His Richmond agent was directed to acquire as many iron spikes as possible for all the gunboats, though the pressure was on to complete the Edwards Ferry ironclad and floating battery.

With alternating layers of yellow pine and oak having been attached to the casemate's interior walls, joint reinforcements in the form of oak knees would have been bolted under all deck beam ends where they met the hull. That process created the strongest joint then known. The final work of finishing the interior casemate walls was that of ceiling. By covering the walls with smoothly finished planks, injury to personnel by splintering would be diminished in the event of penetration by enemy fire.[51]

When Charles Grice Elliott later wrote of younger brother Gilbert's shipbuilding career, he credited James F. Snell, Gilbert's former master mechanic from Elizabeth City, with setting a high example for his fellow workers and also the carpenters among which were "the faithful gang of negro slaves, who worked as cheerfully as the white men."[52] Under the experienced supervision of both Peter E. Smith and James F. Snell, the difficulties of constructing such a craft in the primitive facilities at their disposal were made to appear negligible.

On July 27 Mrs. Edmondston said that a neighbor informed her of a dispatch from Colonel Martin, of the 17th Regiment at Rainbow Banks, warning of a Yankee force of 3,000 infantry, 6 artillery pieces, and 1 company of cavalry enroute to Weldon via Edwards Ferry. A second column was advancing north of the Roanoke in hopes of reaching Northampton County. The Confederates hoped that a hastily organized supplemental militia, enforcing the 17th, would turn back the invaders.

By the twenty-ninth the northerly column was closest to the shipyard. Throughout an anxious waiting time Mrs. Edmondston made rifle cartridges for the soldiers. Tensions remained high until the afternoon of July 30, when a message arrived telling of the Yankees' retreat to Plymouth. Late that afternoon Cooke and Elliott arrived with news confirming the withdrawal, and said that six companies of the 24th N.C. Regiment met the invaders at Crump's Mill near Jackson, and drove them back. The enemy had advanced to within about twelve miles north of Edwards Ferry.

By dinner time that evening further word came from Colonel Martin that his pickets had been driven in, and the enemy was landing troops from small gunboats.[53] Late the same evening came a final dispatch from Martin with news that "the enemy had finally retired back towards Plymouth."[54]

On Saturday August 1, 1863, Mrs. Edmondston accepted an invitation from Commander Cooke for a courtesy inspection of the vessel at Edwards Ferry. Of the event she wrote,

> I rode down to the boat in question with Capt. Cooke...to see the object of so much care & anxiety, [and] found a negro force employed throwing up entrenchments & preparing to mount a couple of small cannon which the Department have sent here to defend it. The boat is much larger than I had supposed & seems a strong & substantial piece of work.[55]

The *Albemarle* under construction at Edwards Ferry shipyard
From an engraving by J. O. Davidson. Battles and Leaders, Vol. IV

After viewing the gunboat and inspecting the facilities, Mrs. Edmondston invited Cooke to accompany her back to Hascosea. Later in the afternoon, while visiting quietly with the family at tea, Cooke received a hasty dispatch from Lieutenant Elliott telling him that, "the enemy were at Rich Square in force and inquiring for the gunboat." Instantly Cooke departed since Rich Square was scarcely five miles from the gunboat. Fortunately for everyone, the river's height temporarily prevented the enemy from hauling their guns near enough to the river's north bank to enable a clear shot at the yard. At dawn they were visited by "Capt. Cooke worn & wearied out having been up all night. The advance to Rich Square was from a third body of troops, from either Murfreesboro or Winton." They had suddenly halted upon finding themselves ahead of the other column, wheeled and scurried to join forces in the withdrawal.[56]

Capt. James L. Manney, temporarily commanding Lt. Col. Stephen D. Pool's Battalion during August, was ordered to garrison and strengthen Fort Branch with Companies B, G, and H of the 10th N.C. Regiment. Manney was responsible for preventing enemy gun boats from ascending the river, and destroying the ironclad on the stocks at Edwards Ferry. The companies of the 10th performed picket and garrison duty at Fort Branch for the remainder of 1863.[57]

From his Flag-Steamer *Hetzel* off New Bern on August 17, 1863, Rear Adm. Samuel P. Lee submitted a routine report of affairs in the sounds of North Carolina to Secretary of the Union Navy Gideon Welles. After proposing that certain vessels be rotated to Norfolk and Baltimore for repairs, he directed his remarks to the Confederate shipbuilding activity.

> The vessel on the stocks at Tarboro, not plated, but probably designed for an ironclad, together with two small light draft river steamers, erroneously reported as gunboats, were recently destroyed in a military raid ordered by General Foster... The ironclad on the Roanoke at Edwards Ferry, 40 miles above Rainbow Bluff, heretofore reported to the Department, is considered by Lt. Commander Flusser as a formidable affair, though of light draft. The fortifications at Rainbow Bluff, and the low stage of water in the river, make it impracticable for the navy to destroy her before completion, which is reported near.

Admiral Lee assured Secretary Welles he had made written application to Maj. Gen. John J. Peck to send an expedition to Edwards Ferry at first opportunity. He then added that if this could not be accomplished, the alternative was to assign Union ironclads to the sounds, but this seemed a useless wish since shoal waters at Hatteras were no more than nine feet, far less than water's depth required for the monitors.[58]

Adam Tredwell arrived at Edwards Ferry on August 24. He brought from Wilmington the payment of $10,156.50 for charges Elliott had submitted July 4. It represented an appropriation for labor and wagons used to haul iron plates.

According to Elliott's records, supervision required 55 days at $5.00 per day. During that time period 823 labor man-days were expended among 15 men working 15 hours per day at $3.50 per day. Concurrently with the labor, 350 wagons & teams-days were expended for 18 teams costing $20.00 per day for about 6.4 teams.[59]

Tredwell's Voucher #37 could have been the culmination of those fruitless negotiations for used railroad iron between Governor Vance, Flag Officer Lynch, and Jonathon D. Whitford, President of the Atlantic & North Carolina Railroad. A relatively short railroad, its trains ran on tracks of 4 ft. 8^1/$_2$-in guage connecting Morehead City to New Bern, and on to Goldsboro.

Commander Cooke hastily responded to Lynch's order of the preceding second of February when Lynch stated,

> You will...proceed without delay to Kingston [Kinston] and make the best arrangement you can, for the speedy transportation of rail road iron below that point, using your best judgement in determining whether it shall be brought across the Neuse or conveyed by wagons to the Wilmington and Weldon rail road.[60]

Cooke had gathered men, mules and wagons for the Herculean task of loading and carting 450 tons of rail road iron stored at Besse's Station. Whoever he had selected as supervisor performed his task expeditiously. But there was another possibility of where this iron might have come from. Lynch had mentioned, in his March 9 letter to Maj. Gen. Daniel H. Hill, that a quantity of rails had been located near Laurinburg, N.C. A portion of those might have been included in this acquisition.

The important fact was that procurement of railroad iron had proven successful. It can be assumed the rails were shipped to Tredegar in Richmond, since they had stated "30 tons of plates could be rolled daily."

It's probable that the long delayed shipment of iron plates were being applied to the floating battery. There might have been an outside chance a few plates were being fitted to the ironclad, but they would not have applied very many while she was high and dry on the stocks before launching.

Considering the crude circumstances under which they labored, they would not have had means to move a vessel of enormous weight into the water. However, if iron plates were being fitted during a lull in the ironclad's construction, that might have been when Elliott and Smith began to realize that the method of drilling bolt holes required improvement.

The drilling machine earlier promised by Lynch on June fourth turned out to be old and quite worn. It was one of those pieces of equipment removed from Norfolk just before the Union Navy took possession. Although it worked to satisfaction with wood, in the drilling of iron it was a failure. Peter Smith must have conducted tests, for Elliott wrote,

> The work of putting on the armor was prosecuted for some time under the most disheartening circumstances, on account of the difficulty of drilling holes in the iron intended for her armor. But one small engine and drill could be had, and it required, at the best, twenty minutes to drill an inch and a quarter hole through [a] plate, and it looked as if we would never accomplish the task.[61]

Drill bits at that time performed their task by grinding the metal, thus removing residue in the form of fine powder.

Catherine Edmondston wrote of a curious event on September 8.

> Capt Cook was off yesterday [Monday]. At short notice he received orders to report to Governor Vance for the reception of his orders respecting a cargo of cotton which the State of North Carolina wishes shipped to Nassau. Commander Cook, C.S.N., is to command the vessel. We gave him commissions [authority to procure], some shoes, tea, etc., but thank God our wants are not many.[62]

Cooke may have received such an order to convene with Governor Vance, but it seems inconsistent with Naval policy that he would have been allowed to command a ship for the State, especially as he was superintendent of a shipyard under threat of enemy assault at any time.

Meanwhile, Union authorities were gravely concerned about persistent reports of Confederate vessels then building in the North Carolina rivers. Navy Secretary Gideon Welles wrote Secretary of War Edward Stanton suggesting "an attack to insure the destruction of an ironclad...and a floating battery, reported nearing completion up the Roanoke River. Should they succeed in getting down the river, our possession of the sounds would be jeoparded *(sic)*."[63]

September brought a decided improvement of the yard's security, when companies E and H of Capt. William G. Graves' 56th N.C. Regiment arrived. He commanded companies E [of Northampton County] and H [of Alexander, Caswell, and Orange Counties primarily] in protecting the ironclad and floating battery under construction at Edwards Ferry. Joined with the 17th Regiment nearby, their presence was a detriment to any plans the enemy might have had to destroy the yard. Mrs. Edmondston wrote of Captain Graves, on the twenty-second, that he and Dr. Watkins (Ass't Surgeon of the 25th Regiment) had visited her husband Patrick on the preceding Saturday for a brief moment of rest from the weariness of camp life.[64]

Elliott and Smith must have had serious discussions about the unforeseen difficulties encountered in drilling $1^{1}/_{4}$-inch test holes in 2-inch thick iron plates. Evidently they became convinced of the problem while working on the floating battery, because of the disadvantages of working in a primitive environment while using drilling techniques of the day, Elliott envisioned substantial cost overruns in applying the armor plates. He decided to request of Secretary Mallory an amendment to the contract, which would have provided supplementary payment for installing the plates. On September 22, 1863, Elliott addressed his proposal to Mallory.[65]

To further demonstrate how very dull and inactive the shipyard could often become, Lena Hill Smith, oldest daughter of Peter E. Smith, and her two nephews Arthur R. and Walter J. Smith, ages thirteen and eleven respectively,[66] were permitted "to spend Saturdays playing around the ironclad. They were even allowed to drive some nails into the ram."[67]

But beyond the pastoral vista beside the Roanoke, Flag Officer Lynch, in asserting his rank, nearly scuttled plans for the ironclad.

Becoming increasingly distressed by the enemy's forays towards Edwards Ferry, Lynch directed Commander Cooke to order the vessel launched. Cooke later wrote Mallory in vindication of his belated obedience to Lynch's surprise order to launch "at the first possible opportunity[,] even provided the river was favorable before the holes were bored for the shafts."[68]

Lynch must have considered it prudent to move the vessel upriver to the Halifax yard where greater protection was offered. He probably surmised the location would be a greater deterrent to the enemy than the small troop detachment at Edwards Ferry. And of course he had sold his idea to Secretary Mallory, who in turn endorsed the recommendation.

When Elliott learned of Cooke's orders to launch the ironclad well ahead of schedule, he had no alternative but to make necessary arrangements. That included acquisition of teams of horses, mules and yokes of oxen. Barrels of lard to grease the ways were probably collected from neighboring farms. The on-site sawmill dressed logs to supplement those upon which the vessel would slide hesitatingly to the river's edge. Ropes and hawsers were assembled with which to pull her immense weight into the water, and then to hold her against the river's current. As September began to wane, the tempo of preparations increased in hopes of launching at the full moon when the river's level would be highest.

On Wednesday September 30, Adam Tredwell met Elliott at the Halifax yard with three vouchers in hand. He required receipts from Elliott for Vouchers #5 and #6, representing ironclad payments of $5,000 each for the sixth and fifth increments respectively.

Voucher #7, amounting to $1,480.00, represented Elliott's charges of September 1 directly related to processing iron plates. It revealed 170 days labor drilling iron @ $4.00 per day, 240 days handling materials @ $3.00 per day, and 20 days work on the boring machine @ $4.00 per day. This last charge may have been for performing service or repairs to the machine.[69] In accordance with Lynch's directive, Cooke had endorsed initial approval of Elliott's charges.

Cooke realized he was rapidly becoming embroiled in a politically untenable position. On one hand, his reputation for fairness to Elliott could be compromised. On the other, he had pledged himself to Secretary Mallory in the matter of collecting iron for his 'charges' on the Roanoke. Then too there was Lynch, his superior Naval officer, from whom he must receive and obey orders pertaining to Naval affairs.

As superintendent of the Edwards Ferry yard, his greatest concerns had been the acquisition of iron plates, and protection from the aggressive Union Army. That was enough responsibility for anyone, but the primary authority to please was Richmond. He could well have been alarmed that Lynch had perhaps omitted Elliott from any preliminary discussions prior to the launch order.

What Cooke didn't know, however, was how fervently Lynch wished for Elliott's removal as contractor. Lynch might have envisioned that if he could remove Elliott, then the vessel's destiny would be under his control, and if it turned the Union tide into a Confederate victory, he would enjoy the rewards.

As Cooke weighed his options, the Roanoke rose slowly. An unexpected drop in the water level would further delay launching an unfinished vessel. No doubt he hoped it would happen. He and Elliott discussed strategy pertaining to an untimely launch, and Contractor Elliott assured him that all would be in readiness when the Superintendent passed the order. Men, mules, horses and oxen were standing by, with only the workers being perturbed about the hasty launch plans.

Someone suggested the vessel be launched in the time honored manner by breaking a wine bottle against her bow. Consequently, Miss Mary Spottswood was invited to christen the vessel, and of course she readily accepted. The date and time of the occasion was indefinite, and depended on whether or not the river's level was adequate, whether or not the vessel could be moved because of her weight, and whether the yard might then be under assault at the planned moment.[70]

Indeed the launch was delayed, but to the spectators the bustle and confusion appeared normal. There were animals heaving on taunt lines with teamsters encouraging them on with shouts and the cracking of whips. Other workers were seen using long poles with swabs attached, with which they applied more grease to the ways. Elliott was observed by all, as he hurried from one area to another offering encouragement to some, and words of caution to others. The actual launch date was October 6, 1863.

Catherine Edmondston recorded the incident on Wednesday October 7, 1863.

> On Monday Sue & I...went down to see the gunboat launched, but like most of her sex she was uncertain & disappointing & beyond seeing all our neighbors assembled[,] we had our ride for nothing. She, however, took her future element without accident we heard[,] at three o'clock the next morning, [with] her builders being forced to wait for the moon to rise ere they could persuade the coy maiden to venture upon the slippery 'ways' that lead to the water.[71]

Of the long awaited event Elliott later wrote,

> Seizing an opportunity by comparatively high water, the boat was launched, though not without misgivings as to the result, for the yard being on a bluff she had to take a jump, and as a matter of fact was 'hogged' in the attempt, but to our great gratification did not thereby spring a leak.[72]

Chief Constructor Porter reported the launch to Secretary Mallory. An extract of that report provides a reason for Elliott's "misgivings as to the result." Porter said "the launch occurred when the water level was 6 feet too low, and because of this the vessel was hogged $5^{1}/_{2}$ inches."[73] This condition was best described by visualizing similar points of the keel's bottom at stem, center, and stern; with the stem and stern points being $5^{1}/_{2}$ inches lower than the point at center keel.

As the hull slid stern first down the ways the stern extended out above the water, instead of being buoyed upon it, since the water's level was too low. When the keel's midpoint neared the way's end, the vessel could have been likened to a teeterboard. Finally the heavy stern dropped to the water, but by then excessive strain had caused the keel's 'hogged' state.

Most likely she was launched diagonally upriver. Because her enormous weight augmented the launch momentum, her water surface speed was neutralized by the downriver current. For a moment she was practically motionless, thus enabling the workers to pull her against the bank for mooring. To all who beheld her, she appeared majestic in her watery element as she rode the ripples on an even keel.

Perhaps J. Thomas Scharf, formerly of the Confederate Navy, expressed the event most succinctly.

The building of the iron-clad, under all the disadvantages of place and circumstances, was viewed by the community as a chimerical absurdity. Great was the general astonishment when it became known that the indomitable commander had conquered all obstacles and was about to launch his bantling. On the appointed day 'Cooke & Company' committed their 'nonesuch' to the turbid waters of the Roanoke, christening her, as she glided from the launching ways, 'the good ship *Albemarle.*'[74]

In Elliott's own words, so often repeated over the years, "No vessel was ever constructed under more adverse circumstances."

CHAPTER 9

THE ALBEMARLE BECOMES AN IRONCLAD

The *Albemarle's* premature launch, as directed by Flag Officer Lynch, was the beginning of a series of written acccusations, rebuttals, and complaints, each of a recriminatory nature. Principals in the unfolding tableau were Flag Officer Lynch, Commander Cooke, Gilbert Elliott, Governor Vance, and Secretary Mallory. Difficulties included a jurisdictional dispute over how and when the vessel would be completed, and who would be responsible for the work.

As the 1863 fall season approached, with his construction schedules thwarted by the lack of iron plates, Elliott had remarked to someone that further effort to finish the ironclad might be futile. His opinion became known to Flag Officer Lynch, who shortly thereafter decided to remove the *Albemarle* to Halifax. Perhaps he reasoned that would effectually relieve Elliott of his responsibility in finishing the vessel.

Since he was under official contract with the Navy Department Elliott disputed the move, for in his opinion any such order should have originated with Secretary Mallory. As most of his workers were already idle because of the supply shortage, he slowed their work pace until the matter was resolved. In later years when he wrote of the *Albemarle*, Elliott diplomatically remarked that, "for many reasons it was thought judicious to remove the boat to the town of Halifax, about twenty miles up river,...."[1]

While at Halifax on October 12, Lynch wrote Cooke at Edwards Ferry in response to Cooke's letter which he had received two days earlier. Lynch referred to a machine that Cooke ordered, but its specific identification was not mentioned.

> The machine will be sent down as desired, but no step be taken which will one instant detain the boat below this point. Everything must yield which may come in conflict with that measure. With that exception you will proceed with the work upon the boat inside and out.

Then, as an afterthought, he added, "the Department directs that the boat be called the *Albemarle*."

In conclusion, Lynch then requested of Cooke, "say to Mr. Elliott that upon the strength of Mr. Carr's statement I have suggested the building of a tender upon the Roanoke." Lastly, Lynch offered a warning to Elliott.

> Inform him that when he throws up his contract for building the gunboat, the Department will decide whether he does not thereby incur the forfeit of what would otherwise be due. Should he throw up, employ the workmen for the Government and place them in charge of Mr. Thomas, apprising me of the abandonment in order that I may send Mr. Roberson to value the unpaid work. In the meantime make the best arrangements you can to feed the men.[2]

That very same day Elliott received Mallory's response to his letter of September 22, in which he had requested a contractural amendment allowing separate payment for installing iron plates. His proposal had been denied.[3]

Assistant Paymaster Adam Tredwell paid H. W. Peel of Wilson, N.C., $90.00 on October 16 for seventeen days work as Superintendent at Halifax Yard. The labor charge amounted to $5.00 per day, with an additional $5.00 for roundtrip railroad fare between Wilson and Halifax.[4]

A sorrowful loss occurred for Peter E. Smith and his wife Rebecca on October 17, 1863, when their second child Susan Evans Smith, at age 6 or 7, succumbed to the ravages of diptheria. The loss of his child following so closely upon a narrowly avoided launching disaster, placed a severe strain upon Peter and his family.[5]

Within a day or so after October 17, Lynch's command to move the *Albemarle* was executed. She was towed by river steamer from Edwards Ferry to Halifax. Chief Naval Constructor John L. Porter finally sent a report of his October 21 Edwards Ferry inspection visit to the Navy Department and Flag Officer Lynch. It briefly stated,

> I proceeded thence to Scotland Neck and examined the new ironclad steamer built under contract by Mr.

Elliott. This vessel is a very rough and inferior piece of work in labor and material[.] She is not properly fastened and has been launched before she was in a proper state of forwardness and also when the water was too low by six feet, the consequence of which has been to hog the vessel 5½ inches. I gave directions to use such means as were necessary to straighten the vessel and secure her, and think she will be brought back to her original position when her armor is on. Flag Officer Lynch has directed her to be brought to Halifax for completion.[6]

On October 24 Catherine Edmondston gave a civilian's view of naval politics in action.

> Yesterday, [Friday the 23rd] came Capt. Cooke, Capt. Graves, & Lt. Elliott to dine. They told us that the gunboat had been towed up to Halifax to be finished at a heavy expense to government, but that little great man, Comm. Lynch, could not get a house large enough for his dignity short of the town & that bag of wind, Sec. Mallory, listened to him in preference to men of sense & capacity, but he is so stuffed with conceit, so utterly empty headed himself, that I suppose he cannot distinguish good counsel from bad. I have seen this Secy Mallory, seen & heard him, & he is just the man to be blinded by a dose of flattery skillfully administered. He is emphatically as I said before, "a bag of wind." The boat is to be named the *Albemarle*. God grant that she may free her namesake Albemarle Sound from Yankee sway.[7]

Flag Officer Lynch increased the pressure on Elliott, by requesting Commander Cooke to join his intimidation scheme. His October 26 letter to Cooke began,

> Upon receipt of this, you will address a note to Mr. Elliott asking whether, or not, it is his intention to complete the gun boat for which he is contractor, and transmit a copy of his reply, certified by yourself, to me at Wilmington.
> In directing you to send up the materials prepared for the gunboat, I had no reference to the sheds which are

private property, and which, as expressed to Mr. Elliott by Hon. William F. Porter with my sanction, the Government is willing to purchase at a fair price.

For a number of days, Elliott had remained silent to the demands of Lynch by standing on his position as bonafide contractor. He might have wondered why Mallory had not initiated an inquiry. Lynch continued his letter by briefing Cooke on the latest intelligence reports of Union Navy aspirations.

As it seems to be ascertained that General Foster [Maj. Gen. John C.] is fitting out a flotilla of light draft vessels at Fortress Monroe, and the Roanoke may be his destination, you need not move the gun at present but let it remain in readiness for defences. A guard should be kept on the magazine. In the mean time this floating battery must be brought up [to Halifax] as soon as possible, and you will be pleased to do your utmost to effect it. The requisition of repairs of machinery of *Cora* was returned to you approved.

Before closing his letter, Lynch said he understood one of the men sent to Halifax reported that Elliott had transferred everything to Cooke. Acting without confirmation of the allegation, he impulsively requested Cooke to send all the white workmen to Lieutenant Johnston at Halifax so work on the vessel could continue. Cooke was to notify the men their services were required by the Government, and if any should refuse the Halifax assignment, their names would be forwarded to Wilmington from where, if they had been detailed, they would be ordered back to their commanding officers. Their alternative was to report to their district conscript officer. He cautioned Cooke to be vigilant in the pursuit of this matter.[8]

The river steamer *Cora* freely plied rivers and sounds of Eastern North Carolina before navigating hazards were introduced by the Union Navy. From the time Plymouth was first occupied by the Federals, the *Cora* kept to the waters of the Roanoke, Cashie, and Chowan Rivers. She was highly valued by planters and tradesmen alike, along the Roanoke, as an economical means of moving products to market. As the Edwards Ferry yard became operational, repair of government vessels was possible. By March of 1862, the C. S. Navy Department had purchased the *Cora* while retaining D. D. Sirmond as her Master.[9]

She was a frequently used supply ship for Col. Collett Leventhrope who commanded the 34th Regiment at Hamilton. A mile or so down river from Hamilton was Fort Branch, strategically located high on a bluff above the Roanoke. Lynch was known to have authorized Cooke's approval of work contracts as required.[10] Further service to the *Cora* had been provided, for Lynch informed Cooke that requisitions for machinery repairs had been approved.[11]

With the *Albemarle's* departure upriver to Halifax, the spirits of many were no doubt dampened, while others found it difficult to conceal their disgust at the turn of events. Among the latter group was Catherine Edmondston who, on October 31, expressed an impression as seen from the eyes of a civilian.

> Capt. Graves and his command are, to our sorrow, ordered to [Greenville], there being no immediate prospect of the gunboat's being finished. Comm. Lynch, that little great man, is ordered to Wilmington & has interest enough to get the iron intended for the *Albemarle* transferred with him to that point[,] to be put on a gunboat in process of construction there. It was originally brought from Wilmington[,] so that the freight on it going & coming & the expenses incident to so many handlings will make it mount up to $5 per lb, before it is finally fixed in its place. But what can we expect of a pudding headed bag of wind like Secy Mallory & a man who has weakened the little judgement he originally possessed by opium eating, as Comm Lynch has done, when they meet in conjunction. "Woe worth the fate!... Woe worth the day."[12]

The departure of Captain Graves from Edwards Ferry left the yard with little or no protection. Since the *Albemarle* had been moved to Halifax, and the cherished iron plates were being shipped elsewhere, military authorities probably thought there was little remaining to guard.

About seven miles north of Halifax was Weldon. Well dispersed Confederate troops guarded the bridges there, since Weldon was an important North Carolina railroad junction. The military authorities headquartered there felt they were of sufficient strength to repel any Union threat towards Halifax. Mrs. Edmondston's critical observations of Lynch and Mallory might have been reflecting a public resentment of removing the *Albemarle* from Elliott's control, or her strong personal opinions.

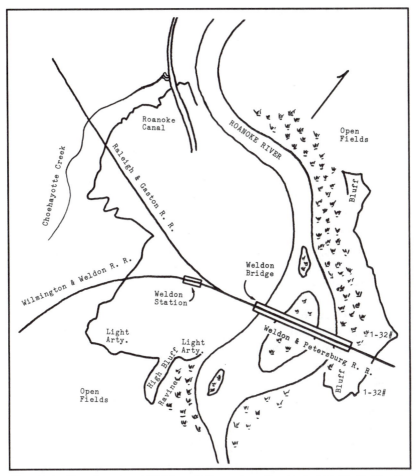

The vital railroad center at Weldon, N.C. was heavily guarded by North Carolina forces. They could quickly respond to repel invaders intent on destroying the Halifax and Edwards Ferry Shipyards.

Author's Sketch

While at his Halifax Yard office, Commander Cooke received a note from Lynch to which had been attached his reply to a Navy Department request for an explanation of proceedings at Edwards Ferry. With it was an extract of Constructor Porter's unfavorable report on the *Albemarle's* untimely launch. Lynch's message to the Department had a conciliatory tone, as he first pointed the finger of blame at Cooke and then accepted a portion of it himself for not being diligent in assigning an on-site inspector.

I have the honor to acknowledge the receipt of your letter of the 21st [October] instant calling my attention to an extract from a report of the Chief of Naval Construction and requesting me to inform the Department who is responsible for the inferior character of the materials and work upon the gunboat at Scotland Neck[,] and for launching her. With the exception of a comparatively brief period, Commander Cooke has been under orders to supervise the construction of the Roanoke gunboat.

Early in the present month [October] the constructor, in writing, reported the gunboat ready for launching and on the 9th on my way to the boat[,] I met Comdr Cooke who answered the report. I instructed him then and again the next morning to have all in readiness for launching as soon as the water rose sufficiently[,] and returning to Halifax, watched the conditions of the river in order to ride down (a distance of 17 miles) whenever the water approached the level which would justify a launch.

The latter took place unexpectedly to me and as foreman Thomas reported[,] against his protest or declaration that he would not be answerable for the consequences.

In reply to your first question I think I am censurable for not having sooner sent Mr. Roberson to inspect the work upon the gunboat. All I can say in palliation is that we were very much pushed for iron and as he was the only energetic man I could find to collect and transport it from near the enemy's lines below Kinston.

For launching inopportunely I consider Comdr Cooke responsible[,] but am convinced that his error of judgement was caused by his patriotic participation in my anxiety to get the vessel afloat. I respectfully ask that he be punished with a copy of this letter, or so much thereof as refers to him.[13]

Flag Officer Lynch may have thought his explanation of what had occurred at Edwards Ferry would satisfy the Department and Mallory. Little did he realize how the tables would be turned, and he would become the scapegoat.

The time had come for Commander Cooke to take pen in hand and defend himself against Lynch's accusations. The future of the

Albemarle was in jeopardy. His career could suffer irreparable damage if his views of the controversy were muted. Elliott and his associates who had performed a miracle in just completing the hull in the corn field, were about to see that their labor had been for naught.

At Scotland Neck on November 5, 1863, Cooke wrote his explanation in ink on simple lined paper. Frayed and worn, with a few small holes here and there, the report was addressed only to 'Sir' though doubtless it had been written to Secretary Mallory.

> In reply to your communication of the 31st, ultimo [October], I have to state in reply the extracts from constructor Porters report the contract calls for no [particular] finish [and] that I consider ___ the vessel strongly put together. There were no rings used [on bolts] for the simple reason at that ___ the contractor was unable to get them, but the heads of the bolts were flattened and well secured [by blacksmiths]. At the material, I must beg leave ___ most decidedly as the timber and planking [were] of the best kind and Mr. Thomas approved of the end of the shield being ___ when the vessel ___ to splinter ___ she was perfectly tight.
>
> When I was ordered on this duty I informed the Department that I was not acquainted with ship building and recommended a competent inspector be appointed to inspect the work[,] and Mr. Roberson at my solicitation [was] appointed for that purpose ___ from other duty[,] therefore I consider myself in no manner responsible for the [quality] of construction ___ report. [I pursued my duties] entirely by instructions of Flag Officer Lynch. In view of the danger to be apprehended from raids of the enemy, so long as the boat remained in the stocks, Flag Officer directed me to launch at the first possible opportunity, even 'provided the river was favorable before the holes were bored for the shafts.'
>
> I hesitated to launch the boat but as my orders were positive, I could only obey them. I therefore do not claim any responsibility in connection thereunto having been subservient to the orders of Flag Officer Lynch in my actions.

> In conclusion I must state ___ Constructor Porter was not at Edwards Ferry, ___ the gun boat but a very cursury scanning to indulge more in argument than in inspection.[14]

Peter E. Smith and James F. Snell exercised their best craftsmanship and ingenuity when creating the *Albemarle*. They "made do" with what materials and facilities that could be mustered at their Edwards Ferry rural site. Lynch's proposal to launch before propellor shaft holes were bored, was a decision made without respect for consequences. Perhaps Porter's visit was planned to benefit Lynch. On November 7, the day he received it, Cooke responded to Lynch's letter of October the thirtieth which had been misdirected to Clarksville, Virginia. Cooke assured Lynch that all construction timber at Edwards Ferry had been shipped to Halifax, and all bills awaiting Lynch's approval were certified for correctness. One item in particular was a machine for drilling holes in iron plates. An ancillary item was the assembly of a drilling press in accordance with Lynch's order to do the work.

Cooke also remarked to Lynch that he had received from Secretary Mallory an abstract of Constructor Porter's launch report. Then Cooke requested clarification of his current orders.

> Your letter of the 26th directs me to remain at Edwards Ferry and not to move the gun or ammunition at present. I wish to be informed if I am still to continue here as there is only a guard of 8 men detailed for the gun and two of them are sick and I have ordered them to be sent to the hospital.

Cooke then interjected an opinion that in the event of an enemy incursion toward Fort Branch, the gun mounted on an aged Navy carriage that Lynch had furnished would command little respect among intruders steaming up the river.

In response to Lynch's earlier request to tow the incomplete floating battery to Halifax, he remarked he was waiting to secure the services of the *Cotton Plant* and the schooner then in use at Halifax. It all depended on the appropriate rise of the river water. Cooke clearly revealed the state of chaos created by Lynch's impulsive decision to move operations to Halifax when he told his superior, "there is no commissary here to supply these men with their rations and I have purchased their supplies at my private expense."[15]

Clarksville was the community closest to Edwards Ferry. Scotland Neck was an indefinite rural area rather than a particular municipality. Their names were often used interchangeably.[16] The Smiths of Scotland Neck owned the river steamer *Cotton Plant*. She usually had plied between Norfolk and Halifax, serving local planters with a means of transporting their products to market.[17] During the war years she was also active carrying crucial supplies for troops stationed along the Roanoke.

When first recruiting workers, Elliott had been able to tap two sources if he agreed to certain conditions. Col. William F. Martin, commanding the 17th Regiment, had detailed several soldiers with some shipbuilding experience, providing that when their services were no longer required they would be returned to the Regiment. They were; Jno T. Harrell, Co. A; C. Patrick, Co. B; Z. Smith, Co. D; W. A. Burroughs and I. L. Swain, Co. E; I. R. Lynch and Staton, Co. F; and Joseph Herrington, Co. G. On November 7 Elliott performed his obligatory duty and ordered these men returned without delay to their respective companies in said Regiment.[18]

Other craftsmen among Elliott's work force were subject to conscript duty. With work on the *Albemarle* halted for an indefinite time, his orders of long standing had been to transfer these men to Col. Peter Mallett, Commander of Conscripts at Camp Holmes near Raleigh. The nine men were; James F. Snell (master mechanic from Elizabeth City who had worked for Gilbert since the fall of '61), W. P. Williams, D. R. Daniel, I. W. Treviathan, O. Liscomb, H. W. Martin, G. L. Winbum, Edward Sikes, and Mr. Peal.[19]

Quite properly, copies of both lists were forwarded to Flag Officer Lynch who might have considered that Elliott had released the men intentionally, for he had received no communication from Elliott since the *Albemarle* was towed away to Halifax. Most likely Elliott was tying loose ends at the yard, while waiting for the matter to be resolved by Secretary Mallory.

From his Wilmington headquarters on November 11, Lynch wrote the Secretary accusing Elliott of several violations. In Lynch's opinion, any one of the charges was a sufficient reason for the Department to commandeer the *Albemarle*. Lynch's comments also revealed how unacquainted he was with matters pertaining to the everyday workings of a shipyard, especially one located in a corn field.

He began with an outright suggestion that the Department assume superintendence of the vessel.

> I respectfully submit to your consideration[,] whether the Department should not take the *Albemarle* in hand for speedy completion. It is now three weeks [from October 21] since she was brought to Halifax and the contractor has not come near her. It is necessary to caulk the lower part of the shield preparatory to putting on the sponson iron, but when the caulkers were sent for, Commander Cooke, who remained at Edwards Ferry in charge of Government property replied that the caulkers were slaves hired by Mr. Elliott and that he had otherwise disposed of them. In addition, the latter, by note herewith enclosed[,] has called upon Lieutenant Johnston by direction as he states, of Colonel Martin for all men detailed by the latter for the work upon the gunboat. Col. Martin, it should be borne in mind was a partner in the contract for building the boat.
>
> There is a difficulty also as to wages. Mr. Elliott refused, as the workmen allege, to pay those sent from Richmond and [from] this place [Wilmington] what they have been receiving. In reply to a call from me, Mr. Elliott promised to resume the work but up to this morning when I left Halifax he had not made his appearance. I know how much the Department has to annoy it, and have foreborne troubling it with this matter in the hope of better things, but I am now impelled by a sense of duty to ask its decision.
>
> Constructor Porter can give some idea of the difficulties I have [had] to encounter in the construction of this boat, difficulties elsewhere unknown. Whatever may be the decision, I earnestly ask that it be speedily communicated for time is slipping away.[20]

Gilbert's fourth contract of September 17, 1862, had been open, allowing for the construction of one or more vessels. It carried a primary endorsement of Secretary Mallory and letter of authority from Cdr. James W. Cooke. Strict adherence to the contract's terms may have been Elliott's reason for awaiting developments and not communicating with Flag Officer Lynch.[21]

Without question the caulkers were slaves from the several Smith family members involved in the *Albemarle's* construction. When their services were no longer needed, because of the vessel having been towed up the river, they were returned to their respective owners. Any misunderstanding about workers wages not having been paid, may have been attributed to an overdue increment payment from the Department.

Flag Officer Lynch received a mild rebuke from Chief Constructor John L. Porter in the nature of a request for clarification of labor expense charges submitted by Lynch on November 11. In his letter of November 14, after a typical salutation, Porter remarked,

> I suppose the two first items of 78 and 55 days work were for preparing to cut and drill the iron. The third item of 182 days was the drilling of the plates. The fourth item of 72 days for handling I suppose was done by negro laborers who are not entitled to $4.00 per day under any circumstances. The fifth item of 72 days blacksmithing was for cutting the iron and bending. I feel confident that the greater part of this work was done by negro laborers, for which four dollars per day has been charged in every instance and which is more than has been paid by the Department.[22]

Here was a direct reference to specific work being performed in fabricating the iron plates. Peter Smith, with his blacksmiths, may have begun covering the *Albemarle* before she was towed to Halifax, or perhaps the plates were instead being prepared for the floating battery. It also may have been about the time Smith had developed the 'twist drill.'

The traditional method of drilling iron at that time produced only iron dust. With full realization that it would have been next to impossible to drill hundreds of holes within a reasonable time, Smith had retired to his personal forge and within a short while emerged with the innovative 'twist drill' which produced iron shavings while cutting. Before it had required twenty minutes to drill an inch and a quarter hole through the 2-inch thick plates, but with Smith's invention the drilling time was reduced to four minutes per hole.[23]

The prodigious *Albemarle*, being fitted with armor and guns at Halifax, was slowly developing the appearance of a war vessel. After she had been moved to Halifax, together with all the tools and materials, there remained at Edwards Ferry an assortment of scrap wooden blocks.

Peter E. Smith was then senior warden in the Scotland Neck area for Dr. Joseph Blount Cheshire, priest of Calvary Episcopal Church in Tarboro. Construction of the church had begun about the time Elliott's ironclad was being built. Smith thought wood scraps of the *Albemarle* could serve the parishioners spiritual needs, so he gave them to Dr. Cheshire to be made into furniture for the new church. By such a presence the *Albemarle* would become a participant in the parishioners' divine worship.

Dr. Cheshire soon engaged a newly arrived English woodcarver who had worked on the restoration of Litchfield Cathedral in England. The wood carver created two altar pieces to which he attached suitably engraved small brass plates attesting to their origin.[24]

In the afternoon of Friday November 20, just after closing Hascosea for the season, and becoming settled in their winter residence at Looking Glass, the Edmondstons had two unexpected visitors. Of the event Catherine Edmondston wrote,

> Scarce were we here when up came Mr. Peter Smith & Capt Cook[e], the former bringing a large hen hawk which he had shot at our gate. Acknowledging my debt of a chicken pie to serve the time honored demand which the shooter of a hawk has a right to make upon the nearest house, I had also to thank him for the promptness with which he mended my spectacles for me, at a time too when they were much needed by me.[25]

The silence of another player in this drama of the *Albemarle* was broken on November 28, 1863, when Governor Zebulon Vance extended his personal impressions of the *Albemarle* fiasco to Secretary Mallory.

> I beg to call your attention to the enclosed letter from Lt. G. Elliott in regards to the gun boat *Albemarle*. I endorse the statement fully in regards to the delay and blunders of Flag Officer Lynch. I am satisfied of his total and utter incapacity for the duties of his position, which has for some time been evident to the whole State.
>
> The iron furnished by the State under the express promises of both himself and you has been applied to other

purposes and our rivers are yet at the mercy of the most contemptible boat of the Yankee Navy.

The *'Neuse'* has been launched and her iron plates put on without her machinery and in the face of the known fact that it will all have to come off before the machinery does go in. Many other ridiculous things have been done meerly to keep the hands employed and deceive the public[,] for it cannot deceive the enemy.

In short Sir, I am so out of heart in the matter that if the water defenses of NC are to continue in the hands of Commander Lynch, I feel it useless and will decline to furnish any more iron or other assistance whatsoever. It would be labor and machinery thrown away. I desire of course that Lt. Elliott should be allowed to finish the boat.[26]

Flag Officer Lynch seemed to have had a propensity for launching vessels before work below the water line had been completed. The *Neuse*, with minor variations of her sister ship *Albemarle*, was ironed and launched before machinery installation. As well, he had ordered Cooke to execute a similar procedure as the *Albemarle's* launching was being planned.[27]

In his annual report to Congress on November 30, 1863, Navy Secretary Mallory emphasized the necessity of properly training naval officers. It was, he emphasized, "a subject of the greatest importance." He further reported that construction activities had been terminated in the western sector, but were continuing at Richmond, Wilmington, Charleston, Savannah, Mobile, and on the Roanoke, Peedee, Chattahoochee, and the Alabama rivers. Mallory emphatically asserted Confederate Navy problems were two-fold; the lack of skilled labor to build ships, and the inability to obtain adequate iron plates to protect them.[28]

Further into his report Mallory defined the type and place various vessels were being built. He described activities on the Roanoke River most succinctly: "One ironclad gunboat of 2 guns has been launched and is now receiving her armor and machinery. One ironclad floating battery launched and ready for armor."[29]

On December 1 Lynch sent a brief note to Cooke at the Halifax Yard advising him that if an enemy attack upon Kinston by way of the Neuse River became imminent, Cooke would consult first with the Commanding Military officers, order the river barricades retained, and endeavor to move the *Neuse* to a safer position further upstream.[30] A followup note about Halifax Yard business was sent by Lynch the next day to Commander Cooke at Kinston.

> You will inform the Hon. Secy of the Navy direct, when, according to the contract with Martin & Elliott, the gunboat on the Roanoke was to be completed, also, any other particulars of the contract within your knowledge.[31]

Surely it would have been more appropriate to send this request for an administrative report via the usual routing to Cooke's Halifax office. Depending on circumstances at Kinston, the time of day Cooke received the note, and availability of transportation, it could well have been two days or so before he would return to Halifax. Cooke might have wondered why he was ordered to Kinston, when personnel there could have coordinated with military commanders about moving the *Neuse*.

The final paragraph of Lynch's letter to Cooke on the third of January, 1863, was quite contrary to Cooke's orders from Lynch on December 1, 1863, when Lynch ordered him to Kinston to supervise implementation of safety measures for the *Neuse*.[32]

Secretary Mallory received another letter adding fuel to the flaming controversy engulfing Flag Officer Lynch. Written by James N. Joiner on December 4 at Kinston, Mallory read that two days earlier Joiner had been directed by Lynch to apprise the Secretary of when the gunboat on the Roanoke was to be completed, and to also advise of any other particulars of the contract within his knowledge. Mr. Joiner said that he believed Elliott's contract was made and signed with the Navy Department, but he had no copy. His only contractural documents were copies of those for the vessels on the Neuse and Tar rivers. Joiner added that he knew Elliott was granted an extension against the gunboat contract in order to finish the floating battery. He then requested additional time to provide other required information, since his records were not readily available.

Mr. Joiner then told Secretary Mallory that he had in hand a December 2 letter copy from Lynch to Mallory in which Lynch was,

> Accusing me of insubordination and deposition to rather to retard by complaint than sustain the efforts of

his command, and that I took 8 days to obey an order in reporting thereupon.

To all these accusations I feel myself innocent and respectfully request that you will grant me a Court of Inquiry to establish my defence. I will not here enter a detail of my defence but will take up the last accusation. On the night of the 24th ultimo I received the enclosed copy of an order of the 22nd to relieve Commander Kerr. The order was received late at night. The next day I had to procure a conveyance to Halifax, which I could not obtain until the following day, the 26th. I immediately left and took the train for this place but there not being any connection with the Wilmington and Kinston Rail Road, I did not arrive until the 27th which occupied just 3 days from the receipt of the order.

How F. O. Lynch can accuse me of taking 8 days when his order was dated Wilmington the 22nd and he acknowledges the receipt of a letter from me of the 30th allowing no time for the transcription of his orders and my time to travel to Kinston, I am at a loss to conjecture.

My address was Scotland Neck, having been ordered to remain there and F. O. Lynch sends me an order directed to Halifax, care of M. McMahon which through the kindness of a friend I received after dark and I am accused of taking 8 days to obey this order.[33]

Mr. Joiner apparently had been at Edwards Ferry when he received Lynch's message to relieve Lieutenant Kerr at Kinston. As on-site representative of Flag Officer Lynch it was Joiner's duty to interface with the contractor and Lynch's Wilmington office. Mr. M. McMahon, of Halifax, who initially received the letter addressed to Mr. Joiner, was vendor of ships supplies.[34]

Lieutenant Kerr had been Naval Ordnance officer at Halifax with orders to oversee the powder magazine, and naval armament at Edwards Ferry. Mr. Joiner continued to expound upon his grievances to Secretary Mallory by asking for his judgement on the matter. Further, he stated that although he had not visited his home since the preceeding September, he had not made a side trip in this instance. Kerr had been ill when he visited with Joiner in Kinston and had left in time to reach Wilmington by Monday November 30. Then, after citing several other grievances, Joiner respectfully requested Mallory assign him to service afloat.[35]

On December 4 Flag Officer Lynch composed a lengthy letter of self vindication to Governor Vance. Lynch began in a conciliatory tone.

> In order to preserve harmony between yourself, the representative of the majesty of a soverign State and the head of one of the Departments of the Confederate Government [Secy Mallory], I deem it my duty to submit the following statement.
>
> The gunboat *Albemarle* was removed from Edwards Ferry to Halifax by direction of Mr. Mallory[,] a precautionary measure taken in consequence of a letter from the military commander of the District. Mr. Elliott had been paid by installments, [and] had received more than the contract would have justified upon a survey and the boat was the sole property of the Government.

Lynch was indeed covering all options. He had originally said it was Commander Cooke who had given the order to launch. It was also true that Elliott had been paid in installments, but if he had been overpaid it was by approval of Lynch, after his inspector and Commander Cooke had certified the requisitions. Lynch asserted that for three weeks Mr. Elliott had ignored his invitations to continue the work, causing the Department to remove the vessel from his responsibility. The "removal from his responsibility" seems to have been only that of actually moving the *Albemarle* from Edwards Ferry to Halifax. There was no evidence of a contractural penalty. The craftsmen had followed with the boat, taking time to establish living huts and workshops after their arrival at the Halifax yard. A lack of laborers and caulkers principally caused an immediate work slowdown.

Lynch then mentioned the 435,000 pounds of iron he had caused to be sent to Atlanta, as well as another 125,000 pounds to Richmond, all to be rolled into plates.

In his own defense he attested to Governor Vance that not a single iron plate acquired for the Naval Defense of the State had been diverted to other use. He remarked that he was honor bound to support the Navy Department in its project of building gunboats in North Carolina. His concluding remarks could well have caused a demand for satisfaction on a field of honor, had they been made in earlier times.

Your Excellency has done me a great injustice but
self respect prevents the tending an unsought explanation. It is in my power[,] by written evidence with names
and dates[,] to disprove every assertion made by Mr. Elliott.
His platitudes about exalted patriotism and personal sac-
rifice are worse than trash, for they are untrue. When[,] as
the 10th [of] February, 1862, Elizabeth City, his place of
residence, if not his native place, was attacked by the enemy, he fled and I remained to defend it. As to personal
sacrifices, I can only say that his bills against the Government indicate a keen regard to individual interest.[36]

Perhaps Flag Officer Lynch was unaware that Elliott, as contractor for the Navy Department, had been engaged in the building
of a vessel at Elizabeth City on February 10, 1862. Perhaps Lynch
also didn't know that Elliott had moved immediately after the fall of
Elizabeth City to the vicinity of Gosport, Virginia, for the purpose of
again building a vessel under contract to the Navy Department.

A celebration was planned for December 10, 1863, by Peter
Smith. In keeping with tradition of the landed gentry, he had invited neighbors and friends to partake of the host's hospitality at his
plantation known as 'Sunnyside.' The occasion was the twentieth
birthday of the Smith's house guest, Lieutenant Gilbert Elliott. Another guest was Lucy Ann Hill, Rebecca Smith's sister.

Elliott and Lucy Ann may have been introduced earlier, but
with certainty they were to become acquainted at the party honor-
ing Elliott.

Five days later, after lengthy contemplation, Lt. Gilbert Elliott
effected a decisive change in his military career. In an honorable
gesture of good faith, he wrote a letter on December 15, 1863, to
Col. William F. Martin, the 17th Regimental Commander at
Wilmington, North Carolina, offering to resign both as Regimental
Adjutant, and from the Army. He cited as reason his activity as contractor to the Navy Department in building the *Albemarle*.[37]

At Camp Burgwyn near Wilmington, on December 18, Colonel Martin inscribed the first endorsement.

Offer of resignation with reasons assigned within approved and respectfully forwarded with the remark that
Adjutant Elliott has been absent with leave engaged in
the construction of gun boats since August, 1862. Believ-

ing he is rendering efficient services in the work in which he is engaged, my own conclusion is that his resignation ought to be accepted.

Then followed a second endorsement of approval on the nineteenth from Brig. Gen. James Green Martin at his Martin Brigade Headquarters in Wilmington. The same day there was a third endorsement by Maj. Gen. William H. C. Whiting. He grumpily conveyed a contrary message.

> Respectfully forwarded, disapproved. I consider every man employed on ironclad gun boats thrown away as far as the defences of the country is concerned.

A fourth and final endorsement was respectfully submitted to the Secretary of War at Richmond, on January 7, 1864. It was approved effective January 20, 1864.[38]

CHAPTER 10

THE BUSTLING HALIFAX YARD

With the advent of New Year 1864, General Robert E. Lee wrote President Jefferson Davis. In his January second letter he called the President's attention to the importance of planning a long contemplated attack upon New Bern, N.C. Lee stated that he could then spare the troops, since winter weather in Northern Virginia prevented large scale operations there. He represented to President Davis that New Bern could be taken with two brigades plus gun boats on the Neuse River, all assisted by the two ironclads under construction, the *Neuse* and *Albemarle*.

The ironclads' task would be to clear the waters of the enemy, capture the Union troop transports, and support the attack upon New Bern by shelling the town from the river. Lee explained briefly how it all might be accomplished. Then he asked the President whether the ironclads were available.[1] President Davis' January 4 response was not encouraging.

> The progress on the boats of the Neuse and Roanoke
> is slow and too uncertain to fix a date for completion,
> [but] your suggestion is approved.

He questioned Lee about who would execute the campaign. As he saw it, Lee himself should lead the offensive, "otherwise I will go myself, though it could only be for a very few days, Congress being in session."[2]

That development would not necessarily have concerned Cooke and Elliott since the continuing shortage of iron, and Flag Officer Lynch's interference, had put the *Albemarle* well behind schedule.

Nonetheless work upon the *Albemarle* at the Halifax Yard was steadily progressing, as evidenced by three vouchers paid on January 13, 1864. Voucher #14 amounting to $1,397.50 was paid by Adam

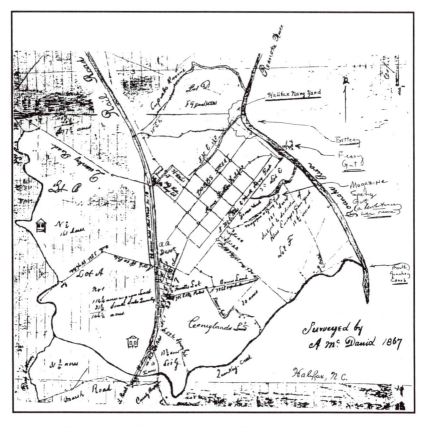

On this 1867 map of Halifax, N.C., the Halifax Navy Yard site is identified.
It is accessible only on foot with permission of owner Vernon T. Bradley of Halifax.

Map Courtesy of Johnny M. Kelly, Weldon, N.C.

Tredwell to John A. Thomas. The itemized charges were for; 104 days blacksmithing at $4.00 per day; 134 days labor at $3.00 per day; 226 days labor at $2.00 per day; 75 days labor at $1.00 per day; and 5 days rental of oxen and cart at $8.00 per day. The voucher tabulated to $1,381.00, but the amount paid was $1,397.50.[3]

Voucher #17 was for $1,886.50, payable to Gilbert Elliott. Summarized, the charges were for barrels of tar; hauling an engine; loading engine on a barge; 4,500 feet of pine plank; oak knees; 33 days mechanics labor on gunboat at $5.00 per day; 7 days labor on gunboat at $3.50 per day; and 54 caulkers at $5.00 per day.[4]

Lastly, Voucher #18 in the amount of $815.00 was payable to Elliott also. Interestingly, the invoice date was November 6, 1863. Summarized, the voucher allowed payment for two large pine spars; 32 days labor cutting and hauling same; the hire of four yokes of oxen for hauling same; 15 days labor loading same on barge for transport; 118 days putting engines on gun boat; the hire of four mules and wagon for 2 days to send workmen to Halifax, and 40 days hire of mules and wagons to transfer officers to and from Clarkesville Ferry.[5]

A noteworthy milestone was the fact that there was the first direct mention of engines being placed in the *Albemarle*. The event could very well have taken place shortly after the *Albemarle* had arrived at Halifax. A barge carrying the engines was probably securely moored alongside the *Albemarle*. Workmen then erected a hoist to lift and swing the engine components over a deck opening, before lowering them below to be fastened to the bedplates. The fact that officer personnel were being transported daily from Clarkesville Ferry (Edwards Ferry) to Halifax and return, implied that residential quarters were in short supply at Halifax. Lastly, a charge made in error had a line scrawled over it. The claim, "and damage to land at Edwards Ferry from building fort magazine," was for $200.00, but was deleted from payment.

Early in the month of January 1864, Commander Cooke was summoned to Wilmington by the Navy Department's Office of Orders and Detail in Richmond. He was assigned to Naval Court Martial duty. By January 14 an order superseding the former was dispatched to him from the same office. Ensign K. Mitchell, commander in charge, advised Cooke by telegraph,

> You are hereby detached from the Naval Court Martial at Wilmington, N.C., and will report to Flag Officer William F. Lynch, commanding, for the command of the *Albemarle*, at Halifax, N.C., where you will proceed and relieve Lieutenant Johnston. By Command of the Secretary of the Navy.[6]

This order amounted to a reward for Commander Cooke, one he had probably long anticipated, and certainly well deserved. There were few opportunities such as his, in which he labored to find construction materials, watched his vessel grow to completion and then commanded her in battle. On Friday the fifteenth Cooke wired his reply to Richmond.

Your telegram of the 14th instant, directing me to report to Flag Officer Lynch for the command of the *Albemarle* at Halifax was received today, and in compliance therewith I reported to Flag Officer Lynch and received from him the following order, viz:

You will proceed to Halifax and assume command of the gun boat *Albemarle* now under construction at that place and exert your utmost in expediting her completion. You will also take the floating battery in charge and put her in a safe position for putting on her armor. Direct Lt. Johnston to report for duty at this place.

Cooke explained further to Lt. Mitchell.

I did proceed [to engage space on] the train which left Wilmington today [the 15th] to obey the orders from the Department and Flag Officer Lynch, but I was directed to await a reply to a telegraphic dispatch he had transmitted to the Department asking for a revocation of my orders. If, however, no further orders reach me in the meantime and the President of the Courts Martial permitting it, I shall leave for Halifax on the train of tomorrow [the 16th].[7]

The same day that Cooke was arranging for railroad passage to Halifax, Secretary Mallory was composing a long letter of instructions and assurances. Mallory's letter exonerated Cooke of alleged improprieties charged by Flag Officer Lynch.

You have been ordered to Halifax to take charge of the completion of the gunboat *Albemarle*. This charge has been made upon representations to the Department that your acquaintance with the people and resources of the district in which the vessel is being built renders you peculiarly qualified for the duty, and because the Department is anxious to adopt any measure which looks to an early completion of the vessel.

To one so familiar with the whole subject it is needless to dwell upon the great importance of the utmost prompt and energetic action in getting the vessel ready, and you are expected to leave nothing undone to effect this object. That your judgement may be untrammeled, you are relieved from duty under Flag Officer Lynch, and will correspond directly with this Department.

Notwithstanding it is reported that there are as many men employed as can work to advantage, I have this day sent Acting Constructor Graves [William A. of Norfolk] with 21 men to report to you, believing that their services will be important. You have been requested to keep these men together, not only with the view of stimulating the work on the vessel by their competition with those already there, but that they may return here at the proper time.

You are expected to command the *Albemarle*, and you will push on all parts of the work upon and for her as far as practicable at the same time. Consult with Constructor Graves, who has charge of the work, and read him so much of this letter as you may deem necessary to secure his energetic cooperation.

Your ladders, gratings, hatches, racks, hammock cloths, hooks, eyebolts, magazine work, etc., should all be looked after at once. Your guns will be got in readiness here. You will make a weekly report of your progress, and you will not hesitate to adopt any measure necessary to the prompt completion of the work. Under Constructor Porter's arrangement with Mr. Elliott, employing him and his force by the day, it is clearly his interest to protract the work, a circumstance which you will not fail to note.[8]

The *Albemarle's* engines, and where they were obtained, have long been a subject of wonder and discussion. Most authors have merely said, "the engines were installed with other machinery." One wrote they were built of "odds and ends."[9] The former Commander of the *Neuse*, Benjamin F. Loyall, remarked on January 19, 1897, at the occasion of Robert E. Lee's birthday dinner in Norfolk that, "the engine of a large saw mill was altered and made to serve for her propelling power."[10]

A publication circa 1897, Ironclads in Action, mentioned in passing,

The engines procured from the Tredegar Works, at Richmond, were two, each driving one screw, and had a nominal horse-power of 100 apiece.[11]

In his 1887 History of the Confederate Navy, J. Thomas Scharf said of the *Albemarle's* engines,

The engine was adapted from incongruous material, ingeniously dovetailed and put together with a determined will that mastered doubt, but not without some natural anxiety as to derangements that might occur from so heterogenous a combination.[12]

Although there has been widespread uncertainty about where her engines were procured, substantial knowledge of their construction and engineering features has been acquired. Each of the two engines was capable of generating 200 horse-power, contrary to "a nominal horse-power of 100 apiece," as earlier alleged.

Because of low headspace, the non-condensing engines were mounted horizontally, side by side. Cylinders of 18 inches diameter encased pistons whose stroke was 19 inches. (Elliott said each cylinder diameter was 20 inches). A link motion design allowed both pistons to expend their thrust simultaneously, thus transmitting their energy through four gears to both propellor shafts.[13] Non-condensing engines operated at higher steam pressure, as opposed to the low pressure condensing type.

Draft, or the flow of air through the furnaces, was by "natural draft," created by the rising column of heated gases in the funnel. This method worked satisfactorily unless the funnel became seriously perforated.[14]

Both engines were powered by cast iron steam producing boilers. A furnace for each was connected to the single funnel by flues 1'9" high and 9" wide. The boilers measured 15'4" long, 5'2" high, and 4'7" wide. Within each boiler were 120 tubes, 1'10" long with an outside diameter of 3¼".

Each furnace was 4'6" long by 4' wide, having two elliptical and vertical water tubes for return. Diameter of both steam drums was 2'8", and their height was 1'6". The diameter of both large drive wheels (gears) at pitch line was 2'9½", and the pinions (gears) were 2'6" at pitch line. Faces of all wheels measured 9 inches.[15] There were two three-bladed propellers of 9 feet pitch, being the distance a given point in a screw propeller would move in the direction of its axis if turned through one complete revolution in a solid, fixed medium.[16]

Two propeller shafts with exterior housings for same as well as both propellers were fabricated at the C.S. Navy Yard at Charlotte, North Carolina.[17] The shafts were enclosed in wooden passageways named shaft alleys, which extended from the engines to the stern through which the shafts passed. Both boilers were installed amidship at the single funnel, with the furnaces and gear train mounted abaft.

On January 20, 1864, General Robert E. Lee responded to President Davis' letter of January 4. He continued their discussion of campaign plans against New Bern, N.C. Lee had wished to know when the *Neuse* and *Albemarle* would be operational, since their participation in the assault would be of prime importance to its success. After announcing the time had arrived for the execution of the attempt on New Bern, Lee remarked,

> I regret very much that the boats on the Neuse and Roanoke are not completed. With their aid I think success would be certain. Without them, though the place may be captured, the fruits of the expedition will be lessened and our maintenance of the command of the waters in North Carolina uncertain. I think every effort should be made now to get them into service as soon as possible.[18]

Secretary Mallory and General Lee shared a common problem as they pursued their individual goals. Lack of rail transportation of iron plates was as frustrating to those building the *Albemarle*, as was Lee's discouragement in his futile efforts to obtain adequate food supplies by rail for his Army of Northern Virginia. One can only wonder if Lee really knew why the *Albemarle* was behind schedule.

Commander Cooke was now and then physically disabled by an undisclosed ailment. His health problem, combined with assigned duties, had delayed his writing Governor Vance in response to Mallory's communication of December 11, 1863. He therefore requested Elliott, as a courtesy to the Governor, to present the facts pertaining to the Lynch matter. Elliott's letter explained events from October 1863 to January 27, 1864.

My attention has just been directed to a communication from the Honorable Secretary of the Navy, dated December 11, 1863, in answer to your letter to him of the 28th November last, in which you enclosed [a] statement from me in relation to the ironclad gun boat *Albemarle*, endorsed by several prominent citizens of Halifax County.

It is proper for me to state that, at the present time I am engaged in the completion of the *Ablemarle* without being at all inconvenienced by Flag Officer Lynch. The Hon. Secy[,] in the closing paragraph of his letter[,] informs you that receiving your letter and learning the course which the Contractor had pursued sent the Chief Naval Constructor, Jno. Porter[,] to Halifax with orders to adopt best means available for the earliest completion of the vessel and that "he acted accordingly." He might also have informed you that the means adopted by Mr. Porter consisted in the making [of] a new contract with me for the "completion of the vessel." The work is now progressing under the superintendence of Commander Cooke as rapidly as can be expected and his operations are untrammelled by Flag Officer Lynch, but I think it due the gentlemen who endorsed my letter to you, to your Excellency and to myself that I should reply to the letter of the Hon. Secy even at this late day.

I informed you that Flag Officer Lynch removed the boat to Halifax for the "ostensible" purpose of completion, because no evidence had been furnished to show that such was the "real design of that Officer," after the lapse of nearly two months of invaluable time, as will be shown by the resolution of the County Court of Halifax, forwarded to the Hon. Secy early in December last, a copy of which is herewith enclosed marked 'A.'

As evidence that the removal of the boat from Edwards Ferry to Halifax was unnecessary and not considered by well informed persons a wise measure, I enclose copy of a letter upon the subject from Col. William F. Martin to the Hon. Secy, marked 'B.' Col. Martin, as you know, commanded Fort Branch below Hamilton, on the Roanoke River. He was in command there at the time of this unfortunate removal and certainly had opportunities of ascertaining whether such a move was advisable.

To show that Flag Officer Lynch did regard the boat as out of my hands in removing her to Halifax, I enclose copy of certificate from Commander J. W. Cooke, delivered to me on the day of seizure, marked 'C,' and copy of certified copy of letter of instructions from Flag Officer Lynch to Commander Cooke, written October 19, 1863, marked 'D.'

If Flag Officer Lynch expected me to complete the vessel it is strange that he should have ordered the forcible seizure not only of the *Albemarle* but of my private property with which I was expected to complete the work as will be shown by papers 'C' & 'D.'

The seizure of materials did take place and all my private property at Edwards Ferry was removed to Halifax by direction of Flag Officer Lynch.

The Hon. Secy asserted that I had no right to terminate the detail of hands detailed from the Army to work for me. Inquiry into this matter will show that Contractors are compelled to swear that the men will be returned as soon as their services shall no longer be needed. In accordance with my oath so to do, I ordered the return of the men as soon as I ceased to need their services.

The Hon. Secy also states that my subsequent offer to complete the boat was coupled with the condition that I should receive $25,000 for so doing. If this was wrong the question naturally presents itself, "Why did Mr. Porter by order of the Secy Navy make a new contract with me for completing the boat, instead of compelling me to finish her for $10,000 as he alleges it was my duty to do?"

Again, if, as the Hon. Secy states, additional expense became necessary from the inefficient manner of constructing the vessel, I submit that the Govt would have been spared this expense if the vessel had been left at Edwards Ferry and completed by me under my original contract "to the satisfaction of the Constructor detailed to report upon same."

If Flag Officer Lynch ever "stood high as an intelligent, faithful, zealous and energetic officer" it is sadly to be regretted that he has now so completely lost his standing. As your Excellency well knows, Flag Officer Lynch is universally looked upon in this State as incompetent, inefficient and almost imbecile. His management of the Roanoke Island fleet convinced the people in my district of his utter incapacity. He retreated to Elizabeth City where he must have known his fleet would inevitably meet the fate that befell it. Why did he not bring the boats up the Roanoke or carry them through the new canal to Norfolk?

If Flag Officer Lynch has made "faithful, zealous and energetic" efforts to build and equip vessels in North Carolina, where are the material results of his endeavours? Has he a boat at Wilmington able to inflict damage upon the blockades, after all the money spent for the 700 tons of iron to which the Hon. Secy alludes? Has he finished the *Neuse* or did he launch her without her propellors and without reason? Has he finished the *Albemarle* after taking her out of my hands with so much flourish, or has the Hon. Secy overruled him in this matter and taken the vessel entirely out of his control?

So long as Flag Officer Lynch remains in command in this State, I can assure your Excellency that his Paymaster will be busily engaged but I doubt whether the other Officers under him will be allowed to distinguish themselves as much.[19]

Governor Vance received one more explanatory letter pertaining to the furor about Flag Officer Lynch. Commander Cooke wrote the Governor, (for the record) on January 28, 1864.

In consequence of severe indisposition I have been unable to answer the communication of the Secy of the Navy to you, and therefore referred it to Mr. Elliott to give you all the facts, as regards himself, and I herewith enclose this reply and copies of letters marked A,B,C,& D.

I think the Secretary is mistaken as regards the quantity of iron furnished by the State of N.C. There was taken from the N.C. road on the south bank of the Neuse [River] about 450 tons and from the Rutherford road between 6 and 700 tons, a part of which was exchanged with the Wilmington Road for the worn out rails. I can't say where this iron was sent to be rolled.

As regards the boat on the Neuse, had she been permitted to remain on the stocks until holes of her propellor shafts had been bored, the great expense of constructing a coffer dam would have been avoided, and the expense of the boat greatly lessened[.] The removal of the boat incurred such additional expense in the transportation of timber for her completion, a large portion of which was lost by the overturning of the rafts, which necessarily had to be resupplied[.]

A portion of her armour or plating was put on the shield and taken off by the order of Flag Officer Lynch, of which fact you can refer the Secretary to Mr. Porter, the Naval Constructor. I am at a loss to know what Flag Officer Lynch has done to entitle him to the high compliment as here bestowed by the Secretary. There has been little or nothing accomplished in Wilmington and I think had there been a proper degree of harmony existing between him and the commanding General[,] much property could have been saved.

Had there been constructed two or three boats such as are known by the name of "Beaufort flats," boats of 59 or 60 feet, keel drawing from 2½ to 3 feet, carrying from 100 to 150 barrels,...[greater success might have been achieved on our rivers at an earlier date.]

To the remark "as his efforts to build and equip vessels in North Carolina had to encounter difficulties and entanglements not generally understood," this paragraph of the Secretary's letter is to me so very ambiguous that I think it requires some explanation, as I am not aware that Flag Officer Lynch had any entanglements or difficulties to encumber. With feelings of consideration of respect and esteem, I am very truly yours.[20]

With Commander Cooke's letter, the lively exchange of accusations and posturing for control of the *Albemarle's* destiny abruptly ended. It had cost nearly two months of down time and countless dollars to retain idle workers. And perhaps General Lee's campaign plans, against the Union forces at New Bern, might have been negatively influenced by the unfinished *Albemarle*, since iron plates that had been shipped sat on railroad sidings where so many cars had been shunted.

Perhaps to view conditions at the Halifax yard through the eyes of an independent observer, Governor Vance apparently requested James W. Hinton to visit the yard and report. That was Col. James W. Hinton, commanding the 68th Regiment, since the regiment had been headquartered a month earlier at Murfreesboro, N.C.[21] Colonel Hinton was another Elizabeth City native, one with whom Elliott was acquainted. Hinton addressed a brief report from Halifax to the Governor on February 4, 1864.

> I arrived at this place late yesterday evening. Captain Cooke has arrived here and the work on the gunboat is progressing finely. He is not trammeled at all by Lynch's old fogyism. We have no two-inch iron here, the difficulty being to get transportation for it on the Wilmington Road. I have just dispatched Elliott to Wilmington with an urgent appeal to the master of transportation to let the iron come up at once. If the boat is not delayed for want of iron, she will be completed in thirty days. I have sent a young man across the river for your pork. I am expecting it every day.[22]

General Lee's campaign plans against New Bern were proceeding to the extent that Brig. Gen. Innis Newton Palmer, U.S.A., Administrative Commander of the Sub-District of New Bern, circulated a number of reports throughout his command about the approaching Confederate assault. Confederate prisoners and deserters had provided much information.

Palmer's concern for protection of water approaches to New Bern was strongly pronounced, since Cdr. John Taylor Wood, C.S.N., had led a small-boat force on February 2, 1864, in the successful capture and destruction of the U.S.S. *Underwriter* in the Neuse River near New Bern. Wood's boats had been assembled at Petersburg, Virginia, shipped by rail to Kinston, North Carolina, and launched upon the Neuse River at that point. The plan had been to capture the 4-gun sidewheel steamer, but after boarding her it was discovered she had no steam pressure with which to run her engines.[23]

General Palmer sent an advisory report on February 7 to Assistant Adjutant General R. S. Davis, which also included his latest intelligence of Confederate ironclad activity on the Neuse.

> One of the prisoners informs me that he had been detailed to work on the rebel ironclad ram, now building

at Kinston. He says they are finishing the work on her as fast as possible; that the engine is not yet in her, but it was thought that a few weeks would complete her. She has four embrasures; can carry four heavy guns, and is plated with 4-inch iron and built after the model of the Merrimac. This is a matter for serious consideration. A vessel like the one described, could she get into the harbor, would do incalculable damage.I think there is no doubt of the truth of this statement.[24]

What a dilemma he must have experienced, real and imagined, when he later learned of Confederate plans to combine the *Neuse* and *Albemarle* in an assault on New Bern.

Secretary Mallory, who was informed of General Lee's intent to assault New Bern, proclaimed his ever present worry about the shortage of iron for the two North Carolina ironclads then under construction on the Neuse and Roanoke. On February 8, he dashed off a short letter again expressing how critical was the matter of timely transportation of iron. To Major John N. Whitford, C.S.A., and President of the Atlantic and North Carolina Railroad at Goldsboro, he appealed.

> The construction of naval vessels in North Carolina and particularly that on the Neuse and Roanoke has been greatly retarded by the difficulty of getting iron armour for them over the railroads. Commander [John Taylor] Wood who has just returned from North Carolina informs me that if called upon by this Department you would give it important aid in this request.
>
> I take liberty therefore of requesting whatever assistance you may be able to afford in the transportation of iron from the rolling mill in Atlanta to Kinston and Halifax. Flag Officer Lynch at Wilmington can give you all necessary information upon the subject and will apprise you of the difficulties in the way.
>
> I know of no more important service, than getting this iron to it's destination, that I would feel at liberty to call upon you for.[25]

In keeping with terms of Elliott's new Department contract, payment for labor and supplies became a frequent routine. With authorization of vouchers approved by Halifax Yard Superintendent John A. Thomas, it was the duty of Assistant Paymaster Adam Tredwell to make five payments on February 9, 1864.

Workman A. Hopkins was paid $20.50, the balance of his $33.00 claim, of which $12.50 had been paid in cash. It covered two days round-trip travel cost from Wilmington to Edwards Ferry for $12.00; 1 day fitting suitable living quarters for $6.00; and 2½ days work on the gunboat.

Frankin Dunn was also paid similar amounts for travel and quarters, but he had worked 19 days on the gunboat for $95.00. Of this amount he had been earlier paid $76.00 in cash, so he received $37.00 from Tredwell.

Carter Hogwood received similar travel and quarters amounts, and had worked on the gunboat 11 days for $66.00. An earlier cash payment of $55.00 lowered his final amount to $29.00.

Those vouchers were simply dated 1863. Possibly the workmen had been unfortunate victims of the untimely transfer to Halifax of both the *Albemarle* and Elliott's records. As well, Tredwell paid 2 vouchers to Elliott for yard expenses. The first, amounting to $6,481.96, covered charges for 4,702 feet of pine plank at $75.00 per thousand feet; 1,682 feet of oak plank at $80.00 per thousand; 332 bushels of charcoal; 53 oak knees @ $27.50 each; 797 and ½ days labor @ $5.00; and 33½ days quarters per man @ $6.50. The second voucher paid Elliott, amounting to $550.00, provided him with one 3-inch fall, two 2-inch falls and blocks, and a single 2-inch fall and block.[26]

As the construction tempo at Halifax began to mount, it appears that a shortage of certain supplies became imminent. Frequent appeals to the Quartermaster Department had afforded no relief, which caused Elliott to address a question of policy to Secretary Mallory on February 12. Four days later Mallory responded to Elliott at Halifax with a rather cryptic note.

> Your letter of the 12th inst. is received. I can perceive no objection to the exchanges you propose to make to obtain provisions to enable you to carry on the work and complete the *Albemarle*.
>
> Trading directly or indirectly with the enemy must not be countenanced but, between good and loyal citizens of the Confederacy cannot be objected to.[27]

Throughout the Confederate military there had been random incidents of trading with the enemy. Most often such reports were about close contact opportunities between troops of both sides when the men traded coffee, tobacco, sugar and like items.

Catherine Edmondston had business in Halifax at County Court on Monday, February 16, 1864. When the proceedings were concluded her carriage driver took her down to the Halifax Yard, where she could inspect the *Albemarle* and visit with Commander Cooke and Elliott. In her Journal she recorded her impressions.

> Went to see the Navy Yard and the gunboat *Albemarle,* our old acquaintance upon whom we waited until dark last summer at Edwards Ferry to see her take her proper element. She is now nearly completed, engines & propeller in & will, if the Department at Richmond send on the iron to complete her armour, steam down the river next month. Captain Cooke is in command of the station & his energy & decision in getting so much accomplished in so short a time is surprising. We saw some of the famous Brooke Guns, much smaller in the bore than I had supposed.[28]

She gave eyewitness testimony that the engines, shafts, and propellers were installed on the *Albemarle,* although no official record of the accomplishment has thus far been discovered. From Mrs. Edmondston's observations, at that time, only the bolting on of the armor plates remained to be completed before the *Albemarle* could be commissioned into service.

The same day, Lt. Robert D. Minor reported to Flag Officer Lynch about the C.S.S. *Neuse* then building at Kinston, N.C.

> Lieutenant Commdg. [William] Sharp has a force of one hundred and seventy-two men employed upon her.... As you are aware the steamer has two layers of iron on the forward end of her shield, but none of either broadside, or on the after part.
>
> The carpenters are now caulking the longitudinal pieces on the hull, and if the iron can be delivered more rapidly, or in small quantities with some degree of regularity, the work would progress in a much more satisfactory manner. The boiler was today lowered into the vessel

and when in place, the main deck will be laid in.... The river I am told is unprecedentedly low for the season of the year.... I am satisfied not more than five feet can be now carried down the channel.... And as the steamer when ready for service will draw between six or seven feet, it is very apparent that to be useful, she must be equipped in time to take advantage of the first rise.[29]

Lieutenant Minor's concern for the need of sufficiently deep water would later be justified when the *Neuse* grounded on a sand bar while steaming into battle.

Further evidence the Department had adopted a serious policy of management, to assure early completion of both the *Neuse* and *Albemarle*, appeared in a letter of February 17, 1864, written by Lt. Robert D. Minor, C.S.N., to Admiral Franklin Buchanan, C.S.N., in Mobile. The letter was largely that of a communication between old friends, but it did contain a significant statement pertaining to Minor's assignment to command the *Neuse*.

I was tendered the command of her, but upon some representations being made to the Secretary that I could advance the public service by completing, or rather hurrying the completion of this vessel and the ironclad steamer *Albemarle*, Commander Cooke, at Halifax[N.C.], on the Roanoke River, than I could by being confined to one vessel as her commanding officer, my orders were so framed that I should have authority to push forward the material and the completion of both vessels, and I hope soon decided success will crown my efforts.[30]

Back at Halifax on the Roanoke, word of an impending Union expedition up the Roanoke came to Cooke and Elliott. Because the river at Halifax was relatively narrow, with hazards of shoal waters during the season of drought, it was generally considered safe from enemy intrusion. On February 22, Lt. Cdr. Charles W. Flusser, commanding U.S. Naval Forces, Albemarle Sound, issued an order to Acting Master William N. Welles of the tinclad U.S.S. *Whitehead*. Welles was to advance up the Roanoke to wreak all possible destruction.

As a result of the incursion, the greatest Confederate loss was that of a corn mill just below Hamilton near Rainbow Bluff. Flusser reported later that torpedoes were found planted in the river above that point, an indication he observed that "would argue rather, fear of our advance than an intention on their part to attack." His remark was made in the wake of repeatedly expressed concern of a rumored massive Confederate attack on Union positions in the North Carolina sounds.[31]

In accordance with his orders from Secretary Mallory, after concluding his inspection of the *Neuse*, Lieutenant Minor had visited the Halifax Yard to view progress on the *Albemarle*. Minor's report to Mallory on February 28 portrayed the ironclad nearing completion,

> With the exception of some little connecting work to be completed [the ironclad] may be considered as ready. Steam will probably be raised on Friday next [March 4]. The iron is all on the hull...the carpenters are now bolting the first layers of plate on the shield, and as long as iron is available the work will progress. The rudder is in place. Shell room and magazine prepared. Office quarters arranged and berth deck ready for either hammocks if allowed the ship[,] or bunks if the canvas cannot be obtained.... The ship is now afloat and when ready for service will I think draw between 7 to 8 feet.... The guns, carriages, and equipment have not yet arrived, but are expected on the 4th of March.[32]

Minor's graphic description of the nearly completed *Albemarle* rapidly being readied at the Halifax Yard, appeared to have absolved Elliott of every criticism proffered by Lynch. Although not related to the Yard's activites, the next day Elliott's resignation from the army was noted on the 17th Regiment's muster for Monday, February 29, 1864.[33]

Flag Officer Lynch was no longer associated with the *Albemarle*, and neither was his Assistant Paymaster Adam Tredwell. When Mallory had ordered Cooke to command the *Albemarle's* construction at Halifax Naval Station, the Navy Department provided an onsite Assistant Paymaster. Beginning with the first of March, invoices were paid by P. M. DeLeon, C.S.N. He settled five accounts that day, none over one month old. In all cases the vouchers were countersigned by Commander Cooke.

The first (unnumbered) was payable to Seth K. Cordin for materials. Included in the list were: 1 pair trace chains [for horse or mule harness], 3 pairs of hanes, 5 hinges, 3 pounds copper wire, 1 box Crone Yellow, 10 pairs butts, 4 dozen 2-inch screws, 10 dozen 1-inch screws, $1\frac{1}{2}$ and $\frac{3}{4}$-inch brads, 12 sheets sand paper, 2 dozen screws, and $\frac{1}{2}$ dozen nabs. The amount paid Corbin was $85.75.

Peter E. Smith had submitted a bill for sixty-seven pounds of greenstone. Considering freight to Wilmington and hauling to Halifax, Voucher #24 provided payment amounting to $72.55. The acquisition of greenstone strongly indicated that Smith was probably modifying his Halifax forges to permit the generation of greater heat. Greenstone, a solid mineral often mixed with clay, was used in foundries to line the interiors of furnaces or cupolas within which metal was heated to a molten state, before being poured into molds to produce castings. The emphasis of work upon the *Albemarle* had turned to iron installation and fabrication of iron components. In all likelihood greater heat was required of his forges, and to make certain they would withstand the elevated temperatures he probably planned to line them with greenstone.

Ships stores proprietor M. McMahon received $3,040.67 for supplies ordered by Cooke. These included 1 barrel of turpentine, rope, salt, and 2 bales of cotton @ $1272.50 each.

As contractor, Elliott's charges for labor were lumped into man-days. February labor charges totaled $6,430.50, equating to 1238 general labor man-days at $5.00 per day, and 34 Foremen man-days at $6.50 per day. There was an unaccounted difference of $19.50 unpaid.

A final voucher paid to the contractor that day amounted to $5,198.72. It was for assorted materials such as; pine, cypress, and oak planks, oak and ash timbers, borax, lock and lantern, 17 barrels of tar, a supply of butts, screws, flat hooks, knobs, locks, and files, 805 bushels of charcoal, 100 pounds of tallow, and 4 months use of a steam engine, and 4 months rental of the schooner *Julia Frances*, both from February 1 until May 1.[34]

The name of the person who designed the method of attaching rolled iron plates to the *Albemarle's* casemate was unrecorded. Possibly it was Peter E. Smith with his natural mechanical genius. As earlier mentioned, the casemate was to be covered with two courses of iron plates. Each plate measured 7 inches wide by 2 inches thick, but their length was not known. It's conceivable that Smith or Elliott had specified individual lengths when the plates had been ordered rolled.

When Elliott wrote of the *Albemarle* in July 1888, he stated the first course, laid horizontally, was bolted to a wooden backing sixteen inches thick. A drawing of the *Albemarle* probably made when she was being surveyed for Admiralty Court proceedings in April 1865, showed specific measurements of the plates to have been 6 ³/₄ inches wide.[35] This varied slightly from Elliott's recollection in 1888.[36]

Three laminated wooden layers formed the casemate's side walls. The interior layer was of vertically placed yellow pine 12 by 13-inch frame timbers, each bolted to the other side by side. Horizontally nailed on the exterior were 5-inch thick pine planks, and on their exterior were 4-inch thick oak planks vertically attached.

The first armor course was laid lengthwise from deck level against the casemate's oak planking. In Elliott's 1888 account, he stated that the plates were laid leaving a 2-inch space between each two layers of iron. This narrow space was filled with wood leaving a clearance between the inner plate pairs for the bolting of outer plates

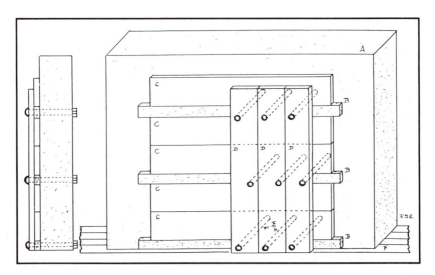

The method of attaching casemate iron plates is best described in Gilbert Elliott's words. "The iron plating consisted of two courses 7 inches wide and 2 inches thick. The first course was laid lengthwise over a wooden backing 16 inches in thickness. A 2-inch space filled with wood being left between each two layers to afford space for bolting the outer course through the whole shield. The outer course was laid flush, forming a smooth surface."

Note: Casemate wall, 'A'; 2-inch thick wooden spacers, 'B'; horizontal iron plates, 'C'; vertical iron plates, 'D'; bolt holes drilled through all surfaces, 1¹/₄ inches in diameter, 'E'; deck surface, 'F'.

Author's drawing

over the inner plates, and through the whole shield. The 1¹/₄-inch holes drilled through each outer iron plate were countersunk to prevent protruding bolt heads from defacing the smooth iron surface. Since 1¹/₄-inch diameter bolts about 26 inches long were required to penetrate the thick shield wall, in all probability their nonstandard size supports the supposition that Smith made the bolts in his forge.

During the preceding fall on November 6, 1863, Cooke had written Mallory offering his explanation to allegations by Constructor Porter that iron washers had not been used in bolting iron plates. Cooke had asserted,

> There were no rings used [on bolts] for the simple reason that...the contractor was unable to get them, but the heads of the bolts were flattened and well secured [by blacksmiths].[37]

On March 7 Elliott learned that 14 carloads of armor plates had been delivered to Flag Officer Lynch.[38] Some of the shipment was meant for the *Albemarle*. Cooke and Elliott must have been elated with the news, as they anxiously waited for the plates to arrive from Wilmington.

Flag Officer Lynch again entered the arena on March 8, when he wrote Mallory revealing his frustration over delayed iron shipments.

> Fourteen carloads of plate iron arrived last evening, and for a week past we have had two carloads waiting transportation to Kinston and Halifax. The whole capacity of the road, except passenger trains, has been monopolized by the Army, and I fear the completion of the gunboats at those places will be delayed.[39]

Three days later on the eleventh, Mallory dispatched a message to James A. Seddon, Secretary of War. He again called attention to the predicament of those building the ironclads in North Carolina, since there was as yet insufficient iron transportation. Mallory's sense of urgency was imparted in an extract from the letter.

> ...to have the iron plates referred to [be] transported to Kinston and Halifax at the earliest moment. The gunboats at those points are completed with the exception of the iron plating, and the mechanics are delayed in their

work waiting for it. The work upon these vessels has been delayed for months by want of transportation, and now that they are very near completion I respectfully urge that no further delay on this account may be had,... The subject is of so much importance that I suggest the detail by the Quartermaster General of an officer specially charged with it.[40]

When Seddon directed the request through channels to Quartermaster General Alexander R. Lawton, it was endorsed back to Seddon with a cryptically brief response.

Respectfully returned to honorable Secretary of War. At present forage and food necessary for our armies in the field demand our entire transportation.[41]

Though railroad owners had inclinations to expedite shipment of the most profitable freight, deciding the criticality of materials and supplies should not have been their province. They even might not have shipped ammunition had they been approached with more profitable freight.

When Lynch had removed the *Albemarle* from Edwards Ferry, there was due Elliott and Martin the sum of $2,500. Lynch might have delayed payment authorization as an assertion of his authority. At any rate, Adam Tredwell visited Halifax on March 14, 1864, where he acquired Elliott's receipt for the full amount. As the receipt stated, payment was for work completed "at the time it was taken from our hands."

The spectacle of a nearly completed ironclad being fitted out at the Halifax Yard naturally became news. Rumors or reports from informers had provided the Union with constantly changing views of the *Albemarle's* progress. From his headquarters at Plymouth, Lt. Commander Flusser had prepared a routine dispatch to Rear Admiral Lee on March 16, in which he remarked, "the ram was reported to have two layers of iron and to be ready to proceed to Williamston on 1 April." Two days later he informed Lee that the *Albemarle* was "to have 7 inches of plating.... The reporters are putting on the iron rather heavy. I am inclined to believe her armor is not more than stated in one of my former letters, 3 inches."[42]

Mallory had written Elliott on February 16, 1864, in response to Elliott's request for clarification of the Department's policy of trading with the enemy for scarce materials. Mallory had, of course, said the Department would not approve, but between "good and loyal citizens of the Confederacy [it] cannot be objected to."

With the tacit approval on paper, Elliott selected a Plymouth gentleman and prepared for him a handwritten identification.

> Mr. B. J. Spruill is my Agent to exchange Cotton & Cloth & Tobacco for Bacon, Lard & Tallow, which provisions are necessary for the use of the Navy on Roanoke River. Gilbert Elliott, Contractor for *Albemarle*, Halifax, N.C., March 20, 1864.[43]

Among the records extant, between October 26, 1863, and January 15, 1864, Elliott's floating battery had been mentioned infrequently. On the latter date, Cooke had repeated Lynch's last orders by telegraphing them to Lieutenant Mitchell. He had been requested to "take the floating battery in charge and put her in a safe position for putting on her armor."[44]

Anticipating a seasonal shortage of pork products, Elliott had ordered a substantial quantity of lard. It could have been used for machinery lubrication as well as for nutritional purposes. On March 24, Paymaster P. M. DeLeon paid Elliott the sum of $5,616.00 for 1,404 pounds of lard @ $4.00 per pound. It would prove to have been one of the most valuable stores purchased.[45]

That same day Flusser reported to Rear Adm. Samuel D. Lee stating, "intelligence which would seem reliable," indicated the ironclad ram was at Hamilton, and the torpedoes placed by the Confederates in the Roanoke River below Williamston were being removed to permit her passage downstream.[46]

Others in the Federal command were optimistic that they would prevail should the dreaded ironclad make an appearance. From his headquarters at New Bern on March 26, Maj. Gen. John J. Peck sent a routine report to Maj. Gen. Benjamin F. Butler, commanding Department of North Carolina at Fortress Monroe. In closing Peck boldly proclaimed, "I feel entirely sanguine that the ironclad in the Roanoke will be destroyed if she attacks Plymouth."[47]

P. M. DeLeon paid a mechanics board bill with Voucher #45 on March 31, 1864. Mr. W. R. Williams received $1,247.83 for services during February and March. He could have been a boarding house proprietor, or manager of communal housing at the Halifax Yard.

Partakers of his hospitality were craftsmen working on the *Albemarle*. They were machinists Mahony, Stokes, Long and McLinchlin; coppersmiths Fisher and Fuqui; and boilermakers Lee, Mackii and O'Neal. Their daily rates of $6.00 per man had been charged during February, but by March the daily rate had increased to $10.00 per day per man.[48]

In order to appreciate the *Albemarle's* massive strength and degree of complexity, in spite of her crude beginnings, a summary developed from information provided by persons during the *Albemarle's* career and afterwards showed her peculiar characteristics as they appeared on April 1, 1864.

Elliott set forth the hull specifications; length 152 feet between perpendiculars; an extreme beam of 45 feet; depth from gun deck to keel was 9 feet; when empty her draft was 6½ feet though it became 8 feet when loaded; the ram of solid oak extending 18 feet back from the bow was covered with 2 inches of iron which tapered forward to a 4-inch pointed edge; and the hull sides from the knuckle to 4 feet below the deck were covered with iron plates 2 inches thick. Of the casemate, Elliott said it was octagonal and 60 feet long at deck level, and all interior surfaces were sided [smooth finished] to prevent splintering, [and probably painted in light color].[49]

John L. Porter drew his plans calling for a length of 152 feet between perpendiculars; an extreme beam of 34 feet at the knuckle above water; and depth of hull to be 9 feet from gun deck to rabbet,[50] with total tonnage to be 376. His plan located the crews quarters forward below the gun deck near the magazine; boilers flanked the center stack; engines and fire room were immediately aft the boilers; and further aft of the engine room were officers quarters, with a small ward room still further aft.

Additionally he called for 2 ladder ways on starboard and port from gun deck to below deck; 1 engine hatch aft of stack; 2 grating covered deck hatches, 1 each forward and aft; and an anchor winch midships and forward of stack below helmsman's cupola.

Lastly, Porter's plan specified a 20-foot Captains gig to be chock mounted on the after deck; on the forward deck at the bow were a pair of 6-foot anchors attached to 6-inch chain; and mounted on the casemate's exterior walls forward and aft were ladders fastened to the gun port's right, each reaching from deck to casemate top. At rear of the casemate top was a flagstaff from which flew the Second National Flag.[51]

JOHN L. PORTER'S PLANS

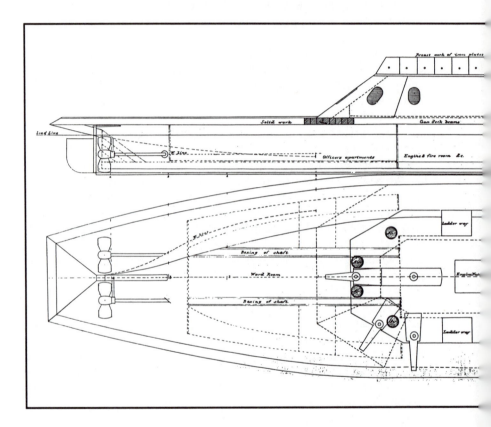

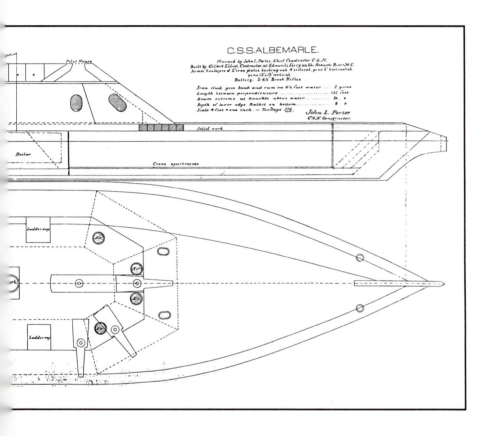

John L. Porter, Chief Constructor, C.S.N., drew these top and side plans of the C.S.S. *Albemarle*. In building the ironclad, the hinged iron breastwork plates atop the casemate were eliminated, as were the forward and aft quarter gun positions.

Courtesy of: 3-5-27 Record Group 19, National Archives

W. E. GEOGHEGAN'S PLANS

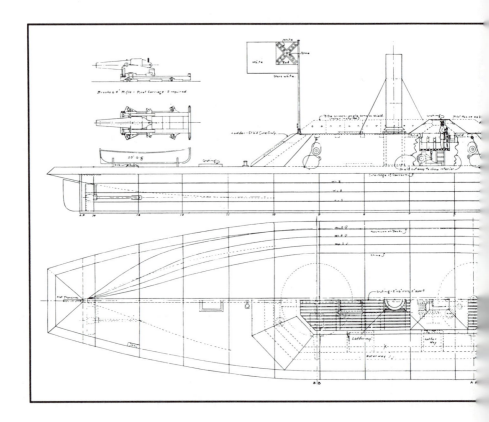

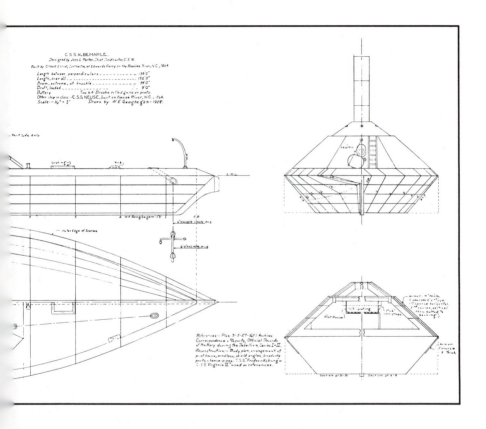

This revised top and side plan of the C.S.S. *Albemarle* was drawn by W. E. Geoghegan. He incorporated Porter's plan with "Correspondence and Reports, Official Records of the Navy during the War of The Rebellion, Series I-II." Reconstruction: Body plans, arrangement of pilot house, windlass, shield angles, broadside ports, hawse pipes. C.S.S. *Fredericksburg* and C.S.S. *Virginia* II used as reference.

Courtesy of: 3-5-27 Record Group 19, National Archives

When the U.S. District Court ordered a survey of the captured *Albemarle* to supplement Case 146 on May 18, 1865, three U.S. Navy officials examined the vessel where she was moored in Norfolk Navy Yard. In their joint report they stated her extreme length was 158 feet; extreme beam was 35 feet 3 inches, and deck width as 32 feet; hull depth from top of beam to top of floor [over bilge] was 8 feet 2 inches; her loaded draft was 9 feet; she was flat bottomed with straight sides; and plated from 2 feet below the knuckle to the deck with two layers of 1-inch iron. The survey report also stated the forward and aft decks were covered with 1-inch iron plates, and the casemate had 2 layers of 2-inch iron plating on outside surfaces. Sketches relating to the survey revealed little known details such as; the casemate grating top was 46 feet long and 15 feet 6 inches wide; gun deck headroom within the casemate was 7 feet from floor to grating top; all casemate sides were angled 35 degrees from vertical providing proper deflection angle; there were 2 each gunports on port and starboard, and 1 each forward and aft, consisting of holes 22 inches wide and 2 feet 6 inches high; that gunport shutters measured 2 feet 8 inches wide and 5 feet 6 inches high; and all shutters were covered with 2 layers of 2-inch iron as were the casemate walls.[52]

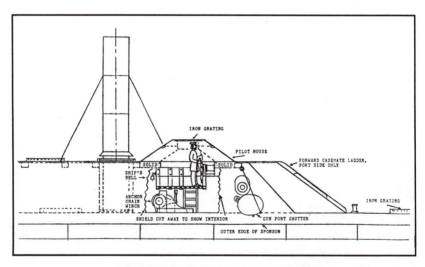

DRAWING BY W. E. GEOGHEGAN

Record Group #19-National Archives

CHAPTER 11

DOWN THE ROANOKE TO BATTLE

During the first seventeen days of April 1864, observers could see accelerated activity on board the *Albemarle*. There were iron plates to be fastened. Interior wood work was being finished with special attention paid to surface smoothness. Ships stores had to be assembled and loaded on board. Even the engineers were busy adjusting machinery, firing the boilers, and raising steam to test both engines.

Halifax Yard's Voucher #83 illustrated the concerted labor effort expended to complete the *Albemarle*. Elliott's March labor bill amounted to $6,925.00. On April 1 Paymaster DeLeon paid the itemized labor bill. It accounted for 50 men for 27 days @ $5.00 per day, or $6,750.00. The foreman's labor was for 35 days at $6.50 per day, making a total of $227.50. The slight discrepancy of $52.50 was not accounted for.[1]

As the *Albemarle* had begun to settle deeper into the water while the iron plates were being applied, Elliott and Cooke realized that the river's low level might create a problem when she would begin the tortuous voyage downriver to Plymouth. At Halifax the Roanoke was marginally narrow with a greater possibility of hidden shoals. Perhaps that was the most important reason for moving the *Albemarle* downriver to Hamilton as the last plates were being attached.

Whether she made the trip under steam, or was towed, Cooke brought her downriver shortly after April 1. The crew were much distressed while they worked at Hamilton to complete the ironclad, because they were separated from their usual rations and quarters.

In Plymouth at his naval headquarters on April 5, Flusser reported another rumor from up the Roanoke to Admiral Lee. Reports were circulating that the large ship was of such light draft "that she may pass over our obstructions in the river without touching them."[2]

The *Albemarle's* loaded draft of approximately nine feet had been erroneously reported by Flusser on March 27 as being "6 to 8 feet," according to a carpenter who had worked upon her.

From his Richmond Headquarters on April 12, General Braxton Bragg issued comprehensive orders to Brig. Gen. Robert F. Hoke. In preparation for the long awaited assault to retake Plymouth, N.C., he was to confer with Commander Cooke to elicit from him a realistic date when the ironclad would be ready for battle.

When Hoke visited Cooke at Hamilton, Cooke finally learned of the urgent need for the *Albemarle* on the eighteenth. Hoke's manner was very persuasive. With full understanding of the *Albemarle's* importance to the campaign, and in response to Hoke's question of readiness Cooke laconically said, "in fifteen days, with ten additional mechanics."[3] Hoke rendered assistance as promised. In turn, he requested that Cooke have the *Albemarle* in readiness with armament and supplies loaded. He also had further assurance additional crewmen would arrive in a few days. Bragg had even suggested that Hoke provide Cooke with his plans of attack, in order that Cooke and his vessel would be fully prepared when they reached Plymouth.[4]

Brig. Gen. Henry W. Wessells, U.S.A., commanding at Plymouth, suspected General Hoke's assault plans against Plymouth. Wessels alerted Captain Judson, Assistant Adjutant General, District of North Carolina, on April 13 with information from disconnected sources that amounted to a warning.

A large Confederate force (stated at 10,000 to 12,000) has assembled near Hamilton on the [Roanoke] river, designing, in conjunction with an iron clad to make an attack on Plymouth this week.[5]

There can be little doubt that Cooke briefed Elliott about his conversation with General Hoke, and his agreement to leave on the seventeenth, ready or not. Since there remained much work to prepare the *Albemarle* for battle, they decided to continue construction while floating downriver. On Sunday, April 17, 1864,

The C.S. Steamer *Albemarle* was placed in Commission this day at 2 o'clock P.M. The Officers ordered to her hitherto awaiting her completion will be entered on your Books as on duty afloat from this date inclusive. I am very respectfully, J. W. Cooke, Commanding C.S.N.[6]

As Assistant Paymaster P. M. DeLeon set his hand as witness, workmen began loading aboard iron plates yet to be attached. Portable forges were installed on the *Albemarle's* flush decks, and several might have been set up along with extra materials on the flat to be towed behind. In addition, a number of carpenters and blacksmiths had been assembled to continue working as the *Albemarle* headed downriver.

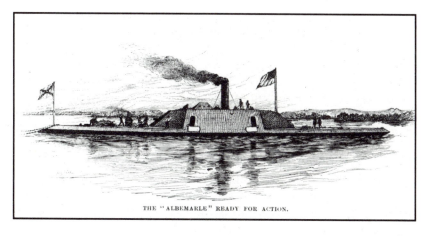

THE "ALBEMARLE" READY FOR ACTION.

An engraving by M. H. Hoke shows the *Albemarle* steaming stern first down the Roanoke. She dragged chains from her bow to assist in navigating the river's numerous twists and turns.

Century Magazine, July, 1888

Because of the river's current with its many twists and turns, Cooke ordered heavy chains to be dragged from the bow when the *Albemarle* would begin drifting stern first downstream.[7] He believed it would be easier to steer the vessel by this method. By about 3 P.M., all was in readiness. With all hands aboard and at their stations, Cooke ordered "Cast off all lines." The assistance of a small steam tender could have been necessary to ease the *Albemarle* into the center stream's current, but she was on her way by April 17, 1864, as planned.[8]

The *Albemarle* had not drifted many miles before she encountered the steamer *Cora* carrying the sailors promised by General Hoke. Transfer of twenty seasoned sailors was effectively made without apparent delay to her downriver drift.[9]

The folks at Williamston were waiting for the *Albemarle's* arrival. In fact, for two days inhabitants of the countryside had been gathering for that event. Visitors arrived by carriage, canoes, pirogues, on horseback, and afoot. All available rooms in the community were taken, and the Yellowley Hotel was "filled to triple its capacity. Folks slept in carts or wagons and ate where they could." Because the river was in full freshet "the multitude assembled had to view the event from the river hill," and the hill was also the vantage point for those soldiers stationed at Williamston for the vessel's protection. A picnic with a band playing on the hill top could have been Cooke's first vision of Williamston.

As he eased the vessel to the bank where lines were attached, speeches were being made to the throng by Judge Asa Biggs, Dennis Simmons, Jesse Stubbs and Mr. Bagley. It was a historic day for the people of Williamston. For months the town had seen Union troops marching in her streets, as they fanned out across the countryside to raid and attack other places in North Carolina. For the moment it was glorious to be free.

At five in the afternoon, Cooke stopped only briefly to put ashore unnecessary men, materials, and equipment. Several mechanics, carpenters, and blacksmiths were kept aboard as a precaution, should repairs be required before reaching Plymouth.[10] Friendly hands probably helped Cooke cast off as he left Williamston. As the village faded into the distance over the bow, Cooke called for another gun drill. His inexperienced crew were drilled by Cooke himself. Amid the confusion of workmen applying iron plates, he assumed a position on the gun deck just below the pilot's cupola. From there he could have been heard loudly commanding, "drive in Spike No. 10!" He then followed with, "on nut below and screw up! Invert and sponge. Load with cartridge!" Then the next command was, "drive in No. 11, port-side, so! On nut and screw up hard! Load with shells, prime!"[11]

Later in the evening about 10 P.M., a drive shaft coupling gave way. Bolts fastening the coupling to a propeller shaft sheared, either from excessive torque, or from not having been sufficiently hardened. The *Albemarle* was moored to the river's bank while mechanics disconnected the coupling. Blacksmiths lit their forges on the flush deck, and began the task of making new bolts. Every effort was expended to increase the degree of each new bolt's hardness.

Six hours later, about four in the morning on Monday the eighteenth, Cooke once more slipped the lines and resumed floating down the Roanoke. Two hours later, about 6 A.M., the rudder head fractured, probably weakened from excessive pressures while steering stern first. After a four hour delay carpenters and mechanics had repaired the damage. The *Albemarle* was once again on her way by about ten that morning.

Monday April 18 must have been chaotic aboard the ironclad. Anvils rang as cherry red iron was being pounded to form. Fitters outside hammered bolts fastening iron plates to the casemate, and above it all Cooke shouted commands to both gun crews, as they drilled and drilled. Perhaps they sent a practice shot or two up or down the river.

By five in the afternoon Cooke thought it prudent to heave to along the river's bank, and put ashore excess men, equipment, and materials. The decks were cleared for action, and soon the *Albemarle* was on her way again.[12]

Where the river widened, he turned the vessel so she headed downriver bow first. The entire voyage had been conducted only with an agreed upon departure date from Hamilton. Cooke had no information regarding Hoke's plans. More importantly, he had no knowledge of when he was expected to arrive off Plymouth, or what targets Hoke wished him to fire upon. Cooke knew only one thing definitely, the Union Navy would be encountered.

Meanwhile, about eight that evening in his quarters on board his flagship *Miami,* Flusser was making two reports. The first was to Cdr. Henry K. Davenport, Senior Officer, Sounds of North Carolina.

> The ram will be down tonight or tomorrow. She was, just after daylight this morning, foul of a tree 6 miles above Williamston. I think, if she does not stay under cover of their battery established above Fort Grey, that we shall whip her. I had to destroy the obstruction in the Thoroughfare, as the *Whitehead* was above and could not run by the battery placed below her on the Roanoke.[13]

He varied his message to Rear Adm. Samuel P. Lee. Repeating only his estimate of when the *Albemarle* would arrive, he continued,

> I fear [that], for the protection of the town, I shall have to abandon my plan of fighting the ram, lashed to

the Southfield.... I today gave to Fort Grey 100 projectiles for [the] Parrott 100-pounder rifle.[14]

Ever present in Cooke's mind must have been the question of subsurface obstructions ahead, as well as undetected enemy shore batteries. At ten Monday night he dropped anchor three miles above Plymouth. Cooke summoned the officer staff to discuss alternatives and strategy. All probably felt the *Albemarle* would float safely over any obstructions, since the spring freshet had raised the river's level to what some old timers had said "was the highest in memory."

Of the meeting Elliott later reflected,

> An exploring expedition was sent out, under command of one of the Lieutenants, which returned in about two hours, with the report that it was considered impossible to pass the obstructions. Thereupon the fires were banked, and the officers and crew not on duty retired to rest.[15]

Elliott was among those with whom Cooke conferred. He had volunteered as Cooke's aide. When he thought of lying there all night contemplating an attempt to cross hazardous obstructions in daylight, Elliott reacted to a "then or never" impulse and volunteered to make a personal inspection. Cooke cordially assented. A small boat was readied for Elliott, Pilot John Luck, and two experienced seamen. They departed downriver at 11 P.M. carrying a long pole. Visibility on the open river must have been enhanced by a full moon overhead. Arriving at the obstructions he and Luck took soundings.

> To our great joy it was ascertained that there was ten feet of water over and above the obstructions. This was due to the remarkable freshet then prevailing.... Pushing on down stream to Plymouth, and taking advantage of the shadows of trees on the north side of the river, opposite the town, we watched the Federal transports taking on board the women and children who were being sent away for safety, on account of the approaching bombardment. With muffled oars, and almost afraid to breathe, we made our way back up river, hugging close to the northern bank, and reached the ram about one in the morning, reporting to Captain Cooke that it was practicable to pass the obstructions provided the boat was kept in the middle of the stream.[16]

Elliott had also reported the location of two batteries on the river's south bank. Submerged obstructions were upriver from Plymouth, located above and below the batteries. Cooke ordered all hands to rest and be prepared for a two-thirty departure that same morning, the nineteenth of April. Right on time Cooke ordered the anchor raised and slowly headed towards Plymouth. It had taken about thirty-two hours to travel down the river from Hamilton to their anchorage above Plymouth.

In the shadows aft the *Albemarle,* the *Cotton Plant* also had anchored. Little has been learned about the *Cotton Plant's* sailing with the *Albemarle,* but she was known to have troops aboard with shoulder arms, ensconced behind rifle screens. Perhaps she remained at anchor until daylight, or until the sound of cannon fire had diminished before steaming on to Plymouth.

Cooke probably stood beside the helmsman as both peered through small cupola ports into the misty darkness. He ordered "all ahead, slow" as he quietly directed the helmsman to steer towards mid-stream. His intention was to ride the river's flow and float over the obstructions. The plan worked. Within moments the *Albemarle* was safely in deeper water.

Cooke's momentary illusion of safety was partially dispelled as they neared the first battery. Passing by the heavy guns at night was moderately safe, though there was always the chance of receiving a lucky direct hit. Cooke had worked a year for the moment at hand. His ship was under steam, guns were loaded, he had faith in his crew, they were snug inside their iron cocoon, and his destined encounter with the enemy vessels was minutes ahead.

Lieutenant Commander Flusser, Senior Naval Officer at Plymouth, knew Cooke's silent voyage was underway. The *Albemarle's*

COMMANDER CHARLES W. FLUSSER, U.S.N.
ordered the *Southfield* and *Miami* to be tied together with chains and ropes in hopes of snaring the *Albemarle.*
Century Magazine, July, 1888

anticipated arrival time had been variably forecast since Sunday April 17, so Flusser ordered early warning lookouts posted upriver.

Accordingly, the U.S.S. *Whitehead* was assigned guard duty just below the uppermost obstructions. At 2:00 P.M. on the seventeenth, Acting Ensign George W. Barrett, commanding the *Whitehead*, accepted Flusser's orders to relieve the U.S.S. *Ceres* which had been temporarily on station for brief periods. As the *Whitehead* anchored in a strategic position at Hyman's Ferry, enabling an unchallenged view upriver as far as the next bend, the *Ceres* weighed anchor and headed downstream. By 6:10 P.M. the *Ceres* had returned with a message from Flusser that "sharp lookouts be detailed." The *Ceres* had departed again for Plymouth by 8:00 P.M.

At 8:10 P.M. on the eighteenth, lights of two steamers were sighted moving slowly around the river's bend above the barricade. Barrett immediately passed orders to slip the cable, the boatswain piped 'to quarters,' and the *Whitehead* steamed downstream heading for the north bank, though she did hesitate momentarily to observe if the approaching vessels successfully passed over the obstructions.

Complying with orders, Barrett ordered a rocket fired to warn Flusser's observers of the approaching enemy. Moments later a rocket flared across the dark sky from where the enemy was supposed to have been. Cooke had probably mistakenly thought the previous rocket was from General Hoke's pickets, when he ordered a responding flare to be fired. The *Whitehead's* safe passage down river was by then cut off by a Confederate battery, along the south shore, commanding the river west of Fort Grey.

Barrett's only chance to escape being fired upon by the approaching enemy, and of avoiding an exchange of fire with the Confederate battery commanding the river west of Fort Grey, was to pass through a very narrow and crooked natural sluice, connecting the Roanoke and Cashie rivers. To some locals it was known as the Upper Thoroughfare, while others called it Ryan's Thoroughfare. Upon entering the narrow sluice, strong currents swept the *Whitehead* against the bank where she grounded. Barrett ordered a bow line fastened to the opposite bank, and by winching slowly the bow swung into the channel, but her stern was still mired. Tension was great not only with Barrett, but also with his crew. The approaching enemy vessels were very close, and unless his ship could break free of the bank the *Whitehead* would, if seen, be subjected to heavy fire

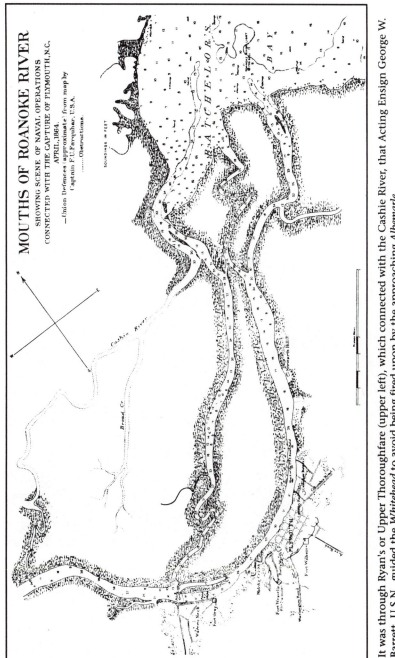

It was through Ryan's or Upper Thoroughfare (upper left), which connected with the Cashie River, that Acting Ensign George W. Barrett, U.S.N., guided the *Whitehead* to avoid being fired upon by the approaching *Albemarle*.
Official Records of the Union and Confederate Navies in the War of the Rebellion, Ser. I, Vol. IX

from the ironclad. With engines "all ahead full," she finally moved off the bank and surged ahead towards a pile blockade some fifty yards further. It was Barrett's intention to force his way through the piles, to avoid possible discovery by the ironclad, but when he tried to do so the *Whitehead* stuck fast.

All engines were immediately stopped. Perfect silence was ordered. Thus it was that in the dull gloom of approaching morning, the *Albemarle* steamed past the sluice without seeing what could have been her first victim.

With the ironclad below the sluice Barrett steamed through the piles, but in so doing wrenched off the shoe which kept the rudder's heel and iron sternpost in place. By 12:30 A.M., on the nineteenth, he was anchored at Plymouth reporting to Flusser.

About 3:15 A.M. the *Ceres*, which had been coaling alongside the Plymouth wharf, arrived with the news that the enemy was com-

To the west over the Roanoke River a nearly full moon would have cast it's reflected light upon Cdr. James W. Cooke, and the *Albemarle* as they neared Plymouth, N.C. There would have been sufficient illumination to have aided Cooke as he maneuvered the *Albemarle*, even though the moon was about 15 degrees above the horizon at 3:40 A.M. when he engaged his adversaries. Plymouth's observing location is 076 42' W & 33 47' N.

Hayden Planetarium, American Ephemeris & Nautical Almanac, 1864, U.S. Naval Observatory Computer generated photo print courtesy of M. Barlow Pepin, Deltona, Fla.

ing. Flusser immediately signaled the *Southfield* to again be lashed to the *Miami*. Both ships were then at the lower picket station below Plymouth. Before all hawsers were secured, Flusser had signaled an order to steam towards the ironclad. Their encounter point would be about one mile below Plymouth off the Roanoke's south bank. Low in the western sky an almost full moon set by 3:45 A.M.[17]

As Fort Grey at Warren's Neck became dimly visible, the thunderous blast of a 100-pounder Parrott broke the pre-dawn silence as it belched forth solid shot on Tuesday morning April 19. Located on the south side of the Roanoke opposite Tallow (or Tabor) Island, about $1^1/_2$ miles above Plymouth, the fort guarded upriver approaches to the town. When the reverberations and echoes faded into heavy darkness, they were replaced with a staccato snapping and crackling of small arms fire, until the illusive target disappeared in the mists.

A casual observer, about three-thirty that morning, would have been left with an impression the gunners at Fort Grey were practicing their craft by merely firing into the swirls of fog rising from deep shadows neath trees bordering the Roanoke's north bank. Their real target though was a ghostly apparition of dark iron floating down river with the current.

From a point above Fort Grey, to another location about a mile downstream, were river obstructions in the form of sunken hulls, torpedoes, and piles blocking the channel. Flusser had hoped they would impede or prevent passage of the long awaited iron monster, but recent spring freshets had raised the river's level preventing them from serving their purpose. Much to the delight of Cooke and his crew, disaster was avoided by floating safely over those obstructions, with no damage from the fort's battery.

Wisps of steam and smoke puffed from the vessel's tall funnel, but not a light was visible from the silent leviathan. Smoke alone disclosed that men were inside. Through the swirls of first-light-tinted fog, eddying around the foreboding hulk, could be seen subliminal glimpses of the Confederate States' Second National Flag also known as the 'Stainless Banner.'

The ensign waved gently in the breeze from the peak of a staff atop the casemate, aft of the funnel. It was the Confederate ironclad *Albemarle* that gunners were firing at, but their shot and shell were ineffective.

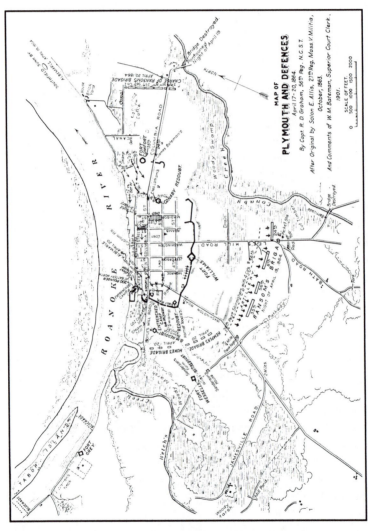

Map of Plymouth, N.C., in October 1863. Note where the *Albemarle* engaged and sunk the *Southfield* at upper right corner.

Clark's North Carolina Regiments, Vol. V

Recalling the occasion in later life, Elliott had observed,

> Protected by the ironclad shield, to those on board [,] the noise made by the shot and shell as they struck the boat sounded no louder than pebbles thrown against an empty barrel.[18]

Without answering fire from Fort Grey, the *Albemarle* continued to drift slowly with the current, though minimum speed was maintained to provide steerageway. At the east end of Tabor (or Tallow) Island, nearly midway between Fort Grey and Welch's Creek, there was another barricade across the Roanoke constructed of similar debris used above Fort Grey. About a mile further downriver was Battery Worth. The battery was adjacent to an entrenched Union camp situated on the river bank at Plymouth's western boundary. A 200-pounder Parrott was mounted there. Perhaps because the *Albemarle* had not been detected the battery did not open fire as she steamed by, though Commander Cooke said later in his report "the river is only 200 yards wide at that point."[19]

Once below Battery Worth, Plymouth lay before him on the starboard. Lookouts were promptly posted, one in the hatch topside the casemate, and another forward on the main deck. Easterly, the sky's color announced a hint of dawn as the *Albemarle* steamed slowly and quietly downriver. Her course, probably just north of center stream, allowed abundant room for maneuvering.

As Cooke perceived, he was abreast of Plymouth where the river ran straight for a short distance, he ordered gun shutters covering portholes to be opened. An exterior mounted levered chain device, operated from inside the casemate, allowed the gun crews to swing the iron covered shutters down to one side. Forward and stern 6.4-inch Brooke rifles rested upon roller-mounted tube carriages placed on center-pivoted carriages, permitting rotation and firing through a 180° sweep. Rollers of the latter carriages were mounted so that they would traverse the circumference of a circle, the centers of which were the carriages pivots. When in the withdrawn position, gun muzzles could swing either way without interfering with the casemate's structure, but when rolled forward on their tracks, the muzzles protruded outside the casemate. Twin sets of heavy blocks and falls were attached either side of the guns to ring-mounted bolts through the casemate, and larger ropes through each gun's cascabel absorbed their explosive recoil.

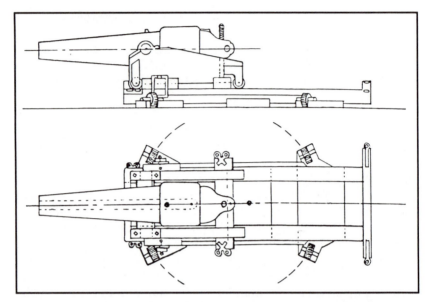

BROOKE 6.4" RIFLE - PIVOT CARRIAGE - 2 REQUIRED
Typical Gun Mount Configuration Used on the *Albemarle*
Drawing by W. E. Geoghegan - Record Group #19 - National Archives

When the *Albemarle* was abreast of Plymouth, Cooke's look-outs saw running lights of two ships ahead. He then had ordered his gun crews to load solid shot and standby for orders. The smaller wooden steam tender *Cotton Plant* had lingered behind to avoid in-volvement in the battle. The *Albemarle* was on her own.

Although nautical twilight began at 4:07 A.M.,[20] Cooke did not immediately see the hawsers and chains linking the two ap-proaching vessels, but when he had realized the implications of such a tactic he lost no time in signaling "all ahead, full." His position to their starboard and across the river was ideal. Cooke may have feinted avoidance of the linked ships, but at the opportune moment he or-dered an abrupt turn to starboard. At full speed, though of only about five knots, the 376-ton *Albemarle* headed straight for the space be-tween the bows of both vessels. His angle of approach might have been about 30° off their line of approach.

In seconds, the battle-ready *Albemarle* was upon the enemy. Outside were heard shouted commands of officers aboard the *Mi-ami*. Heavy guns of the *Southfield* and *Miami* had begun firing. Clos-est to the *Albemarle's* course was the *Miami* who lay slightly to port, between the *Albemarle* and the *Southfield* dead ahead. The curved section of the *Albemarle's* port knuckle rammed the *Miami* at her port bow. For about ten feet along the hull at the waterline, two planks were nearly gouged through by the impact. At practically the same instant the *Albemarle's* ram penetrated the *Southfield's* starboard bow, crashed through her forward store room, and came to rest in the fire room ten feet inside the hull.

The *Southfield* began sinking at once. Depth of penetration, and the *Southfield's* sudden list to starboard, caused the *Albemarle's* bow to have become jammed in the wreckage. Cooke probably had ordered "all engines, stop" at the moment of impact.

With his propellers briefly motionless, momentum caused the ram to penetrate the *Southfield's* wooden hull. Calling for "all astern, full" as momentum ceased, Cooke depended on full reverse thrust to release his bow. For what seemed an eternity, his judgement appeared to have failed. Gradually the *Albemarle's* bow began to sink with the *Southfield.* Later in his report of the battle, Cooke said of the occurrence,

> I immediately commenced backing the *Albemarle,* but was unable to extricate her from the sinking vessel for some time. In the meantime the weight of the vessel so depressed the forward deck of the *Albemarle* as to cause the water to run into the forward port.[21]

The *Southfield's* uninjured crewmen below decks scrambled topside, hastily lowering small boats in which to escape. Others leapt into the water. Some tried to throw debris overboard to which they could cling. When their forward lashings parted, the *Miami's* stern swung towards the *Southfield's* starboard aft rail, enabling other surviving officers and men to climb aboard. Blended with the turmoil of commands, shouts, curses and screams of wounded sailors, was the screeching of escaping steam. The crescendo of sound was enhanced by the creaking and groaning of ships timbers that strained to resist such overwhelming forces.

During the brief moments from when the *Albemarle* had struck the *Miami,* and while she was trying to extricate herself from being pressed under the water by the sinking *Southfield,* Flusser ordered several broadsides fired at the *Albemarle's* port casemate. It may have been during one of those broadsides that he was killed. Flusser's zeal in the pursuit of his determination to sink the *Albemarle* was widely known. He had asserted his intention to Commander Davenport only the night before.

The *Albemarle*, foreground, engaged the *Southfield*, right, in the Roanoke River about a mile east of Plymouth on April 19, 1864 at approximately 3:45 A.M. The *Southfield* was rammed on her starboard bow and sunk within less than five minutes. Looming behind the *Albemarle* is Commander Flusser's *Miami*.

Engraving by J. O. Davidson, Courtesy of Hampton Roads Naval Museum

The *Miami's* armament consisted of six 9-inch Dahlgrens; one 100-pdr. Parrott; and one 24-pdr. rifle, though Cooke reported she had carried thirteen guns. About eighteen hours earlier the *Miami* had been shelling Plymouth with Dahlgren shells employing 10-second fuses. Flusser personally fired the first three shots from the bow gun. This could have been during the barrage Cooke reported when the *Albemarle,* with her port side laying under the Miami's bow, had been jammed within the *Southfield.*

At point blank range of probably about thirty feet, Flusser fired his third shot. It was his last moment alive. Some have said the shell ricocheted back from the *Albemarle's* casemate, exploding in the air directly over Flusser's gun, instantly killing him and wounding several of his gun crew.

With his vessel stuck inside the *Southfield,* Cooke was unable to use his Brooke rifles. Rising to the challenge, he ordered all idle crewmen to be armed and clamber to the casemate's top, where they engaged the *Miami's* crew in a brisk small arms skirmish.

When the *Southfield* touched the river's bottom her hull rolled slightly, thus freeing the *Albemarle's* ram. As Cooke felt the surge of release he probably reaffirmed his order "all astern, full." From the time the *Albemarle* had crashed into the *Miami,* until the ram's release from the sunken *Southfield,* reports stated she had sunk in from 3 to 5 minutes. Only her superstructure remained visible above water.

Cooke's intention was to quickly maneuver the *Albemarle* for an attack on the *Miami.* William N. Welles, the *Miami's* Acting Master and Executive Officer, had a similar intention. But before he could have brought his bow gun to bear on the *Albemarle,* he had to reverse his engines to prevent grounding on the river's bank.

During the time of straightening the *Miami,* the *Albemarle* had righted herself, turned towards the *Miami,* and was steaming at "all ahead, full." Although some distance away, Cooke's gunners were firing the forward Brooke rifle loaded with solid shot. If a shot or two may have struck the *Miami,* the damage wasn't evident to Cooke.

Welles had second thoughts about risking the *Miami* in light of the *Southfield's* fate, so he turned away and steamed downstream towards the Sound's friendly waters. As the encounter was ending the *Whitehead* and *Ceres* had arrived from downriver, but were of no assistance to the *Miami.* They did, however, escort the injured *Miami* eastward to safer waters, while firing a few shots at the *Albemarle* to cover their retreat. By sunrise at 5:11 A.M.,[22] a brassy glow was being

Frustrated by his failure to sink the *Albemarle* while she was stuck inside the *Southfield*, Flusser personally fired his bow-mounted XI-inch Dahlgren. Both vessels were so close that pieces of the fused shell bounced back over Flusser's gun position killing him and wounding many of his crew.

Century Magazine, July, 1888

cast over the embattled waters of the Roanoke River at Plymouth. Acting Lt. Charles A. French, late commander of the *Southfield,* had assumed command of the *Miami* when, after climbing aboard from the sinking *Southfield,* he had learned of Flusser's death.

Satisfied his enemies had retired, Cooke ordered the *Albemarle* anchored about one mile below Plymouth to await further orders from General Hoke. Taking advantage of the enemy's departure, he ordered a damage report. It was found only nine iron plates had been fractured. Still intact was the small boat which had been used to rescue eight crewmen from the sunken *Southfield.* These prisoners were later turned over to Hoke.

The *Albemarle's* baptism of fire produced only one casualty, and that because of curiosity. At the height of the exchange with the *Miami,* crewman Harris sought a quick glimpse of the noisy clash. Someone at the *Miami's* rail saw Harris peek from a gun port and dispatched him with a pistol shot.

There was one crewman on the *Albemarle* who must have welcomed the battle's end more than most aboard. He was Benjamin H. Gray, a twelve-year-old black youth who had enlisted as powder boy when Cooke was signing his crew. For the six months while the *Albemarle* was at war, his major duty was carrying powder bags from the magazine below to the gun deck above, although he also may have occasionally served as cabin boy.[23]

Victorious Commander Cooke, from atop the scarred *Albemarle,* watched the humbled Union flotilla as they resolutely steamed downriver to safer haven in the open Sound. He had given orders to anchor about one mile below Plymouth allowing his crew

BENJAMIN H. GRAY
in later years.
When age 12 he enlisted as powder boy
on the *Albemarle* for which he received
a Confederate pension.
Harry Thompson Collection, Windsor, N.C.

time to recover, clean up battle debris, and make their vessel ship-shape. Also he needed to make contact with General Hoke. As Cooke was at a loss to know what course to pursue,

Mr. Elliott again volunteered and took Pilot Hopkins
with a boat's crew and proceeded down to the mouth of
the river and up a creek in the rear of Plymouth, distant
from the boat by water about 12 miles. He communicated
with General Hoke and sent me dispatches.[24]

At 6 A.M., French ordered the *Miami's* Acting Paymaster, Frank
W. Hackett, to report of the encounter to Cdr. Henry K. Davenport,
Senior Officer, Sounds of North Carolina. Hackett wrote that Captain French held a consultation of officers to weigh their options.
The opinion of all who saw the ram and witnessed the effect of solid
shot upon her "agree that another attack would result only in the
sinking of the *Miami*." In conclusion, he stated French was on a
reconnoiter with the *Whitehead*, and would report officially upon
his return. His postscript revealed heretofore unsubstantiated information, as he noted, "the ram was accompanied by the *Cotton Plant,*
steamer."[25]

Although the *Cotton Plant* had remained above Plymouth while
the *Albemarle* engaged the enemy opposite Plymouth, she rendez-
voused near Cooke during the final moments of his encounter with
the *Miami*.

By 6:30 A.M. Captain French had returned to the anchored
Miami near the Roanoke's mouth, and had written a brief dispatch
to Admiral Lee. He notified Lee that "we fired solid shot from both
vessels, which glanced upward from her slanting sides." In closing,
he said a comprehensive action report would be presented by Mr.
Hackett upon his arrival at Hampton Roads.[26]

Acting upon dispatches forwarded by Elliott from General Hoke,
Cooke ordered sporadic firing with his two 6.4 Brooke rifles at enemy targets in and around Plymouth. His floating two-gun battery
would serve to weaken the Union's resolve as they fought to retain
their emplacements.[27]

Later in the day, Roanoke Island's Post Commander Lt. Col.
William W. Clarke dispatched a brief memo to Captain A. J. Judson,
the Ass't. Adjutant General. He announced the *Ceres,* on her way to
New Bern, had just arrived with Captain Flusser's body.[28]

Near midnight on the nineteenth, Cooke had stationed the
Albemarle somewhat over a mile downriver on a line opposite
Ransom's Brigade. A full moon lit the perfectly calm and cloudless

sky. The *Albemarle* was to shell the 200-pound Parrott in Battery Worth at Plymouth's west boundary. Although the extent of her firing accuracy seems not to have been recorded, every indication points to success as the battery's position was known to Cooke. To the battery's gunners his ironclad must have appeared as a small indistinct target somewhat less than two miles distant.[29]

In the morning of the twentieth, Cooke steamed towards Plymouth. Anchoring off Jefferson Street, his gunners had an unobstructed view of Fort Williams' less fortified river side. Both gun crews resorted to using fused shells. By late morning after several shells had exploded overhead, together with repeated requests to surrender, Brig. Gen. Henry W. Wessells, U.S.A., at 10 A.M. accepted terms from Confederate Maj. Gen. Robert F. Hoke.[30]

Captain Ira B. Sampson, Chief of Artillery, Sub-District of the Albemarle personally commanded Fort Williams. General Wessells ordered Sampson to lower the garrison flag. Not desiring the delegation of such disagreeable duty to any subordinate, Captain Sampson carried out the order himself.[31]

From New Bern at 12:30 P.M. on the twentieth, Maj. Gen. John J. Peck sent a message to Maj. Gen. Benjamin F. Butler. The Unions' former optimism regarding the *Albemarle* appeared to have been reversed when he said "the ram is heavy and formidable, and none of the gunboats here can stand against its power. The *Southfield* is sunk and the rest disabled."[32]

The *Ceres*, commanded by Acting Master Henry H. Foster, arrived off New Bern later on the twentieth. In his report to Davenport, Foster related that he had intercepted the *Miami's* withdrawal downriver, and accompanied her to the north side of Edenton Bay, where Lt. Commander Flusser's body was transferred to the *Ceres*. He had then stopped at Roanoke Island before proceeding on to New Bern.[33]

The capture of about 200 tons of anthracite coal benefitted both Cooke and the *Albemarle*. Having been bunkered at Plymouth by the Union Navy it was a rare commodity, since only low quality bitumonous coal was available from mines located in eastern Virginia.[34]

In his battle report to Mallory, Cooke complimented Lt. Francis M. Roby for his coolness and firmness, Master Shelly for bravery and excellence with further recommendation he be commissioned Lieutenant for the war, and Midshipman Hamilton for gallantry. In concluding Cooke acknowledged,

I had only 20 seamen, those sent from Charleston, and without them I should have been almost powerless. The damage to the *Albemarle* was slight, only nine bars [of] iron being broken, and she now lies at Plymouth undergoing repair and completion.[35]

As Confederate ground forces began to restore order from chaos in Plymouth, Cooke gave serious consideration to raising the sunken U.S.S. *Bombshell*. Once afloat she would have become a welcome addition to his two-ship flotilla. Cooke had probably felt that the large quantities of captured ship stores, materials, and equipment would be sufficient to accomplish the task.

The *Bombshell*, a U.S. Army transport, was believed to have been a former Erie Canal steamer. She was armed with one gun and two small light pieces, having made her first appearance in North Carolina waters during the Burnside expedition.

On Monday the eighteenth when Fort Grey was under assault by Ransom's Brigade, shells from Dearing's artillery struck the *Bombshell* below her waterline as she withdrew from Fort Grey. Her commander, Acting Ensign Thomas B. Stokes, U.S.N., successfully navigated her downriver to Plymouth, where she sunk at the wharf.[36]

The Union Navy Command of Albemarle Sound wrote many letters as a result of the *Albemarle's* victory. Maj. Gen. Benjamin F. Butler summed it up on April 21, when his dispatch to Assistant Secretary of the Navy Gustavus V. Fox ended with, "great consternation there."[37]

From his Flagship *Minnesota* off Newport News on the same day, Rear Admiral Lee voiced concern to Secretary of the Navy Gideon Welles that "the draft of the ram is not known and it may not be able to pass Croatan Sound."[38] Late that afternoon Admiral Lee again dispatched a note to Secretary Welles at 6 P. M. He expressed what might have been his real concern by observing, "an attack by land and water upon New Bern is apprehended. Her draft is unknown."[39] Before the day had ended, Assistant Adj. General J. A. Judson in New Bern had issued General Order No. 66, in which he lamented,

But for the powerful assistance of the rebel ironclad ram and the floating iron sharpshooter battery, the *Cotton Plant*, Plymouth would still have been in our hands.[40]

Col. John Taylor Wood, Aide-de-Camp to President Jefferson Davis at Plymouth, addressed a brief memo to Davis on the twenty-first in which he announced,

Heaven has crowned our efforts with success. General Hoke has captured this point with 1,600 prisoners, 25 pieces of artillery, and Navy cooperation.[41]

At midnight on April 22, General Butler posted a long letter to Assistant Secretary Fox at the Navy Department. Butler seems to have been grossly misinformed when he told Fox,

The ram is 125 feet long, draws 8 feet of water, has two independent propellers, can make about 4 knots, has two guns, only 20 pounders. She will have done all the mischief she can do, probably.[42]

An overconfident Admiral Lee optimistically telegraphed Secretary Welles on April 24.

The ram and rifle-screened *Cotton Plant* were in the Roanoke River, and *Tacony, Miami,* and other gunboats at mouth river waiting for her, confident of destroying her when she enters the sounds.[43]

Lt. Albert G. Hudgins, C.S.N., eventually to command the repaired *Bombshell,* mentioned to Lt. Robert D. Minor on April 29 that "the *Albemarle* had convoyed a steamer captured by the army on [the] Alligator River."[44]

An extract from Secretary Mallory's April 30 report aggrandized the April 19 Plymouth victory.

The signal success of this brilliant naval engagement is due to the admirable skill and courage displayed by Commander Cooke, his officers and men, in handling and fighting his ship against a greatly superior force of men and guns. A copy of Commander Cooke's report is herewith submitted.[45]

CHAPTER 12

ONE AGAINST SEVEN

Cooke's control of the Roanoke had been established on April 19. Therefore after Gilbert Elliott and Pilot Hopkins had ventured forth to find General Hoke, Elliott was no longer of assistance to Cooke. As a civilian, he made his way back to Edwards Ferry and Halifax.

At Halifax Yard on May the first he received $6,575.00 from P. M. DeLeon, representing April labor charges claimed for the *Albemarle.* Judging from the invoice figures, 74 men worked for 17 days @ $5.00 per day, for a total of $6,290.00, while the foreman drew $305.50 which amounted to 47 days @ $6.50 per day.[1] He was paid $20.50 less than the claim.

From Plymouth on Sunday May 1, General Martin wrote his wife Hetty. He told her Sunday morning service had been conducted in Mr. Watson's church, which had benefitted from the efforts of an Episcopal Chaplain in General Wessell's command. Without revealing any secret information, he kept her informed of military events.

> We have been able to raise one of the gunboats [*Bombshell*] and I think will have benefit for service in two or three days. If we get the steamer I mentioned to the General[,] we shall then have three steamers besides our ironclad.[2]

At Kinston the same day, General Pierre G. T. Beauregard wrote Brig. Gen. Robert F. Hoke in the field near New Bern. He was aware that Hoke was called to Virginia by General Lee, and desired that Beauregard command the campaign against New Bern. Beauregard wrote that he regretted the loss of the combined use of the *Neuse* and *Albemarle* in the forthcoming campaign to recapture New Bern.

He outlined how best to employ the ironclad tactically. In a text book sequence Beauregard planned for the *Albemarle* to sink all gunboats defending New Bern, destroy all bridges across the Trent river, and "take such position in the Neuse as to cut off from New Bern all communications from forces north of that river." In conclusion he remarked "the *Albemarle* should cooperate" with Hoke's attack "by flanking the enemy's works and defending direct approaches to the city."[3]

Late Monday afternoon Cooke safely returned from a trip to the Alligator River. The river's mouth, about forty-five miles east of Plymouth, emptied into the Sound on the south shore. Enemy vessels had been sighted and chased, but had retired further east towards Roanoke Island. With the *Albemarle* safely moored at Plymouth, Cooke summoned Frank P. O'Brien on board. For some time O'Brien had served as scout for Col. George H. Wortham of the 50th Regiment. With the arrival upon the scene of Cooke and his ironclad, Wortham had responded to an inquiry from Cooke and recommended O'Brien as an experienced scout.

After opening remarks, Cooke asked O'Brien if he could safely cross the Sound to Edenton to learn of the fleet's nightly habits, their anchorages, and any related intelligence of benefit to Hoke's expedition. Such information could also be used by Cooke in planning his voyage to New Bern. O'Brien replied without hesitation that he would obey Cooke's command. He then requested Cooke's permission to select a partner, someone in whom he placed implicit confidence. After Cooke's consent, O'Brien selected Signal Officer Arthur Chalk. He had chosen Chalk for two reasons. He was expert in paddling a canoe, and had a reputation of remaining calm in an emergency. On this expedition O'Brien pondered whether he would use a canoe of about fifteen feet in length or another of about twenty-five feet.

They quietly cast off about 5:30 P.M. on May 2, and by 8 P.M. were at the Roanoke's mouth. Rounding a thick stand of cypress they observed the *Whitehead* about a half mile off shore. She was stationed to guard entrance to the Sound, so they glided amongst the cypress knees to observe. From there they saw the *Commodore Hull* in relatively the same position above the river's mouth.[4]

After Cooke had dismissed O'Brien on May 2, he turned to matters of his ship. From Union coal bunkers he was replenishing his fuel supply, augmenting it with as much wood as space allowed. Meanwhile, the same day he received a letter from John T. Wood, his friend of long standing. Under the circumstances a response was necessary, so after acknowledging Wood's compliments relating to his encounter with the *Southfield*, Cooke continued,

> I returned this evening from an expedition in the Sound to the mouth of the Alligator River where I departed on Thursday last [Apr. 28] to bring a small steamer, barge and schooner captured by some of our men, loaded with some 3 or 4 thousand bushels of grain and lumber.
>
> On Friday [Apr. 29], on entering the Sound I...chased three of the enemy's gunboats and a transport, but was unsuccessful in overhauling them. I am induced to believe...the reports they carried of my presumed attack...caused the evacuation of Washington, N.C.
>
> I was able to bring off the steamer. The other two vessels [were] up the river and my boat [was] unable to ascend. We have succeeded in raising the *Bombshell* and expect to have her ready by Wednesday [May 4]. The *Southfield* we will not be able to raise at present but intend to attempt to get her gun off. I am quite unwell with a bilious attack but hope to be up in time for work.[5]

Elsewhere in Plymouth that evening, General Martin again wrote his wife Hetty. Inserted among personal remarks was Martin's customary overview of the day's events.

> The ironclad will be ready to leave here to join in the attack on New Bern in two or three days. She went out into Albemarle Sound a few days ago and I think caused the evacuation of Washington, N.C. The enemy's gunboats left in a great hurry. It is reported the enemy burned Washington N.C. before leaving it. I should like very much to go with the ironclad and take Roanoke Island and Hatteras.[6]

O'Brien's first intention had been to follow the shore until near the Chowan's river mouth, then cut across to Edenton Bay a mile below town. Because of the two strategically located gunboats, O'Brien was "forced to adopt a new course. An additional hazard not earlier noticed, was the approach of two other vessels steaming from the Chowan towards the *Commodore Hull*."

They weighed their chances of crossing the nearly nine-mile wide sound in whispered words, until Chalk said, "Frank, there is no place you can try to reach that I will not follow you in the attempt to do your bidding."

About half way across the sound they found themselves between two gunboats, so close that they distinctly heard the tread of sentinels on decks of both vessels. With the moon hidden behind heavy clouds, they lay flat and motionless in the canoe making not a sound. It took about thirty minutes before both vessels had passed and proceeded another quarter mile. O'Brien and Chalk then tried to make up for lost time. Around midnight they beached their canoe in Edenton Bay. Selecting a nearby creek in which to hide the canoe under brush, they surveyed the area before wrapping themselves in blankets to protect their hands and faces from mosquitoes.

Sleep came quickly. At daybreak they awoke and snacked from their knapsacks. Before departing from their hidden camp they donned civilian clothing over their uniforms, but they were more concerned about being sighted by 'Buffaloes' than by soldiers.

In many areas of eastern North Carolina there were citizens whose conduct was generally lawless, and with the presence of invading forces in the area they saw it profitable to prey on their neighbors. A Buffalo was to the Southern cause what a Tory had been to the cause of liberty during the days of the Revolution, and was held in as much contempt.

By sunrise O'Brien and Chalk had reached Mr. Gregory's house. It was said he kept the best hotel in Edenton. Upon entering a modest office they "found an elderly black man sweeping the office and arranging things in general. After guarded conversation we learned there were no overnight strangers within." They were invited to take seats, and before he left the room, the old man said "Marse Fred would be down in er minet *(sic)*."

About ten minutes later Mr. Gregory descended the stairs, and in feigned surprise exclaimed, "Good morning gentlemen, what can I do for you?" as he passed them by and entered another room.

When he returned a moment later,

> He gave the negro *(sic)* instructions to go upstairs and attend to his room. After the negro *(sic)* was gone I introduced Arthur Chalk to Mr. Gregory and requested him to arrange for a private meeting.... He asked us to follow him at once to the attic, which proved the very place...where we could make known our mission in safety.

Gregory cautioned them to remain quiet while he returned downstairs to warn his wife, and for the benefit of the listening servant said, "I could not find out what those fools wanted and sent them on their way." Gregory must have often resorted to this deception since he seldom knew when Federals were in the vicinity, and domestics were sometimes paid to tattle. Satisfied that his wife would be observant of approaching Federals, and that she would send the old man from the hotel by some subterfuge if it became necessary to warn him in the attic, Mr. Gregory began to brief his guests.

A short time later she came up the stairs and told her husband the *Sassacus* was entering the bay. Mr. Gregory hastily led the two men to a trunk closet built into a far niche of the attic, and directed them to hide in one of the large nondescript chests.

The first thing they did after Mr. Gregory left was to remove their civilian clothes and hide them inside an old trunk. If it were discovered that they had been so clothed when entering the enemy's territory, they could have been court martialed as spies. Cooke's two agents remained in hiding until evening when Mr. Gregory returned with welcome information that the ship had steamed down the bay.

Gregory did tell them, however, that through an exchange with a Warrant Officer whom he had befriended he learned that,

> The ironclad was to leave at such a day and time which was one week later than Capt. Cooke was to sail, and also the Sound fleet was to be strengthened by the addition of three other double enders of large armament.

O'Brien and Chalk left at once, and with nothing in sight at seven that evening they hurried to launch their canoe. Rapidly paddling across the Sound in the darkness, they sighted the fore-top lights of a vessel which appeared to be in the direction of the Roanoke's mouth. Using the lights as a guide, they later determined the vessel "was a guard boat anchored to the west of the channel." Blessed with unusually smooth Sound waters they had made good time in their silent canoes, for they reached Plymouth at 2 A.M.

Boarding the *Albemarle*, O'Brien had the Officer of the Deck waken Cooke to hear his report.

> When the Old Captain was informed that the Yankees had knowledge of the proposed trip down the Sound, he stormed and swore like a dozen troopers with the as-

sertion that there must be some traitor in the Navy Department at Richmond, as he had imparted the knowledge to no one but the officers of his ship.

As O'Brien told him they had set the time of leaving one week later than he had planned, he said "damn them, I will fool them yet." Cooke then had Lieutenant Roby wakened and ordered him to "get the ship ready to sail as he intended to move on the second day thereafter, or on the fifth of May." Chalk was also given orders to have his signal flags ready for action. Before turning in, Cooke composed a message to authorities in Richmond telling them of his change of plans and the reasons for it. The paddle trip to Edenton and return had taken thirty-two and one half hours.[7]

General Hoke expressed great optimism in his May 3 dispatch to Brig. Gen. William S. Walker. A message from Cooke included a report of his recent excursions about the Sound, his satisfaction with the *Albemarle's* ability of weathering rougher waters between Plymouth and New Bern, and that "he will be with us."[8]

On the afternoon of the third, Cooke was visited by his scout O'Brien. Although O'Brien had wished to learn if another assignment was awaiting him, Cooke turned the tables by asking the young man if he wished to join the ship's company on the next engagement. Although he knew the trip to Cooke's intended destination would be risky, O'Brien said yes without hesitation. As an invited crewmember who was to be trained as a Regular Seaman, O'Brien took the liberty of asking Cooke if he would also accept a volunteer sharpshooter. Once Cooke became convinced the volunteer would not jump overboard when, as he said, "the Music began," and that O'Brien would be responsible for his friend, he agreed to detail Mortie Williams as a First Class Volunteer.[9]

For almost a week craftsmen and workers were repairing, loading supplies, and performing regular maintenance on the *Cotton Plant* and *Bombshell*. Both were scheduled to accompany the *Albemarle* in convoy to Alligator River.[10] Some speculated that the *Cotton Plant,* which drew nearly as much water as the *Albemarle,* was to lead the way in sounding for river obstructions.

As the convoy steamed from Plymouth towards the Sound, a small boat was sent carrying orders from the *Albemarle* to the *Bombshell* requesting transfer of seaman John B. Patrick back to the ironclad. Patrick had served aboard the *Albemarle* at the time the *Bomb-*

shell had sunk at Plymouth, and was required as second front leverman on the *Albemarle's* stern Brooke rifle.[11] The *Cotton Plant* was carrying troops, while the armed *Bombshell* was laden with provisions and coal.[12]

At 2 P.M. on the fifth of May Cooke's flotilla of three entered the Sound.[13] Dead ahead were the *Ceres, Commodore Hull, Whitehead,* and transport *Ida May.* Their intended mission had been to place two lines of torpedoes across the river, but the unexpected appearance of Cooke's flotilla cancelled their plans. In contemplation of the ironclad's early arrival while placing torpedoes, their orders were not to engage. The *Ida May,* their fastest vessel, was sent to warn the fleet some twenty miles down the Sound, while the remaining three turned about and withdrew.[14]

Steaming behind, Cooke noticed they set a course E.N.E. generally in the direction of Sandy Point. For nearly ten miles he followed the retreating picket vessels. About four or five miles ahead, lying just on the horizon below Bluff Point, he sighted three large double-ended gunboats. On top of the casemate, with glass to his eye, Cooke recognized they were of a more formidable class than those he had followed. He estimated they carried from ten to twelve guns each. Perceiving that an unequal contest was imminent, Cooke immediately prepared the *Albemarle* for action.

At that point he had requested Signal Officer Chalk to hoist flags ordering the *Cotton Plant* and *Bombshell* to turn about and steam towards the Roanoke. The *Cotton Plant*, with a number of launches in tow, immediately obeyed her command and escaped, but for some reason the *Bombshell* was delayed and lost her opportunity to evade the aggressors.[15]

Capt. Melancton Smith, senior officer of the Federal flotilla,

CAPTAIN MELANCTON SMITH commanded Union naval forces in the Sound during the May 5 engagement with the *Albemarle.*
Courtesy of Frederick C. McKean, Naval Historical Center

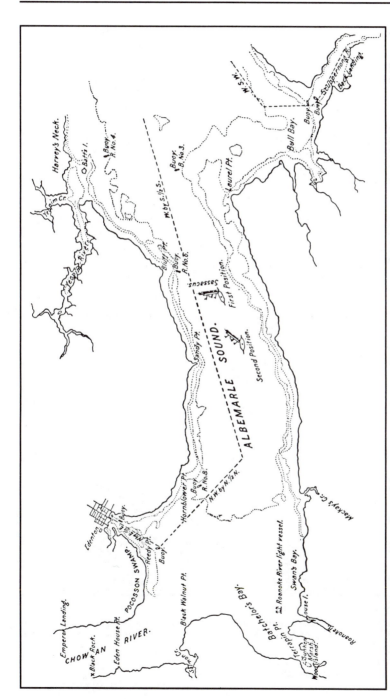

The approximate location of the *Albemarle*'s encounter with seven Union gunboats on May 5, 1864, is indicated in this map of Albemarle Sound's extreme west end.

Official Records of the Union and Confederate Navies in the War of the Rebellion, Ser. I, Vol. IX

had prepared an order of steaming for two columns of four gunboats paralleling each a half mile apart. In conformity with his plan signal flags were hoisted at 4:40 P.M. Smith had ordered each vessel "to run its guns out and steam past the *Albemarle* and *Bombshell*, giving them a broadside at every opportunity."[16] Adherence to such rigid orders was soon found not practical with seven vessels fighting one.

Leading the first line of attack upon the *Albemarle* was Captain Smith's Flagship, the *Mattabesett*. A vessel of 974 tons, she carried four 9-inch Dahlgren smooth bores; two 100-pdr. Parrott rifles; two 24-pdrs.; one 12-pdr. heavy smooth bore; and one 12-pdr. rifle.[17]

As the *Mattabesett* was closing on the *Albemarle,* Cooke began a sweeping turn to starboard. Extended from its port side was the after Brooke, and from the starboard was the forward Brooke. The after gun had two shots away before Smith's fleet began to fire.

Both shots from the after gun struck the *Mattabesett,* the first destroying the launch, its davits and spars, and the second cutting away some of the standing and running rigging.

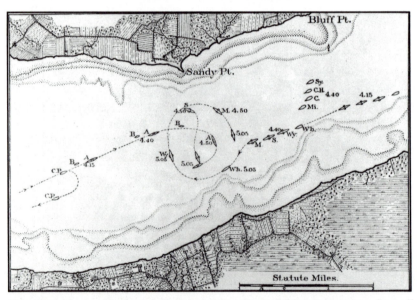

The *Albemarle*, A, with *Bombshell*, B, and *Cotton Plant*, C.P., met the enemy fleet off Sandy Point in Albemarle Sound. The *Albemarle* avoided being embraced by the enemy's double line of battle and maneuvered in such manner that the battle became disorganized.
Her most severe threat came when the *Sassacus*, S, rammed her, but Cooke prevailed when he disabled the *Sassacus* with two well-placed shots.

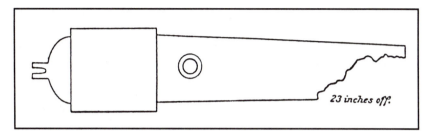

23 inches off.

Commander of the *Miami,* Lt. Richard T. Renshaw, included a sketch of the *Albemarle's* damaged stern Brooke 6.4" rifle in a report to Capt. Melancton Smith on June 3, 1864.
It had been suggested in a previous report that the third or fourth shot fired by the *Mattabesett* was credited with having inflicted the damage.
In his after-battle report Cdr. James W. Cooke noted the damaged gun, but failed to identify which vessel may have fired the lucky shot.
　　　Official Records of the Union and Confederate Navies in the War of the Rebellion, Ser. I, Vol. IX

The arc of Cooke's turn positioned the *Albemarle* parallel to, but to the starboard of, the *Mattabesett's* line of attack. As seaman Patrick later said,

> They steamed right up in line of battle, passing us on the port side firing right into us...It was the first broadside that knocked a hole in us, but not all the way through, [only] splinters of wood flew about.

"The third or fourth shot fired by the enemy broke off 20 inches of the muzzle of the after gun of the *Albemarle,*" Cooke later reported, however "the gun remained in use."
As the *Mattabesett* ceased firing on her parallel run to port of the *Albemarle,* Cdr. John C. Febiger feared the ironclad was about to alter course to ram him.

> The helm was ordered to starboard, sheering [the vessel] to port, thus causing us to pass at a greater distance than was our intention.
> At 4:45 P.M. ranged up alongside the ram and engaged her from about 150 yards with the starboard battery, firing pivot and IX-inch with solid shot.[18]

Momentum carried the *Mattabesett* sufficiently beyond the *Albemarle,* where at 4:50 P.M. she engaged the *Bombshell.* When nearly abeam the *Albemarle's* consort, Febiger ordered starboard howitzers and a forward rifle fired.

Midshipman Hamilton, Signal Officer Chalk, sharpshooter Mortie Williams, and Frank P. O'Brien were outside the *Albemarle's* casemate on the after deck near the hatch, as the *Mattabesett* rounded the *Albemarle's* port bow. Though ordered inside the casemate by Cooke, they observed the *Mattabesett* steaming for the *Bombshell* before they entered the casemate. Over the din of battle O'Brien said Cooke was heard ordering Lieutenant Roby to "give the Yankee his bow gun."

So promptly was the order executed that,

> One of the *Mattabesett's* guns was dismounted and it seemed to us that every man at that gun was either killed or wounded. Another shot was delivered from the port side. This shot cut away spars and otherwise injured another gun.

Vision of the outside from within the casemate was meager at best, but with dense grey gunsmoke blended with coal smoke from the stacks darkening the exterior scene one could hardly see friend or foe.

The *Bombshell,* though hit by the *Mattabesett's* guns, continued to change positions, thus preventing her antagonist from running close along her starboard.

By then the *Albemarle* was surrounded. The *Wyalusing* and *Sassacus,* having overtaken her, were then steaming around her bow, the latter having given the ironclad a broadside in passing. Moments later the *Mattabesett* was on her quarter with engines stopped. The *Sassacus* was abeam, and off her starboard bow was the *Wyalusing.* The two latter gunboats were also of 974 tons each, as was the *Mattabesett.*

Heaviest armed of the three was the *Wyalusing.* She carried four 9-inch Dahlgren smooth bores; four 24-pdr. Howitzers; two 100-pdr. Parrott rifles; two 12-pdr. rifles; and two 12-pdr. heavy smooth bores.

Armament on board the *Sassacus* consisted of four 9-inch Dahlgren smooth bores; two 100-pdr. Parrott's; two 24-pdr. Howitzer rifles; one 12-pdr. rifle; one 12-pdr. heavy smooth bore, and two 20-pdr. Dahlgren rifles.

The *Albemarle,* of 376 tons weight, was opposed by three opponents weighing a combined 2922 tons. It was a ratio of about one to eight.[19] After her encounter with the *Mattabesett,* the *Bombshell* was still able to maneuver and fire. Closest to her was the *Sassacus* which immediately became a target for her three rifle howitzers and one 20-pdr. Parrott.

Captain Smith's three most powerful vessels surrounded the *Albemarle* in an unsuccessful attempt to sink her. From the left is the *Wyalusing, Sassacus,* center, the *Albemarle* floating low in the water, and the *Mattabesett.*

Painting by Acting Second Engineer, Alexander C. Stuart, U.S.N., 1864, from Surgeon H. P. Babock, U.S.N., Naval Historical Center

The *Sassacus'* Acting Master, C. A. Boutelle, made detailed entries of the event in the ship's log. Increased powder charges with solid shot had been ordered for the *Albemarle's* broadside, but in sheering hard aport around the ironclad's bow, they had encountered the *Bombshell* which began shelling them with their rifled pieces. Broadsiding the *Bombshell* in retaliation, they hulled her in three places. Because of such damage, the *Bombshell* hauled down her colors and displayed white flags. When hailed, "have you struck your colors?" from the *Sassacus* running close abeam, and receiving a "yes," the *Bombshell* was ordered to cross their stern and anchor. The order was promptly obeyed.

Commander Francis A. Roe, of the *Sassacus*, then ordered the army steam tug to bring her alongside and anchor. Next, the *Ceres* was ordered to approach the *Bombshell*, and after making fast alongside, officers and men were transferred as prisoners. Roe then ordered a prize crew to board the captive, start her fires and raise steam. Meanwhile, the *Albemarle* was conducting intermittent fire upon the *Sassacus* and other vessels, and in maneuvering had become broadside of the enemy.[20]

While surrounded by the *Mattabesett, Sassacus,* and *Wyalusing,* the *Albemarle* was a sitting target for the combined firepower of the three double-enders. Union gunners tried to aim shots into her open gun ports, cast powder bags down her stack, lob explosives onto her open latticed iron casemate top, riddle her smoke stack and cut her color's mast. They had success with only the two latter targets.

Because it was involved with the *Bombshell's* capture, the *Sassacus* had drifted away from the *Albemarle* which had been maintaining a moving station between her assailants. The distance of about 300 to 400 yards was perceived by Commander Roe as advantageous.

> Seeing that we had some room to gather headway and a good opportunity to strike her, [we] rang four bells again and started for her [at] full speed, working our battery as long as we could train [upon him] and pouring into him solid and chilled-end shots. The hour was about 5:05 P.M.

As he watched the battle action from a viewing port near his helmsman, Cooke became enraged at the persistency of the double-enders. Perhaps because he was brewing a defensive plan, Cooke

The *Sassacus* rammed the *Albemarle* while steaming at about 11 knots. Within a few minutes the *Sassacus* was disabled when the *Albemarle* fired one shot through her boilers.

Battles and Leaders, Vol. IV

instructed Pilot Hopkins to relieve his assistant John Luck, with the admonition that he promptly obey every order.

Cooke's attention focused on the rapidly approaching *Sassacus* bearing down upon the *Albemarle's* starboard beam. It appeared to him the intended impact point might be where the casemate joined the after deck. He ordered "full steam ahead," and though he felt his ship responding, it moved too slowly to avoid being struck by the heavy double-ender. Reacting to the emergency, his crew rapidly assumed escape positions near hatches and ports. Someone was heard to shout an order, "stand by small arms and repel boarders."

Crewmen of the *Sassacus* also prepared themselves for the impact, though the shock to them was to be far less than that felt by those inside the *Albemarle*. As smoke clouds parted momentarily, the ironclad was seen dead ahead making way slowly to their starboard. Seconds before impact, the crew were ordered, "all hands, lie down!"

In the fleeting moments before colliding with the *Albemarle*, Commander Roe had observed his ship was steaming about 10 to 11 knots with her engines making 22 revolutions per minute under 30 pounds steam pressure.

Responding to Cooke's shouted order, eight men ran out the *Albemarle's* already loaded, but damaged, starboard aft Brooke rifle. Gunner Hamilton had seconds to sight the gun at the *Sassacus'* bow looming ever larger, before it would crash into their starboard knuckle. His was a point-blank shot.

With the crackling of splintering wood and the crunching screech of torn iron, the *Sassacus* struck the *Albemarle* just abaft her starboard beam where the ram's casemate rear joined the hull.

> To those inside the ironclad the impact felt like an earthquake, sending many tumbling to the deck. Even the small open lamps were extinguished. Captain Cooke was standing in the hatch and was knocked down. Mr. Shelly and Roby were unshaken. Some water came in the open ports, but no shots.

That first shot fired while the *Albemarle's* gun was almost touching the *Sassacus'* bow, entered ten feet abaft the stem and three feet above her hull's copper covering on the starboard side, passed through the storeroom, crossed the berth deck and went out the port side.

Water poured through the *Albemarle's* stern starboard port when the *Sassacus* struck bow-on. Moments later the gun crew fired point blank into the *Sassacus*, and followed with another which passed through her boilers.

Century Magazine, 1888

Assistant Surgeon Edgar Holden was at that instant watching the action through a damaged starboard shutter on the *Sassacus*, when he saw the jagged muzzle of a Brooke rifle pointing his way. In another second with a sharp roar, it belched forth a solid shot enveloped in flame. Holden was whirled around in shock by the great concussion and flung to the deck.

The *Albemarle* careened to starboard only enough to take water through her open aft starboard port.

> Some of the crew became demoralized, but the calm voice of the undismayed Captain checked the incipient disorder, with the command, "Stand to your guns, and if we must sink let us go down like brave men."

Her ironclad knuckle had sliced into the *Sassacus'* bow like a huge knife. The *Albemarle* had four 1-inch waterline plates loosened, though her starboard beam was by then about three feet underwater.

As the *Albemarle* listed to starboard under the *Sassacus'* weight, Roe ordered Master Boutelle to sustain the engines' revolutions. For about ten minutes Roe forced his ship against the ironclad hoping that the immense pressure would depress her deck beneath the water and sink her. While retaining his stuck position, Roe's men threw grenades towards the *Albemarle's* deck hatches and tried in vain to get powder charges down her smokestack. Through it all they sustained volleys of musketry from Cooke's sharpshooters Williams and O'Brien, who had stationed themselves in firing positions atop the casemate.

Notwithstanding the starboard list, the taking on of water, and the solid grip of the *Sassacus'* shattered bow, Cooke maintained forward way.

The *Sassacus'* position, when she was about to strike the ironclad, permitted Hamilton to fire only that single shot into the *Sassacus'* bow. With both vessels locked together at their point of contact, and their engines providing forward movement to each, "the headway of the two vessels, exerted at right angles, forced her gradually round on our starboard bow," said Commander Roe. As this fact became apparent to those aboard the *Albemarle*,

> Captain Cooke ordered Pilot Hopkins to put his tiller "Hard-a-port." By that means the *Albemarle's* stern swung to port, loosening the *Sassacus'* grip, and allowing Cooke to order "All ahead, slow." The stern's movement had wrenched her free.

Sliding from the twisted mass of the *Sassacus'* bow, Cooke maneuvered the *Albemarle* in a tight arc to starboard. He was nearly parallel the *Sassacus* less than his ship's width away, starboard to starboard. His loaded forward gun had been pivoted in accordance with the maneuver. Cooke's signal to the gun crew came at once. The gun was run out the starboard forward port and fired point-blank. So close was the muzzle that its blast scorched the *Sassacus'* paint.

> The second shot, which was fired by their Brooke rifle from the starboard forward port entered the side abreast of the foremast 4 feet above the water, on the starboard side, cutting through planking and frames diagonally, kept on through the back of one knee and the throat

of the next, smashing the dispensary and from there passing through the forward coal bunker, entered the starboard boiler, going clear through it, keeping on through the engine room, passed between the cylinders and main condenser, cutting off a 3-inch iron stanchion, thence through the steerage and wardroom bulkheads, smashing doors and furniture, and passing through the magazine screen, struck with spent force on an oak stanchion and glancing at right angles lodged in one of the starboard state rooms.

At the moment the shot struck the boiler, steam rushed up in terrible volume, scalding all the men in the fire room, killing one coal handler instantly, also badly scalding First Assistant Engineer J. M. Hobby who was at the starting bar.[21]

Surgeon Edgar Holden had no more recovered from the effects of the *Albemarle's* first shot when the second shell crashed through. A cloud of steam and boiling water immediately filled the forward decks as the *Sassacus'* overcharged boilers were pierced by the shot. Their contents emptied with such a shrill scream that the roar of guns was drowned for an instant.

As the great weight of water in the boilers was expended, the ship surged heavily to port. Over the cry "the ship is sinking" came the shout, "all hands, repel boarders on the starboard bow."

The men from below, who had escaped the scalding steam, sprang to the ladders with pistols and cutlass', and gained the bulwarks. Others had climbed the rigging with muskets and hand grenades, and with well directed fire soon discouraged the Confederates from attempting to board.

Commander Cooke was, by then, fairly aroused to battle. He gave orders to get alongside and prepare to board ship. Moments later, there were about twent-five of the *Albemarle's* crew assembled on her forward deck with pistols and cutlass' in hand. When Chalk and O'Brien were climbing through the bow port they heard the loud cry "stand by to repel boarders" from the *Sassacus'* quarter deck. Looking towards the sound they saw that the decks, spars, and every part of her works were crowded with sailors and marines prepared to defend their ship to the last. Cooke reluctantly withdrew his order, but still continued to pepper the enemy from bow to stern until she seemed to be settling.

After disengaging from the *Albemarle*, the *Sassacus'* starboard wheel passed across the *Albemarle's* after deck as she rounded the *Albemarle's* stern to starboard, and crossed her bows again while heading for safety east down the Sound.

Century Magazine, July, 1888

By the time orders to repel boarders had been cancelled, the *Sassacus'* bow was completely free. Roe ordered Boutelle to head down the Sound. Though both vessels were nearly touching, Boutelle ordered the helm hard-a-port as he began to maneuver forward and around the *Albemarle's* stern. He misjudged how little clearance there was between both vessels, with the result that "our starboard wheel passed over her stern, crushing a launch which she was towing and injuring buckets and braces of our wheel on her hull."

Boutelle guided the disabled *Sassacus* away from the *Albemarle*, though he was unable to outdistance her shells fired at him as he withdrew. The chief engineer had reported their engines were working on vacuum alone, and would soon fail. His only alternative was to continue towards Sandy Point. To cover their withdrawal, Commander Roe ordered his gun crews to continue firing upon the *Albemarle* until,

> We drifted out of range. I tried to ricochet several 9-inch shot, so that she might be struck on her bottom by the upward bound of the shell, but I had the mortification to see every shot strike the water inside of her and rise on the opposite side of her.

About two miles further the engines failed, so he dropped anchor. His maneuver cleared the waters for others to shell the *Albemarle*.

Later one of the eyewitnesses on the shore recalled,

> Sometimes the whole number, the ram included, were completely shrouded in thick white smoke which lay upon the blue, rippling, glancing waters like a thunder cloud in a clear summer sky, while naught else was seen of the fierce combat behind it but columns of snowy spray, rising successively in long lines as the balls ricochetted across the waters.
>
> Then the soft smooth south wind would lift the curtain just in time to disclose the red flashes of new broadsides from the enemy or the jet of lurid fire which preceded one of the sonorous, metallic voices of the iron monster.
>
> Now one of the enemy's largest vessels has withdrawn the fight and steams rather slowly behind Sandy Point,

where she still lies at this moment badly crippled; the ram meanwhile steadily pursuing her course towards Roanoke River, and firing leisurely as she moves. The fire of the enemy somewhat slackens, and only the two remaining large vessels continue the pursuit.

Reporting about his withdrawal after anchoring about 5:30 P.M. Roe said,

> She played musketry upon us severely all the time...she is too strong for us...I regret most profoundly that I was obliged to drift out of the fight just as it was becoming interesting and when my services were still neeeded, but I fear I am now totally *hors de combat.*

In a subsequent after-battle report, Roe declared a tribute to the *Albemarle's* designer, builder and commander when he observed, "Yet I am forced to think that the *Albemarle* is more formidable than the *Merrimack* or *Atlanta,* for our solid 100-pounder rifle shot flew into splinters upon her iron plates."[22]

The Miami with eight guns led the opposite battle column, and had begun firing at the ironclad simultaneously with the *Sassacus'* first engagement with the *Bombshell.* With the *Albemarle* and *Sassacus* dueling at point blank range, the *Miami* was forced to lay back and wait for a clear shot. When the *Sassacus* drifted away from her hull-to-hull encounter with the *Albemarle,* Lt. Charles A. French, the *Miami's* commander, received signals from the *Mattabesett* to torpedo the ram. The boom-mounted explosive device on the *Miami's* bow required expert maneuvering by French to explode it beneath the *Albemarle's* hull. His maneuvering proved futile.

> I used every endeavor to get at her, bow on, but the *Miami* proving herself so unwieldy and so very bad to steer, the enemy (who was probably well aware of my purpose) succeeded in keeping clear of us by going ahead and backing and turning. We did not cease our fire, however, all this time.

Cooke's gunners scored several hits upon the *Miami* while maintaining a steady fire to disrupt her attempted torpedo emplacement. Of the several hits sustained, one nearly disabled her rudder. Unable to employ her bow-mounted torpedo, the *Miami* broad-sided the *Albemarle* with her six 9-inch Dahlgrens, a 100-pdr. Parrott and a single 24-pdr. rifle from a distance of one ship's length.

Lt. Cdr. Walter W. Queen, commanding the *Wyalusing*, steamed into range once the *Miami* was perceived to lie-to. He had ordered the *Mattabesett* and *Sassacus* to fire at the ironclad, but soon found both could be damaged from such an encounter. Queen reported that when the *Albemarle* had cleared from her encounter with the *Sassacus*, random firing from the *Wyalusing* had cut the ironclad's signal halyards. When he saw her flag being hauled down, he supposed she was surrendering, but was soon convinced to the contrary.

At 5:55 P.M. the *Mattabesett* hoisted a cease fire signal for the *Wyalusing*, and repeated the same at 6:45 P.M. Queen had been told in the meantime his ship was sinking. He again signaled his condition, but within minutes the engineer reported she was taking on no more water than usual. Queen then steamed to overtake the *Albemarle*, and from one hundred yards again broadsided her with little effect. An observer did, however, report seeing a small piece fly off from the forward port side plating.

A crewman from within the Albemarle's casemate watched while,

> The *Miami* attended by the *Wyalusing* came up in line and opened on us with their entire armament and with the other boats doing all they could for thirty minutes, the shot striking our sides produced such a concussion nearly every man on board bled from the ears and nose.

Next to take her turn against the *Albemarle* at about 6:30 P.M. was the *Commodore Hull*. Acting Master Francis Josselyn reported they,

> Ran across the ram's prow, keeping up a brisk fire to keep her from opening her ports. Ran a seine across her bow so that it might catch in her screw, but it did not succeed. [We] expended in the engagement 81 rounds, 60 30-pdr. Parrott and 21 24-pdr. howitzer.

When Cooke observed that the *Sassacus* had been seriously crippled, he ordered Pilot Hopkins to bring her about and return to the Roanoke. The *Albemarle* steamed W.S.W. at about 5 knots while several of the Union fleet circled and fired upon her. Her speed was slowly but steadily diminishing because her upper stack was riddled with holes, her draft was insufficient, and her fuel supply was exhausted. The once roaring fires in her furnaces were becoming only smoldering clumps of ash. Steam pressure had fallen to nearly zero.

Cooke knew that once his antagonists realized he was dead in the water he would certainly be rammed and sunk. His order, passed to all hands, was to dismantle all interior wooden structures and feed the furnace. Bulkheads, doors, cabin furniture, interior casemate planking, literally anything that would burn was piled on the grates, but the fire wasn't hot enough because there was no draft. Aside from the wood, there was on board a large quantity of bacon, ham, and lard. An enterprising individual ordered the fires fed by the meat and lard. Characteristically that fuel required no draft to burn, and a blistering hot fire resulted. Steam pressure rose, the propellors turned, and the *Albemarle* steamed towards the Roanoke.

Because she seemed impervious to damage, the Union fleet was hesitant to attack her further. How fortunate for the *Albemarle*, since her tiller ropes had parted and mechanics sweated in the darkening interior to make spliced repairs. At the Roanoke's mouth Cooke brought her about. Facing the *Albemarle* were the *Commodore Hull* and *Ceres*, while further down the Sound about $2^{1}/_{2}$ miles were anchored the *Miami, Wyalusing, Whitehead,* and *Mattabesett.*

Out trundled the bow Brooke which belched a parting shot towards his pursuers. Then, slowly turning against the current, the *Albemarle* steamed a crooked course towards Plymouth. John B. Patrick later explained that the reason she steamed so erratically was that a large piece of plating, which had been partially blown off, was hanging over the bow into the water, and was neutralizing the rudders' effect. "She would not steer at all, running first into one bank and then the other," he said. By 7:30 P.M., on Thursday May 5, 1864, the battle had ended.[23]

At 8:00 P.M. that evening, Brig. Gen. James G. Martin wrote his wife telling her of the great excitement that morning when the *Albemarle* and her consort, the *Bombshell*, steamed from Plymouth supposedly on their way to New Bern.

At four o'clock this afternoon we heard heavy firing which we inferred was a fight, as we had heard that the enemy had returned to this vicinity yesterday in greater force of gunboats than he had yet shown.

A towboat went out with the other two from here to bring up a large barge loaded with corn from the Alligator River and with orders to return if there was any danger. A short time since this last boat returned, [the Captain brought] us an account of the attack by seven gunboats on our ironclad. He saw the fight for about an hour[,] at the end of that time he was several miles distant, but could distinctly see that all the enemy gunboats had drawn off from the ironclad.

He was under the impression three of the enemy's gunboats were disabled and the tender of the ironclad disabled. The ironclad continued to go ahead. I suppose we shall not have anything definite or satisfactory till sometime tomorrow after this letter leaves here.[24]

While the *Albemarle* was steaming up the Roanoke back to Plymouth, Acting Gunner Hugh McDonald prepared his report of expended ordnance for Executive Officer Lt. F. W. Roby. His very brief notations indicate only 27 shots may have been fired at the enemy.

Charges of 10 lbs.	14
Charges of 8 lbs.	13
Percussion shells	6
Cast iron bolts (shells)	21
Percussion primers	20
Friction primers	15
1 Rammer belonging to No. 2 gun.	1 [25]

By 2 A.M., May 6, the *Albemarle* was docking at Plymouth "in rather dilapidated condition." McDonald then prepared for John Mercer Brooke, C.S.N., Chief of Ordnance Bureau, a report of 'Ordnance and Ordnance Stores Expended' during the engagement of May 5. He prefaced the report with comments not included in Roby's.

Gun No. 2 has got twenty one & one half inches broken off the lower portion of the muzzle. Dimensions of gun as follows: Calibre, Rifle 6.40; Pattern, Brooke; Weight, not on; Date Fabr., 1862; Marks, J.R.A.& Co./F.F.; No., 19. The rammer for gun No. 2 was lost overboard during the action.[26]

After-battle reports of the seven Union vessels, who had failed miserably in their combined assault on the *Albemarle*, graphically illustrate how correct had been Mallory's early policy of developing an ironclad fleet.

Upon the seven gunboats eight types of naval guns are known to have been mounted. Among the combined total of sixty guns that would have been fired at the *Albemarle* were: eighteen 9-inch Dahlgren smooth bores; eight 100-pdr. Parrott's; four 30-pdr. Parrott's; eighteen 24-pdr. rifles; two 20-pdr. Parrott's; two 20-pdr. Dahlgren rifles; four 12-pdr. rifles; and four 12-pdr. smooth bores.

Ordnance expended was equally impressive. Gleaned not only from individual after-battle reports of the vessels involved, but also from authoritative published sources, totals of ordnance expended compare favorably. Broken down to types of shot and shell, the figures reveal how impassioned was the Union to rid the Sound of the single ironclad. It was not to be accomplished in battle; a fact they learned after nearly three hours of uninterrupted firing.

Solid shot	400		
Chilled tip, solid	61		
Cannister	5		
Percussion	13		
Hotchkiss	21		
J. A. D.	29		
Shrapnel	28		
Total Union Expended	557	Total guns	60
Total for *Albemarle*.	27	Total guns	2 [27]

When Brig. General Martin spoke with Commander Cooke a few hours after his return, and learned of the battle's ferocity, he immediately wrote his wife to set her mind at ease.

> Captain Cooke has returned with his ironclad safe, but lost his tender. He had a terrific fight with nine of the enemy's gunboats, (three very large just in from the blockading squadron). This is the substance of what he has written to Gen. Hoke.
> They ran all around him and attempted to enclose him in a seine, but the ropes gave way. He is talking about going out in the morning again. I doubt if his crew can endure a repetition so soon.[28]

In an act of compassion for one of his crew with whom he had shared the previous day's battle, Commander Cooke approved a ten-day furlough for seaman James R. Smithwick.[29]

On the seventh Cooke received a letter from his close friend Maj. Gen. Robert F. Hoke. Their personal ties had recently been strengthened when Hoke captured Plymouth with the able assistance of Cooke and the *Albemarle*.

> Thank God for your safe return. A great relief is given me by the reception of your letter as I am ordered to another field. I have just written Commodore Pinkney that I had taken the River Road and had command of the river and the enemy completely surrounded when I had my orders to proceed to another field which I deeply regret, but the summers work can still be accomplished and I hope with the aid of the Almighty to do it as soon as my troops are not wanted elsewhere. The Almighty is certainly with you in your movements. Take care of Plymouth.[30]

Hoke had revealed to Cdr. Robert F. Pinkney that Richmond was his destination, and requested Brig. General Martin be advised. Though he expressed optimism that New Bern could still be taken, deep concern about Richmond was evident when he added, "Everything is being concentrated around Richmond where the big fight of the war is to take place, and with the aid of the Almighty we must be successful."[31]

Although Cooke was known as a crafty and tenacious naval warrior who, when sufficiently aroused, would press his opponent unmercifully, his crew's safety and welfare were ever-present responsibilities. Having been delayed one day by circumstances, he addressed the question of the *Bombshell's* prisoners. His dispatch was hand carried to the U.S. Naval Commander, Albemarle Sound.

> I send Lt. Roby in charge of a Flag of Truce to inquire as to the fate of Lt. Albert G. Hudgins and crew of the steamer tender *Bombshell* captured by your forces in Albemarle Sound on the evening of the 5th inst.
> You will oblige me by allowing the letters and funds sent to be transmitted to Lt. Hudgins.[32]

Officers and crew of the captured *Bombshell* were:[33]

COMMANDER, Albert G. Hudgins
FIRST OFFICER, Henry Roberts
ASS'T SURGEON, J. S. Tipton
ASS'T ENGINEER, R. J. Hackley
BOATSWAIN, A. G. [J.] Wilson
CREW; Ball, Thomas M.

Brant, A. B.
Brennan, Michael
Bright, J.
Clemens, George
Crocker, William D.
Davenport, S. B.
Davis, B. W.
Dowd, W. H.
Farraday, Andrew
Fitzgerald, Thomas
George, Thomas
Henry, David
Hodges, Jacob
Jackson, C. W.
Kilby, W. A.

King, J. C.
McCulloch, E. D.
McFarland, William
Mitchell, A. S.
Morton, William
Phipps, William H.
Roberts, W.
Rodgers, R. B.
Sugenbuhl, J. J.
Sumner, J. J.
Thornton, James
Weeman, R. E.
Wesley, John

The crew was held in double irons and officers under sentry.

Ever aware his success was entirely dependent upon his crew, Cooke commended to Commodore Pinkney on the seventh those who had served with distinction.

I can not speak too highly of the officers and crew, especially of the following named men, viz, John Benton, James Cullington, J. B. Cooper, H. A. Kuhn, John Smith, H. P. Hay, Thomas Wroten, John Steely and T. Nichols. The pilot, J. B. Hopkins, deserves great credit for the manner in which he maneuvered the vessel, and bringing her safely back to port.[34]

CHAPTER 13

REPAIRS & REFLECTION

Three days after his memorable encounter, Cooke obtained approval from Commodore Pinkney to write Mallory advising the building of an additional gunboat within established facilities along the Roanoke. He called Mallory's attention to certain deficiencies in the *Albemarle's* design, all the while recommending solutions to her problems. He declared that the May 5 battle in Albemarle Sound proved the *Albemarle* drew too much water to safely navigate the Sound, and she had insufficient buoyancy.

That feature contributed to the sluggish helm response frequently experienced when fighting his ship in close proximity to the enemy. He further observed,

> Her decks are so near the water as to render it an easy task for the enemy's vessels to run on her, and any great weight soon submerges the decks.

Cooke recommended that a second ironclad be built without delay. Appropriate design changes would limit loaded draft to 6½ feet of water. Two courses of 1-inch iron plates would seem preferable to one of 2-inch iron. He explained that 2-inch iron would crack or break, while 1-inch would bend while absorbing severe impacts. Four guns would be better than two, by adding the extra two as port and starboard broadside guns.

> I find the shifting the guns in action a very great disadvantage; while the gun is being shifted the enemy's vessel, being close aboard, has time to change position....
>
> I feel no doubt but that we should have had an entire victory in our late fight if there had been two broadside guns in addition to the two now mounted on the *Albemarle*.[1]

On the eighth Catherine Edmondston entered in her Journal her personal observations of what had occurred on the Sound.

> Our Ram, the *Albemarle,* is carrying everything before her in the Sound. She last week captured a small steamer, a schooner, 2 barges and 300 barrels of corn. She had gone into Pamlico [Sound] and her appearance it was which caused the rapid evacuation of Washington.... The *Bombshell*, the Yankee gunboat sunk at Plymouth has been raised and now acts as a tender to her.[2]

The *Albemarle*, though hit forty-four times, sustained little damage during her three-hour bout with seven enemy gunboats. Her stern Brooke rifle was struck on the muzzle by the third or fourth shot she sustained. It may have been the *Mattabesett* that fired such a shot. Just over twenty inches of the muzzle's underside was broken off. Her small boat towed astern was destroyed, along with assorted gear stowed on her after flush deck, when the *Sassacus* had disengaged herself after the thunderous ramming. Two or three starboard knuckle plates were displaced by the *Sassacus'* impact.

Five of her six gun-port shutters had vanished after having been struck by random shots. A staff on top of the aft casemate was hit, but her colors were saved. Sustained firing at the port quarter casemate had cracked and broken several 2-inch plates. One of the dislodged plates hung overboard creating a condition which interfered with her steering. The stack was completely riddled with holes which literally terminated her furnace's draft. Luckily the power loss, known only to those within the *Albemarle*, hadn't occurred until she was well on her way back to the Roanoke.

These sights met observers eyes shortly after daybreak when they viewed the *Albemarle*. She was tied to a dock in front of property on which, sixty-three years later, stood the Riverview Hotel.

Notwithstanding the heavily armored casemate sides designed with a proper angle to deflect the most powerful shots imaginable, there might have been another reason so many point-blank hits glanced off the iron plates. Byron Josephus Woodhull was a crewman on the *Ceres* that followed the *Albemarle* back towards the Roanoke.

In his diary he made a brief observation of those final moments, which could be construed as an excuse why the seven gunboats were unable to dispatch the ironclad. When darkness was coming on, as they steamed west towards the river, reflected light from the setting sun caused them to see what appeared to be tallow smeared upon the *Albemarle's* sloping sides. He reasoned that shots would have glanced off more readily if that were true.[3]

Capt. Melancton Smith, on board the flagship *Mattabesett*, prepared a report for Rear Adm. Lee. His once proud fleet was grossly indisposed. Extracts of his report present a forlorn image of his tattered command.

> The *Hetzel* and *Lockwood* are reported to me as worthless. The *Louisiana* and *Tacony* are repairing boilers...in consequence of the disabled condition of the *Sassacus*...I have ordered the *Commodore Barney* to proceed to this place without delay, as I must have three vessels with heavy guns to meet the ram, should he make his appearance again...The *Whitehead* may at any moment lose her rudder...the *Mattabesett* is obliged to work by hand after reversing engine...the *Wyalusing* can use but one of her rudders...the *Miami* requires very extensive repairs on boiler, engine and engine frames.
>
> I am of the opinion that the *Southfield* will be raised and accompany the *Albemarle*...and I have to assist me in repelling an attack from these vessels the *Mattabesett, Wyalusing, Miami, Ceres, Whitehead,* and the *Barney,*...which I trust will not be considered too large a force for an iron vessel and a very formidable wooden one...if there did not appear to be a great scarcity of vessels, I should feel it my duty to ask for vessels capable of ramming in addition to my force. If they were heavy and without guns, I would be satisfied.[4]

By May 9, Secretary of the Navy Gideon Welles personally responded to a resolution passed by the House on May 2 directing the Secretary of the Navy furnish the House,

> With all the information in his possession concerning the construction of the rebel ram which participated in the recent rebel attack on the United States forces and vessels at and near Plymouth;
>
> Also to inform the House why the construction of said ram was not prevented, whether any steps were taken

to prevent the same, or to guard against the action of said ram;

Also what action was taken in relation to the subjects of this enquiry, and why the same was not effective.

Welles reminded the House that fault was theirs since no shallow draft ironclad gunboats, designed for service in the sounds and rivers of North Carolina, had ever been delivered. In fact, they were nearly eighteen months overdue. Regional arguments as to where shipyard facilities would be located also hindered the completion of these vessels. The Secretary also reminded the House that his often recommended establishment of government construction sites, for building and servicing ironclad vessels, would be in the government's best interest.[5]

On the tenth Catherine Edmondston wrote further of Cooke's adventure on the Sound. Her news sources lacked their usual credibility.

> Captain Cooke has had a severe fight with Yankee gunboats in Albemarle Sound. His smoke stack was so riddled with shot that he could not burn coal & but for a supply of lard & bacon he would have been taken. He kept up his fires with these, however. Sunk two steamers & fought his way back to Plymouth with one gun disabled & her smoke stack with holes in it through which a man might creep. He lost his new tender, the *Bombshell*. She was sunk & her crew captured. Ten men were killed on the deck of the *Albemarle*. She engaged eleven boats at once & escaped them all. They threw a net made of rope over her but the ropes which held it to the steamers parting, it fell harmless off her sides into the water. For her preservation God be thanked.[6]

When Gilbert Elliott had returned to the Halifax Yard after Plymouth's recapture, he informed Mallory of how the *Albemarle* had performed against the *Southfield* and *Miami*. Fortified by Cooke's letter of May 8, the Secretary was encouraged to consider seriously the construction of another ironclad more closely to Cooke's battle tested specifications. After receiving a request for proposal from Chief Constructor Porter, Elliott wrote Governor Vance on May 11 from Scotland Neck. He opened with Porter's quotation.

We are disposed to build an ironclad at Edwards Ferry if we can procure the iron[.] Do you know where 275 tons of iron could be gotten in North Carolina, if so it could be rolled into armor iron here[?] We have vessels now built which require 3000 tons to clad them, and it would hardly be of any use to build without a prospect of getting iron to clad them.

Will you interest yourslf and write me immediately what the prospect is?

Elliott then continued with his plea for Vance's assistance.

Considering the vast importance of immediately constructing other ironclad boats on Roanoke River to cooperate with the *Albemarle*, I have determined to appeal to your Excellency for assistance in procuring the iron. The aid you so generously rendered us in furnishing the iron with which the *Albemarle* was built resulted in the glorious recovery of a portion of our State and I do not think I shall appeal to you in vain when I ask that you will again provide us with sufficient iron to cover a boat.

I am informed upon the best authority that a large quantity of iron can yet be obtained from the A & NC Road [Atlantic and North Carolina] below Kinston and if you will give permission to take it, I pledge myself with the assistance of the Almighty to have another boat finished in six months. I have proposed to contract for the entire work to be delivered in six months and some grounds for hoping that iron may be procured is all that is needed to induce the Secretary of the Navy to accept my proposal. Only about four miles of the road will be needed and I trust that you will give us permission to take it.

One portion of our State has been relieved from Yankee rule and despotism mainly by the efforts of Commander Cooke in the *Albemarle*. The completion of that vessel is an earnest of my interest in the cause, for as you had opportunity to know, I built her under manifold disadvantages. The operations of the *Albemarle* however have inspired such confidence among the people that I feel sure my path hereafter will be a smooth one.

There is no hope of building an additional boat and by that means saving the entire Albemarle section[,] unless your Excellency agrees to furnish the Confederate Government with 275 tons iron and with the confident hope of receiving a favorable reply to this communication at an early day, I am very respectfully your obt servt, Gilbert Elliott. [7]

Having earned her aggressors' respect, the *Albemarle* was in turn now respected by the Confederate high command. In times past Elliott and Cooke had to plead repeatedly for her protection during her construction. Becoming a successful warrior had earned the right to protection, and plans for such were being devised in the event that the waters, where she reigned supreme, eventually became overrun with returning invaders.

On May 12, Ass't Adjutant and Inspector General Giles B. Cooke at Petersburg, Virginia, wrote Commander Cooke at Plymouth with the notification that Brig. Gen. William H. C. Whiting was being placed in temporary command of the Department of North Carolina and Southern Virginia. Whiting was given instructions to protect the *Albemarle* in case the enemy should make serious advances against Plymouth. A.A.I.G. Cooke asked Commander Cooke to communicate with Whiting in case it became necessary to abandon Plymouth and to plan to,

Withdraw the *Albemarle* from Plymouth and ascend the Roanoke River, at least to a point beyond Hamilton, where Gen. Whiting has been directed to concentrate the troops now garrisoning Plymouth, and to mount the necessary heavy guns to prevent the enemy from passing the fort located at that place.

The general commanding instructs me to thank you, and, through you, the officers and men of your command, for your and their gallant action in the late attack made on you in Albemarle Sound by nine of the enemy's war vessels. [8]

One may recall that it was General Whiting who, on December 19, 1863, disapproved Lt. Gilbert Elliott's request for resignation to build ironclads with his negative endorsement.

I consider every man employed on ironclad gunboats thrown away as far as the defences of the country is concerned.[9]

Meanwhile the enemy was busily engaged in reconnaissance. Their objective was the *Albemarle*. On May 12, Captain Smith reported the observations to Admiral Lee. Acting Ensign John R. Peacock and a boat's crew from the late *Southfield* had ascended about six miles up the Middle River, where after landing, they endured a fatiguing four-hour tramp through the swamps. At about 5 P.M. they reached a place of observation about 200 yards opposite the *Albemarle*.
Peacock reported,

The ram [is] lying at the coal yard wharf, lower end of the town, with smokestack down and a number of men engaged upon the repairs. The vessel seems to have been lightened, as he appears much higher out of water forward and aft than when we engaged him in the sound, but the sides of his casemates are even now touching the water.

[We] could not see that the roof plating was at all broken or displaced, and nothing of the stack of the *Southfield*, which would have been visible if the vessel had not been raised or her smokestack removed to supply one for the *Albemarle*. The last suggestion seems to be most probable.

A free colored man was captured on the way down,...just from Plymouth by the way of the Roanoke River, who states that he heard from an engineer of the *Albemarle* that one of the large guns was split open by one of our shot, and that there was a great quantity of water in the cabin on the arrival of the vessel at Plymouth.

His roofing and casemates are covered with narrow plates of iron. Only two regiments remain at Plymouth, three having left for Virginia last week.[10]

Capt. Melancton Smith prepared a detailed attack plan against the *Albemarle* in case the ironclad would again make an appearance in the Sound. On May 13 it was dispatched to Lt. Richard T. Renshaw commanding the *Miami*. The next day he sailed with the *Wyalusing* to the Perquimans River in hopes of deceiving the Confederates.

Guarding the Roanoke and Cashie rivers were the *Miami, Commodore Hull, Commodore Barney* and *Ceres*. If the *Albemarle* appeared, they were to retreat into the Sound far enough to maneuver successfully. They would there be joined by the *Wyalusing* and her consorts. Smith emphasized one precaution.

> Do not on any account attempt to engage in the river, as his guns [are] as heavy as yours and are equal in range, and it is already proved to our satisfaction that our shot can not injure him very materially at close quarters.
>
> His next effort will perhaps be to outgeneral us by slipping by in the night from the mouth of the Cashie [river].[11]

The combined assault of seven Union gunboats against a single Confederate ironclad on May 5 had ended as darkness enveloped the scene. Seven of the Unions' select battle fleet, commanded by Capt. Melancton Smith, had produced the inglorious statistics of four killed, twenty-five wounded, one of the three 974-ton gunboats completely disabled with three others seriously damaged. Flagship orders had signaled the "cease fire," after which the pursuit had been limited and casual. Surely these facts were not welcome in Washington City.

Exclusive of enclosures, Admiral Lee's letter of May 14 to Navy Secretary Gideon Welles made the Union Navy look better than reality dictated.

> I transmit enclosed report...of the gallant fight on the afternoon of the 5th instant in Albemarle Sound between our wooden gunboats and the rebel ironclad *Albemarle*, in which the latter was repulsed and her tender captured.
>
> I ask the especial attention of the Department to the signal bravery displayed by Captain Smith and the officers and men engaged with him in this remarkable action, which adds a brilliant page to the exploits of the Navy.[12]

Another reconnaissance was conducted on May 17 by Captain Smith. His observers retraced their earlier route from the Middle River to a vantage point from which the *Albemarle* and *Southfield* could be seen. He learned that the *Southfield* was lying where she had been sunk, her upper deck just awash and smokestack standing. It also appeared the smokestack of the ram had been repaired and replaced. Men were heard working upon the vessel, and no damage was evident on the starboard side which faced the observers.[13]

Aboard the *Albemarle* on the eighteenth, Cooke composed a letter to Governor Vance in which he related how he had urged the Navy Department to construct another ironclad as quickly as possible. Saying he expected to be named project superintendent, Cooke candidly admitted the object of his letter.

> Request that you will aid me in procuring the iron to cover her with. One boat carrying [only] two guns I am confident that we can't succeed in getting possession of the sound and I demonstrated that fact in my last engagement with the enemy on the 5th inst., but give me another ironclad carrying two broadside guns in addition to the bow and stern ones and I feel confident that the sounds will once more be ours, and this iron[,] Governor[,] can be very easily procured from the refuse iron in the NC roads.

With pencil Vance wrote on the reverse, "say that I will assist him in getting iron as far as possible." [14]

On Tuesday May 24 the *Albemarle* ventured downriver stern first. The Union command noted that it was the first time she had been observed away from her dock since May 5. She had been accompanied by a rowboat moving diagonally across the river as if dragging for torpedoes. Captain Smith reported later to Admiral Lee that the *Whitehead* "fired a shell which exploded near his stern, when the *Albemarle* immediately steamed up the river." Smith added that the *Southfield's* guns had been raised. One had been sent away while two remained on the wharf awaiting transportation.[15]

Smith, intent on destroying the *Albemarle* without a fight, devised a plan and asked for volunteers. Based on intelligence gained from surveillance, he imagined that torpedoes could be floated downriver and guided against the ironclad's hull. About 2 P.M. on May 25 five volunteers from the *Wyalusing* departed in a dinghy borrowed from the *Mattabesett*. Two 100-pound torpedoes with appendages were accompanied by coal heaver Charles Baldwin, cockswain John W. Loyd, fireman Allen Crawford, fireman John Laverty, and coal heaver Benjamin Loyd.

They ascended the Middle River without incident and reached their preparatory location shortly after dark. Leaving Benjamin Loyd as boat keeper, the other four men used a stretcher to transport both torpedoes across the island swamp, where they carefully assembled all their gear on the river bank in the dark. Leaving Crawford ashore to detonate the charges upon a signal from Baldwin, John Loyd and Baldwin then swam the river with a line. Once ashore on the Plymouth side they pulled both torpedoes across. The torpedoes were connected at each end of a bridle, and to the bridle was attached a guiding line.

About 11 P.M. Baldwin entered the river with the explosive device. He slowly floated along while guiding it towards the unprotected vessel. Loyd remained in place on the south bank playing out the line as Baldwin drifted downstream. Baldwin's task was to adjust the bridle to enfold the ironclad's bow. A few yards from his target he was seen. The wharf sentry hailed him and fired two shots. A musketry volley followed.

Hearing the challenge and firing, John Loyd cut the guiding line, threw away the ignition coil, and swam across the river. There he met Laverty who was custodian of clothing and small arms. They thrashed through the swamp to rendezvous with boat keeper Benjamin Loyd. Without waiting for the others they left the scene. By morning on the twenty-seventh they moored alongside the *Wyalusing*.

Luckily, Baldwin escaped the random shots, and more fortunately, the shots missed the torpedoes. He joined Crawford and together they made their way back to the fleet by Sunday, May 29.

Their plan was perfectly executed, except for two mistakes. First, Baldwin was sighted, and secondly the vessel nearly blown up was a schooner anchored in the river.[16]

Miss Sarah Mackay of Savannah received a letter on May 30 from James C. Long aboard the *Albemarle* at Plymouth. Although he had been transferred from the C.S. *Savannah* to the *Albemarle* on May 3, he stopped to visit his family in Griffin, Georgia. Subsequent travel delays as well as poor postal service from Plymouth had delayed his mail. For these reasons he offered apologies for not writing sooner. Arriving on May 12 he "found that all of the army had been withdrawn, except one regiment, to reenforce the Army of Virginia." Long continued with a graphic description of the Plymouth scene.

The town of Plymouth contained immense quantities of stores such as bacon, flour, etc. Sutlers stores were also abundant, and our soldiers supplied themselves well with clothing.

The officers of the *Albemarle* have been living well on Yankee spoils, such as coffee, sugar, oranges, lemons, jellies, fruit in cans, in fact everything nice.... The *Albemarle's* armor was penetrated in several places by wrought iron bolts fired from 100-pdr. Parrott guns. We have taken a new Brooke 100-pdr. gun on board, and the engines have been put in splendid order, but we have been unable to repair her armor for want of iron. We would have attacked the enemy before this but they have obstructed the river with torpedoes and rope netting.

Captain Cooke intends to make an attack in two days from this time, in spite of these obstacles.... The town of Plymouth is almost deserted by its inhabitants. The few who remain here are disloyal. I do not think there is a refined lady in the town, all the Southern people have moved to the interior of the State. [17]

Commodore Robert F. Pinkney, Commanding Naval Defences at Kinston, wrote Governor Vance May 31 thanking him for offering to provide iron for another gunboat on the Roanoke. Pinkney continued with a,

Request you give me such authority as will enable me to procure it. There will be required for the object intended about four hundred tons of rails, and its preparation for use should be begun immediately to make it available within convenient time.[18]

Sometime before May 30 seamen J. H. McCann and John Williams, along with carpenter William Schafer and fireman William Daley deserted from the *Albemarle*. At Roanoke Island, aboard the *Miami*, they were questioned separately with statements taken on June 3 by Cdr. Richard T. Renshaw. Renshaw, who was the *Miami's* commander, desired specific information concerning the rumored iron basket surrounding the *Albemarle's* propellers. McCann stated he had heard Elliott tell Cooke "not to be afraid of anything fouling the propellers as they are protected." Maybe, he surmised, there was an iron basket. Williams said there was no shield over the propellers, as he had at different times hooked off lines that had caught and fouled the same. All four generally confirmed the ironclad's damage previously described. A sketch depicting the damaged stern Brooke gun was prepared for Renshaw from the deserters descriptions.[19]

The same day Admiral Lee reported to Secretary Welles the unfortunate failure of a gallant attempt to blow up the Albemarle.[20] For weeks Melancton Smith had engaged in torpedo tests. Their emplacement in the Roanoke had long been practiced, but emphasis had been redirected to the *Albemarle's* immediate destruction.

On June 6, Smith reported to Lee about an experiment to best foul a boat. The plan involved towing a torpedo-loaded boat in such a manner it would contact an enemy vessel. Initial trials had been successful. Smith's confidential description of his proposed plan varied from a procedure earlier approved,

> By placing torpedoes in the Roanoke River, to be exploded by friction matches,...trigger wires were to be watched by selected men during the day, as it is believed...the ram will never attempt to come down the river at night for fear of getting aground. I have no idea he will make his appearance in the sound until the floating batteries that are building at Weldon are ready to cooperate.[21]

For the men of Smith's command who would have been detailed to sit on the river bank awaiting the Albemarle's appearance, the proposal of towing torpedo-laden boats probably met with their approval.

On June 8, Smith ordered another tactic to force the *Albemarle's* appearance in the Sound. His strategy was to send the *Whitehead* far enough upriver to shell Plymouth's lower battery. Then she was to quickly withdraw and join the *Commodore Barney* in the Middle River opposite Plymouth, from where they both would shell the battery. The shelling's purpose was to entice the *Albemarle* into open water. Cooke ignored the challenge.[22]

For an undisclosed time Cooke had experienced failing health. Acting in the best interest of the Navy, he requested from Mallory to be relieved of duty aboard the *Albemarle*. In support of Cooke's request, the Office of Orders and Detail in Richmond generated an order to Cdr. John N. Maffitt on the ninth of June.

> Sir: Proceed to Plymouth, N.C., and report to Captain R. F. Pinkney, commanding, etc., for the command of the C.S. [ram] *Albemarle*. You will report by the 22d instant, or as soon thereafter as practicable. By command of the Secretary of the Navy.[23]

Commander Cooke's achievement in gallantly fighting the Union's best gunboats on two separate occasions was officially acknowledged when he received Secretary Mallory's June 10 notification.

> You are hereby informed that the President [Davis] has appointed you by and with the advice and consent of the Senate as Captain in the Provisional Navy of the Confederate States, for gallant and meritorious conduct on the 19th, 20th, and 21st days of April 1864 in attacking the enemies ships and batteries and in cooperation with the army in the capture of the town of Plymouth NC[,] and in the action of the 5th of May, 1864 between the sloop *Albemarle* under your command and nine of the enemies gun boats in Albemarle Sound. You will please acknowledge the receipt of this appointment.[24]

For Distinguished Valor and Skill Commander James W. Cooke was promoted to Captain, C.S.N., effective June 4, 1864.

On June 11, a day before departing for New Bern, Captain Smith instructed Cdr. John P. Bankhead, of the *Otsego*, how to dispatch the *Albemarle* if she made an appearance in the Sound. With the *Wyalusing* as command ship, his priority instruction included an established preference of enticing the ironclad from the river where greater maneuvering would benefit the fleet. He cited the danger of an upriver encounter. The Cashie was also mentioned as the ram's possible avenue of escape.

Smith provided Bankhead with the latest plan of using a towed vessel loaded with torpedoes with which to impact and explode the ram. He told Bankhead of three torpedoes placed near the river's first bend and that,

They are watched during the day by an officer and four men, two of the latter to be relieved every second day (by the double enders) and furnished with their rations.[25]

Floating batteries rumored near Weldon caused increased anxiety for Admiral Lee which prompted him to suggest, "a portion of the light-draft monitors should be fitted either as submarine prodders or as torpedo vessels" which, in his opinion, would require the removal of their guns and part of their turrets for the purpose.[26]

From the Navy Department in Richmond an order was issued on June 17, 1864, relieving Captain Cooke as the *Albemarle's* commander.

> Sir: On the reporting of your successor, Commander Maffitt, you will consider yourself relieved of the command, at your request, of the C.S. [ram] *Albemarle,* to await orders. By command of the Secretary of the Navy.[27]

Commander Maffitt had no doubt been chosen to command the *Albemarle* because of his reputation as former commander of the famous blockade runner C.S.S. *Florida.* In any event his name probably caused deep concern among those commanding the Union fleet in Albemarle Sound.

Catherine Edmondston commented on that change of command when on the same day she wrote,

> Capt. Cooke has at his own request, in consequence of his health, been removed from the command of the *Albemarle* & Capt. Maffitt of the *Florida* memory assigned to the duty. Poor gentleman, I pity him. How he will chafe cooped up in this narrow crooked river after roaming at will the broad bosom of the sea in search of Yankee commerce.[28]

As result of Bankhead's reconnaissance of the *Albemarle* on June 24, it became known to the Union command that John N. Maffitt then commanded the ironclad. A party which had penetrated the swamp to observe activities reported,

> The work upon her appeared completed; her smokestack replaced by that of the *Southfield*; guns mounted and in all respects ready for work.[29]

On June 25, 1864, Commander Maffitt reported for duty to Commander Pinkney at Halifax Yard from where, after a short inspection of facilities in the company of Pinkney, he probably took a small boat downriver to his new command at Plymouth.

Having become settled after his transfer to the *Albemarle* from the *Savannah*, James C. Long wrote his friend Midshipman Hubbard T. Minor, Jr., on the twenty-eighth of June. He noted that Commander Maffitt had taken command of the vessel and that ship's repairs were complete. He then cautioned Minor not to expect too much of the *Albemarle* for,

> She is the poorest ironclad in the Confederacy. Her sides are plated with four inches of iron [but] her spar deck is not covered at all. A portion of her forward flush deck is covered with one inch iron [and] the other portion is not covered with anything. Her after flush deck is partially covered with one inch iron, the rest of it with ¼ inch sheet iron.
>
> I received my commission as Master a few days ago to date from June 2. [30]

COMMANDER JOHN NEWLAND MAFFITT was assigned command of the *Albemarle* after Commander Cooke requested reassignment due to health reasons. Maffitt won fame as a blockade runner.
Naval Historical Center

That revelation of iron plating deficiencies, mentioned by a credible witness assigned to the *Albemarle*, made her survival of the terrible bombardment on May 5 all the more remarkable. Probably the penetrating energies of impacting shots were neutralized when striking the flush decks as glancing blows.

After having received an earlier report about floating batteries on the Roanoke at Weldon, Admiral Lee notified Commander William H. Macomb, commanding Union naval forces off New Bern, North Carolina, that "I have ordered four tugs to be fitted with torpedoes and sent to you at the earliest practicable moment." The tugs were to have mounted on their bows 20-foot long spars, at the end of which was suspended a 150-pound powder cannister.[31]

Although Elliott had returned up the Roanoke shortly after the recapture of Plymouth nearly two and one half months earlier, he was paid $353.56 on July 1 for an overdue timber expense voucher from the preceding February. The timbers, which may have been used in finishing the *Albemarle*, consisted of 3,796 feet of 1-inch pine, and 2,413 feet of 4-inch oak.[32]

Maffitt's assignment as the *Albemarle's* commander brought with it varying degrees of anxiety. Among Union commanders he was widely known as a wily, aggressive, and successful blockade runner. His being teamed with the feared ironclad had prompted Union commanders to explore every possible way, other than battle, of defeating the *Albemarle*.

Maffitt's verbal instructions from Secretary Mallory to "attack the enemy's fleet in the Sound with the *Albemarle*" brought greater attention by Confederate authorities. Many felt, as did Commodore Pinkney and Captain Cooke, that she should remain within the river's protection as a deterrent to further invasion. Cooke offered a further opinion that in all probability she would be captured or sunk by venturing into the broad waters of the sound.

It was felt within the Army that strong local protection of Plymouth by land and water forces would indefinitely discourage another Union invasion of eastern North Carolina. If the *Albemarle* was captured or destroyed after venturing into the Sound, the door would be opened for the Union's return.

The *Albemarle's* static presence served to protect the Roanoke valley and Washington, North Carolina. Confederate Naval officers, other than those at Plymouth, agreed with that premise. On July 2 Col. George Wortham, post commander at Plymouth, assessed the dangers in a letter forwarded to the Secretary of War by Brig. Gen. Laurence S. Baker, commanding the Second District, Dept. of North Carolina and Southern Virginia at Goldsboro. His concluding remarks were meant to be alarming.

> It is risking much, with fearful odds against us, for the doubtful prospect of an inconsiderable advantage. My condition here with a small garrison would be very precarious if the ironclad came to harm. I most respectfully

request that the honorable Secretary of War be informed of the state of affairs, so that he may take such steps to prevent an impending calamity as his good judgement may dictate.

Perhaps a personal interiew with the Secretary of the Navy might enable him to procure a revocation of the order to Captain Maffitt.[33]

General Baker, pursuing his goal of limiting the *Albemarle's* use, wrote Commander Maffitt on the sixth of July cautioning against a proposed attack upon the enemy's gunboats in the Sound. He urged Maffitt to refrain from the engagement unless he was certain of success. Baker went on to remind Maffitt of the river's importance to the Confederacy, and of the U.S. Government's serious plans to use great numbers of their largest gunboats to destroy the ironclad. In conclusion Baker observed,

I have no doubt that in event of an attack by you the most desperate efforts will be made to destroy your boat, and thus open the approach to Plymouth and Washington.

I hope, Captain, you will appreciate the importance of the matter which has induced these suggestions, and pardon the liberty taken. [34]

From his Flagship *Shamrock* off the Perquimans River, Cdr. William H. Macomb reported to Admiral Lee on July 7. He enumerated the thirty-two ships of his command. His larger vessels had been positioned off the Perquimans River, rather than below Edenton, because of the Sounds' breadth and deeper water in which to maneuver. Pickets were to maintain their positions off the Roanoke's mouth. Frequent reconnaissance expeditions had resulted in hearing only what was thought to have been the *Albemarle's* bell. No sightings were reported, leading them to believe the ironclad was hidden from view. Numerous strategy sessions had been conducted with all ships' commanders present. From those conferences a battle plan was then developed.

He also reported that five men in charge of torpedoes in the Roanoke River had been captured. Their leader was named Baldwin. He might also have been one of the swimmers in the abortive attempt to float two torpedoes against the *Albemarle's* hull.[35] On the same day Commander Macomb sent Admiral Lee a report of the Confederate vessels under construction on the Roanoke.

> I have received reports from intelligent refugees...that
> the rebel ironclad *Albemarle* is lying at Plymouth ready
> for service, and that Captain Maffitt, late of the U.S. Navy,
> has command. The new ironclad vessel at Halifax, [N.C.]
> will be ready in three weeks or a month. The floating bat-
> tery at Rainbow Bluff is finished also, they say. It is sup-
> posed that they will operate together.[36]

In his frantic effort to have Maffitt's verbal orders revoked,
General Baker wrote Secretary Seddon on July 8. He reiterated Colonel Wortham's plea to Seddon, and his own to Maffitt adding,

> I beg leave most respectfully to suggest that steps be
> taken to obtain an immediate revocation of the order to
> Captain Maffitt...[while] communicating at the same time
> with General Beauregard.[37]

Baker followed this letter the same day with another to Capt. J.
M. Otey, Ass't Adjutant General, Dept. of North Carolina and Southern Virginia, at Petersburg,. Virginia. He repeated introductory comments of his earlier letters before adding,

> In the opinion of Commodore Pinkney and Captain
> Cooke, both thoroughly acquainted with the capacity, etc.,
> of the gunboat *Albemarle,* there is a great danger of her
> capture if she goes out into the Sound for this purpose.

Baker mentioned others with whom he had registered his concern before concluding with the observation,

> Immediate steps in the premises to procure a revoca-
> tion of the order to Captain Maffitt, as the loss of the
> *Albemarle* would probably necessitate the evacuation of
> the country recently recaptured by our forces, and now so
> important to the Confederacy. [38]

On July 9 Commander Macomb, aboard the *Shamrock* in the
Sound, reported to Admiral Lee what he termed reliable information gained from an Edenton citizen. In the exchange he had learned
that,

> Large quantities of bacon and other supplies have
> been sent to South Mills, at the southern end of the Dis-
> mal Swamp Canal on the Pasquotank River, and are there
> sold to rebel agents for the supply of the rebel Army.
>
> It is said that this bacon, etc., is sent from Norfolk by
> permit from United States authority in that district.[39]

Admiral Lee informed Secretary Welles on the ninth that Lt.
William B. Cushing had arrived on the scene four days earlier. Lee
broached the subject of destroying the *Albemarle* by means of a torpedo attack. Although Cushing proposed a large scale assault, he
agreed to Lee's recommendation that a limited expedition be planned
using a small torpedo equipped vessel with which to attack the ironclad. When Admiral Lee received Cushing's July 9 response from
Hampton Roads, where Cushing was aboard the *Monticello*, he was
pleased when Cushing agreed that,[40]

> Deeming the capture or destruction of the rebel ram
> *Albemarle* feasible, I beg to state that I am acquainted with
> the waters held by her, and am willing to undertake the
> task.

With that opening remark, he then elaborated upon the type
of vessels he desired to support the task, how they would be equipped,
and that he desired to superintend equipping the vessels.[41]

Apprehensive that unattended torpedoes would fall into enemy hands, Macomb ordered their removal from the Roanoke on
July 10. Since the attending parties had recently been captured, he
declined to risk losing more men. Therefore, an armed launch party
was detailed to raise the torpedoes. If removal was impossible they
were to be detonated to prohibit use by the enemy. A line of concussion torpedoes styled to explode on contact were left in place at the
river's mouth.[42]

True to his word, Governor Vance initiated contact on July 16
with Col. John D. Whitford, President of the Atlantic and North
Carolina Railroad.

> Mr. Elliott informs me that his company is desirous
> of contracting for rail road iron to build a gun boat upon
> the terms proposed by your company that is to say, to pay
> for the iron in funds which can be made available to pay
> the debt of the company to the State.

The Treasurer of the State will receive State Bonds or Treasury Notes. Mr. Elliott visits you to make a contract and I hope you can come to some satisfactory arrangement.[43]

Brig. Gen. Innis N. Palmer, in command at New Bern, reported on the nineteenth that,

The rebels are vigorously pushing the work upon their ironclad fleet in the Roanoke River. I have good reason to believe that besides the ram *Albemarle* two others are being built, and if they can succeed in coming into the Sounds together we have no naval force to cope with them....Captain Maffitt now commands the ram *Albemarle,* and we all know that he is not the man to sit down at Plymouth. He was ordered there to do something, and if he can get a fleet of these rams before we receive any iron vessels we must expect disaster.[44]

On July 24 Master Henry H. Foster, aboard the *Ceres,* reported a suggestion to Macomb. For long the *Ceres* had been detailed to picket the Roanoke's mouth and report the *Albemarle's* movements. The night time hours were of greatest concern, since it was believed the ironclad could easily slip out unobserved and get between the picket and the fleet. Foster envisioned a plan whereby a boat would be stationed at the rivers' mouth with a signal light pointing towards the fleet to the east. Thus, if the ironclad came down the river, its approach could be discreetly signalled.

By adopting this procedure, Foster was convinced the ram could not get out unobserved. Impulsively he had sent out a boat the evening before, but at the same time he sought approval of his plan from Macomb.[45]

Acting Masters Mate John Woodman, also of the *Ceres,* was an ambitious crewman selected by Foster on Monday July 25 to reconnoiter the *Southfield* and *Albemarle*. Little information had been regularly collected on either vessel during brief observation excursions. He left the *Ceres* on Tuesday at 12:30 A.M. in a cutter with three men. They headed for a landing point at the swamp along the Middle River opposite Plymouth, and from there he trudged through dense growth to a vantage point opposite the *Southfield.*

She appeared to be in the same condition as when sunk, though her hurricane deck was about three feet higher above water level than when last seen in May. Woodman reported her smokestack, lookout ladder, and forward pilot house were yet standing. On her starboard was a barge of about 500 or 600 tons, and a schooner of 150 or 200 tons on her port. There was no purchase rigging for raising the *Southfield* onto these vessels, and neither did he observe anyone at work though it was nearly 10 A.M.

He then proceeded upriver until he was opposite the *Albemarle* lying at the wharf near the steam sawmill. He observed no one working there either. The only person visible was the quartermaster on top her casemate. All was quiet in the town. Few people were moving about. Blacksmiths and carpenters could be heard working in their shops near the river, and when he turned to ask Henry Hatch for his glass with which to better view the *Albemarle*, Henry was gone. Woodman said he waited a half hour before returning to the small boat, but Henry had not returned. Two days rations, with a message to wait for help, were left before Woodman and his two boatmen departed. Upon Woodman's return, Macomb sent a search party for Hatch who was found and safely rescued.[46]

On Saturday July 30, Secretary Mallory prepared a statement for Secretary Seddon in reponse to his receipt of letter copies from General Baker, Colonel Wortham and others who wished revocation of Maffitt's orders to fight the *Albemarle*.

Mallory stated his policy and position in two sentences.

It is evident from these papers that the military authorities immediately in charge at Plymouth regard our tenure of Plymouth, Washington, and the rich valley of the Roanoke as dependent upon the ironclad *Albemarle*; and hence their protest against alleged verbal orders given her by the Navy Department to attack the enemy.

The importance of this vessel in holding the country she greatly aided to recover is apparent, even if the water fronts of Plymouth were strengthened, but she was not designed to act as a floating battery merely, and while her loss must not be lightly hazarded, the question of when to attack the enemy must be left to the judgement of the naval officer in command, deciding in view of the relations she bears to the defenses of North Carolina.[47]

CHAPTER 14

A QUIET TIME BEFORE THE STORM

The months of August, September, and part of October were quiet times for the *Albemarle* and her crew. She remained the captive of political maneuvering. Lethargy permeated the atmosphere around her. Summer's heat, boredom, inactivity, and isolation were relieved only occasionally when brief excursions downriver were ordered to observe the enemy and show the flag.

Secretary Mallory sought to keep Maffitt thoroughly informed of all official correspondence that passed between himself, Wortham, Baker, Maffitt, Seddon, Pinkney, and others in the brewing controversy over fighting the *Albemarle*. A number of enclosures accompanied his letter of August the fourth.[1]

At 4 A.M. on Saturday August 6 the *Albemarle* made an appearance at the Roanoke's mouth where she halted. Picket boat *Chicopee* slipped her cable and stood out slowly with other picket boats fully expecting the ironclad to follow. Despite an open battle invitation, the *Albemarle* remained steadfast. Lining the river banks were groups of people who were expecting to watch a naval battle before their very eyes.

Cdr. Abram D. Harrell, of the *Chicopee*, later reported to Macomb that it appeared the ironclad lay in the river blowing off steam. For long minutes there was no move by either party, which encouraged Harrell to believe the ironclad would not advance but,

> Should she do so, however, I will endeavor to draw
> her toward the fleet. I shall now pay my respects to those
> gentlemen on the beach in the shape of a few shells.[2]

While the *Albemarle* had been in final construction stages at Halifax and Hamilton, necessary materials, equipment, and supplies had been procured by routine processes. Before the Navy Department could authorize payment, all vouchers had to be endorsed by the Yard superintendent. When the *Albemarle* was being readied for its initial encounter at Plymouth, Commander Cooke was still superintendent. In fact he had signed Yard vouchers as late as June 30.

Several vouchers submitted by Elliott had been withheld from payment. The first was for workmen sent from Halifax to Hamilton in an attempt to raise the *Cora*. The second was for iron spikes that had been acquired for fastening planking to the *Albemarle's* spar deck and pilot house sides. The third was for malls that had been Elliott's property at Edwards Ferry yard, of which same were used at Halifax, some were lost at Hamilton and the remainder taken to Plymouth. The fourth was for ship's timbers acquired to repair the *Cora* and *Cotton Plant*.

Sometime in late July Cooke returned the unsigned vouchers to Elliott, stating that it was not his responsibility to sign them since he had been aboard the *Albemarle,* and not present at Halifax as superintendent.

On the sixth of August Elliott composed a long letter explaining to Cooke that those charges had occurred on his watch. He reminded Cooke that he possessed letters requesting Mr. Taylor and his hands be sent to Hamilton for purposes of raising the *Cora*. In accordance with Cooke's wishes twelve men accompanied Taylor, but their efforts had been unavailing. Elliott admitted that the Yard was within Captain Pinkney's command at the time, but he had not dealt with him. He then added,

> If it is necessary for Captain Pinkney to approve the account we will forward it to him, but it certainly first requires your signature if we can take the numerous bills settled under Flag Officer Lynch's adminstration as a precedent.

In response to Cooke's supposition that the spikes had been Yard property under Lt. John J. Guthrie's command, Elliott reminded Cooke that they had been especially purchased for the *Albemarle*. By mutual agreement he and Cooke had returned 5-inch nails shipped in error from Tredegar. As a consequence Elliott had been compelled to arrange a country-store trade with Tredegar. For three pounds of spikes he had traded one pound of bacon [at $4 per pound] and paid transportation costs to and from Greensboro, North Carolina, making the spikes cost $1.50 per pound.

In an explanation of charges for the malls Elliott stated, "it was expressly understood and stated in the contract for ironing the gunboat that all tools should be furnished by the Government." Since the Halifax Navy Yard could not supply the malls, Elliott provided the Yard with his company owned malls. Some had been worn out at Halifax, a few broken from hard use, some lost at Hamilton, and those remaining went to Plymouth when the *Albemarle* was repaired after the April 19 battle. Special Agent and Naval Inspector J. J. Roberson had used the malls during the April repairs. In conclusion Elliott reminded Cooke that he personally had ordered timbers for repairing the *Cora* and *Cotton Plant*. Both sustained damage while running on the Roanoke before and after the fall of Plymouth.[3]

Very shortly after midnight, on Sunday morning August 7, the *Albemarle* ventured down the river. At 2:25 A.M. she was observed outside the buoy at the river's mouth. From aboard his picket ship *Ceres*, Lt. Cdr. William T. Truxton observed that the ironclad blended so well with the seascape that it could hardly be distinguished, as his ship passed it near their stern's side.

At 10 A.M. Monday, Mr. William Atkinson was escorted aboard. He was from Plymouth, and had permission from the military commander there to visit Edenton. Truxtun detained Atkinson for some time, and after extended conversation Atkinson was allowed to proceed. From the interview Truxtun learned,

> The ram will come down frequently and endeavor to pick up one of us, or will risk an engagement with two double-enders. A boat expedition is to be sent to Edenton [with] two launches containing about fifty men each. He saw the floating battery at Halifax three weeks ago....has never heard of another ram at Halifax. A steamer is building there, to run on the Roanoke River, but is not to be ironed, that's what Atkinson says.[4]

Having been humiliated by the fact their cannonading had produced such insignificant damage to the *Albemarle* on May 5, the Union command soon concluded why. They believed that too light powder charges had been used in the 9-inch and 100-pdr. guns. Therefore, the *Mattabesett* and *Chicopee* had been ordered to Norfolk where each would receive one 11-inch gun. They would be fitted to be fired with thirty pounds of powder and solid shot. Consequently, on August 9 Admiral Lee advised Commander Macomb,

That even using XI-inch guns the vessels should touch the ram while engaging her and the XI-inch guns be fired with 30 pounds of powder and solid shot. The Department still is of the opinion that ramming at full speed is the best course.[5]

While the Union command worried and fretted on how best to subdue the *Albemarle*, Capt. James W. Cooke, in quiet reflection, observed his fifty-second birthday on August 13.

Colonel David W. Wardrop, commanding Sub-District Headquarters at Roanoke Island, wrote Commander Macomb on August 15 with news of varying and opposing rumors concerning activities on the Roanoke. He cited information from "heretofore reliable sources" that the enemy was fitting their vessels with torpedoes, and planned to combine forces with the *Albemarle* on August 23. Another source confidentially stated the second ram would be completed in a fortnight. Wardrop's personal opinion of the increased traffic between Plymouth and towns upriver meant only that "there is something there that they are trying to keep to themselves."

He sincerely believed they had light-draft boats each capable of carrying fifty men; that the boats were torpedo equipped, though their use would be only to support a combined attack upon the fleet. Almost apologetically Wardrop concluded that he found it most difficult to believe anyone, since each informant told a different story.[6]

In a routine report to Admiral Lee on the same day, Commander Macomb advised that informants from Edenton and Plymouth had reported large numbers of mechanics being employed to complete the Halifax ironclad. He had further assurances that rebel ironclads were ready to attack the Sound's squadron momentarily; his belief was strengthened by the fact that the *Albemarle* had shown herself several times within recent days. Macomb also mentioned he had learned that the trading of bacon, salt, sugar, etc. with the Confederates at South Mills continued unabated. He had first alerted Lee of this circumstance on July the ninth.[7]

During the several weeks from June 1 through August 15 at Plymouth, the *Albemarle* underwent repairs of damage suffered during the May 5 battle. A special procurement agent from Wilmington, Mr. J. J. Roberson, was engaged to procure iron for repairs, coal from Washington, and negotiate for numerous ancillary services and supplies. He traveled between Wilmington, Goldsboro, Kinston, Wilson, Halifax, Plymouth, Washington [N.C.], and Tarboro. With the exception of travel to and from Wilmington, his horse provided local transportation. For his 41 days services he was paid $879.50 on August 15. The voucher breakdown noted his $7.50 per day labor charge totaled $307.50, while room, board, and road expenses amounted to $572.00.[8]

What may have been Elliott's contested voucher was paid on August 17. Dated May 1, it amounted to $4,681.00. Included in the charges were day rates for a foreman and laborers, 12 pin malls, 23 cords of wood, and 2,531 pounds of spikes @ $1.50 per pound.[9]

The next day, in a letter to Cooke acknowledging receipt of payment, Elliott announced,

> I am now making arrangements to commence hauling the iron on the Atlantic & North Carolina rail road, and will start the work in a few days. After the contract is made for hauling the iron I do not see how Secy Mallory can avoid contracting the ram. The molasses I promised you was sent to Mr. McMahon's Express office some time ago, but I learn today that it has not been shipped. I will endeavour to get it off and hope you will receive it in a few days.[10]

Captain Cooke endured a long spell with ill health after resigning the *Albemarle's* command. Once recovered, Cooke sought reassignment to duty. He had applied to the Navy Department for command of the Halifax Yard.

On August the twentieth, Cooke received a response from the Office of Orders and Detail in Richmond. With probable disappointment he read, "the Department regrets to inform you that it cannot be granted." The news was not encouraging. In explanation he was informed,

> Captain R. F. Pinkney, Commanding Naval Defences in that section of North Carolina including Kinston and Plymouth was directed on the 10th inst. to make his headquarters at Halifax. With special reference to the superintendency of the Naval Works at that point.
>
> There is no place vacant for you at present, but you will be placed on duty as soon as possible.[11]

Another reconnaissance of the *Albemarle* was being planned for August 23 by the Union fleet. Master's Mate John Woodman was again selected to lead such a mission. From the *Valley City* anchored off the Roanoke, he left at 8 P.M. in her dinghy accompanied by four crewmen. About midnight he entered a creek leading from the Middle River opposite Plymouth. At dawn the next morning, after instructing his crew to remain with the boat, he started across the swamp towards Plymouth. By 10 A.M. he had arrived at the Roanoke.

The *Albmarle* was lying alongside a wharf, her hull protected by timbers extending completely around her. Upriver three large open boats were being repaired on the shore. Woodman estimated they could have held from eight to sixteen men each. He also noted a large barge under water, with the exception that her bow rested on the bank. At the lower wharf a steam barge was undergoing repairs.

He then shifted his position until opposite the *Southfield*, and noticed that her hurricane deck appeared to be about eighteen inches above water. On the *Southfield's* starboard, to the rear, were moored a barge and schooner. Four large timbers lay across the barge's deck with one end of each resting on the *Southfield's* main deck.

On the port side towards the river's south bank was a large schooner with shears, a hoisting apparatus of several upright spars, erected on her after deck. Attached to the shears was heavy tackle with the fall leading to a windlass upon which men were heaving, but "I could not make out what the lower block was attached to." At sundown Woodman returned to his small boat and they were aboard the *Valley City* at 9 P.M.[12]

The long awaited fifth contract to build a larger, more powerful ironclad was awarded on August 29, 1864. The contractor was Gilbert Elliott & Company, a Halifax County partnership between Gilbert Elliott, Peter E. Smith and his younger brother William H. Smith. As parties of the first part they were to furnish one ironclad gunboat, in accordance with annexed specifications, to Chief Naval Constructor John L. Porter, and the Confederate States as parties of the second part.

The partnership was to construct the boat, complete in all its parts, ready to receive the engines, boilers, etc. which would be placed on the boat by the party of the second part. Government furnished iron armor and bolts were to be installed by the partners. Delivery date was six months. Navy supplied fixtures such as castings, rudder, pumps, wheel & yoke, ventilators, coal scuttles, cables & anchors, boats & davits were to be installed by the partners.

Of the appropriated sum of $286,895.13, twelve increment payments were to be made upon completion of each twelfth of approved work. Partners were to perform necessary alterations, for which additional time would be allowed and payment made.

In the event of interruption or destruction by the enemy, partners were to receive payment for work completed to that date. Signatories were Gilbert Elliott, Peter E. Smith, William H. Smith, and John L. Porter.[13]

Commander Maffitt organized a raid to capture the Union mail boat *Fawn*. She routinely made a circuit from Norfolk to Plymouth to Roanoke Island. Besides mail, she also carried paymaster's funds. No doubt the raid was prompted by the boredom of inactivity at Plymouth. On August 31, Maffitt ordered Pilot James B. Hopkins to command the raiders and proceed to the Dismal Swamp Canal near Elizabeth City where they were to, "capture the mail boat, and if you can not bring her into this port, destroy her by fire and retreat to this place with your prisoners."[14]

On September 5, Master James C. Long submitted to Commander Maffitt an operational plan against enemy vessels in the Sounds. He requested a boat and ten or fifteen men for an expedition through Welch's Creek, into the Pungo River, the Pamlico River and finally Pamlico Sound. By hiding in the numerous creeks and bayous they could intercept and burn enemy sailing craft. He saw little chance of discovery by the gunboats, since they could be seen earlier than his small craft could be detected.

Perhaps his most noteworthy goal was to burn or blow up the Hatteras lighthouse, the lack of which would have caused great inconvenience to the enemy in navigating the Hatteras Banks. [15]

On the seventh, Commander Macomb reported to Admiral Lee that a former *Southfield* crewman had escaped and was being questioned. He had revealed to Macomb the fact that the *Albemarle* was moored head down the river. Maffitt was still in command, and attempts at raising the *Southfield* had been progressing for a month. Macomb also learned the vessel building at Halifax was to be the *Albemarle's* tender, and the floating battery at Halifax was square shaped with about thirty men working on both vessels.[16]

Frank P. O'Brien was one of twenty in the September 9 raiding party ordered by Maffitt on August 31. He later recalled that their plans had been to force the drawbridge tender's obedience to the *Fawn's* signal as she approached, and then at the last minute to close the bridge. Raiders had been concealed in the bushes bordering the canal. On signal of a pistol shot they were to step aboard. That feat was easily accomplished since there were numerous places along the bank where one could step aboard a slow moving boat.

Henry Disher, the third assistant engineer of the *Albemarle*, had the pistol. He had also been ordered to take the captured *Fawn* down the canal to the Pasquotank River, into the Sound, across to the Roanoke, and up to Plymouth. In the excitement Disher discharged his weapon too early, and by so doing ensured a warm reception from the *Fawn's* defenders.

All twenty raiders boarded safely, but amid the confusion someone threw mail and other bags into the vessel's furnace. There were seven killed or wounded among the *Fawn's* passengers and crew. Twenty-nine prisoners were taken, including one colonel, two majors, soldiers, government employees and citizens. The raiders left the burning hulk effectively blocking the canal. Major Jenney and Mr. George W. Julian, M.C., were released at Elizabeth City and allowed to proceed to Roanoke Island.

With more than eight hours start on their pursuers, Hopkins and his men herded their prisoners about twenty-five miles west to the Chowan River where friends saw to it they had passage across.[17] Once safely back at Plymouth, Hopkins and his men were probably surprised to learn their commander was leaving. The Navy Department had issued transfer orders to Commander Maffitt on September 9.

> You are hereby detached from the command of the C.S. [ram] *Albemarle,* and will proceed to Wilmington, N.C., and report to Flag Officer William F. Lynch, commanding, for the command of a blockade runner.[18]

Maffitt's new command was the blockade runner *Owl.*

On September 10, the *Albemarle's* new commander was ordered to duty at Plymouth. Flag Officer Commanding Afloat, William W. Hunter at Savannah, relayed contents of a telegram from Richmond to Lieutenant Commanding, Alexander F. Warley, Provisional Navy C.S.

> By a telegram dated Richmond, Va., September 9, 1864, from Captain S. S. Lee...I am ordered to direct you

to proceed to Plymouth, N.C., and report to Captain Pinkney for the command of the *Albemarle*. You will therefore please proceed forthwith to Plymouth in obedience thereto.[19]

At his residence in Warrenton on September 13, Captain Cooke may have smiled when he read the dispatch from Richmond granting his request.

> Proceed to Halifax, N.C., without delay, and relieve Captain Robert F. Pinkney, Provisional Navy C.S., of his present duty, commanding naval defenses, etc. By command of the Secretary of the Navy.[20]

LIEUTENANT ALEXANDER F. WARLEY, C.S.N., was the *Albemarle's* third commander. He had the dubious distinction of being in command when she was sunk by a torpedo placed by Lt. William B. Cushing, U.S.N.
Century Magazine, July, 1888

During the process of changing command for the Halifax Yard, work continued as usual on several vessels. On September 30, Captain Cooke endorsed a voucher from P. M. DeLeon for a partial payment of $15,000.00, payable to Gilbert Elliott & Company for the new ironclad being built at Edwards Ferry.

The J. C. Randolph Company was a vendor of ship's stores at Halifax. Captain Pinkney signed the payment authorization for September acquisitions amounting to $380.00, which accounted for sixty 5½-inch spikes and one stock with six dies.

M. M. Mahon, another Halifax Yard supplier, received $3,165.00 for open account charges from April 30 to September 30. Yard Superintendent Lt. John J. Guthrie had endorsed payment for an assortment of paints, varnish, brushes, linseed oil, putty, white lead, matches, glue, rosin, long screws, a large oven, express charges, and a mule collar. There was even a charge for cooking food for wounded men from Plymouth.[21]

Commander Maffitt's departure might have forecast the *Albemarle's* eventual demise. Politically enforced inactivity, persistent repair difficulties, and the sense of apathy which likely prevailed among the crew affected Warley when he assumed command. The small garrison of troops occupying Plymouth had become dependent on the *Albemarle* for their security. Perhaps because of boredom, James R. Smithwick had asked Lieutenant Warley on October 5 to grant him a fifteen-day furlough to visit his family in Warren County. Ordinary seaman Smithwick probably was an Acting Hospital Steward, since his leave request was approved by Acting Surgeon George A. Foote, and endorsed by Warley and Cooke. Warley did, however, alter the leave date to November 7.[22]

On the same day Admiral Lee ended a routine report to Headquarters Blockading Squadron with an inquiry.

> I have not learned what means the Department has provided for destroying the rebel ram *Albemarle*, to which I invited its attention in a confidential communication of July 9, sent by Lt. Cushing.[23]

Ten days later on October 15, Rear Adm. David D. Porter, Commanding North Atlantic Squadron at Hampton Roads, sent an order to Commander Macomb.

> On the arrival of Lieutenant W. B. Cushing you will supply him with all the men he will need in the performance of the duty assigned him.[24]

Master's Mate John Woodman conducted another reconnaissance expedition to the *Albemarle* on Saturday the fifteenth of October. He began preparations at 3 P.M. by boarding the *Tacony* where he obtained its second cutter with a crew of seven men. At 7 P.M. they went alongside the *Valley City* where they remained until 2 A.M. Then they proceeded up the Middle River to their usual landing site in the swamp. At daylight, Woodman and a companion named Green made their way through the undergrowth to the Roanoke where at 10 A.M. they arrived opposite Plymouth.

> I had a good view of the rebel ram *Albemarle*. She was moored alongside the wharf, head downstream, apparently having no steam. On her port side, which was towards the stream, there are timbers extending from the

wharf and lapping on her prow and stern one-quarter her length from each end, one half her side being protected by piles, the other half being unprotected. At 10:30 A.M. I proceeded down the river toward the *Southfield* and arrived opposite her at Meridian. The *Southfield* is in the same position as last I saw her...except her smokestack being removed. There are two vessels forward, one on each side and two aft, one on each side, having timbers extended across for the purpose of raising the *Southfield*. The work seems to be abandoned for the present.[25]

The next day Rear Adm. David D. Porter in Norfolk confirmed his orders to Secretary Welles. Suspicious of an accident to one of Cushing's two launches, he had sent Cushing who searched with an Army tug to no avail. He then concluded,

> As time is passing and Mr. Cushing was confident of succeeding with one launch, I have sent him to execute his orders.[26]

Porter's concern was centered around the fact that Cushing had lost one of his two launches somewhere in Chesapeake Bay above Norfolk. They were of Cushing's design to be used in his attempt to destroy the *Albemarle*.

From his Headquarters in Norfolk on Saturday October 22, Porter sent further instructions to Macomb. He presented an elaborate review of alternatives which, in his opinion, would "capture that vessel in ten minutes."

His suggested methods were wide ranging. While using canister to fire into her ports, another vessel would strike her stern disabling the rudder. Four gunboats were to approach, two on each side at stern and bow. Riflemen would lay covering fire against the ports preventing their opening for the Brooke rifles. By using grapnels the four vessels could prevent the ironclad from moving by dropping their anchors. Thus boarders could employ hand grenades or flood hot boiler water into the ironclad's hatches and air holes.

With apparent pessimism he concluded,

> I have directed Lieutenant Cushing to go down in a steam launch, and if possible destroy this ram with torpedoes. I have no great confidence in his success, but you

will afford him all the assistance in your power, and keep boats ready to pick him up in case of failure.[27]

All Union plans had been completed. The aggressive leader and his volunteers were enthusiastic. Their target remained oblivious to impending disaster. In five days their plan would be tested.

CHAPTER 15

NOBLE TO THE END

Upon his arrival at the place where the Union fleet was guarding the Roanoke River's mouth, Lt. William B. Cushing immediately reported to Commander Macomb who read the dispatches presented. In short, Cushing needed more men for his unique assignment and Macomb agreed to furnish them. Without stating the duty, commanders of the other ships were asked to request volunteers who would then report aboard the *Shamrock*.

To the volunteers assembled on the *Shamrock's* after deck, Cushing revealed their mission for the first time. He stated his plan grimly.

> Not only must you not expect, but you must not hope to return. I can promise you nothing but glory, death or, possibly, promotion. We will have the satisfaction of getting in a good lick at the rebels, that is all.

Then followed broad details of the planned journey to Plymouth. Under lowering clouds, at about 9 P.M. on October 26, Cushing ran his launch alongside the *Otsego* to pick up additional volunteers for the hazardous assignment. Casting off from the *Otsego*'s anchorage, Cushing di-

LT. WILLIAM B. CUSHING, U.S.N.,
who devised the successful plan to sink the *Albemarle* by a hand placed torpedo on October 28,1864.
Century Magazine, July, 1888

rected helmsman Samuel Higgins to steer the launch for the river's mouth about a mile distant.

A rapidly ebbing tide soon caused the launch to run aground. Not until 2 A.M. on the twenty-seventh was the launch again floating, too late to continue safely, but Cushing decided to proceed anyway. His justification was the feared risk of losing the crew's enthusiasm by waiting another day. Perhaps five hundred yards upriver they were hailed by what turned out to be one of their own army picket launches. Under the visible threat of a bow-mounted howitzer pointing their way they were boarded, examined and recognized. Lieutenant Wilson, the picket commander, offered his apologies for the inconvenience, and in departing respectfully remarked, "got to be careful, Sir." It was then 3 A.M., too close to dawn to continue.

On the trip downriver Cushing recalled how easily the army picket had discovered his launch. Discussing the matter with Master Mates William L. Howorth and Thomas S. Gay, they decided to enclose their engine with a box and muffle the sound with a tarpaulin.

When they were once again aboard the *Shamrock* his crew rested while carpenters boxed the engine. During an early morning conference on the twenty-seventh with Commander Macomb and the *Shamrock's* Executive Officer Lieutenant Duer, they discussed recently received intelligence pertaining to picket and guard strength along the river. They decided that the launch would tow a cutter carrying two officers and eleven heavily armed men.

Lieutenant Duer addressed the ship's crew requesting volunteers for a "dangerous mission from which probably none will return. Only those young men without encumbrances will be accepted." All 275 men stepped forward.

The cutter's crew was to capture pickets on the *Southfield*, thereby preventing advance warning of their attack as they neared the wharf to which the *Albemarle* was moored. It was not until the launch and cutter were well beyond hearing distance of the *Shamrock* that the mission goals were revealed to all hands. By then the time was 8:30 P.M. on the twenty-seventh.

Light winds of sixty-five degrees were southerly. Skies were cloudy with intermittent chilly rain. Almost two hours later by 11:28 P.M. the launch and cutter had reached the Roanoke's mouth and started upriver. It began raining harder as chilly winds increased. Cushing had ordered strict silence as both friendly and hostile sentries lined the eight miles of river banks to Plymouth. For two hours not a sound would be made.

Cushing's crew of fourteen men had been hand picked by their leader. He believed that each was the most capable, experienced, and dependable of those comrades he could have chosen. He believed if his crew was successful in avoiding sentries, and if the *Albemarle* was moored to the wharf as reported, they could capture her by overpowering the watch. Once on board they would cast her loose, start the fires, and steam away. He felt this tactic would be relatively safe since everyone would be within the armored casemate. In anticipation of success he had even brought along the Union flag to fly from her staff.

To avoid being seen, Cushing had plotted a course along the river's right bank [the launch's left] almost under the overhanging trees. About a mile from Plymouth Ensign Gay, who was on the forecastle manning the 12-pdr. howitzer, first saw a schooner's shadowy outline. As the launch silently closed with the schooner, between it and the river bank, the *Southfield's* hulk emerged as a darker shadow in the distance to their starboard.

Because of his previous experience upon the Roanoke John Woodman, as pilot, stood next to helmsman Samuel Higgins. Paymaster Francis Swan sat just behind Cushing and Howorth who were standing aft the forecastle deck. All the men froze in their respective positions as pilot Woodman expertly guided the launch and cutter-in-tow within twenty yards of the silent vessels. They were so close that it would have been impossible to have steered around towards midstream, so Woodman cautiously piloted both boats between the river bank and the vessel's port sides. Luckily they were neither hailed nor fired upon.

The twenty-eight men must have felt triumphant. They would next encounter the *Albemarle*. After silently steaming upriver for another ten minutes, the ironclad's dark mass was silhouetted against a distant light. When abeam the shore light they observed the ironclad was then slightly astern. Circling back, the *Albemarle* could be seen moored to a wharf. To Cushing it appeared the ironclad's capture might yet be successful, but it was destined not to be so easy. As he sheered towards the wharf a nodding sentry's small dog commenced barking. Startled by the persistent barking the sentry hailed the intruders, and began firing towards the two indistinct floating objects. Within seconds a fusillade of shots spattered across the dark waters as someone lit a prepared bonfire nearby. It was about 3 A.M. October 28, 1864.

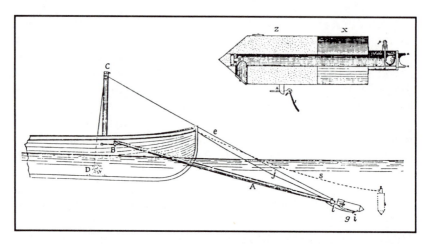

A line drawing of Cushing's launch. The hand operated boom was lowered into position, and by using several hand lines he disengaged and triggered the torpedo.

Century Magazine, July, 1888

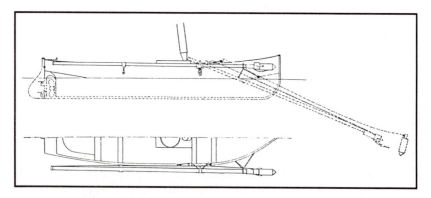

Side and deck elevations of Lt. Cushing's steam launch are reasonable facsimilies of the original concept. A torpedo boom was horizontally rigged for transport. To deploy, it was extended forward through a sling device. Cushing stood forward of the stack and manipulated the torpedo's placement, release, and subsequent firing by pulling on various lanyards.

The launch's size was sufficient to accommodate Cushing and his crew of fourteen volunteers.

Official Records of the Union and Confederate Navies in the War of the Rebellion, Ser. I, Vol. X

About a week earlier Col. John N. Whitford had assumed command of the Plymouth garrison with the 67th Regiment. Their duty was to guard the *Albemarle*. Within several days Colonel Whitford, Lieutenant Warley and Captain Lee had been duly informed of a torpedo boat's presence at the river's mouth.

Acting on this information Warley had doubled the *Albemarle's* watch and taken extra precaution since rumors suggested the Union was up to something. Several artillery pieces commanded by Captain Lee had been emplaced along the river bank adjacent to the ironclad.

Earlier in the evening of the twenty-seventh there had been a "grand bacchanalian feast and dance in Plymouth" which may have accounted for the snoozing sentry. The barking dog also alerted the officer of the deck who sighted the approaching boats. He rang the bell, and opened fire with the watch who had quickly joined him.

Officers and men aboard scrambled to quarters. The shutter port facing the enemy's boat was opened, grape shot was hastily loaded into the Brooke, its muzzle was depressed to the limit and the command to fire was awaited. Though numbers of soldiers had begun firing from the shore, the artillery battery remained silent except for one piece which, when fired, was too late.

With shots arriving like hail Cushing shouted, "cast off, Peterkin, and go down and get those pickets on the schooner near the *Southfield*." The launch leaped forward as the cutter's drag was eliminated, and then Engineer William Stotesbury further opened the steam valves when Cushing called "ahead fast." Because of poor visibility Cushing had to exercise special care in the launch's approach, since accuracy of placement was necessary to assure maximum damage from the torpedo's detonation.

By the bonfire's flickering reflections off the water and the ironclad's casemate, Cushing detected exactly where the protecting log boom was located. To emplace the torpedo it was necessary to be inside the log's semicircle. Shouting "full speed" to Howorth, he ordered Woodman to guide the launch towards the stream in a sweeping turn to head towards the logs. Standing erect aft the casemate with bullets whistling like swarming bees, Cushing ordered Gay to swing the torpedo boom around into place. In an instant Cushing pulled the howitzer's lanyard sending a dose of canister buzzing against the iron casemate. Some of it spattered into the mass of men standing fire-lit upon the shore.

Artist's conception of how Cushing's launch rode over the *Albemarle's* protective log boom as he steamed to attack. *Naval Historical Center*

The canister momentarily diverted the *Albemarle's* gunner's attention, allowing Cushing's launch to strike the log boom with a grinding crunch where it balanced with bow out of water. Cushing stumbled, but quickly regained his footing. As he looked up he stared into a Brooke muzzle about ten or fifteen feet away. From inside he could hear commands being given to load and fire. He had just seconds left. In his right hand was the torpedo release cord, in his left was the trigger pin cord. Both had to be slowly but steadily pulled, the release first, the trigger last. From the moment of impact the torpedo boom was being winched down. Standing calmly, waiting for the torpedo to be completely submerged, Cushing was hit several times by shots from the *Albemarle's* riflemen. The back of his coat was torn away, and a bullet removed the sole of one shoe. He firmly pulled the release cord, counted to five as the torpedo rose under the ironclad's hull, and then pulled the trigger cord.

There was no time to duck. Two dreadful explosions occurred together. An immense wave of water erupted from beneath the hull engulfing the launch as it descended. Simultaneously the Brooke's

Blasts from the torpedo and cannon were simultaneous. Riflemen on the *Albemarle* joined with those on shore in firing at Cushing's launch. An immense wave of water was thrust upwards and into the launch, just as the cannon blast tore above Cushing's men.

Unidentified artist, author's collection

blast slammed everyone in the launch, though the grape passed just over their heads. The flame and hot air belching from its muzzle may have accounted for injuries to some of Cushing's men. The launch was flattened, swamped with water, and the crew devastated.

Lieutenant Warley had been standing on the gun deck as the Brooke was fired and simultaneously heard,

> A report as of an unshotted gun, and a piece of wood fell at my feet. I called for the carpenter and told him a torpedo had been exploded, and ordered him to examine [the hull below] and report...saying nothing to anyone else. He soon reported "a hole in her bottom big enough to drive a wagon in." I found her resting on the bottom in eight feet of water, her upper works above water.

The torpedo had exploded just beneath the port quarter knuckle. Water rushed through the huge hole so fast all efforts to stem the

While some jumped, others of Cushing's crew were thrown into the water when the wave hit their launch. Only four swam away, and of those, two survived the cold water.

Unidentified artist, author's collection

flow were in vain. Within a few moments the *Albemarle* was on the
bottom with only her shield and smokestack above water.

There was one known casualty among the *Albemarle's* crew of
sixty. Acting Masters Mate James Charles Hill sustained severe injury when the hatchway fell upon him while he was asleep in his
bunk as the explosion occurred.

Amidst the scramble for survival outside the *Albemarle*, Cushing
staggered to his feet after the blast while stripping off his pistol,
sword, coat and shoes as he shouted to his crew, "men, save your-
selves" before he dove into the cold river. Several others took to the
water also, but they were soon separated in the darkness. Searchers
with torches in small boats were then approaching. Some survivors
were found clinging to the launch, and others were holding to the
logs around the ironclad.

Unobserved in the darkness, Cushing and three companions
swam away from the wreck. Edward J. Houghton escaped as did
Cushing. John Woodman and Samuel Higgins were subsequently
drowned from exhaustion in the cold water. Cushing swam towards
the struggling Higgins who was calling for help, but could not reach
him in time. Much later after being carried by the current he encountered Woodman, but was unable to get him ashore. On several
occasions when searchers came too close, Cushing would submerge
beneath the water until they had passed.

When well below Plymouth he managed to reach the shore,
but was too weak to crawl from the water until daylight. After traveling through a swamp for several hours he encountered a black
man whom he sent for information. It was by this means that
Cushing learned the *Albemarle* had truly been sunk. Through that
day and into the night he floundered in the swamps until he luckily
acquired a skiff. He paddled down the river and into the Sound until
he sighted the anchored *Valley City*. Able to hail the ship only once
at about 10:15 P.M. he collapsed in the skiff, where he was later
found by Ensign Milton Webster commanding an armed boat crew
sent to investigate. By 11 P.M. on October 28 he was confirming the
Albemarle's destruction to authorities on board the *Shamrock*, where
he had been transferred from the *Valley City*.

Lieutenant Warley reported the destruction of his ship on October 28 in a letter to Secretary Mallory. He sought to absolve himself of responsibility since the pickets below had given no advance
warning of the approaching launch, even though it was known such

The *Albemarle* resting on the Roanoke River bottom at Plymouth. Note the open gunport shutters and forward starboard casemate section that was blown out by orders of Lt. Warley.
An engraving from a photograph by J. O. Davidson. North Carolina Division of Archives and History

a craft was nearby. Also contributing to his ship's demise was the absence of artillery protection, although one piece did fire belatedly. Warley concluded his report to Mallory by requesting a Court of Inquiry to establish "on whose shoulders rests the blame of the loss of the *Albemarle.*"

A serious accusation of the guard force's incompetence was implied in a letter soldier J. U. Edmundson wrote.

> A member of Col. Whitford's regiment who was cognizant of the facts informs me "that his Adjutant neglected to give the pickets who were stationed in the river a few miles in the direction of the Sound any signal or countersign."

After Warley had surveyed the *Albemarle's* damage, and determined to his satisfaction she could not be refloated, he assigned half the crew to sink the schooner near the *Southfield.* The remaining crewmen set up two 8-inch guns on platforms commanding the upper river approaches. From the *Albemarle* they fished out tackles, a few shells, and waited.

Messrs. Long and Shelly performed a creditable job in manning the guns, but were overwhelmed by the returning Union fleet. Before Warley was forced to leave he administered a coup de grace to the sturdy vessel, that had prevailed against the enemy's longest odds, when he ordered an explosive charge be detonated inside her forward casemate which blew out both forward and top sections.[1]

By the morning of October 29, 1864, a flurry of messages applauding Cushing's exploit had begun to circulate among commands of the Atlantic Blockading Squadron, and to Secretary Welles. With the *Albemarle's* threat eliminated, Union forces anticipated their return to Eastern North Carolina via the Roanoke River. A condensed report of the explosive encounter resulting in the *Albemarle's* sinking was prepared by Commander Macomb for Admiral Porter on the twenty-ninth. In that report he had omitted mention of the fact that an expedition was then underway to retake Plymouth.[2]

Seeking the advantage of surprise, knowing that great consternation had spread at Plymouth over the *Albemarle's* loss, Commander Macomb steamed through the Middle River on Sunday October 30, with a fleet of five gunboats to attack the defenses above Plymouth and shell the town from long range.

The next day Macomb formed a battle line with the *Commodore Hull* in the van. Following in order were the *Tacony*, with the *Whitehead* lashed to her port; the *Shamrock* with the tug *Bazely* lashed alongside; the *Otsego* with tug *Belle* also lashed alongside, and the *Wyalusing*. The flotilla bombarded batteries and rifle pits at close range. After an enormous magazine explosion Confederate forces began their evacuation, whereupon Macomb signalled a cease fire. His forces landed, occupied Fort Williams and again hoisted the Stars and Stripes over Plymouth as Monday, October 31 ended.[3]

On the same day Catherine Edmondston had acknowledged in her Journal the *Albemarle* had been sunk. She also noted their young seventeen-year-old neighbor James C. Hill had been wounded in the ankle.[4]

During Tuesday morning November 1 Macomb appointed a survey team to examine the *Albemarle* and prepare a damage report. When they returned later that day Macomb eagerly reviewed their findings.

She is sunk at the wharf and heading downstream, heeling offshore at an angle of about 10 degrees; the flat part of the casemate on the port side is 22 inches out of the water. We find the entire top of the casemate blown off.... As it is reported that she was again blown up by the rebel authorities after she was sunk by Lt. Cushing, it is impossible to say how much of the damage was done by him. Her armament consists of two 8-inch rifle guns worked on pivots, so as to fire either from the side or ahead; one of these guns is partly out of water, the other entirely immersed. Her machinery is entirely submerged, so that it is impossible to examine it.[5]

Adm. David D. Porter's dispatch at 1:25 P.M. on November 1 to Secretary Welles briefly mentioned Cushing's success in sinking the *Albemarle*. In concluding he reminded Porter, "I promised Cushing promotion to another grade if he succeeded. Hope the Department will honor the promise if the report is corroborated."[6]

The same day Macomb sent Porter further details concerning events of the twenty-eighth. He had examined the *Albemarle* after Plymouth had been retaken and told Porter the ironclad was down as far as her ports, and the top casemate plating was entirely blown off. He had since ordered a survey of which copies were included.[7]

In another report of substantial length to Porter that day, Macomb presented the news that Plymouth was again under Union control. He mentioned the *Albemarle* only to say her colors were captured.[8]

Secretary Mallory produced a periodic Naval Activity report on the first of November. He called attention to increased shipbuilding at Edwards Ferry. On the stocks was a light draft wooden gunboat mounting two guns for use in the Roanoke. Navy Department-furnished engines were ready for installation, but had been delayed because workmen from the Naval Iron Works had been called to the field. He also publicly confirmed that a contract had been signed with Messrs. Elliott & Smith for a light draft four-gun ironclad to be built at Edwards Ferry. Armor for this vessel would be rolled from railroad iron purchased in North Carolina. At Richmond the boilers and some machinery were ready.[9]

By November 2 Catherine Edmondston had received the news from Plymouth, and in her Journal she wrote,

This act of Lt. Warley's cannot be sufficiently con-
demned. It is premature to say the least of it, for until the
Yankees actually entered the place, or the terms of capitu-
lation were about to be discussed, it was his duty to stand
by his ship & resolutely defend her. She lay in water so
shallow that her guns were not submerged & ten days work
would have set her afloat again. But no! The fashion set
by Commander Tatnall, when he blew up the *Virginia*,
must be followed by every other numbskull in the Confederate Navy who, like him, gets drunk and neglects his
duty. The explosion covers up all. He goes off in a blaze of
glory and nonsensical heroism, but takes excellent care
that his own person shall not suffer.[10]

Mrs. Edmondston was expressing the frustration, and disappointment generally felt by her fellow North Carolinians. Then again,
maybe she knew of the midnight party at Plymouth on that fateful
night. However, she made a valid point about fighting the *Albemarle*
from where she lay. With a bow and stern gun she could have held
the river above and below Plymouth. Properly placed shore batteries
up and down the river could have created a deterrence had the fleet
approached. The placing of additional torpedoes below town, and
others above at the Middle River's junction, could also have impeded
the returning Union fleet.

Macomb wrote a question-filled letter to Porter on November
the sixth. After expressing his views on how to contain Plymouth
with his naval forces, he asked if there were plans for the *Albemarle's*
disposition. In his opinion she might be raised if proper submarine
and hoisting apparatus was available. Macomb envisioned a use for
the ironclad in the U.S. Navy, but if Porter thought otherwise, then
it would be dangerous to leave her at the present site "for the rebels
would certainly make use of her armor, so perhaps she should be
destroyed." As an afterthought he added that the steamer *Southfield*
might be raised by the same apparatus.

In responding two days later Porter requested Macomb to, "see
if the ram *Albemarle* can be raised, and tell me what is wanted. There
is a ram building at Halifax, up the Roanoke River. Can you not get
up there?" [11]

On the tenth Macomb sent Porter corrected information pertaining to the *Albemarle's* survey conducted nine days before.

Shortly after recapturing Plymouth, Union soldiers and sailors visited the *Albemarle*.
Photograph by Mayhew & Brothers. Courtesy of The New-York Historical Society, N.Y.C.

I beg leave to correct a mistake made by the board in surveying the late C.S. ram *Albemarle*. They stated that the guns were 8-inch Brooke rifles, but I find by careful measurement that they are but 6 $^{23}/_{48}$ inches bore.

The following day in his correspondence to Porter, Macomb included a captured letter from Secretary Mallory to Captain Cooke. It was dated May 26, 1864, and referred to an imminent launching of the Halifax gunboat. In closing he suggested,

As there is not water enough in this river, except during the freshets, for vessels of this class [*Shamrock*] to ascend as far as Halifax, I would respectfully suggest a land force may be sent to destroy their ironclad before she is completed.[12]

Admiral Porter followed through on the fourteenth with Macomb's suggestion, by recommending to Secretary Welles that the *Albemarle* be raised. He also advised placing a salvage party under contract to begin work as soon as possible. That same day Macomb informed Porter of the three schooners then obstructing the Roanoke's channel. He requested orders for their disposition, and if they could be considered prizes. In closing he stated that "the barricade below the town still remains...has been strengthened, and another has been made above the town and fleet." [13]

Mrs. Edmondston had learned that Captain Cooke was in very bad health. In a neighborly gesture on the seventeenth, she baked him a loaf of bread to relieve the discomfort of severe weather.[14]

Fearing that his previous mail had not been received by Macomb, Admiral Porter again ordered Macomb on November 20 to,

> Dismount all the captured guns and send them to me. Use all the ammunition that will suit for the vessels under your command. Send here all naval stores, copper, lead, or brass. Leave no rebel guns anywhere that may be captured. Raise the *Albemarle* if possible. Communicate with me more often.[15]

Macomb had further news for Porter on the twenty-fourth, when he related that an escaped Union black prisoner, who may have been captured near Fort Branch, brought news from upriver that,

> The rebels are laying torpedoes in the Roanoke below Rainbow Bluff, at a place called Poplar Point. They have eighteen guns at Rainbow Bluff, the largest of which is a 64-pounder. Poplar Point is about 3 miles below the Bluff. The pilot of the *Albemarle*, whose name is Hopkins, was trying to get recruits for Lt. Cushing's [captured] torpedo boat to come down and blow up one of the double-enders. The rebel force was said to be 3,000." [16]

On November 25 Macomb sent a long review of events to Porter. He restated his opinion that the *Albemarle* could be raised with proper equipment, but without it the attempt would be hopeless. If it were left, and Plymouth exchanged captors again, he was fearful she would indeed be raised and worked against the Union. He also confirmed that her guns were being disabled. To insure that Porter would have the latest news, he was sending his latest response by Lt. Cdr. Earl English.[17]

Recommendations that U.S. Army attacking forces invade the upper Roanoke River to capture Fort Branch at Rainbow Bluff were being seriously considered. As set forth in Porter's letter of November 28 to Maj. Gen. Benjamin F. Butler, Commanding Department of Virginia and North Carolina at Fortress Monroe, 1500 troops, or

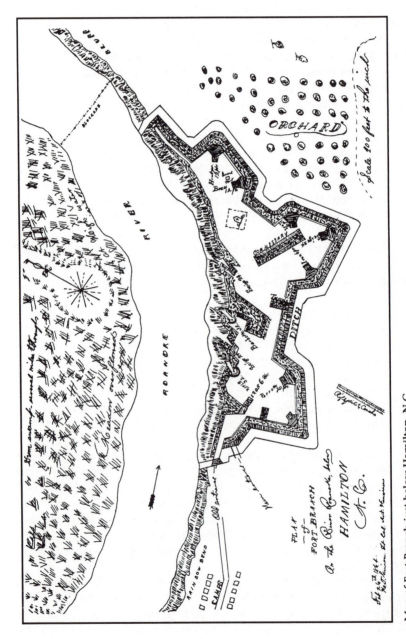

Map of Fort Branch just below Hamilton, N.C.
Drawn by Lt. Col. Henry T. Guion, Artillery & Engineers. Rare book room, William R. Perkins Library, Duke University, Durham, North Carolina

one half of those then at New Bern could be detached for that expedition. By landing six miles below the Bluffs they could easily capture the fort, guns and ammunition. It would then be an easy march to Halifax where the ram could be destroyed.[18]

Macomb's flotilla was cautiously ascending the Roanoke at Jamesville by December 9. By evening Macomb ordered the fleet to anchor while waiting for units of the army to arrive. The Army-Navy campaign to take Fort Branch, on their way to Edwards Ferry and Halifax, had begun. While anchoring at 9:15 P.M. the *Otsego* struck a torpedo and began sinking. Within ten minutes, a second blast under her foremast ripped a larger hole through which water gushed to sink her in 2½ fathoms. The *Bazely* was dropping anchor, but in rushing to the *Otsego's* aid struck a torpedo and sank.

Porter dispatched a preliminary report of the event to Secretary Welles on the twelfth. He had received no confirmation of events from sources at Jamesville, aside from evidence that the torpedoes had been fired by wires from the river's bank.[19]

Attempting to allay Porter's doubt that he was progressing up the Roanoke, Macomb reported from a point seven miles above Jamesville on December 13 that he had every intention of reaching Rainbow Bluff, and of pressing further upriver to destroy the ironclad under construction. Later the same day while torpedo-dragging two miles further upriver, Macomb's boats had found a new nest of twenty-one torpedoes emplaced in a curve called Shad Island Bend. In spite of these delays, he claimed progress of five miles each day. [20]

Without Commander Macomb's knowledge, army units commanded by Col. Jones Frankle waited in vain at Williamston on December 11 for the navy to arrive. Pushing on that night they arrived at Spring Green near Hamilton about 1 A.M. on the twelfth. Learning the Confederate forces were entrenched north of Butler's Bridge over the Coniho creek, Frankle's troops engaged the defenders near dawn at the bridge, but later they retreated back to Williamston.

The coordinated Army-Navy attack upon Fort Branch, Edwards Ferry and Halifax was a failure, for the navy had been delayed by removing unforeseen numbers of torpedoes from the Roanoke River.[21]

By December 15 a submarine diver had arrived at Plymouth and inspected the *Albemarle*. He must have been optimistic about raising her, since he quickly left to assemble his equipment on the same day. Not being aware of that turn of events, Macomb had asked Plymouth authorities to send the diver to examine the *Otsego*. The same day he also received Colonel Frankle's message that he was falling back to Plymouth for recruiting and rest. Macomb decided to proceed alone.[22]

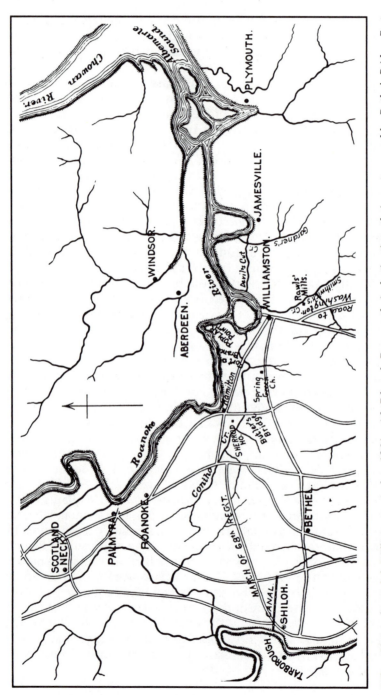

When Union forces left Williamston in late 1864, with Edwards Ferry as their destination, their route passed by Butler's Bridge, Fort Branch, and Hamilton.

Catherine Edmondston comprehended the invader's ultimate goal when she wrote on the twentieth,

> Their object is supposed to be the destruction of the gunboats now building within two miles of us. Since the wanton destruction of the *Albemarle,* I have not the enthusiasm I once had in the construction of gunboats. It seems but time and labour lost.[23]

The vessels mentioned were one light draft 2-gun wooden gunboat, and one light draft 4-gun ironclad being built at Edwards Ferry.[24] On December 21 she noted that the invaders were returning via Bertie County on the river's north side. From all reports "their destination was again the Edwards Ferry yard" said Brig. Gen. Collett Leventhrope, commanding Confederate forces at Hamilton.[25]

Among the regiments protecting Fort Branch during mid-December was the 68th Regiment, N.C. Infantry. It may have been known to Gilbert Elliott that his cousin from Elizabeth City, Lt. William Harrison Elliott of Company B, was among those defending the Fort.

As the year 1865 began, the Union increased its attention to shipbuilding along the Roanoke. With increasing frequency there were routine exchanges of messages between commanders calling for action to destroy the vessel, or proposing how best to accomplish the fact. On January 24, 1865, Brig. Gen. Innis N. Palmer, Commanding District of North Carolina at Fortress Monroe, wrote Lt. Gen. Ulysses S. Grant at City Point explaining in great detail the strategy required to retake eastern North Carolina. Everything hinged upon destroying the new ironclad under construction at Edwards Ferry. Palmer recommended "that it would require but little ingenuity to carry one of our ironclads or rams over the bar at Hatteras Inlet, and I cannot too strongly urge this matter to your attention."[26] When Grant received Palmer's letter, he added his endorsement in a followup message to Secretary Welles citing mounting concern about the new Roanoke ironclad.[27]

Mrs. Edmondston's Journal entry on the twenty-sixth told of a Yankee column advancing in Northhampton County. Their object was destruction of the Edwards Ferry yard and the ironclad a short distance from her home.[28] The next day she had gratifying news that the Yankees were retreating. Upon visiting the gunboat, her husband had learned that two companies of cavalry had been ferried across the river after dark the night before. For the crossing they had borrowed her father's flat.[29]

On January 31 Secretary Welles acknowledged General Grant's endorsement of General Palmer's January 24 letter, and suggested the same day to Admiral Porter that measures be taken against disaster.[30] In the absence of the diver who was to raise the *Albemarle*, Porter sent equipment plans to Macomb in hopes a pumping devise could be made on site. On February 6 he directed Macomb to continue working night and day to raise the ironclad.

Referring to the pump plans he sent earlier, Porter thought they would raise her in a few hours "if you can get canvas over the hole." He closed by asking "if the submarine man was there, and had he done anything?" [31]

Porter addressed a letter of assurance to Grant on February 11, in which he reviewed precautionary measures then in place to prohibit the suspicioned ram from entering the Sound. In conclusion he said, "the ram *Albemarle* is being raised, but could not be made available in four months, except to sink as an obstruction."[32]

By the fifteenth Macomb revealed further details concerning efforts to raise the *Albemarle*.

> I had 12 more [box pumps] made here and sent them to Plymouth. The diver states that he has stopped the leaks in the bottom of the ram...but the casemate, which is partially submerged, is much shattered...which the rebels exploded in her after she sank. Mr. Underdown, the head of the submarine party, wrote me yesterday from Norfolk stating he would get his steam pump down on the 11th, and he had no doubt but he could raise the *Albemarle*.[33]

The Edwards Ferry yard welcomed two visitors on the twentieth when neighbors Mr.and Mrs. Edmondston stopped by to inspect the gunboat. In her Journal that day Mrs. Edmondston remarked,

> I had no idea how rapidly the work had gone on nor of what a fine large boat it is! Messrs. Smith and Elliott, the contractors, deserve the greatest credit for the energetic manner in which they have carried it so near to completion.

The next day they again visited the Yard in company of Captain and Mrs. Cooke who were entertaining a group of young people from Scotland Neck.[34]

Commander Macomb had good news for Admiral Porter when his report of March 20 was prepared. Two days earlier the submarine operators had succeeded in raising the *Albemarle,* and had kept her afloat for two days by running the pumps continuously because a few leaks were unsealed. Macomb repeated the remarks of work party chief Mr. Brown, who had told him that he "would have to strip off all the iron from the casemate in order to lighten her sufficiently to stop leaks near the overhang." Brown held a conversation about raising the ironclad with naval constructor Mr. Lenthall who was prompted to say "the casemate would have to be taken off when the ship was being repaired at the Navy Yard." In a tone of finality Macomb said,

> So I see no objection to the armor being stripped from her casemate now. It is very doubtful whether she could be taken through the canal without relieving her of this great weight.[35]

Two escaped prisoners, an army captain and lieutenant captured by the Confederates at Kinston, reported to Macomb on March 24 with news from a black man who had worked on the Roanoke ironclad that she was planked, but had no iron attached, and they had no certainty if iron would be delivered. They had not learned if engines were installed.[36]

During the day on April 7 a squad of pickets visited the Edmonstons at Looking Glass, their river home, with news that the enemy was approaching from Northampton with intention of burning the ram. Being advised to conceal their valuables as quickly as possible, she and Mr. Edmondston buried money, title deeds, his Confederate Commission, and other important articles in a large jar and anxiously awaited the worst. Just as it became dark,

> The whole hemisphere was suddenly lighted up with lurid flames whose origin none could be blind to. It was the gunboat!
> Silently & solemnly it burned on, whilst we stood an excited group & listened for some sound indicating the presence of the enemy, but none came. When reassured we went into our tea, when a sudden heavy footstep on the piazza sent all the blood to my heart, but it proved to

be only Captain Cooke, who after ordering the firing of this boat came over to bid us adieu, as orders are out for the evacuation of this whole country...so we concluded that as the burning of the gunboat gave us little respite that we would go out there ourselves the next day & by burning & concealing our valuable papers try and prepare for this interruption of irresponsible vandals upon us.

On the eighth, while at Hascosea [west of Hills Cross Road] we sorted private papers, destroying some, and made preparations for the future.[37]

William Waggner was an accountant working at Edwards Ferry, so it became his duty on Saturday April 8, 1865, to certify that,

At the time of the destruction by fire of the Ironclad Gunboat building by Messrs. Gilbert Elliott & Co., according to the foregoing contract with Constructor John L. Porter, C.S.N. at this place, which burning took place on the night of April 7th, 1865, by order of Captain J. W. Cooke, C.S.N., seven twelfths of the work was done upon said vessel.

I further certify that the amount now due Messrs. Gilbert Elliott & Co. under said contract is Eighty Seven Thousand Three Hundred and sixty two & $^{49}/_{100}$ dollars. Witness in presence of E. L. Price.[38]

Catherine Edmondston kept her Journal throughout the war from June 1860 through the end of hostilities. Though consecutive in style, her entries were not always from day to day. For news of the conflict beyond her immediate neighborhood, she depended heavily upon news print, letters, and the spoken word of friends, family, and strangers. In cases where she recorded events from far places, the news was often stale.

During the preceding days she had known Confederate forces were steadily being diminished at Petersburg, Richmond, and closer to home those of General Joseph Johnston. The Edmondstons probably feared the worst. Unknown to them within their home along the Roanoke, General Robert E. Lee, after thoughtfully weighing his options, would make the most difficult decision of his career. Little did the Edmondstons and their friends know that General Lee would surrender his spent forces to General Grant in the Wilmer McLean house at Appomattox Courthouse on Sunday April 9, 1865.

On the day the war ended Lt. Charles L. Franklin, of the *Iosco*, submitted a report of his reconnaissance up the Roanoke to locate evidence of a floating battery said to have been seen below Jamesville. He found the battery sunk on a middle-of-the-river sand bar nearly nine miles above Plymouth. It rested in about 2½ to 3 fathoms of water with only about two feet of the casemate being visible. Since he had ordered the mission, Macomb read the detailed report with great interest.

> I found it to be a four-sided box, 20 feet square at the top, with sides sloping at an angle of about 45 degrees. Height between decks, 8 feet, the box composed of heavy timber frames with a layer of yellow pine 1½ feet thick. On two of the sides this pine was covered with 6-inch oak, bolted athwart-ships [from side to side as opposed to fore and aft]. I found two ports on either side. [I] sounded with oars and boat hooks over her floor, but could discover no evidence of scuttling...to complete her ruin I cut in the pine end three beds for seating fires, and after filling them with combustibles and pitch wood I fired the work myself, withdrew my men and returned. The fires were blazing as long as I could see her in my glass.

When he read that a local fisherman spoke of hearing what he had supposed were one or two guns firing upriver on the fifth near the *Ceres* at the obstructions, Macomb judged a torpedo had been responsible for the sinking.[39] No doubt it was Elliott's unfinished floating battery of which so little was recorded.

One day after Appomattox the *Albemarle* was floating upon the Sound. Being towed by the *Ceres* with escorts *Martin* and *Belle*, she left Plymouth in the afternoon headed for Norfolk. Once across the North River bar the *Belle* returned to Plymouth.[40] The *Albemarle's* destiny would eventually be determined after it's arrival at Norfolk Navy Yard.

The New York Herald published a short story on Saturday April 15 about the *Albemarle* having been raised from the Roanoke River. They described her structure, evidence of battle damage, and items found within her hull after being pumped dry by salvager Underwood and Company.

> The celebrated rebel ram *Albemarle* has been raised...and is now lying in North River, N.C., at the mouth of the canal waiting to be towed into Norfolk. They have been nearly a month in getting her up....She is not seriously injured...her boilers and machinery are uninjured and she is at present under steam.
>
> The *Albemarle* was one of the most formidable rams of the Confederacy...she has several indentations in her sides from the different shots and shells fired at her, and an unexploded shell was found buried under her iron plating. In her were found officers clothing, arms, and twenty-eight cans of powder. She had Liverpool coal on board, which must have run the blockade.[41]

The *Albemarle* was moored in ordinary storage at the Norfolk Navy Yard in April 1865. Numerous iron plates had been removed from her casemate and hull to reduce weight before she was towed from Plymouth to Norfolk. The route of her last journey was across Albemarle Sound to North River, through North River Canal, up Currituck Sound to a canal connecting with the Elizabeth River and on into the Norfolk Yard.
U.S. Army Military History Institute, Carlisle, Pa.

On April 27, 1865, Capt. John M. Berrien, Commanding Naval Station Norfolk, proclaimed to Navy Secretary Gideon Welles in Washington, D.C., "I have the honor to inform the Department that the *Albemarle*, late rebel ram, arrived at this yard today in tow of the U.S.S. *Ceres*." [42]

Norfolk officials wasted no time in surveying the *Albemarle* to estimate her value. On May 18, 1865, an in-depth review of her structure was completed by Commander Henry N. T. Arnold, Naval Constructor J. Hanscom, and Chief Engineer John H. Long. To Commandant of the Navy Yard John M. Berrien they submitted their findings.

> In obedience to your order annexed we have carefully examined the hull and engines of the rebel ram *Albemarle* and beg leave to report that we have estimated her value as follows, viz:

Hull and Plating	$77,444.00
Steam Machinery	15,000.00
Total Worth	$92,444.00
Repairs to Hull	20,000.00
Repairs to Machinery	1,500.00
Total Repairs Cost	$21,500.00

> The dimensions of the vessel are as follows, viz: Extreme length, 158 ft.; Extreme Breadth, 35 ft. 3 in.; Breadth of beam on deck, 32 ft.; Depth of hold from top of beam to top of floor, 8 ft. 2 in.; Load draft, 9 ft. She had a flat bottom and straight sides, as will be seen by the enclosed midship section, and is built of yellow pine. The frame, deck beams and planking are fastened with iron and treenails. The vessel was plated two feet below the knuckle and to the deck above with two thicknesses of one-inch. Forward and aft of the casemate the deck was covered with one-inch plating and the casemate with two thicknesses of two-inch iron. All the plating above the knuckle and part of that below has been taken off. Two sections of the casemate have been started by explosion. The torpedo exploded against her side, broke one of the planks and sprung five timbers. The bottom is not covered with anything to protect it from the worms, and in the repairs it is contemplated to cover it with sheet zinc.

There are two horizontal non-condensing engines fitted with the link motion to two propellers by means of four gear wheels. Diameter of cylinders, 18 inches; Stroke of cylinders, 19 inches; Diameter of driving wheels at pitch line, 2 ft. 9½ in. Diameter of pinions at pitch line, 2 ft. 6 in.; Face of wheels, 9 inches; Diameter of propellers, 6 ft; Number of blades, 3; Pitch, 9 ft.

There are two boilers each containing one furnace, and having two elliptical and vertical water tubes for the return. Length of boilers, 15 ft. 4 in.; Height of boilers, 5 ft. 2 in.; Width of boilers, 4 ft. 7 in.; Diameter of Shell, 4 ft. 7 in.; Length of furnace, 4 ft. 6 in.; Width of furnace, 4 ft.; Height of flue, 1 ft. 9 in.; Average width of flues, 9 in.; Number of tubes in each boiler, 120; Diameter of steam drums, 2 ft. 8 in.; Height of steam drum, 1 ft. 6 in.; Outside diameter of tubes, 3¼ in.; Length of tubes, 1 ft. 10 in. All the pipes connected with the engines and boilers are of cast iron. There is a small piece broken off one blade of each propeller, and the smoke pipe is gone. The engines and boilers are in fair condition and need but few repairs. [43]

Upon conclusion of the Washington Prize Court deliberations, the *Albemarle* was purchased by the Navy for $79,944.00. The Navy had made no immediate plans for rebuilding the *Albemarle* so she was taken into service, and placed in ordinary [laid up, out of commission] at Norfolk Naval Yard.[44]

After determining that her hull had deteriorated beyond repair, the Navy ordered Commodore Augustus H. Kilty to dispose of surplus vessels at public auction. They were the *Agawam, Seneca,* Confederate ironclads *Texas, Columbia,* and ram *Albemarle.*

For sixteen months the *Albemarle* had remained moored to an obscure wharf in the Norfolk Yard. Her hull was constructed without exterior surface worm protection, and after being tied to a remote wharf for about sixteen months yard authorities became aware of the deteriorated wood. With her iron plating removed, additiional wood damage might have been evident to early bidders' inspections.

A brief human interest story appeared in the October 9, 1867, Norfolk Journal. The reporter related having met "the distinguished Confederate Captain James W. Cooke walking on crutches." When queried about his injuries, Cooke replied "he had fallen from the roof of his house but had broken no limbs."

Before the *Albemarle* was auctioned on October 10, 1867, the Yard commander is said to have invited Mrs. James W. Cooke to board the vessel and be photographed. It was further related he had the picture framed in oak and presented as a gift. One of the two ladies standing on the fore deck may well have been Mrs. Cooke.

Credit story, The Scotland Neck Commonwealth, Feb. 16, 1922.
Photograph courtesy of Naval Historical Center

A part of Elliott's life was placed on the auction block at Norfolk Navy Yard the next day. On the same page of the <u>Norfolk Journal</u> announcing the Navy Yard sale, was an advertisement by Smith, Elliott & Co. Groceries, offering refined sugars from Porto Rico and Cuba [sic.], molasses, coffee, candles, flour, fish, salt, whiskey, gin, rum and brandy.

Gilbert Elliott's *Albemarle*, having been held in ordinary since May 1865, was one of five ships to be sold on October 10, 1867 at 11 A.M. The *Albemarle* was simply advertised.

> Having 2 non-condensing engines, 18-inch cylinders, 20 inches stroke, 2 propellers, 2 vertical tubular boilers, 1 furnace in each boiler. The articles herein expressed will be sold with the vessel, and nothing more.

Buyers and speculators from Boston, New York, Philadelphia, and Baltimore were present. Auctioneers Messrs. Maupin & Hatton conducted the sale. It was stipulated in advance that terms would require "twenty percent of purchase money to be deposited by purchaser at sale's conclusion, and the remainder within two weeks when the vessels must be removed by their owners. Bills of sale will then be made." It was reported in the <u>Norfolk Journal</u> of October 11, 1867, that Mr. J. Wilder acquired Elliott's creation for $2,500.00. [45]

When Secretary Mallory first proposed his defensive ironclad fleet, there were those who envisioned it to be ineffective, and others who were optimistic. As the ironclads became waterborne and were baptized by combat their numbers began to dwindle. Most often, when overcome by superior fire power or force of numbers, their commanders would order them exploded, burned to avoid capture, or as it happened to some, they were grounded in error.

So repetitious was their destruction that a crewman from the *Savannah* asserted that "if we are attacked we will follow the course of the other ironclads and either blowup or get captured."

Such a pessimistic attitude was not shared among the *Albemarle's* officers and crew. From commissioning on April 17, 1864 until after the May 5 encounter with seven of the Union's fleet in Albemarle Sound, their esprit de corps and loyalty to their commander and ship was not exceeded elsewhere.

The *Albemarle*, broken and stripped of its armor waiting salvage. Note the ruptured casemate section which had been blown out by Lt. Warley just after she was sunk.

U.S. Army Military History Institute, Carlisle, Pa.

In all, Mallory's armored fleet numbered over fifty-two hulls, of which more than thirty were laid down but not finished, and twenty-two completed and launched. Of these, four were captured while the rest were destroyed by the Confederates to prevent capture. All, that is, except the *Albemarle*, who earned the distinction of having been the only Confederate ironclad destroyed by enemy action.

Aside from Captain Cooke, his officer staff, and the few professional seamen delivered by General Hoke, the rest of her crew was mostly composed of local folk determined to defend their families and property. Known ages of those aboard ranged from twelve to fifty-two. As individuals they would forever proudly remember having served aboard the Ironclad of The Roanoke.

EPILOGUE

It may have been because of the war, or of his shipbuilding obliga-
tions, that Gilbert and Lucy Ann Hill had not married during the
war years. In all probability they saw each other frequently, since
Edwards Ferry Yard was not far from Kenmore, her family's estate.
With the war's end, and his naval shipbuilding career over, Gilbert
Elliott began a lifelong commitment.

On April 13, 1865, he and Lucy Ann Hill were married at Trinity Church on the outskirts of Scotland Neck. Officiating at the cer-
emony was Rev. Joseph Blount Cheshire who, in what may have
been a courtesy to his friends the Smiths, had travelled from his
parish in Tarboro for the occasion.

Lucy was the daughter of Whitmel John Hill, and his wife
Lavinia Dorothy Barnes. The couple were first introduced at Gilbert's
birthday party hosted by the Peter E. Smiths on December 10, 1863.
Immediately after the reception, which probably was also hosted by
the Smiths, Gilbert and his bride left by carriage for Oxford, North
Carolina. While there, they enjoyed a long delayed visit with his
mother and remained in Oxford for several months.[1]

It's reasonable to assume the newlywed couple contemplated
their future, with lengthy discussion of Gilbert's career to be. Of
immediate concern to him was the threatened loss of his personal
property at Edwards Ferry Yard. When the Federal forces wrested
control of eastern North Carolinian's lives and property, they initiated a series of property seizures. The military considered that any
property which had been associated with the Confederate government was subject to confiscation. Because of this policy, Elliott, Smith
& Co. suffered inventory and property loss at Edwards Ferry.

In June 1865, Elliott filed a claim with Commander William H.
Macomb at Plymouth who then requested instructions regarding
seized property from Commodore William Radford, Commanding
North Atlantic Squadron.

I have received a communication from Gilbert Elliott & Co., owners of the shipyard at Edwards Ferry, who state that that yard was a private one, and that the ironclad built there was by contract to the rebel Government, in proof of which they enclosed me their contract, which is signed on the part of the rebel Navy Department by John L. Porter, Chief Naval Constructor of the rebel Navy. It follows from this, they say, that the property taken by our naval forces from that yard, viz, a steam sawmill and some lumber, did not belong to the rebel Navy, and therefore are not liable to seizure. I do not consider this claim worth anything; in fact, I think that this contract would render all the property of this firm confiscable.[2]

Secretary Welles directed a message to Commodore Radford on June 23, in which he expressed firm disapproval of private property seizures. To support his assertion, reference was made to endorsements of Generals Grant and Schofield, and Colonel Frankle supporting his seizure policy. An order received by Welles from Schofield in mid-May implementing that policy was sent to Radford on the thirty-first. Welles concluded with the admonition,

There is no necessity for the Navy to make further excursions or expeditions. Such unnecessary and improper seizures as those indicated must cease, and you will give immediate instructions accordingly.[3]

Macomb's response to the Secretary on July 8 was a convoluted explanation of why he had performed such acts of seizure. In closing he had respectfully pleaded innocent on the grounds that such orders had never come to his attention.[4]

Whether or not Elliott's claim was ever settled is not clear though for a young man, who had proven himself attentive to busines detail, it's proper to assume he spent several months settling old business affairs.

Elliott and his bride returned to Kenmore near Hills Crossroads by early fall. Their cohesive circle of mutual friends, coupled with the presence of Lucy's kin, may have influenced their choice of residence. His claim against the Union for seizing his personal property may never have been settled, but Elliott spent several months in reuniting himself with civilian life.

In spite of the devastation caused when Union troops had occupied the area, it must have been relaxing for Gilbert and Lucy to have lived in the peaceful countryside at Kenmore. Comforts may have been sparse, but among their friends they were wealthy. Their first child, a son whom they named Gilbert III, was born there on January 5, 1866.[5]

Faced with the growing responsibilities of an uncertain future, Elliott discussed all options with his close friend William Henry Smith who had helped in building the *Albemarle*. From early on, both probably dismissed any thoughts of living off the land as recovery would be long and tedious.

Gilbert's older brother Charles had settled in Norfolk after having been discharged in May, 1865, from General Johnston's army at Greensboro, North Carolina. In 1866 he rented a farm near the Roanoke River in Northampton County, North Carolina, but after a severe drought he returned to Norfolk. Before moving, he was invited to meet with William Smith and Gilbert. Their conversations resulted in organizing a wholesale grocery partnership in Norfolk, Virginia. By January 1867 they were advertised in the Norfolk City Directory as Smith, Elliott & Co., Wholesale Grocers, 12 Roanoke Square. Elliott's Norfolk grocery venture was indeed a family affair. He, Lucy and their son, Gilbert; his elder brother Charles with his bride Jeanette Tunsall Cooper of Oxford, North Carolina, whom he married on March 28, 1867; and younger brother Warren Grice resided in what must have been a very large house at 30 West Freemason Street.[6] For obscure reasons, in 1868 the wholesale grocery partnership was dissolved. When the *Albemarle* was auctioned on October 10, 1867 it's probable that Elliott knew of the event, and quite possibly he was among the spectators. The year ended on a brighter note, however, when their first daughter Nannie Hill Elliott was born in Norfolk on October 29, 1868.

All the while Elliott was developing other career avenues, for the 1869 City Directory listed him as Secretary of four Building and Loan Associations. They were, The People's Building Association; The Old Dominion Loan Company; The Homestead Loan Association; and the Real Estate Loan Company. Additionally, he was serving as Director of The People's Bank of Norfolk at the corner of Main and Commerce Streets. For the first time Elliott advertised himself as Attorney-at-Law with office at 24 West Main Street.

His younger brother Warren, a Notary Public, was Librarian in the Tazewell Society, one of Norfolk's three literary associations.

That year Elliott's old friend William F. Martin, former Colonel of the 17th Regiment and Elizabeth City lawyer, opened his law office at 50 Bank Street. In the meantime, the Elliotts had moved their residence to 38 Boush Street.[7]

By 1870, Elliott's career in finance was blossoming. He was President of the Cooperative Loan Company; Secretary of The People's Building Association, The Old Dominion Loan Company, The Homestead Loan Association, and Real Estate Loan Company; as well as a Director of Virginia Building Company. He also served as a Director of The People's Bank of Norfolk. His personal Law Office remained at the same address, though it appears he was associated with his old friend in the firm of Martin & Elliott, Attorneys-At-Law, with offices under the Atlantic Hotel on West Main Street. The Elliotts common residence had become 5 West Freemason Street.[8]

An event occured in late spring which encouraged Elliott to seek another Norfolk residence. Their second daughter, Elizabeth Grice Elliott, was born on May 29, 1871.

By 1872, Elliott and his brother Warren's law office was located over the Citizens Bank. Their residence addresses had also changed. Gilbert and family had relocated to 44 York Street, and Warren found quarters next door at number 42.[9] There were no changes of the brothers' business and residence listings for 1872-1873, but the firm of Martin & Elliott had been dissolved. Elliott's career advanced when he was promoted to Secretary and Cashier of The Mercantile Bank of Norfolk.

Their fourth child, and third daughter, was born in Norfolk on September 21, 1873. She was named Rebecca Norfleet Elliott.[10] When the 1874-1875 city directory was released, Elliott was listed as Secretary and Cashier of The Mercantile Bank of Norfolk. Their residence was unchanged. Brother Warren's law address was 117 Main Street, and he resided at 46 York Street.[11]

Elliott was still Cashier of The Mercantile Bank of Norfolk in 1875-1876, but Warren had moved his office next door to 119 Main Street, though their residences remained the same.[12]

Gilbert Elliott may have sensed limited opportunity in Norfolk, or he simply wished to seek fortune elsewhere, because by 1877 he and his family were living in St. Louis, Missouri. He immediately made application for admittance to the Missouri Bar, and on February 12 he was approved. Shortly thereafter he established his law office on the fourth floor of a building at the S.E. corner of Chestnut Street. Elliott's family was then living on Pine Street near Sixteenth Street.[13] The only event known to have happened in 1878 was that the family again moved to 2417 Buena Vista.[14] One year later a Commission Agency known as Joseph Lathrop & Company engaged Elliott as an attorney, and the family was in a new home at 1560 LaFayette Avenue.[15]

By 1880 Elliott was Secretary of the St. Louis Commission Agency. They found a larger home at 1836 California Avenue after their fourth daughter was born on September 16, 1880. She was named Jeanette Cooper Elliott.[16] There may have been a business downturn in 1881, because Elliott became associated with The Bradstreet Company as a Clerk. The position supplemented his regular legal business. Bradstreet's offices were beyond his at 421 North Third Street. They were probably renting their house at 1836, because they moved right next door to number 1838.[17] Elliott moved his law office to the same address as Bradstreets' by 1882. Son Gilbert was by then a Junior Clerk with the Excelsior Mfg. Co., and their residences remained unchanged.[18]

The Bradstreet Company promoted Elliott in 1883 to Assistant Superintendent of their Vine Street office. Son Gilbert worked at the same job, but was living again with his parents at 1630 South Compton Avenue.[19] In the year 1884 the family endured no changes, but Elliott moved his office to 315 Olive Street.[20] Son Gilbert resigned his job as a junior clerk and became a law student. During the year the family moved to 2755 Allen Avenue.[21] Elliott's law firm expanded its reputation in 1887 by becoming St. Louis Counsel for the Bradstreet Company.[22]

In 1888 his firm's address was next door at 317 Olive St. His affiliation with the Bradstreet Company continued uninterrupted; their residence was unchanged; and after having passed the June Term exam, son Gilbert was admitted to the Missouri Bar on the fourth.[23] From 1890 to 1892 Elliott's law firm remained at the same address, but his son was elsewhere. In 1892 Gilbert and his family moved once more to 3621 Cook Avenue.[24]

For perhaps the same reason Elliott had left Norfolk years before, sometime between 1892 and 1893 he moved his family to the vicinity of New York City. Before leaving St. Louis he and his son established the Gilbert Elliott Collection Company at his law firms' previous address. He and Gilbert III were listed as President and Vice President respectively.[25]

Upon arrival in New York City. Elliott purchased the Sharp-Alleman Law & Collection Agency. Giving it his own name, the father with his son opened their law practice in 1893 at 206 Broadway, New York City. Gilbert Jr. lived in Brooklyn at 454 Eighth Street, and Gilbert Sr. established residence for his wife and four daughters near Fort Wadsworth, Staten Island, New York.

The firm prospered until Gilbert Elliott, Sr., at age 51 years and 5 months, suffered an attack of Erysipelas and died at home in Edgewater, Staten Island, on May 9, 1895. Obituaries in The St. Louis Post Dispatch and New York Daily Tribune credited Gilbert Elliott as builder of the Confederate ram _Albemarle_. The Norfolk Virginian stated he was a native of Elizabeth City, North Carolina.[26] Burial was in The Green-Wood Cemetery, Brooklyn, New York. His was an unsuitably identified center grave of a three-grave plot. In 1987 the _Albemarle's_ youthful builder was honored when this author caused an appropriately inscribed Confederate Veteran's grave marker to be emplaced.

GILBERT ELLIOTT
1ST LT 17 NC REGT
CONFEDERATE STATES ARMY
DEC 10 1843   MAY 9 1895

BUILT CSS _ALBEMARLE_

Gilbert Elliott's final resting place in Green-Wood Cemetery. Brooklyn, N.Y.
Photograph by John Mauk Hilliard, Lehman College, Bronx, N.Y. Author's collection

Albemarle memorabilia and artifacts were probably saved by many families of those who either served aboard, or helped build the ironclad. Many of these unidentified families in eastern North Carolina may still have cherished letter collections, diaries, photographs, or possibly artifacts from the *Albemarle*

None-the-less the paucity of memorabilia is somewhat offset by a few significant relics preserved for public scrutiny.

THE *ALBEMARLE'S* FORWARD 6.4-INCH BROOKE RIFLE
John Mercer Brooke devised a method of banding his guns, a feature which added strength and safety. This gun is preserved and displayed in front of the old NATO Headquarters, Norfolk Naval Base.

Author's photograph

THE *ALBEMARLE'S* FUNNEL

was riddled by shot and shrapnel during the May 5 encounter. Because of this damage, her furnaces were unable to draw sufficiently and her steam pressure dropped. It was then that all bacon, ham and lard was burned. Such fuel required no draft, thus steam was raised to allow an escape into the Roanoke River's mouth. Visitors to the North Carolina Archives and History may see the funnel.

Courtesy of the North Carolina Division of Archives and History

THE *ALBEMARLE'S* BELL

measuring 15 inches across the bottom and 15$^{1}/_{2}$ inches high resides in Post 10, G.A.R. Museum, Worcester, Ma. It was removed from the vessel by members of the Massachusetts Twenty-Fifth Regiment. Chaplain Horace James brought it from Plymouth to Worcester where it was later presented to the museum by his widow.

Photo courtesy of City of Worcester, Ma.

This Second National Flag of the Confederacy was flown aboard the *Albemarle* . It is preserved at the Museum of the Confederacy, Richmond, Va.

Photograph by Katherine Wetzel. Courtesy of the Museum of the Confederacy, Richmond, Va.

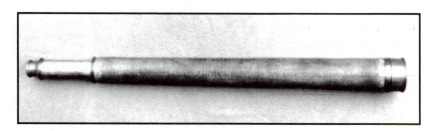

Telescope taken from the *Albemarle* after she was sunk at Plymouth. It measures 2.75" by 26", and extends to 38". Marked on brass, "Spenser, Browning & Co., London, Improved."

It was presented to Lt. William B. Cushing, U.S.N. by Commander William H. Macomb, commanding Union naval forces that recaptured Plymouth on October 29, 1864.

Photograph courtesy of Paul and Patricia DeHaan, Kalamazoo, Mich.

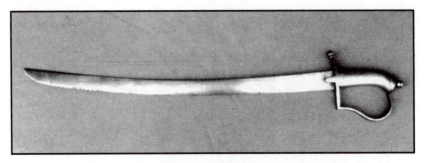

A NAVAL CUTLASS,
28" in length, was manufactured by Schnitzler and Kirschbaum of Solingen, Germany for the Confederacy. Inscribed on the handle, "Taken from the C.S. Ironclad *Albemarle*, October 28, 1864," and on the reverse side "Presented to Admiral S.P. Lee." Acting Rear Admiral Samuel P. Lee commanded the North Atlantic Blockading Squadron.

Photgraph courtesy of Paul and Patricia DeHaan, Kalamazoo, Mich.

This anvil and sledge is said to have been used by Peter Evans Smith as he fabricated iron parts for the *Albemarle*. The anvil's uneven top surface is indicative of many years harsh use.

Photograph courtesy of Dorothy Shields Gregory, great granddaughter of Peter Evans Smith

THE FORWARD 6.4-INCH BROOKE RIFLE: It can be viewed in front of CINCLANT Headquarters, Norfolk Naval Base, Norfolk, Va.

THE SMOKESTACK: The <u>St. Louis Republican</u> published an interview with Gilbert Elliott on November 3, 1885. Their story was of Elliott's former responsibility for building the *Albemarle*. Learning of Elliott's manuscript about the vessel for <u>Century Magazine</u>, the reporter asked to view the ironclad's smokestack which had recently arrived. Elliott escorted the reporter to the Transfer Company's warehouse on Poplar Street, where a sketch was made to illustrate the article.

Having heard of Elliott's forthcoming <u>Century Magazine</u> essay George Lynch, his Weldon, North Carolina friend, had it shipped to St. Louis for display. Judge Lynch, as he was then widely known, was in Norfolk for the auction in 1867, and was able to acquire the smokestack. It was said Lynch stored it outside his Weldon home for years.

Captain John N. Maffitt's September 23, 1880, article in the Weldon <u>Roanoke News</u> stated, "the *Albemarle's* smokestack riddled with cannon ball and grape shot lies in Judge George Green Lynch's grove near Weldon." The stack may be viewed in the North Carolina Division of Archives & History at Raleigh.

THE SHIP'S BELL: It measures 15 inches across the bottom and is 15¹/₂ inches high. While she lay foundered at Plymouth, it was removed from the *Albemarle* by members of the Massachusetts 25th Regiment. On April 6, 1876, it was presented to Post 10, G.A.R., in Worcester, Massachusetts by Mrs. Horace James, widow of Chaplain Horace James who brought the bell from Plymouth.

HER COLORS: She flew a typical Second National ensign measuring roughly 90 inches by 120 inches. The flag was removed from the *Albemarle* by U.S.N. Sailing Master George F. Ford. In 1909 it was presented to The Museum of The Confederacy in Richmond, Virginia, by Dr. Thomas A. Warrell, formerly of Company B, 97th Pennsylvania Volunteers. The museum has a slightly larger flag of identical composition measuring 105 inches by 200 inches which is said to have also been the *Albemarle's* flag.

MASTER'S LOG: Measuring roughly 8 by 13 inches, the slate pages are engraved with chart lines for recording winds, course, coal fuel, etc., and is divided into A.M. and P.M. hours. It rests in The Museum of The Confederacy at Richmond, Virginia.

SINGLE 1-INCH IRON PLATE: Measuring approximately 30 by 12 inches, it may have been either hull or deck plating. It is preserved at the Portsmouth Shipyard Museum, Postsmouth, Virginia.

OAK PULPIT AND LECTURN: Leftover oak wood from the *Albemarle* was given to Rev. Joseph Blount Cheshire, of Tarboro, by Peter E. Smith circa 1863-1864. It was crafted into pulpit furniture for the new Calvary Church. Both handsomely crafted pieces may be seen in All Saints Chapel at Calvary Church, Tarboro, North Carolina.

PETER EVANS SMITH PORTRAIT IN OIL: It has been loaned by his great granddaughter Dorothy Shields Gregory, Winterville, North Carolina, to the Port O'Plymouth Roanoke River Museum, Plymouth, North Carolina.

PETER EVANS SMITH'S ANVIL: Believed to have been used by Smith on board the *Albemarle*, the anvil has been loaned by his great great grandson Peter E. Gregory to Port O'Plymouth Roanoke River Museum, Plymouth, North Carolina.

PHOTOGRAPHIC PORTRAIT OF GILBERT ELLIOTT: What may be pre war-years likeness in civilian clothes appears as Frontispiece herein. Courtesy of Gilbert Elliott VI, Bloomfield, New Jersey, and author.

TELESCOPE RECOVERED FROM THE SUNKEN *ALBEMARLE*: The instrument, marked "Spencer, Browning & Co., London, Improved," was taken from the *Albemarle* and presented by Cdr. William H. Macomb to Lt. William B. Cushing. Courtesy of Paul and Patricia DeHaan, Kalamazoo, Michigan.

NAVAL CUTLASS: Manufactured for the Confederacy by Schnitzler and Kirschbaum of Solingen, Germany. It was presented to Acting Rear Admiral Samuel P. Lee, U.S.N. Courtesy of Paul and Patricia DeHaan, Kalamazoo, Michigan.

MISCELLANEOUS ITEMS: Two wooden fragments; one 4-inch bolt; one 4x5-inch piece of sheet copper; and one twisted piece of iron. Exhibited at U.S. Naval Academy Museum, Annapolis, Maryland.

Thus ends the *Albemarle* chronicle as presently known.

APPENDIX I

GILBERT ELLIOTT GENEALOGY

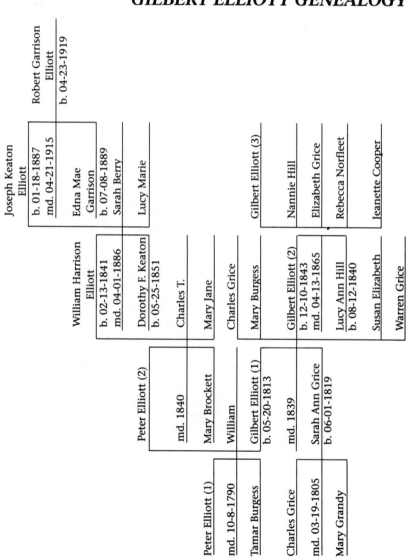

APPENDIX II

SECOND QUARTER, 1864

PARTIAL MUSTER-*ALBEMARLE'S* CREW

Commander	James W. Cooke
	ORN, Ser. I, Vol. IX, 656,657;
	ORN, Ser. II, Vol. I, 274
Lt. (Volunteer)	Gilbert Elliott
	Ibid.
Lieutenant	Francis M. Roby
	ORN, Ser. I, Vol. IX, 656,657;
	Southern Historical Society,
	Sec. XXXV, 295.
Lt. Gunner	B. F. Shelly
	ORN, Ser. I, Vol. IX, 656,657;
	ORN, Ser. II, Vol. I, 274.
Act'g Gunner	Hugh McDonald
	Charles V. Peery, Collection, May 5,
	1864 Ordnance Report;
	ORN, Ser. II, Vol. I, 274.
Gunner	Henry H. Marmaduke
	Confederate Veteran, Vol. I, XXXIII,
	Jan. 1925, 25.
Leverman Aft Gun	John B. Patrick
	ORN, Ser. I, Vol. IX, 768.
Powder Boy	Benjamin H. Gray
	Confederate Pension File, N.C.
	Archives and History.
Master	James C. Long
	Southern Historical Society,
	XXXV, 294;
	ORN, Ser. II, Vol. I, 274.

Act'g Master Mate	James C. Hill Article *Kenmore* in <u>Commonwealth,</u> Scotland Neck, N.C. by Lena H. Smith; Whitmel Joyner, descendant, Hill family of Scotland Neck, N.C.; ORN, Ser. II, Vol. I, 274.
Pilot	James B. Hopkins ORN, Ser. I, Vol. IX, 771; ORN, Ser. II, Vol. I, 274.
Pilot	John Luck ORN, Ser. I, Vol. IX, 656; ORN, Ser. II, Vol. I, 274.
Midshipman	___Hamilton ORN, Ser. I, Vol. IX, 657.
Signal Officer	Arthur Chalk <u>Under Both Flags</u>, 1896, 259, 260.
Coxswain	H. A. Kuhn ORN, Ser. I, Vol. IX, 771; ORN, Ser. II, Vol. I, 274.
Yeoman	J. B. Cooper ORN, Ser. I, Vol. IX, 771; ORN, Ser. II, Vol. I, 274.
3d Ass't Engineer	Henry Disher <u>Under Both Flags</u>, 1896, 259, 260; ORN, Ser. II, Vol. I, 274.
Fireman	William Daley ORN, Ser. I, Vol. IX, 763, 764.
Boatswain Mate	John Benton ORN, Ser. I, Vol. IX, 771; ORN, Ser. II, Vol. I, 274.
Boatswain Mate	John Steeley ORN, Ser. I, Vol. IX, 771; ORN, Ser. II, Vol. I, 274.
Carpenter	William Schafer ORN, Ser. I, Vol. IX, 763, 764.
Scout	Frank P. O'Brien Memoirs, Port O'Plymouth Roanoke River Museum, Plymouth, N.C.
Capt. of Foretop	James Cullington ORN, Ser. I, Vol. IX, 771; ORN, Ser. II, Vol. I, 274.

Capt. of Hold	H. P. Hay ORN, Ser. I, Vol. IX, 771; ORN, Ser. II, Vol. I, 274.
Ordinary Seaman	Thomas Wroten ORN, Ser. I, Vol. IX, 771.
Ordinary Seaman	A. L. Smith Southern Historical Society. XXXV, 296.
Ordinary Seaman	John Smith ORN, Ser. I, Vol. IX, 771.
Ordinary Seaman	James R. Smithwick Smithwick papers, PC 257, N.C. Archives and History; ORN, Ser. II, Vol. I, 274.
Ordinary Seaman	J. H. McCann ORN, Ser. I, Vol. IX, 763, 764.
Ordinary Seaman	John Williams ORN, Ser. I, Vol. IX, 763, 764.
First Courier	Charles S. Smith Article in Commonwealth, Scotland Neck, N.C., Feb. 16, 1922.
Second Courier	Francis J. Smith Claiborne T. Smith, Jr., M.D., *Smith of Scotland Neck*.
Landsman on board	J. T. Game Southern Historical Society, XXXV, 292; ORN, Ser. II, Vol. I, 274.
Landsman	Thomas Nichols ORN, Ser. I, Vol. IX, 771; ORN, Ser. II, Vol. I, 274.
Landsman	M. N. Johnston Lena H. Smith article *Kenmore,* in Commonwealth, Scotland Neck, N.C.
KIA	____ Harris(on) ORN, Ser. I, Vol. IX, 657.

APPENDIX III

THIRD QUARTER, 1864

Muster roll of commissioned, warranted, and appointed officers of the C.S.S. *Albemarle*, as well as crew of the *Albemarle* and Halifax Yard; Alexander F. Warley, Lieutenant Commanding; James W. Cooke, Captain.

Captain	James W. Cooke
Commander	John N. Maffitt
Lt. Commander	Alexander F. Warley
1st. Lieutenant	W. W. Roberts
1st. Lieutenant	Edward Lakin
1st. Lieutenant	John Lewis
Ass't Paymaster	P. M. DeLeon
Master	James C. Long
Act'g Master	B. F. Shelly
Act'g Master	T. J. Burbage
Act'g Master's Mate	Robert Freeman
Act'g Master's Mate	James C. Hill
Act'g Master's Mate	L. D. Pitt
Quartermaster	B. Beveridge
Quartermaster	Spence Gray
Quartermaster	G. W. Hobbs
Quartermaster	Edward Taylor
1st. Chief Pilot	James B. Hopkins
1st. Chief Pilot	John Luck
2nd. Chief Pilot	G. W. Hobbs
2nd. Chief Pilot	Walter Shipley
Act'g Gunner	William Dand
Act'g Gunner	Hugh McDonald
Quarter Gunner	Alfred King
Gunner's Mate	William Pratt

3rd. Ass't Engineer	Henry Discher
3rd. Ass't Engineer	William H. Hardy
3rd. Ass't Engineer	J. T. Robinett
Chief Fireman	James Cullington
1st. Class Fireman	Charles Childs
1st. Class Fireman	John Close
1st. Class Fireman	A. Stuart
2nd. Class Fireman	G. D. Capps
2nd. Class Fireman	Benjamin McClaron
2nd. Class Fireman	John Stafford
Coxswain	Caleb Barker
Coxswain	H. A. Kuhn
Ass't Surgeon	George A. Foote
Ass't Surgeon	Frederick Peck
Surgeon Steward	C. W. Rouzee
Coal Heaver	J. Andrews
Coal Heaver	J. Brown
Coal Heaver	J. B. Snowden
Ship's Cook	M. Payne
2nd. Cook & Baker	Peter Hardy
2nd. Cook & Baker	Benjamin Hayward
2nd. Cook & Baker	James Henderson
2nd. Cook & Baker	George Hooten
Ship's Steward	T. P. Johnston
Yeoman	A. B. Cooper
Boatswain's Mate	John Benton
Boatswain's Mate	J. W. Steeley
Act'g Carpenter	George D. Fentress
Carpenter's Mate	William Cole
Master at Arms	J. W. Reynolds
Captain After Guard	James Waid
Captain After Guard	John White
Chief of the Hold	H. P. Hay
Seaman	William Burgess
Seaman	C. L. Hobbs
Seaman	John Mullins
Seaman	J. A. Nobles
Seaman	Franklin Sikes
Ordinary Seaman	James Belcher
Ordinary Seaman	J. T. Daniel
Ordinary Seaman	R. H. Eno

Ordinary Seaman	J. M. Fulford
Ordinary Seaman	Edward Morton
Ordinary Seaman	James R. Smithwick
Ordinary Seaman	Ezekiel Williams
Landsman	Francis McAdams
Landsman	Shubal Alrid
Landsman	J. T. Anderson
Landsman	J. C. Anthony
Landsman	D. R. Autrey
Landsman	W. H. Aveie
Landsman	J. J. Avant
Landsman	J. W. Avant
Landsman	Erasmaus Ball
Landsman	Simeon Barber
Landsman	John Barton
Landsman	Wilson Beal
Landsman	J. P. Breedlove
Landsman	Miles Blount
Landsman	J. H. Cain
Landsman	J. A. Carter
Landsman	Nat Clark
Landsman	W. J. Clifton
Landsman	Robert T. Crews
Landsman	W. J. McDaniel
Landsman	John Davis
Landsman	Joseph Dunton
Landsman	James Flinn
Landsman	Cofield Fountain
Landsman	J. T. Game
Landsman	A. Gibson
Landsman	H. M. Gibson
Landsman	John Griffin
Landsman	John Harrison
Landsman	Hardy Hatly
Landsman	W. H. Hays
Landsman	H. C. Hight
Landsman	W. Holmes
Landsman	G. W. Horne
Landsman	W. J. Humble
Landsman	M. N. Johnston
Landsman	Felix Jones

Landsman	Wiley Jones
Landsman	Thomas A. Kate
Landsman	L. H. Lancaster
Landsman	W. S. Layard
Landsman	E. R. Lindsay
Landsman	M. A. Lynum
Landsman	Simon Massey
Landsman	B. B. Mitchell
Landsman	Jno. W. Mitchell
Landsman	William O'Neil
Landsman	Thomas Nichols
Landsman	Amos Noah
Landsman	George Ricketts
Landsman	Moses Stancil
Landsman	J. T. Sanders
Landsman	W. S. Simmons
Landsman	Isaac Simpson
Landsman	W. M. Sorrell
Landsman	Samuel Troutman
Landsman	J. D. Turner
Landsman	William L. Walker
Landsman	T. P. Weeks
Landsman	Charles White
Landsman	Samuel W. White
Landsman	John Wilkins
Landsman	Lewis Williams
Landsman	John L. Wilson
Landsman	Robert Wilson
Landsman	William Wilson
Landsman	Henry Winfield
Landsman	Jerry Woodell
Landsman	John Wright
Landsman	Franklin York

Note: The use of initials in substitution for given names has not been intentional. This Muster has been reassembled from the Third Quarter Muster, 1864, published in ORN, Ser. II, Vol. I, 274.

APPENDIX IV

THE WORKMEN OF THE ALBEMARLE

The following tabulation includes known individuals who, in some manner, worked on the C.S.S. ram *Albemarle* at Edwards Ferry, Halifax Yard, and Plymouth, N.C. Doubtless there are many others whose identities remain unknown.

Included herein are persons in Naval Command, Supervisors, Foremen, Craftsmen, Workers, Vendors, Suppliers, Conscripts, Detailed Military, and Civilian Volunteers.

1st. Lt. John J. Guthrie, C.S.N., Commander, Halifax Yard, N.C.
        Micro Reel M-1091, *Halifax Yard*, N.A.;
        News & Observer, Raleigh, N.C., June 17, 1928.
Mr. Hadley, Accounts & Inventory.
        W. A. Ellison Papers, Martin County, N.C.,
        Historical Society.
P. M. DeLeon, C.S.N., Assistant Paymaster.
        Micro Reel M-1091, *Halifax Yard*, N.C., N.A.
Peter Evans Smith, Superintendent of Construction.
        Confederate Veteran, Vol. I, XXXVIII, 376.
William Ruffin Smith, Jr, Head of Supply Dept.
        Confederate Veteran, Vol. I, XXXVIII, 376.
Robert H. Daniel, Halifax Yard Ship's Stores.
        News & Observer, Raleigh, N.C., Jan. 17, 1928.
William Henry Smith, Supplies.
        Lena H. Smith's undated news article, Scotland Neck
        Library.
J. J. Roberson, C.S.N., Special Agent/Inspector.
        Micro Reel M-1091, *Halifax Yard*, N.C., N.A.
Dr. Halsey, Timber Searcher.
        W. A. Ellison Papers, Martin County, N.C., Historical
        Society.

Benjamin Gordon Smith, Woodland Timber Cutter.
>Confederate Veteran, Vol. I, XXXVIII, 376.
Harry Gibson, Dennis Simmons, Selected Cut Lumber.
>W. A. Ellison Papers, Martin County, N.C., Historical
>Society.
Seth K. Cordin, W. R. Williams, J. C. Randolph, and M. M.
Mahon, Halifax Yard Suppliers.
>Micro Reel M-1091, *Halifax Yard,* N.C., N.A.
A. J. Newberry, Plymouth Supplier.
>Micro Reel M-1091, *Halifax Yard*, N.C., N.A.
H. W. Peel, Halifax Conscript Superintendent.
>Micro Reel M-1091, *Halifax Yard*, N.C., N.A.
D. R. Daniel, O. Lipscomb, ___Long, H. W. Martin, ___Peal,
Edward Sikes, James F. Snell, I. W. Treviathan, M. P. Williams,
G. L. Winbum, Conscript Craftsmen.
>Box 78 Folder 1, Adj. General's Dept., Misc. Records,
>N.C. Archives & History.
Jim Ellison, Cabinet Maker/Carpenter.
>W. A. Ellison Papers, Martin County, N.C., Historical
>Society.
John Ha(o)tten, Machinist/Blacksmith.
>W. A. Ellison Papers, Martin County, N.C., Historical
>Society.
___Mahony, ___Stokes, Machinists.
>Micro Reel M-1091, *Halifax Yard*, N.C., N.A.
John T. Thornton, Engineer/Boilermaker.
>Manuscript Collection, Joyner Library, East Carolina
>University, Greenville, N.C.
Robert Lee, Guy McLincklin, John Mackii, Robert O'Neal, Boil-
ermakers.
>Micro Reel M-1091, *Halifax Yard*, N.C., N.A.
John A. Thomas, E. H. Wilson, Blacksmiths.
>Micro Reel M-1091, *Halifax Yard*, N.C., N.A.
___Fisher, ___Fuqui, Coppersmiths.
>Micro Reel M-1091, *Halifax Yard*, N.C., N.A.
John Thrower, Contract Mechanic/Carpenter.
>W. A. Ellison Papers, Martin County, N.C., Historical
>Society.
Franklin Dunn, Carter Hogwood, A. Hopkins, and Henry Smith
[a black workman of Peter E. Smith], Gunboat workmen.
>Micro Reel M-1091, *Halifax Yard*, N.C., N.A; News &
>Observer, Raleigh, N.C., June 17, 1928, Article men-
>tions Henry Smith.

17th Regiment: Co. A, Jno. T. Harrell; Co. B, C. Patrick; Co. D,
Z. Smith; Co. E, W. A. Burroughs, I. L. Swain; Co. F, I. R. Lynch,
___Staton; Co. G, Joseph Herrington, Detached Military Workers.

      Box 78, Folder 1, Adj. General's Dept., Misc. Records,
      N.C. Archives & History.

Miss Mary Spottswood, Launched the *Albemarle*.

      <u>News & Observer</u>, Raleigh, N.C.,
      Feb. 27, 1927.

Lafayette Thrower, Placed river torpedoes below launch site.

      W. A. Ellison Papers, Martin County, N.C., Historical
      Society.

Note: Omission of given names, or the use of initials in substitution, has been unintentional. In all research material examined,
the persons were identified as shown.

BIBLIOGRAPHY

Ashe, Samuel A. *History of North Carolina,* Vol. II. (Raleigh, N.C.: Edwards and Broughton Co., 1925).

Barrett, John Gilchrist. *The Civil War in North Carolina: The Confederate Goliath,* Chapter X. (Chapel Hill: University of North Carolina Press, 1963).

Bright, Leslie S., William H. Rowland, and James C. Bardon. *C.S.S. Neuse, A Question of Iron and Time.* (Raleigh, N.C.: Division of Archives and History, 1981).

Brooke, George M. *John M. Brooke: Naval Scientist and Educator.* (Charlottesville: University of Virginia, 1980).

Butler, Lindley S. *James W. Cooke: The Dictionary of North Carolina Biography.* (Chapel Hill: University of North Carolina Press, 1979).

Canney, Donald L. *The Old Steam Navy: Frigates, Sloops, and Gunboats, 1815-1865,* Vol. I, Glossary. (Annapolis, Md.: Naval Institute Press, 1990).

City of Norfolk Court Order Book, 1763-1765. Norfolk County Court House, Chesapeake, Va.

City of Norfolk Deed Book II, III,12,15,44, 45, 1791-1812. Circuit Court, Norfolk, Va.

City of Norfolk Will Book 3. Circuit Court, Norfolk, Va.

Civil War Naval Chronology, 1861-1865, 6 Vols. (Washington, D.C.: Government Printing Office, 1971).

Clark, Walter, ed. *North Carolina Regiments, 1861-1865,* 5 Vols. (Goldsboro, N.C.: Nash Brothers, Printers, 1901).

Coggins, Jack. *Ships and Seamen of the American Revolution.* (Harrisburg, Pa.: Stackpole Publishing Co., 1969-1973).

Confederate Veteran Magazine, Vol. XXXVIII. Oct., 1930.

Crabtree, Beth G., and James W. Patton, eds. *Journal of a Secesh Lady; The Diary of Catherine Ann Devereux Edmondston, 1860-1866,* Second Printing. (Raleigh, N.C.: Division of Archives and History).

Dew, Charles B. *Ironmaker of the Confederacy: John R. Anderson and the Tredegar Iron Works,* Reprint. (Chapel Hill: University of North Carolina Press, 1987).

Dictionary of American Naval Fighting Ships, Vol. I, 1964. Marshall W. Butt Library, Portsmouth Naval Shipyard Museum, Portsmouth, Va. (Washington, D.C.: Government Printing Office, 1959).

Durkin, Joseph T. *Stephen R. Mallory: Confederate Navy Chief.* (Chapel Hill: University of North Carolina Press, 1954).

Elliott, Gilbert. *The Career of the Confederate Ram Albemarle.* (New York, N.Y.: Century Magazine, July, 1888).

Elliott, Milton Courtright. *A Century of Elliotts,* 1908. John Page Elliott, Charlottesville, Va.

Griffin, William A. *Ante Bellum Elizabeth City.* Elizabeth City, N.C., 1970.

Johnson, Robert U., and Clarence C. Buel, eds. *Battles and Leaders of the Civil War,* 4 Vols. (New York, N.Y.: The Century Company, circa 1888).

Jordan, Weymouth T., Jr. *North Carolina Troops, 1861-1865: A Roster,* Vol. VI, Addenda, 1990. (Raleigh, N.C.: Division of Archives and History).

Nash, Jaquelin Drane. *A Goodly Heritage: The Story of Cavalry Parish.* Tarboro, N.C., Second Edition, Revised. (Wilmington, N.C.: Broadfoot Publishing Co., 1982).

Official Records of the Union and Confederate Armies in the War of the Rebellion, Ser. I, Vols. XVIII, XXXIII, XXXVI, XL Pt. III, XLVI, Pt.II, LI.

Official Records of the Union and Confederate Navies in the War of the Rebellion, Ser. I, Vols. II, VII, VIII, IX, X, XI, XII, XV. Ser. II, Vols. I, II.

Pasquotank County Deed Book V. Courthouse, Elizabeth City, N.C.

Pasquotank Historical Society Year Book, Vol. I, 1954-1955. Elizabeth City, N.C.

Powell, William S. *The North Carolina Gazetter.* (Chapel Hill: University of North Carolina Press, 1968).

Pugh, Jesse F., and Frank T. Williams. *The Hotel in the Great Dismal Swamp.* By the authors. (Old Trap: Camden County, N.C., 1964).

Scharf, J. Thomas. *History of The Confederate States Navy.* (New York, N.Y.: Rogers and Sherwood, 1887).

Smith, Claiborne T., Jr. M.D. *Smith of Scotland Neck.* By the author, Ardmore, Pa., 1976.

Southern Historical Society Papers. Vol. XXVIII. Richmond, Va., 1900.

Turnball, Archibald D. *John Steven's: An American Record.* New York, N.Y., 1928.

Vickers, George M., ed. Frank P. O'Brien, Article, *Under Both Flags: A Panorama of the Great Civil War.* (Philadelphia, Pa.: World Bible House, 1896).

Waterman, Thomas Tileston, and Frances Benjamin Johnston. *The Early Architecture of North Carolina.* (Chapel Hill: University of North Carolina Press, 1941).

Wilson, Herbert Wrigley. *Ironclads in Action*, Chapter V. Marshall W. Butt Library, Portsmouth Naval Shipyard Museum, Portsmouth, Va. (London: S. Low Marston & Co., 1897).

Wingo, Elizabeth B. *Marriages of Norfolk County, Virginia, 1706-1792*. Vol. I, 22. (Chesapeake, Va.: Greenbriar Printing Co., 1961).

Collections

Anderson, Mary Burton. *The Elliott Lineage*. Unpublished. St. Louis, Mo.

Bond, F. L. Collection 296. J. Y. Joyner Library, Greenville, N.C.: East Carolina University.

Carey, George G., IV. *Diary of Joseph Grice*. Cincinnati, Oh.

Clark, Gov. Henry. Papers. Raleigh, N.C.: Division of Archives and History.

Ellison, W. A. Papers. Martin County Historical Society, Williamston, N.C.

Hill, Daniel Harvey. PC93 Papers. Raleigh, N.C.: Division of Archives and History.

Hill, Lucy Ann. Unpublished biographical sketch. Hill Family Collection, David B. Gammon, Raleigh, N.C.

Mackay and Stiles. Collection 470 Papers. Southern Historical Collection. Chapel Hill: University of North Carolina.

Martin, William Francis. Collection 493. Southern Historical Collection, Chapel Hill: University of North Carolina.

Micro Reel 5, Record Group 45. Confederate Navy Subject File A., National Archives.

Micro Reel M-1091, *Halifax Yard*. Confederate Subject File, Record Group 45. National Archives.

Micro Reel, NA-MC270-252, *17th Regiment, N.C. Troops*. Raleigh, N.C.: Division of Archives and History.

Miscellaneous Records, Box 78, Folder I, Adjutant General's Dept. Raleigh, N.C.: Division of Archives and History.

O'Brien, Frank P. Memoirs, *Albemarle crewman*. Plymouth, N.C.: Port O'Plymouth Roanoke River Museum.

Peery, Charles V., M.D. Collection. Charleston, S.C.

Record Group 19. Confederate Subject File AD. National Archives.

Smith, Peter Evans. Collection P677 Papers. Southern Historical Collection. Chapel Hill: University of North Carolina.

Smithwick. Collection PC257 Papers. Raleigh, N.C.: Division of Archives and History.

Starke-Marchant-Martin. Collection 1549 Papers. Southern Historical Collection. Chapel Hill: University of North Carolina.

Swan, Francis H. *Personal Narrative: Member of Lt. Cushing's crew*. Manuscripts Division. Library of Congress.

U.S. Army Military History Institute. Carlisle, Pa.

U.S. District Court, Case 146. Record Group 21, Admiralty Court proceedings. National Archives.

Vance, Gov. Zebulon. GLB 50.1, GP173, GP177, Papers. Raleigh, N.C.: Division of Archives and History.

Woodhull, Byron Josephus. *Personal Reminiscences*. Crewman on U.S.S. *Ceres*. Plymouth, N.C.: Port O'Plymouth Roanoke River Museum.

Wright-Herring. Collection 3234-2 Papers. Southern Historical Collection. Chapel Hill: University of North Carolina.

Newspapers

Bertie Ledger-Advance. Windsor, N.C., Feb. 21, 1963.

Fisherman and Farmer. Elizabeth City, N.C., May, __, [Perhaps Feb., 1897] J. Y. Joyner Library. Greenville, N.C.; East Carolina University.

Harper's Weekly, Saturday March 15, 1862.

Henderson Gold Leaf. Henderson, N.C., July 7, 1898.

New York Daily Tribune. New York, N.Y., May 10, 1895, p. 7, col. 4.

New York Herald. New York, N.Y., Apr. 15, 1865.

News & Observer. Raleigh, N.C. Issues: Mar. 22, 1925; Feb. 27, 1927; Jun. 17, 1928; and Dec. 6, 1959.

Norfolk Journal. Norfolk, Va. Issues: Oct. 9, 10, 11, 1867.

Norfolk Virginian. Norfolk, Va. Issues: Dec. 14, 15, 1893; May 10, 1895.

St. Louis Post Dispatch. St. Louis, Mo., May 12, 1895.

St. Louis Republican. St. Louis, Mo., Nov. 3, 1885.

The American Beacon Daily. Norfolk, Va., Apr. 6, 1821.

The Commonwealth. Scotland Neck, N.C. Issues: Feb. 6, 1922; Feb. 16, 1922; Jun. 13, 1928; Jul. 6, 1928; Aug. 3, 1928.

The Patron & Gleaner. Rich Square, Northampton County, N.C., J. Y. Joyner Library. Greenville, N.C.: East Carolina University. Jan. 5, 1899.

The Roanoke News. Weldon, N.C., Sept. 23, 1880.

The Southerner. Micro Reel. Edgecombe County Library, Tarboro, N.C. Issues: Oct. 15, Dec. 12 & 17, 1861: Sept. 9, Oct. 17, 1862.

ENDNOTES

NOTES for CHAPTER 1

1. Gilbert Elliott, article, *The Career of the Confederate Ram Albemarle,* (Century Magazine, July, 1888), p. 423.

2. Official Records of the Union and Confederate Navies in the War of the Rebellion, hereinafter abbreviated as ORN, Ser. I, Vol. IX, p. 657.

3. ORN, Ser. I, Vol. IX, p. 637.

4. ORN, Ser. I, Vol. IX, pp. 636-637.

5. Hayden Planetarium, *American Ephemeris & Nautical Almanac,* 1864, U. S. Naval Observatory; M. Barlow Pepin, Deltona, Fl.

6. *Ibid.*

7. ORN, Ser. I, Vol. IX, p. 657.

8. Hayden Planetarium, *American Ephemeris & Nautical Almanac,* 1864, U. S. Naval Observatory.

9. N.C. State Pension Records (Confederate)-1901, N.C. Department of Archives and History; Benjamin H. Gray was born on April 2, 1852. In June 1917, while a resident of Bertie County, N.C., he applied for a Confederate Pension from North Carolina. It was approved in July 1917. After he died on June 11, 1924, his wife Margaret was granted a pension based upon Ben's service. It is said he became a minister in later life.

    The News & Observer, Raleigh, July 13, 1924. An article published by the Windsor Ledger a week earlier, and reprinted by The News & Observer on the thirteenth contained a quotation by Judge Winston. "I call attention to the death of Ben Gray, a very respectful old colored man, a small farmer who lived in the Cedar Landing neighborhood. During the Civil War he was in the Confederate Navy and was aboard the Confederate Ironclad *Albemarle*, which fought the Union Navy in the mouth of the Roanoke River."

NOTES for CHAPTER 2

1. Pasquotank Historical Society, Year Book, Vol. I, 1954-55, p. 54. (Article, <u>Raleigh News & Observer</u>, dateline Elizabeth City, N.C., Nov. 22, 1943.)

2. *Ibid.*

3. Pasquotank County Deed Book V, pp. 15-17;

   Robert G. Elliott, *A Tarheel Confederate and His Family,* self published 1989, p.1.

4. George G. Carey, IV, great-great-grandson of Charles Grice. *Diary of Joseph Grice*, brother of Charles. Cincinnati, Ohio.

5. Pasquotank Historical Society, Year Book, Vol. I, p. 50.

6. *Ibid.*, p. 51;

   William A Griffin, *Ante Bellum Elizabeth City*, p. 27.

7. *Ibid.*, pp. 45, 46.

8. *Ibid.*, p. 74.

9. Pasquotank County Deed Book V, p. 102. This was Lot #6, as drawn on the 1795 plat of 'Elizabeth.' A drawbridge on Route 158 in Elizabeth City spans the Pasquotank River to Camden County. At the west end, the adjoining property immediately south of the bridge was generally where Lot #6 was located.

10. William A. Griffin, *Ante Bellum Elizabeth City*, p. 35.

11. Pasquotank Historical Society, Year Book, Vol. I, p. 51.

12. The origin of Peter Elliott has always remained somewhat clouded. Perhaps the most conclusive evidence of Peter's ancestry is quoted by Milton Courtright Elliott in his 'Word of Explanation,' when he wrote, "... but Colonel Lucien Starke was authority for the statement that Peter came to this country directly from Scotland. Colonel Starke, who was Collector of the Port of Camden County, North Carolina, was an intimate friend of Gilbert Elliott (1), [third] son of Peter, and no doubt had full authority for his statement." Milton wrote this on December 25, 1908, in *A Century of Elliotts.*

13. City of Norfolk, Va., Will Book 3, p. 147. Will of George Wright Burgess, dated Sept. 28, 1794, in which he names Tamar (Burgess) Elliott as his daughter;

    Elizabeth B. Wingo, *Marriages of Norfolk County, Virginia, 1706-1792,* Vol. I. (Chesapeake, Va.: Greenbriar Printing Co., 1961), p. 22.

14. Norfolk County, Va., Deed Book 45, p. 303, dated Nov. 2, 1812. The sale price was $600.00, representing a profit of $125.00 over a three-year period of ownership.

15. Jesse F. Pugh & Frank T. Williams, *The Hotel in the Great Dismal Swamp,* (Richmond, Va.: Garrett & Massie, Inc., 1964), p. 5.

16. Milton Courtright Elliott, *A Century of Elliotts*, 1908, p. 6. Original in possession of his son John Page Elliott, Charlottesville, Va.

17. Robert G. Elliott, *A Tarheel Confederate and His Family*, self published 1989. Peter(2) of Shiloh, Camden County, N.C., was this author's great grandfather.

18. M. C. Elliott, *A Century of Elliotts*, 1908, p. 6.

19. The American Beacon Daily, Norfolk, Va., issue of April 6, 1821.

20. Mary Burton Anderson, St. Louis, Mo., great granddaughter of Gilbert Elliott(2), *The Elliott Lineage,* unpublished manuscript;

    The Hill Family of Bertie, Martin and Halifax Counties, Vol. 3, Pt. 1, Southern Historical Collection, University of North Carolina, Chapel Hill, N.C..

21. M. C. Elliott, p. 6. Charles Grice, after arrival at the town of Elizabeth City, became widely known as a shipbuilder, merchant, real estate entrepreneur, Clerk of the Court, and Sheriff of Pasquotank County.

22. *Ibid.,* p. 6;

    Gilbert Elliott(4), formerly of Kingston, N.Y., a grandson of Gilbert Elliott(2), unpublished manuscript, *Charles Grice Family*, property of author;

    Frances Benjamin Johnston and Thomas Tileston Waterman, *The Early Architecture of North Carolina*. This two story brick house once known as Milford is located on the Ferry Landing Road, about four miles north of Camden village. It stands on a slight rise of land sloping down to the Pasquotank nearly a quarter mile west. In Charles Grice's time the property was of 150 acres. Dr. and Mrs. William K. Wassink, the present owners, have preserved the old home to the best estimate of its original exterior design. (Chapel Hill: University of North Carolina Press, 1941), p. 32.

23. M. C. Elliott, p. 7.

24. *Ibid.,* p. 6.

25. William F. Martin Collection 493, Southern Historical Collection, University of North Carolina, Chapel Hill, N.C.

26. Pasquotank Historical Society, Year Book, Vol. I, final paragraph, p. 76. The property mentioned was Lot #42 on the 1832 plat of Elizabeth City;

    Pasquotank Historical Society, Year Book, Vol. II, p. 131. In her memoirs Mrs. W. D. Temple (Blanche Griffin), of Elizabeth City (1865-1880) said, "...The town had been laid out in blocks of an acre each, only one home to each block...The next block, between Pool and Elliott streets on the south side of Main, was owned by Mr. Gilbert Elliott, a lawyer...His home was rather small, and was located on the west half of the block. He sold the east half to my father, who built a nice colonial house which was occupied by Dr. William G. Pool...The block across the street was vacant for many years, as the old wooden courthouse had been burned in 1862 when the Yankee Navy captured the town. The present courthouse was not built until I was quite grown, about 1884, on the same location as the old one."

27. M. C. Elliott, p. 11. Gilbert remained in Elizabeth City to manage the Martin shipyard after his mother and brother had departed for Oxford, North Carolina. There, Warren attended Horner's Military School and later the University of North Carolina at Chapel Hill. By the time Gilbert was working on the *Albemarle* at Edwards Ferry near Scotland Neck, Warren was to join him as an assistant;

    M. B. Anderson, great granddaughter of Gilbert(2), *The Elliott Lineage*, unpublished manuscript, St. Louis, Mo.;

    4-93, William F. Martin Collection, Southern Historical Collection University of North Carolina, Chapel Hill, N.C. There is ample evidence that Elliott was engaged in ship construction at the Martin shipyard, in the vicinity of Elizabeth City, as early as September 14, 1861. A group of letters from North Carolina Militia Maj. Gen. James Green Martin, C.S.A., Cdr. Arthur Sinclair, Sr., C.S.N., and Elliott, written during September and October 1861, suggests that young Elliott was managing William F. Martin's shipyard while Martin, as Colonel of the 17th Regiment North Carolina Infantry, was on military duty at Hatteras Island, North Carolina.

NOTES for CHAPTER 3

1. *Civil War Naval Chronology, 1861-1865,* I-5.

2. Joseph T. Durkin, *Stephen R. Mallory: Confederate Navy Chief.* (Chapel Hill: University of North Carolina Press, 1954).

3. *Naval Chronology*, 1861-1865. I-11.

4. *Naval Chronology*, I-13.

5. Archibald D. Turnball, *John Stevens: An American Record.* (New York, 1928)

6. *Naval Chronology,* I-14.

7. *Naval Chronology,* I-15.

8. *Naval Chronology,* I-16.

9. *Naval Chronology,* I-17.

10. *Naval Chronology,* I-19;

    Battles and Leaders, Vol. I, p. 717.

11. ORN's, Ser. II, Vol. II, p. 174.

12. Norfolk Virginian, Dec. 15, 1893. On December 14, 1893, John L. Porter died at Portsmouth, Va.;

    Confederate Naval Museum, Columbus, Ga;

    Norfolk Virginian Dec. 14, 1893.

13. William F. Martin Collection 493, Southern Historical Collection, University of North Carolina, Chapel Hill, N.C.;

    A. Robert Holcombe, Jr., Director, Confederate Naval Museum, Columbus, Ga. William P. Williamson died in Norfolk, Va., on October 20, 1870.

14. George M. Brooke, *John M. Brooke: Naval Scientist and Educator,* (Charlottesville, Va.: University Press of Virginia, 1980).

15. Walter Clark, *N.C. Regiments, 1861-1865,* Vol. I, p. 3.

16. Pasquotank Historical Society, Year Book, 1954-1955, p. 105. General Martin was born in Elizabeth City in 1819. His father was Dr. William Martin, a Princess Anne County Virginia physician, who moved to Pasquotank County circa 1800. He became a prominent planter and shipbuilder. His mother was Sophia Scott Dauge, daughter of General Peter Dauge, of Camden County. Younger brother, Colonel William Francis Martin, commanded the 17th Regiment, North Carolina Infantry. He was born in Elizabeth City on July 31, 1821. An attorney in Elizabeth City, William F. Martin became Gilbert Elliott's friend and employer before the war began.

17. Tarboro Public Library, Edgecombe County, N.C., The Southerner, Micro Reel. Many issues are missing, but retained are those of Oct. 15, Dec. 12 & 17, 1861, and Sept. 9, & Oct. 17, 1862.

18. William F. Martin Collection 493, Southern Historical Collection, University of North Carolina, Chapel Hill, N.C.

19. *Ibid.*

20. *Ibid.*

21. Pasquotank Historical Society, Year Book, 1954-1955, p. 78. From an article *The Battle of Elizabeth City*, by G. Potter Dixon.

22. William F. Martin Collection 493, Southern Historical Collection, University of North Carolina, Chapel Hill, N.C.

23. *Naval Chronology*, I-28.

24. William F. Martin Collection 493, Southern Historical Collection, University of North Carolina, Chapel Hill, N.C.

25. *Ibid.*

26. *Ibid.*

27. *Ibid.* Further papers relating to Mr. Cropson's inquiry have not been found in this collection.

28. *Ibid.*

29. Donald L. Canney, *The Old Steam Navy: Frigates, Sloops and Gunboats, 1815-1885.* Vol. I., Glossary. (Annapolis, Md.: Naval Institute Press, 1990), p. 193.

30. William F. Martin Collection 493, Southern Historical Collection, University of North Carolina, Chapel Hill, N.C.

31. *Ibid.*

32. *Ibid.*

33. *Ibid.*

34. *Ibid.*

35. *Ibid.*

36. *Naval Chronology*, I-28.

37. William F. Martin Collection 493, Southern Historical Collection, University of North Carolina, Chapel Hill, N.C.

38. *Naval Chronology*, VI-186. For one to appreciate the crude, but effective, shipbuilding techniques used by Confederate shipbuilders, a portion of the C.S.S. *Chattahoochee* is on display at the Confederate Naval Museum, Columbus, Ga.

39. William F. Martin Collection 493, Southern Historical Collection, University of North Carolina, Chapel Hill, N.C.

40. William A. Griffin, *Ante Bellum Elizabeth City*, pp. 66, 67. Here's an account of constructing the Cobb's Point battery, a Court order to underwrite freight charges on guns brought from Roanoke Island, and the mustering of Militia to man the battery. There can be little doubt Gilbert was not involved, since he was Agent for Adj. Gen. James G. Martin, whose authority also included Pasquotank County;

    G. Potter Dixon, *The Battle of Elizabeth City,* Pasquotank Historical Society, Vol. I, 1954-1955, pp. 77, 78, in which Flag Officer Lynch inspected Cobb's Point battery.

41. William F. Martin Collection 493, Southern Historical Collection, University of North Carolina, Chapel Hill, N.C.

42. Weymouth T. Jordan, Jr., *North Carolina Troops, A Roster, 1861-1865,* Vol. VI., (Wilmington, N.C.: Broadfoot Publishing Company), p. 118.

43. William F. Martin Collection 493, Southern Historical Collection, University of North Carolina, Chapel Hill, N.C.;

    Manuscript Collection, Micro Film. Letter of October 27, 1888, from William J. Griffin to Dr. James H. Dennic of Boston, Ma., in which Griffin says he "has spoken with Mr. James F. Snell, who was 'master mechanic' on the *Albemarle.* Snell and Mr. John Thornton, who superintended construction of her boilers, cannot recall name of another worker who allegedly worked on the *Albemarle.*" East Carolina University, Greenville, N.C.:

    An article by Charles Grice Elliott, *The Ram Albemarle,* a former Captain and A.A.G., Martin-Kirkland Brigade, and the older brother of Gilbert Elliott Written for the Richmond Dispatch, reprinted Jan. 5, 1899, by The Patron & Observer, Rich Square, Northhampton County, N.C., Joyner Library, East Carolina University at Greenville, N.C.

44. William F. Martin Collection 493, Southern Historical Collection, University of North Carolina, Chapel Hill, N.C.

45. William F. Martin Collection 493, Southern Historical Collection, University of North Carolina, Chapel Hill, N.C.;

    Clark, *North Carolina Regiments, 1861-1865*, Vol. I, pp. 135-138. The 1st Regiment N.C. Infantry was organized in the spring of 1861 at the race track near Warrenton, in Warren County. Company A, of 121 enlisted men, was raised in Chowan County which was bordered by the Chowan

River on the west and Albemarle Sound on the south. After the regiment was organized in July 1861 it was ordered to Richmond, and assigned to General Holmes' Brigade at Brooks' Station on the railroad between Fredericksburg and Washington. Acquia Creek, the rail terminal point connecting with Richmond, was the first location on the Potomac River where Confederate Naval officers erected batteries.

46. William F. Martin Collection 493, Southern Historical Collection, University of North Carolina, Chapel Hill, N.C.

47. *Ibid.*

48. *Ibid.*

NOTES for CHAPTER 4

1. William F. Martin Collection 493, Southern Historical Collection, University of North Carolina, Chapel Hill, N.C.

2. *Ibid.*

3. *Ibid.*

4. *Ibid.*

5. *Ibid.*

6. *Ibid.*

7. *Ibid.*

8. *Ibid.*

9. *Ibid.*

10. *Ibid.*

11. *Ibid.*

12. *Ibid.*

13. *Ibid.*

14. *Ibid.*

15. *Naval Chronology,* I-37.

16. William F. Martin Collection 493, Southern Historical Collection, University of North Carolina, Chapel Hill, N.C.

17. *Ibid.;*

    A. Robert Holcombe, Jr., Director, The Confederate Naval Museum, Columbus, Ga., offers an opinion of the three gunboats to have been constructed at Washington, N.C. "As best I can tell, [they] were 150 feet between perpendiculars, *Macon* class wooden sail/steam gunboats...25 feet moulded beam, 10 feet depth of hold...twin screw,...rigged with two rather than three sails."

18. W. F. Martin Collection 493, Southern Historical Collection, University of North Carolina, Chapel Hill, N.C.

19. *Ibid.*

20. *Ibid.*

21. *Ibid.*

22. *Ibid.*

23. *Ibid.*

24. *Ibid.*

25. Jack Coggins, *Ships & Seamen of the American Revolution*, (Harrisburg, Pa.: Stackpole Publishing Co., 1969-1973).

26. William F. Martin Collection 493, Southern Historical Collection, University of North Carolina, Chapel Hill, N.C.

27. *Ibid.*

28. *Ibid.*

29. *Ibid.*

NOTES for CHAPTER 5

1. William F. Martin Collection 493, Southern Historical Collection, University of North Carolina, Chapel Hill, N.C.

2. *Ibid.*

3. *Ibid;* 'Report of Evidence taken before a Joint Special Committee of both Houses of the Confederate Congress to Investigate the Affairs of the Navy Department.' (Richmond, 1863).

4. Records at Raleigh Archives and Pasquotank County Court House have revealed no Elizabeth City shipyard locations, circa 1850-1862. It also appears no such maps are available through the U.S. Corps of Engineers.

5. *Naval Chronology, 1861-1865*, II-9.

6. William F. Martin Collection 493, Southern Historical Collection, University of North Carolina, Chapel Hill, N.C.

7. *Ibid.*

8. William A. Griffin, *Ante Bellum Elizabeth City*, pp. 66, 67.

9. Weymouth T. Jordan, Jr., *North Carolina Troops, 1861-1865, A Roster,* Vol. VI, Addenda, 1990. 7th N.C. Volunteers, (17th Regiment, 1st Organization). N.C. Archives & History.

10. William F. Martin Collection 493, Southern Historical Collection, University of North Carolina, Chapel Hill, N.C.

11. *Ibid.*

12. *Ibid.*

13. *Naval Chronology,* VI-197;

    Southern Historical Society, Vol. XXVIII, pp. 125-132. *Appomattox* formerly *Empire*: She was purchased at Norfolk in 1861, converted to a gunboat, and assigned to North Carolina's coastal waters. Now the *Appomattox*, she helped tow block-ships to be sunk at strategic points in the channels near Hatteras. After fighting valiantly in the battles of Roanoke Island and Elizabeth City in February 1861, she tried to escape north through the Dismal Swamp Canal. At the locks near South Mills it was found her beam was 2 inches too wide for passage. Accordingly, her commander Lt. Charles C. Simms, C.S.N., fired the ship and she exploded.

14. *Naval Chronology,* VI-206;

    Southern Historical Society. *Black Warrior*: She was a large merchant schooner, pressed into service by the Confederates to assist in the defense of Roanoke Island and Elizabeth City. At the end of fighting on February 10, 1862, Acting Master Frank M. Harris, C.S.N., fired her to prevent capture. Her crew escaped into the Pasquotank River marshes.

15. *Naval Chronology,* VI-224;

    Southern Historical Society. *Ellis*: An iron hull tug boat, she was purchased by the State of North Carolina at Norfolk in 1861, and turned over to the Confederates when the State seceded. Cdr. William T. Muse, C.S.N., fought her well in defense of Forts Hatteras and Clark, as well as in the battles of Roanoke Island. Lt. James W. Cooke, C.S.N., was her commander in the Pasquotank battle during which he was badly wounded. The *Ellis* was captured by the U.S. Navy and assigned to the North Atlantic Blockading Squadron. She grounded on November 25, 1862, above the river's mouth at New Bern, N.C. To prevent recapture by the Confederates she was set afire and demolished by the explosion of her magazine. Her last commander was Lt. William B. Cushing, U.S.N.

16. *Naval Chronology,* VI-226;

Southern Historical Society. *Fanny:* Originally an iron hulled U.S. Army steamer, she was mounted with two guns after Confederates captured her at Loggerhead Inlet, N.C., on October 1, 1861. Under command of Acting Master James L. Tayloe, C.S.N., she participated in the battles of Roanoke Island and Elizabeth City. On February 8, 1862, she was run aground and blown up by her Captain, who escaped with her crew to shore.

17. *Naval Chronology,* VI-229;

Southern Historical Society. *Forrest*: Originally the *Edwards,* she was purchased at Norfolk in 1861. In the battles of Roanoke Island Lt. James L. Hoole, C.S.N., her commander, was seriously wounded and the *Forrest* disabled. She was towed to Elizabeth City for propeller repairs, it having been displaced in the battle of Pork Point at Roanoke Island on February 10, 1862. While on the way she was burned to prevent capture.

18. *Naval Chronology,* VI-265. *M. C. Etheridge:* Built in 1859 at Plymouth, N.C., the Confederates used her as a fleet storeship. Attacked by the U.S.S. *Whitehead* while carrying stores on the Pasquotank River, the Confederate crew fired her to prevent capture. Despite all efforts to the contrary, the Union boarded and scuttled her.

19. *Naval Chronology,* VI-299;

Southern Historical Society. *Sea Bird:* A side wheel steamer built in 1854 at Keyport, N.J., she was purchased by North Carolina at Norfolk in 1861 and armed with two guns. Her commander in North Carolina waters was Lt. Paterick McCarrick, C.S.N., and she served as Flag Ship for Confederate Flag Officer William F. Lynch's 'Mosquito Fleet' during the battles of Roanoke Island and Elizabeth City. On February 10, 1862, she was rammed and sunk by the U.S.S. *Commodore Perry.*

20. *Naval Chronology,* II-23.

21. *Naval Chronology,* II-26.

22. M. C. Elliott, *A Century of Elliotts,* p. 11.

23. Richard Benbury Creecy, *The Bombardment,* Pasquotank Historical Society, Year Book, 1954-1955, Vol. I, pp. 75, 76.

24. Charles Grice Elliott, article, *The Ram Albemarle*, first published in Richmond Dispatch, reprinted in The Patron and Gleaner, Jan. 5, 1899, Rich Square, Northampton County, N.C., Joyner Library, East Carolina University, Greenville, N.C.

25. *Naval Chronology*, II-28.

26. Pasquotank Historical Society, Year Book, 1954-1955, Vol. I, p. 78.

27. Charles Grice Elliott, article, *The Ram Albemarle*, first published in Richmond Dispatch, reprinted in The Patron and Gleaner, Jan. 5, 1899, Rich Square, Northampton County, N.C., Joyner Library, East Carolina University, Greenville, N.C.

28. Record Group 45, Confederate Navy Subject File 'AC', Roll #5, National Archives. Capt. Sidney Smith Lee was brother to General Robert E. Lee.

29. William A. Griffin, *Ante Bellum Elizabeth City*, p. 6. "In the year 1700 there was quite a settlement of Quakers at Symons Creek [Pasquotank County], and from the Quakers originated the folk lore story of how New Begun Creek got it's name. There lived at Symons Creek a Quaker by the name of Boyd. One of his brethren owed him some money and would not repay him. This made Boyd mad so he called up the debtor in a meeting, but the Quakers would not make the debtor pay. That made Quaker Boyd more furious so he took all his possessions, and settled in the forest five miles away on the bank of a creek. The Quakers called it 'Boyd's New Beginning,' which in time was shortened to 'Boyd's Newbegun,' and then to simply New Begun Creek." See Ancient Pasquotank County, 1586-1793 by Jerome B. Flora, 1953;

    Wheeler's Historic Sketches of N.C.;

    Albertson's Ancient Albemarle, Lawson's History of North Carolina.

30. *Naval Chronology*, II-47, VI-253.

31. William F. Martin Collection 493, Southern Historical Collection, University of North Carolina, Chapel Hill, N.C. 'Report of Evidence taken before a Joint Committee of both Houses of the Confederate Congress to Investigate the Affairs of the Navy Department.' (Richmond, 1863).

32. *Naval Chronology*, II-54;

    William A. Griffin, *Ante Bellum Elizabeth City*, p. 84.

33. ORN, Ser. I, Vol. VII, pp. 751-752;

    Ralph W. Donnelly, *The Charlotte, North Carolina, Navy Yard, C.S.N.*, p. 73. History of Charlotte & Mecklenburg.

34. ORN, Ser. I, Vol. VII, p. 779;

    Ralph W. Donnelly, p. 73.

35. ORN, Ser. I, Vol. VII, p. 780;

    Ralph W. Donnelly, p. 73.

36. Donnelly, *The Charlotte, North Carolina, Navy Yard, C.S.N.*, pp. 73, 74.

37. *Naval Chronology,* II-62;

    Ralph W. Donnelly, *The Charlotte, North Carolina, Navy Yard, C.S.N.*, p. 73.

38. ORN, Ser. I, Vol. VII, pp. 374, 375.

39. Clark, *N.C. Regiments, 1861-1865*, Vol. I, p. 10.

40. Weymouth T. Jordan, Jr., *North Carolina Troops, 1861-1865, A Roster*, Vol. VI, p. 201, 204. N.C. Archives & History;

    Ibid., Addenda, Vol. VI, p. 730;

    Clark, *N.C. Regiments, 1861-1865*, Vol. II, p. 2.

41. W. T. Jordan, Jr., *North Carolina Troops, 1861-1865, A Roster,* Vol. VI, p. 201. N.C. Archives & History.

42. Clark, *N.C. Regiments, 1861-1865*, Vol. III, p. 227.

43. Clark, *N.C. Regiments, 1861-1865*, Vol. IV, pp. 555, 556.

44. Micro Reel, NA-MC270-252, *17th Regiment, Infantry*, N.C. Archives & History.

45. *Ibid.*, Voucher #716, dated August 4, 1862, N.C. Archives & History.

46. Charles Grice Elliott, Article, *The Ram Albemarle,* for the <u>Richmond Dispatch</u>, and reprinted, <u>The Patron and Gleaner</u>, January 5, 1899, Rich Square, Northhampton County, N.C., Joyner Library, East Carolina University, Greenville, N.C.

47. Clark, *N. C. Regiments, 1861-1865*, Vol. II, p. 2.

NOTES for CHAPTER 6

1. ORN, Ser. I, Vol. VII, pp. 486, 487.

2. Beth G. Crabtree and James W. Patton, eds., *Journal of a Secesh Lady: The Diary of Catherine Ann Devereux Edmondston, 1860-1866,* Second Printing. (Raleigh, N.C.: N.C. Division of Archives & History), p. 218.

3. ORN, Ser. I, Vol. VII, pp. 556, 557.

4. Gov. Henry Clark's Papers, N.C. Archives & History.

5. Micro Reel, NA-MC270-252, N.C. Archives & History.

6. *Ibid.*

7. Contract, Tarboro Ironclad, September 17, 1862, 'Report of Evidence Taken Before a Joint Committee of Both Houses of the Confederate Congress to Investigate the Affairs of the Navy Department.' (Richmond, 1863).

8. Micro Reel, NA-MC270-252, N.C. Archives & History.

9. Messrs. Leslie S. Bright, William H. Rowland, and James C. Bardon, *C.S.S. Neuse, A Question of Iron and Time*, p. 150, N.C. Archives & History.

10. Charles V. Peery, M.D., Collection, Charleston, S.C.

11. Charles V. Peery, M.D., Collection, Charleston, S.C;

    William F. Martin Collection 493, Southern Historical Collection, University of North Carolina, Chapel Hill, N.C.

12. William F. Martin Collection 493, Southern Historical Collection, University of North Carolina, Chapel Hill, N.C.

13. Charles V. Peery, M.D., Collection, Charleston, S.C.

14. William S. Powell, *The Dictionary of North Carolina Biography*, (Chapel Hill: University of North Carolina Press, 1979);

    James Wallace Cooke Collection 176, Southern Historical Collection, University of North Carolina, Chapel Hill, S.C. Cdr. James W. Cooke was to become Gilbert Elliott's friend, instructor, and on-site superintending Naval officer during construction of several vessels under contract in the Roanoke River valley. The congenial relationship lasted through the building of a second ironclad at Edwards Ferry. This final episode ended in April, 1865.

15. Clark, *N.C. Regiments, 1861-1865*, Vol. V, p. 6. Brig. Gen. Walter Gwynn, formerly of West Point, was assigned on October 9, 1862, to examine and defend the Neuse, Tar, Roanoke, and Chowan rivers, by obstructing their channels and placing batteries commanding the obstructions. There were to be works at two points on the Neuse as low as Kinston, on the Tar at Greenville, and the Roanoke at or near Hamilton. By November 8 work was in progress near Hamilton, the vicinity of Tarboro, and at Kinston.

16. William F. Martin Collection 493, Southern Historical Collection, University of North Carolina, Chapel Hill, N.C.

17. Charles V. Peery, M.D., Collection, Charleston, S.C.

18. J. Thomas Scharf, *History of the Confederate States Navy*. (New York: Rogers & Sherwood, 1887), p. 404.

19. Micro Reel, NA-MC270-252, N.C. Archives & History.

20. *Naval Chronology*, II-105,107.

21. ORN, Ser. I, Vol. VIII, p. 844.

22. William S. Powell, *The North Carolina Gazetter*. Whitehall, now known as Seven Springs, was incorporated in 1855, and changed to White Hall in 1881. The original name honored the plantation home of William Whitefield, who built there in 1741. The name was changed to Seven Springs in 1951. A resort operated around seven mineral springs from 1881 until 1944. The hotel and spring house still stand. During 1863 the Confederate ironclad, *Neuse*, was built here. (Chapel Hill: University of North Carolina Press, 1968).

23. ORN, Ser. I, Vol. VIII, p. 845.

24. *Journal of a Secesh Lady*, pp. 291-295, N.C. Archives & History.

25. *Ibid.*, p. 295.

26. War of the Rebellion: The Official Records of the Union and Confederate Armies (Washington: Government Printing Office, 1889-1901), hereinafter abbreviated as ORA, Ser. I, Vol. XVIII, pp. 777, 778.

27. ORN, Ser. I, Vol. VIII, pp. 849, 850.

28. *Naval Chronology,* II-110, 111.

29. F. L. Bond papers, Collection 296, Joyner Library, East Carolina University, Greenville, N.C.

30. Charles V. Peery, M.D., Collection, Charleston, S.C;

    ORN, Ser. II, Vol. II, p. 532.

31. Charles V. Peery, M.D., Collection, Charleston, S.C.

32. *Ibid.*

33. *Ibid.*

34. Micro Reel, NA-MC270-252, *17th Regiment, Infantry*, N.C. Archives & History;

    Clark, *N.C. Regiments, 1861-1865*, Vol. II, p. 677.

NOTES for CHAPTER 7

1. *Journal of a Secesh Lady*, p. 330, N.C. Archives & History.

2. ORA, Ser. I, Vol. XVIII, p. 853.

3. Charles V. Peery, M.D., Collection, Charleston, S.C.

4. *Ibid.*

5. *Ibid.*

6. William F. Martin Collection 493, Southern Historical Collection, University of North Carolina, Chapel Hill, N.C.

7. Micro Reel M-1091, *Halifax Yard*, Confederate Subject File, Record Group 45, National Archives.

8. ORA, Ser. I, Vol. XVIII, p. 853.

9. Charles V. Peery, M.D., Collection, Charleston, S.C.

10. Gov. Zebulon Vance Letter Book GLB 50.1, pp. 104, 105, N.C. Archives & History.

11. *Ibid.*

12. *Ibid.*, pp. 105, 106.

13. Box 78, Folder 1, Adjutant General's Dept., Misc. Records, N.C. Archives & History.

14. Gov. Zebulon Vance Letter Book GLB 50.1, p. 104, N.C. Archives & History.

15. *Ibid.* p. 100.

16. Charles V. Peery, M.D., Collection, Charleston, S.C.

17. F. L. Bond papers, Collection 296, Joyner Library, East Carolina University, Greenville, N. C.

18. Micro Reel M-1091, *Halifax Yard*, Confederate Subject File, Record Group 45, National Archives.

19. Charles V. Peery, M.D., Collection, Charleston, S.C.

20. *Ibid.*

21. ORA, Ser. I, Vol. XVIII, p. 875.

22. ORN, Ser. I, Vol. VIII, p. 859.

23. *Journal of a Secesh Lady*, pp. 360, 361, N.C. Archives & History.

24. Charles V. Peery, M.D., Collection, Charleston, S.C.

25. Micro Reel, NA-MC270-252, *17th Regiment, Infantry*. N.C. Archives & History.

26. Daniel Harvey Hill papers PC 93, N.C. Archives & History.

NOTES for CHAPTER 8

1. Samuel A. Ashe, *History of North Carolina*, Vol. II, pp. 854, 855.

2. Manly Wade Wellman, article, *The Life and Death of the Ram Albemarle*, (News & Observer, Raleigh, N.C., Dec. 06, 1959);

   Ben Dixon MacNeill, article in News & Observer, Raleigh, N.C., March 22, 1925;

   Claiborne T. Smith, M.D., *Smith of Scotland Neck*, pp. 98, 117. Peter Evans Smith, son of William R. Smith, Jr., and Susan Evans Smith, was born on January 20, 1829, at 'Piney Prospect.' It was the Edgecombe plantation of his paternal grandfather Peter Evans, for whom he was named. His scholastic career began at Vine Hill Academy with college preparation at the Bingham School in Orange County, N.C. He graduated from Chapel Hill in 1851. On December 22, 1852, Peter married Rebecca Norfleet Hill, the daughter of Whitmel John Hill of 'Kenmore' near Scotland Neck. At the time of his marriage to Rebecca Norfleet Hill, Peter's father gave him a plantation on the Roanoke to farm. It was thereafter called 'Peters.' As well, he received the Marmaduke Norfleet homesite for a residence. It was just north of the Old Trinity Church, and upon this site Peter built his home which he called 'Sunnyside.'

3. Peter Evans Smith papers P-677, Southern Historical Collection, University of North Carolina, Chapel Hill, N.C. Photographs of the *Albemarle* keel site were contributed in 1888 by Miss Lena H. Smith, daughter of Peter Evans Smith, on which she personally described the scene;

   Miss Lena H. Smith, article, *Edwards Ferry*, (The Commonwealth, Scotland Neck, N.C., Aug. 03, 1928).

4. The Commonwealth, Scotland Neck, N.C., Feb. 16, 1922;

   Claiborne T. Smith, Jr., M.D., *Smith of Scotland Neck*, p. 114;

   Samuel A. Ashe, *History of North Carolina*, Vol. II, pp. 854, 855;

Americana Illustrated, 1932, p. 336;

Burton H. Smith, nephew of Peter Evans Smith, unpublished manuscript, authors collection.

5. Manly Wade Wellman, *The Life and Death of the Ram Albemarle,* (News & Dispatch, Raleigh, N.C., March 22, 1925).

6. Miss Lena H. Smith, article, *Sunnyside,* (The Commonwealth, Scotland Neck, N.C., July 06, 1928).

7. Claiborne T. Smith, Jr., M.D., *Smith of Scotland Neck,* p. 159;

Article, *The Building of the Albemarle,* (The Commonwealth, Scotland Neck, N.C., February 06, 1922).

8. Claiborne T. Smith, Jr., M.D., *Smith of Scotland Neck,* p. 112;

Miss Lena H. Smith, article, *New Albemarle Data Released for First Time,* publication unknown, circa late 1920's.

9. ORN, Ser. I, Vol. IX, p. 66.

10. *Journal of a Secesh Lady,* p. 374, N.C. Archives & History.

11. ORN, Ser. I, Vol. VIII, p. 865;

Naval Chronology, III-58.

12. ORN, Ser. I, Vol. VIII, p. 865.

13. Charles V. Peery, M.D., Collection, Charleston, S.C.

14. Micro Reel M-1091, *Halifax Yard,* Confederate Subject File, Record Group 45, National Archives.

15. *Naval Chronology,* III-74.

16. *Journal of a Secesh Lady,* pp. 392, 393, N.C. Archives & History.

17. Micro Reel NA-MC270-252, *17th Regiment, Infantry,* N.C. Archives & History.

18. Micro Reel M-1091, *Halifax Yard,* Confederate Subject File, Record Group 45, National Archives.

19. John L. Porter, Chief Constructor, C.S.N., plans for C.S. *Albemarle,* Smithsonian Institution, Washington D.C.

20. Gilbert Elliott, article, *The Career of the Confederate Ram Albemarle,* (Century Magazine, July, 1888).

21. *Journal of a Secesh Lady*, pp. 394, 395, N.C. Archives & History.

22. ORN, Ser. I, Vol. X, pp. 135, 136, 263, 264.

23. *Journal of a Secesh Lady*, p. 395, N.C. Archives & History.

24. ORA, Ser. I, Vol. XVIII, p. 853.

25. Charles V. Peery, M.D., Collection, Charleston S.C.

26. Ralph W. Donnelly, *The Charlotte, North Carolina Navy Yard, C.S.N.*, pp. 72-79,

27. ORN, Ser. I, Vol. IX, p. 66.

28. Charles V. Peery, M.D., Collection, Charleston, S.C.

29. *Ibid.*

30. Charles B. Dew, *Ironmaker of The Confederacy, John R. Anderson and the Tredegar Iron Works*, (Chapel Hill: University of North Carolina Press, 1987), p. 117.

31. Micro Reel, NA-MC270-252, *17th Regiment, Infantry*, N.C. Archives & History.

32. Sketch of *Albemarle,* notations of dimensions and armor specifications, Confederate Subject File, #AD, Record Group 45, National Archives.

33. W. E. Geoghegan, *Albemarle* plans of John L. Porter, redrawn and enhanced, original plan #3-5-27, National Archives.

34. Sketch of *Albemarle,* notations of dimensions and armor specifications, Confederate Subject File, #AD, Record Group 45, National Archives.

35. Gilbert Elliott, article, *The Career of the Confederate Ram Albemarle,* (Century Magazine, July, 1888), p. 421.

36. *Journal of a Secesh Lady*, p. 420, N.C. Archives & History.

37. *Ibid.*, p. 423, N.C. Archives & History.

38. *Ibid.*, pp. 423, 424, N.C. Archives & History.

39. Micro Reel M-1091, *Halifax Yard*, Confederate Subject File, Record Group 45, National Archives.

40. *Journal of a Secesh Lady*, p. 425, N.C. Archives & History.

41. Gilbert Elliott, article, *The Career of the Confederate Ram Albemarle*, (Century Magazine, July, 1888), p. 421.

42. Charles V. Peery, M.D., Collection, Charleston, S.C.

43. *Ibid.*

44. *Journal of a Secesh Lady*, p. 435, N.C. Archives & History.

45. William S. Powell, *The North Carolina Gazetteer.* Old Sparta was a town in south Edgecombe County on the Tar River. It was a post office as early as 1830. The community as Sparta no longer is active in municipal affairs. (Chapel Hill: University of North Carolina Press, 1968), p. 363;

    ORA, Ser. I, Vol. XXVII, Pt. II, pp. 963-976;

    Barrett, *Civil War in North Carolina,* (Chapel Hill: University of North Carolina Press, 1963), pp. 164-166.

46. *Journal of a Secesh Lady*, pp. 436, 437, N.C. Archives & History.

47. *Ibid.*, pp. 439, 440. N.C. Archives & History;

    Clark, *N.C. Regiments, 1861-1865*, Vol. IV, p. 80, The 75th N.C. Regiment extinguished the Tarboro river bridge fire.

48. Charles V. Peery, M.D., Collection, Charleston, S.C.

49. ORN, Ser. I, Vol. IX, p. 66.

50. Charles V. Peery, M.D., Collection, Charleston, S.C.

51. Gilbert Elliott, article, *The Career of the Confederate Ram Albemarle,* (Century Magazine, July, 1888), p. 421;

    Donald L. Canney, *The Old Steam Navy: Frigates, Sloops & Gunboats, 1815-1885*, Vol. I, Glossary. (Annapolis, Md.: Naval Institute Press, 1990), p. 193.

52. Charles Grice Elliott, article, *The Ram Albemarle,* Richmond Dispatch, reprinted in The Patron and Gleaner, January 5, 1899, Rich Square, Northampton County, N.C., Joyner Library, East Carolina University, Greenville, N.C. The uncapitalized word negro is a typical representation of its use at that time.

53. *Journal of a Secesh Lady*, pp. 442-445, N.C. Archives & History.

54. *Ibid.*, p. 445, N.C. Archives & History.

55. *Ibid.*, p. 446, N.C. Archives & History.

56. *Ibid.*, p. 446.

57. Clark, *N.C. Regiments, 1861-1865*, Vol. I, p. 495.

58. ORN, Ser. I, Vol. IX, p. 162.

59. Micro Reel, M-1091, *Halifax Yard*, Confederate Subject File, Record Group 45, National Archives.

60. Charles V. Peery, M.D., Collection, Charleston, S.C.

61. Gilbert Elliott, article, *The Career of the Confederate Ram Albemarle*, (Century Magazine, July, 1888), p. 421;

    Charles Grice Elliott, article in Richmond Dispatch, reprinted in The Patron and Gleaner, January 5, 1899, Rich Square, N.C., Joyner Library, East Carolina University, Greenville, N.C.

62. *Journal of a Secesh Lady*, p. 462, N.C. Archives & History.

63. *Naval Chronology,* III-140.

64. *Journal of a Secesh Lady*, p. 468, N.C. Archives & History.

65. Charles V. Peery, M.D., Collection, Charleston, S.C.

66. Claiborne T. Smith, M.D., *Smith of Scotland Neck*, pp. 111, 119.

67. Lena H. Smith, article, *Kelvin Grove,* (The Commonwealth, Scotland Neck, N.C., June 13, 1928).

68. Charles V. Peery, M.D., Collection, Charleston, S.C.

69. Micro Reel, M-1091, *Halifax Yard*, Confederate Subject File, Record Group 45, National Archives.

70. Confederate Veteran Magazine, Vol. XXXVIII, October 1930, p. 406;

    Walter H. Paramore, article, (News & Observer, June 17, 1928);

    C. S. Ausbon, article, (News & Observer, February 27, 1927);

    Samuel A. Ashe, article, (History of North Carolina, Vol. II), p. 855;

    Burton H. Smith, article, (News & Observer, date unknown).

71. *Journal of a Secesh Lady*, p. 474, N.C. Archives & History.

72. Gilbert Elliott, article, *The Career of the Confederate Ram Albemarle*, (Century Magazine, July, 1888), p. 419.

73. Charles V. Peery, M.D., Collection, Charleston, S.C.

74. J. Thomas Scharf, *History of The Confederate States Navy*, (Rogers & Sherwood, N.Y., 1887), p. 404.

NOTES for CHAPTER 9

1. Gilbert Elliott, article, *The Career of the Confederate Ram Albemarle*, (Century Magazine, July, 1888), p. 421.

2. Charles V. Peery, M.D., Collection, Charleston, S.C.

3. *Ibid.*

4. Micro Reel, M-1091, *Halifax Yard*, Confederate Subject File, Record Group 45, National Archives.

5. *Journal of a Secesh Lady*, p. 480, N.C. Archives & History;

   Claiborne T. Smith, Jr., M.D., *Smith of Scotland Neck*, p. 119.

6. Box 78, Folder 1, Adjutant General's Dept., Misc. Records, N.C. Archives & History.

7. *Journal of a Secesh Lady,* p. 482, N.C. Archives & History.

8. Charles V. Peery, M.D., Collection, Charleston, S.C.

9. ORN, Ser. I, Vol. VII, p. 747.

10. Charles V. Peery, M.D., Collection, Charleston, S.C.

11. *Ibid.*

12. *Journal of a Secesh Lady*, p. 485. Scott, *Lady of the Lake*, canto 1, stanza 9, line 166. "Woe worth the chase, woe worth the day..." N.C. Archives & History.

13. Charles V. Peery, M.D., Collection, Charleston, S.C.

14. *Ibid.*

15. *Ibid.*

16. *Journal of a Secesh Lady*, XXXVIII, N.C. Archives & History.

17. *Ibid.*

18. Box 78, Folder 1, Adjutant General's Department, Misc. Records, N.C. Archives & History.

19. *Ibid.*

20. *Ibid.*

21. Box 78, Folder 1, Adjutant General's Department, Misc. Records, N.C. Archives & History; 'Report of Evidence Taken before a Joint Special

Committee of both houses of the Confederate Congress to investigate the affairs of the Navy Department.' (Richmond, 1863).

22. Charles V. Peery, M.D., Collection, Charleston, S.C.

23. Gilbert Elliott, article, *The Career of the Confederate Ram Albemarle,* (Century Magazine, July, 1888), p. 421.

24. Jaquelin Drane Nash, *A Goodly Heritage, the Story of Calvary Parish,* Tarboro, N.C., 1960.

25. *Journal of a Secesh Lady*, p. 493, N.C. Archives & History.

26. Governor Zebulon Vance Letter Book GLB 50.1, p. 373, N.C. Archives & History.

27. *Ibid.*, p. 373, Letter, Nov. 28, 1863, Vance to Mallory;

    Vance papers GP 173, Letter, Jan. 27, 1864, Elliott to Vance, and Letter, Jan. 28, 1864, Cooke to Vance.

28. *Naval Chronology,* III-159.

29. ORN, Ser. I, Vol. IX, pp. 797, 798

30. Charles V. Peery, M.D., Collection, Charleston, S.C.

31. *Ibid.*

32. *Ibid.*

33. *Ibid.*

34. Micro Reel, M-1091, Voucher #35, *Halifax Yard*, Confederate Subject File, Record Group 45, National Archives.

35. Charles V. Peery, M.D., Collection, Charleston, S.C.

36. Governor Zebulon Vance Letter Book GLB 50.1, pp. 377, 378, N.C. Archives & History.

37. Micro Reel, NA-MC270-252, *17th Regiment, Infantry*, N.C. Archives & History.

38. *Ibid.*

NOTES for CHAPTER 10

1. ORA, Ser. I, Vol. XXXIII, p. 1061.

2. *Ibid.*, p. 1064.

3. Micro Reel M-1091, *Halifax Yard*, Confederate Subject File, Record Group 45, National Archives.

4. *Ibid.*

5. *Ibid.*

6. Charles V. Peery, M.D., Collection, Charleston, S.C.

7. *Ibid.*

8. ORN, Ser. I, Vol. IX, pp. 799, 800.

9. John G. Barrett, *The Civil War in North Carolina: The Confederate Goliath*, Chapter X, (Chapel Hill: University of North Carolina Press, 1963), p. 215.

10. Benjamin F. Loyall speech, Jan. 19, 1897, <u>Fisher and Farmer,</u> Elizabeth City, N.C., Friday, May, ____, Front page. Manuscript Collection, Joyner Library, East Carolina University, Greenville, N.C.

11. Herbert Wrigley Wilson, *Ironclads in Action,* Chapter V., Marshall W. Butt Library, Portsmouth Naval Shipyard Museum, Portsmouth, Va. (London: S. Low Marston & Co., 1897), p. 107.

12. J. Thomas Scharf, *History of the Confederate States Navy,* (Rogers & Sherwood, New York, 1887), p. 405.

13. Gilbert Elliott, article, *The Career of the Confederate Ram Albemarle,* (<u>Century Magazine</u>, July, 1888), p. 421;

    C.S.S. Ram Albemarle, specs., The Mariners Museum Library, Newport News, Virginia.

14. Donald L. Canney, *The Old Steam Navy:Frigates, Sloops and Gunboats, 1815-1885.* Vol. I, Glossary. (Annapolis, Md.: U.S. Naval Institute Press), p. 192.

15. Hand written assessment of *Albemarle's* condition, U.S. Navy Yard, Norfolk, Va., May 18, 1865. Case 146, U.S. District Court, Washington, D.C., Record Group 21, National Archives.

16. Donald L. Canney, *The Old Steam Navy: Frigates, Sloops and Gunboats, 1815-1885.* Vol. I, Glossary. (Annapolis, Md., U.S. Navy Institute Press), p. 193.

17. Ralph W. Donnelly, *The Charlotte, North Carolina, Navy Yard, C.S.N.,* p. 78.

18. ORA, Ser. I, Vol. XXXIII, p. 1101.

19. Governor Zebulon Vance papers GP 173, N.C. Archives & History.

20. *Ibid.*

21. ORA, Ser. II, Vol. VI, p. 847

22. Governor Zebulon Vance papers GP 174, N.C. Archives & History.

23. *Naval Chronology,* IV-12, 13.

24. ORA, Ser. I, Vol. XXXIII, pp. 54, 56.

25. Governor Zebulon Vance papers GP 173, N.C. Archives & History.

26. Micro Reel, M-1091, *Halifax Yard,* vouchers 65, 66, 67, 85, and 86. Confederate Subject File, Record Group 45, National Archives.

27. Port O'Plymouth Roanoke River Museum, Plymouth, N.C.

28. *Journal of a Secesh Lady,* p. 526, N.C. Archives & History.

29. *Naval Chronology*, IV-20, 21.

30. ORN, Ser. I, Vol. II, p. 827.

31. *Naval Chronology,* IV-23.

32. *Ibid.* IV-24.

33. Micro Reel, NA-MC270-252, *17th Regiment, Infantry*, (Second Organization). N.C. Archives & History.

34. Micro Reel, M-1091, *Halifax Yard,* Confederate Subject File, Record Group 45, National Archives.

35. *Albemarle* drawing with measurement information. Confederate Subject File #AD, Record Group 45, National Archives.

36. Gilbert Elliott, *The Career of the Confederate Ram Albemarle,* (Century Magazine, July, 1888), p. 421.

37. Charles V. Peery, M.D., Collection, Charleston, S.C.

38. ORN, Ser. I, Vol. IX, p. 803.

39. *Ibid.*

40. *Ibid.* pp. 802, 803.

41. *Ibid.* p. 803.

42. *Naval Chronology,* IV-32.

43. Port O'Plymouth Roanoke River Museum, Plymouth, N.C. In 1860 Benjamin J. Spruill, a Superior Court Judge, was 53. A native of Bertie County bordering the Roanoke on the north opposite Plymouth, Spruill had married a lady from Plymouth and settled there to live. Perhaps Elliott saw in Spruill an effective agent who could quietly negotiate acquisitions from local Union authorities.

44. Lena H. Smith, article, *New Albemarle Data Released for First Time,* possibly in News & Observer, Raleigh, circa 1928. Courtesy of Claiborne T. Smith, Jr., M.D., Ardmore, Pa. In the article Lena, who was Peter E. Smith's daughter, remarked that "the floating battery had proven so unwieldy that it was eventually abandonded."

45. Micro Reel, M-1091, *Halifax Yard,* Confederate Subject File, Record Group 45, National Archives.

46. *Naval Chronology,* IV-32.

47. ORA, Ser. I, Vol. XXXIII, p. 748.

48. Micro Reel, M-1091, *Halifax Yard,* Confederate Subject File, Record Group 45, National Archives.

49. Gilbert Elliott, article, *The Career of the Confederate Ram Albemarle,* (Century Magazine, July, 1888), pp. 419-421;

    The *Albemarle's* specifications during her April 1864 construction stages have been disclosed in five sources: Contractor Elliott; Constructor John L. Porter; W. E. Geohegan; the U.S. Navy at Norfolk, Va.; and the National Archives.

50. Donald L. Canney, The Old Steam Navy: *Frigates, Sloops and Gunboats, 1815-1885.* Vol. I, Glossary. Rabbet: A joint made by a groove or channel in a piece of timber, cut to receive and secure the edge or ends of planks, as planks to the keel, stem, or sternpost. (Annapolis, Md.: U.S. Naval Institute Press), p. 193.

51. John L. Porter, *Plan for Albemarle,* 3-5-27, Record Group 19, National Archives.

52. Case 146, U.S. District Court, Research Group 21, Survey of *Albemarle,* May 18, 1865, by Cdr. Henry N. Arnold, Naval Constructor J. Hanscom, and Chief Engineer John H. Long. Approved by Capt. John N. Berrien, Commandant of U.S. Navy Yard, Norfolk, Va., National Archives;

James C. Long letter to Midshipman Hubbard T. Minor, June 28, 1864, after battle of Plymouth, N.C. Dr. Richard J. Sommers Collection, U.S. Army Military History Institute, Carlisle, Pa.

NOTES for CHAPTER 11

1. Micro Reel, M-1091, *Halifax Yard*, Mar. 1, 1864, Confederate Subject File, Record Group 45, National Archives.

2. *Naval Chronology,* IV-38.

3. J. Thomas Scharf, *History of the Confederate States Navy*, (Rogers & Sherwood, New York, 1887), p. 404.

4. ORA, Ser. I, Vol. LI, Pt.2, p. 858, Apr. 12, 1864.

5. ORA, Ser. I, Vol. XXXIII, p. 281, 5 P.M., Apr. 13, 1864.

6. *Albemarle's* commissioning, Confederate Subject File, Record Group 45, Area 7 File, National Archives. Courtesy Confederate Naval Museum, Columbus, Ga.

7. ORN, Ser. I, Vol. IX, p. 656, Apr. 23, 1864. Cooke's battle report from Apr. 17 to 23, 1864;

   Gilbert Elliott, article, *The Career of the Confederate Ram Albemarle,* (Century Magazine, July, 1888), p. 422.

8. Clark, *N.C. Regiments, 1861-1865*, Vol. V, p. 181.

9. *Ibid.*

10. Martin County Historical Society, N.C., article for Enterprise, from W. A. Ellison papers, Hyde County, N.C;

    Wilson, Herbert Wrigley, *Ironclads in Action.*, Chapter V, Marshall W. Butt Library. Portsmouth Naval Shipyard Museum, Portsmouth, VA. (London: S. Low Marston & Co., 1897), p. 107;

    J. Thomas Scharf, *History of the Confederate States Navy*, (Rogers & Sherwood, New York, 1887), p. 405.

11. Wilson Herbert Wrigley, *Ironclads in Action*, Chapter V, Marshall W. Butt Library. Portsmouth Naval Shipyard Museum, Portsmouth, Va. (London: S. Low Marston & Co., 1897), 107;

    J. Thomas Scharf, *History of the Confederate States Navy,* (Rogers & Sherwood, New York, 1887), p. 405.

12. ORN, Ser. I, Vol. IX, p. 656, Cooke's battle report;

    Shelby Foote, *Red River to Appomatox*, Vol. III, p. 113;

    John Gilchrist Barrett, *The Civil War in North Carolina*, Chapter X. (Chapel Hill: University of North Carolina Press, 1963), p. 217.

13. ORN, Ser. I, Vol. IX, p. 637.

14. *Ibid.,* pp. 636, 637.

15. Gilbert Elliott, article, *The Career of the Confederate Ram Albemarle,* (Century Magazine, July, 1888), pp. 422, 423;

    ORN, Ser. I, Vol. IX, p. 656. Cooke's battle report.

16. Gilbert Elliott, article, *The Career of the Confederate Ram Albemarle,* (Century Magazine, July, 1888), pp. 422, 423.

17. Hayden Planetarium, *American Ephemeris & Nautical Almanac, 1864,* U.S. Naval Observatory.

18. Gilbert Elliott, article, *The Career of the Confederate Ram Albemarle,* (Century Magazine, July, 1888), p. 423.

19. ORN, Ser. I, Vol. IX, p. 657.

20. Hayden Planetarium, *American Ephemeris & Nautical Almanac, 1864.* U.S. Naval Observatory.

21. ORN, Ser. I, Vol. IX, p. 657.

22. Hayden Planetarium, *American Ephemeris & Nautical Almanac, 1864,* U. S. Naval Observatory.

23. N.C. State Pension Records (Confederate), 1901. N.C. Department of Archives and History. In June 1917, while a resident of Bertie County, N.C., Benjamin H. Gray applied for a Confederate Pension from North Carolina, and it was approved a month later in July. After he died on June 11, 1924, his wife Margaret was granted a pension based upon Ben's service. It was said he became a minister in later life.

24. ORN, Ser. I, Vol. IX, p. 657. Cooke's battle report, Apr. 23, 1864, aboard C.S.S. *Albemarle,* off Plymouth, N.C.

25. *Ibid.,* pp. 638, 639

26. *Ibid.,* p. 638.

27. Clark, *N.C. Regiments, 1861-1865,* Vol. V, p. 182.

28. ORN, Ser. I, Vol. IX, p. 647.

29. Clark, *N.C. Regiments, 1861-1865,* Vol. V, p. 183.

30. *Ibid.*, p. 190;

    ORN, Ser. I, Vol. IX, p. 655.

31. Robert G. Elliott, personal collection. A fragment of Ft. Williams' garrison flag has a single star pierced with several holes, evidently from exploding shell fragments. A letter addressed to Ira B. Sampson from Washington City, Oct. 5, 1882, requesting Sampson accept the flag fragment in good faith, "with nothing to be said how it reached your hand." Another letter to Ira B. Sampson from Washington City, June 29, 1885, in response to Sampson's request for glass with which to frame the flag fragment.

32. ORN, Ser. I, Vol. IX, p. 648.

33. *Ibid.*, p. 646.

34. *Ibid.*, p. 657;

    Louis Manarin, Historian, Virginia State Library.

35. ORN, Ser. I, Vol. IX, p. 658.

36. *Naval Chronology,* VI-206;

    Clark, *N.C. Regiments, 1861-1865*, Vol. III, pp. 337, 338;

    ORN, Ser. I, Vol. IX, p. 653;

    J. Thomas Scharf, *History of the Confederate States Navy*, (Rogers & Sherwood, New York, 1887), p. 405, 407.

37. ORN, Ser. I, Vol. IX, p. 649.

38. *Ibid.*, p. 647.

39. *Ibid.*, p. 649.

40. ORA, Ser. I, Vol. XXXIII, p. 295.

41. ORN, Ser. I, Vol. IX, p. 658.

42. *Ibid.*, p. 650.

43. *Ibid.*, p. 651.

44. *Ibid.*, p. 808;

    Naval Chronology, VI-206.

45. ORN, Ser. I, Vol. IX, p. 658.

NOTES for CHAPTER 12

1. Micro Reel, M-1091, *Halifax Yard*, Confederate Subject File, Record Group 45, National Archives.

2. Starke-Marchant-Martin papers 1549, Southern Historical Collection, University of North Carolina, Chapel Hill, N.C.

3. ORN, Ser. I, Vol. IX, p. 810;

   ORA, Ser. I, Vol. LI, Pt. 2, p. 882.

4. Frank P. O'Brien, memoirs, excerpts published in Under Both Flags, A Panorama of the Great Civil War, Edited by George M. Vickers, (World Bible House, Philadelphia, Pa., 1896), pp. 259-261. Port O'Plymouth Roanoke River Museum, Plymouth, N.C. Frank P. O'Brien was a member of the Montgomery True Blues, having enlisted in January 1861.

5. Charles V. Peery, M. D., Collection, Charleston, S.C.

6. Starke-Marchant-Martin papers 1549, Southern Historical Collection, University of North Carolina, Chapel Hill, N.C.

7. Frank P. O'Brien, memoirs. Port O'Plymouth Roanoke River Museum, Plymouth, N.C.

8. ORA, Ser. I, Vol. XXXIII, p. 294.

9. Frank P. O'Brien, memoirs. Port O'Plymouth Roanoke River Museum, Plymouth, N.C.

10. ORN, Ser. I, Vol. IX, p. 770. Cooke's battle report to Cdr. R. F. Pinckney, May 7, 1864.

11. *Ibid.*, p. 768. Statement of John B. Patrick, seaman, late of C.S. *Albemarle*, taken by Capt. John S. Barnes, U.S.N., June 26, 1864.

12. *Ibid.*, p. 753. Lt. Charles A. French, commanding *Miami*, battle report, May 6, 1864;

    Ibid., p. 734. Capt. Melancton Smith, commanding *Mattabesett*, battle report to Adm. S. P. Lee at anchor, May 5, 1864.

13. *Ibid.*, p, 734. Capt. M. Smith's report.

14. Bryon Josephus Woodhull, memoirs. Former crewman on *Ceres*, May 5, 1864. Port O'Plymouth Roanoke River Museum, Plymouth, N.C.

15. ORN, Ser. I, Vol. IX, p. 770. Cooke's battle report;

    Ibid., p. 753. Lt. French's *Miami* battle report, May 6;

    Ibid., p. 755. Ensign George W. Barrett's *Whitehead* battle report, May 6.

16. Byron Josephus Woodhull, memoirs. Port O'Plymouth Roanoke River Museum, Plymouth, N.C.;

    ORN, Ser. I, Vol. IX, p. 770. Cooke's battle report.

17. ORN, Ser. II, Vol. I, p. 139. Statistics of U.S. Ships.

18. ORN, Ser. I, Vol. IX, p. 770. Cooke's battle report, May 7;

    Ibid., p. 768. Seaman John B. Patrick's battle statement, June 27;

    Ibid., p. 734. Capt. Melancton Smith's battle report, May 5;

    Ibid., p. 749. Cdr. John C. Febiger's battle report, May 5;

    Ibid., p. 747. Cdr. John C. Febiger's battle report, May 6.

19. ORN, Ser. I, Vol. IX, p. 747. Cdr. John C. Febiger's battle report, May 6;

    Frank P. O'Brien, memoirs. Port O'Plymouth Roanoke River Museum, Plymouth, N.C.;

    ORN, Ser. I, Vol. IX, p. 734. Capt. Melancton Smith's battle report, May 5;

    ORN, Ser. II, Vol. I, pp. 202, 243. Statistics of U.S. Ships.

20. ORN, Ser. I, Vol. IX, p. 744. Acting Master C. A. Boutelle, *Sassacus* report, May 5;

    Ibid., p. 737. Cdr. Francis A. Roe's battle report, May 5;

    Ibid., p. 738;

    ORN, Ser. II, Vol. I, pp. 202, 242.

21. Frank P. O'Brien, memoirs. Port O'Plymouth Roanoke River Museum, Plymouth, N.C.;

    ORN, Ser. I, Vol. IX, pp. 738, 739. Commander Roe, *Sassacus* battle report, May 6;

    Ibid., pp. 741, 744, 745. Master C. A. Boutelle, *Sassacus* battle report, May 6;

    Ibid., p. 769. John B. Patrick, seaman's statement, June 27, 1864;

Battles and Leaders, Vol. IV, p. 629. Edgar Holden, U.S.N., Ass't Surgeon, aboard *Sassacus*, May 5;

Gilbert Elliott, article, *The Career of the Confederate Ram Albemarle*, (Century Magazine, July, 1888), p. 426.

22. *Battles and Leaders*, Vol. IV, p. 630;

Frank P. O'Brien, memoirs. Port O'Plymouth Roanoke River Museum, Plymouth, N.C.;

ORN, Ser. I, Vol. IX, p. 739. Cdr. Francis A. Roe, *Sassacus* battle report, May 6;

Ibid., p. 741. Master C. A. Boutelle, *Sassacus* battle report, May 6;

Ibid., p. 745. Boutelle's battle report, May 5;

J. Thomas Scharf, *History of the Confederate States Navy.* (Rogers & Sherwood, New York, 1887), p. 410;

ORN, Ser. I, Vol. IX, p. 738. Roe's battle report, May 5;

Newspaper article, *Batchelor's Bay Battle visible at Scotch Hall*, Bertie Ledger-Advance, Windsor, N.C., Feb. 21, 1963. In later years this newspaper article reviewed the memorable battle. It was of particular interest to family descendants of those who had then lived along the northern shores of Albemarle Sound, from Batchelor's Bay above the Roanoke east to Sandy Point. "People standing on the shore at Scotch Hall and neighboring plantations had ring side seats of this battle and there were many who watched.";

William S. Powell, *The North Carolina Gazetter*. (Chapel Hill: University of North Carolina Press, 1968), p. 58. Scotch Hall, in Bertie County, was one of several plantations owned by the Pettigrew family in southeastern Washington and western Tyrrell counties.

23. ORN, Ser. I, Vol. IX, p. 748. Cdr. John C. Febiger, *Mattabesett* after-battle report, May 6;

Ibid., pp. 750, 751. Lt. W. W. Queen, *Wyalusing* after-battle report, May 6;

Ibid., p. 753. Lt. Charles A. French, *Miami* after-battle report, May 6;

Ibid., pp. 756, 757. Master Francis Josselyn, *Commodore Hull* after-battle report, May 6;

Ibid., p. 771. Cdr. James W. Cooke, *Albemarle* after-battle report, May 6;

Frank P. O'Brien, memoirs. Port O'Plymouth Roanoke River Museum, Plymouth, N.C.;

Gilbert Elliott, article, *The Career of the Confederate Ram Albemarle.* (Century Magazine, July, 1888), p. 426;

ORN, Ser. II, Vol. I, p. 143.

24. Starke-Marchant-Martin papers 1549. Letter of Gen. James G. Martin to his wife, 8:00 P.M., Thursday, May 5, 1864. Southern Historical Collection, University of North Carolina, Chapel Hill, N.C.

25. Charles V. Peery, M. D., Collection, Charleston, S.C. Acting Gunner Hugh McDonald's *Albemarle* ordnance report to Lt. F. W. Roby, May 5, 1864.

26. *Ibid.*, Official *Albemarle* ordnance report of May 6, 1864, from Acting Gunner Hugh McDonald to John Mercer Brooke, C.S.N., Chief of Ordnance Bureau.

27. ORN, Ser. I, Vol. IX, pp. 746, 749, 751, 752, 754, 755, 756;

ORN, Ser. II, Vol. I, pp. 54, 63, 139, 143, 202, 239, 242, 243;

J. Thomas Scharf, *History of the Confederate States Navy.* (Rogers & Sherwood, New York, 1887), pp. 411, 412.

28. Starke-Marchant-Martin papers 1549. Letter from Gen. James G. Martin to his wife, May 6, 1864. Southern Historical Collection, University of North Carolina, Chapel Hill, N.C.

29. Smithwick papers PC 257. N.C. Archives & History.

30. Charles V. Peery, M. D., Collection, Charleston, S.C.

31. *Ibid.*

32. *Ibid.*

33. ORN, Ser. I, Vol. IX, pp. 745, 746. Master C. A. Boutelle's report to Lt. Cdr. F. A. Roe, May 6, 1864.

34. *Ibid.*, p. 771. Commander Cooke's after-battle report to Commander R. F. Pinkney, May 7, 1864.

NOTES for CHAPTER 13

1. ORN, Ser. I, Vol. X, p. 627. Cooke's May 8, 1864, letter to Secretary Mallory;

Naval Chronology, IV-56.

2. *Journal of a Secesh Lady*, p. 556. N.C. Archives & History.

3. ORN, Ser. I, Vol. X, p. 641. Cooke's May 16, 1864, report to Cdr. John M. Brooke, Ordnance Department, Richmond;

   C. S. Ausbon, article, *Would Erect Memorial for Confederate Ram.* (<u>News & Observer</u>, Raleigh, N.C., February 27, 1927);

   Diary of Byron Josephus Woodhull, Williamson, N.J., 1864. He was crewman on *Ceres* during battle of May 5, 1864. Port O'Plymouth Roanoke River Museum, Plymouth, N.C.

4. ORN, Ser. I, Vol. X, pp. 31, 32. Capt. Melancton Smith's May 7, 1864, report to Rear Adm. Samuel. P. Lee.

5. *Ibid.*, pp. 37, 38. Navy Secretary Gideon Welles' May 9 response to the House of Representatives.

6. *Journal of a Secesh Lady*, p. 556. N.C. Archives & History.

7. Gov. Zebulon Vance papers GP 177-File, May 10-13, 1864. N.C. Archives & History.

8. ORN, Ser. I, Vol. X, p. 631.

9. Micro Reel NA-MC270-252, *17th Regiment, Infantry*. N.C. Archives & History.

10. ORN, Ser. I, Vol. X, pp. 49, 50. Capt. Melancton Smith's May 12, 1864, report to Rear Adm. Samuel P. Lee.

11. *Ibid.*, p. 55.

12. ORN, Ser. I, Vol. IX, p. 733.

13. ORN, Ser. I, Vol. X, p. 73.

14. Gov. Zebulon Vance papers GP 177-File. N.C. Archives & History.

15. ORN, Ser. I, Vol. X, p. 86.

16. J. Thomas Scharf, *History of the Confederate States Navy.* (Rogers & Sherwood, New York, 1887), pp. 412, 413;

    Naval Chronology, IV-62.

17. Mackay and Stiles papers 470. Southern Historical Collection, University of North Carolina, Chapel Hill, N.C.

18. Gov. Zebulon Vance papers GP 177. N.C. Archives & History.

19. ORN, Ser. I, Vol. IX, pp. 762-764. Reports of Capt. Melancton Smith, June 1 & 4, and Cdr. Richard T. Renshaw, June 3, 1864.

20. ORA, Ser. I, Vol. XXXVI, Pt.3, p. 565.

21. ORN, Ser. I, Vol. X, p. 145.

22. *Ibid.*, p. 135. Captain Smith's June 8, 1864, order to Lt James M. Williams of the *Commodore Barney*.

23. *Ibid.,* p. 687.

24. Charles V. Peery, M. D., Collection, Charleston, S.C. Letter of June 10, 1864, from Mallory to Cooke at Plymouth.

25. ORN, Ser. I, Vol. X, pp. 141, 142.

26. *Ibid.*, pp. 144, 145.

27. *Ibid.*, p. 704.

28. *Journal of a Secesh Lady*, pp. 578, 579. N.C. Archives & History.

29. ORN, Ser. I, Vol. X, p. 211.

30. U.S. Army Military History Institute, Carlisle Barracks, Pa.

31. ORN, Ser. I, Vol. X, p. 220;

    Naval Chronology, IV-91.

32. Micro Reel M-1091, *Halifax Yard*, Confederate Subject File, Record Group 45, National Archives.

33. ORA, Ser. I, Vol. XL, Pt. III, pp. 751, 752. Col. George Wortham's July 2, 1864, letter to Ass't Adjutant General Capt. J. C. McRae, endorsed to Brig. Gen. Laurence S. Baker, endorsed to Secretary of War Seddon.

34. ORN, Ser. I, Vol. X, p. 718.

35. *Ibid.*, pp. 239, 240.

36. *Ibid.*, p. 240.

37. *Ibid.,* p. 751.

38. ORA, Ser. I, Vol. XL, Pt. III, p. 752.

39. ORN, Ser. I, Vol. X, pp. 246, 247.

40. *Ibid.*, pp. 247, 248.

41. *Ibid.*, p. 248.

42. *Ibid.*, pp. 263, 264. Commander Macomb's report to Admiral Lee.

43. Gov. Zebulon Vance Letter Book GLB 50.1, p. 536. N.C. Archives & History.

44. ORA, Ser. I, Vol. XL, Pt. III, pp. 343, 344. Brig. Gen. Innis N. Palmer's July 19, 1864, letter to Maj. R. S. Davis, A.A.G., Dept. of Virginia and North Carolina.

45. ORN, Ser. I, Vol. X, p. 303.

46. *Ibid.*, p. 306. John Woodman's July 26, 1864, recon report to Capt. Henry H. Foster;

   Micro Reel M-1091, *Halifax Yard*, Confederate Subject File, Record Group 45, National Archives. Blacksmith E. H. Wilson worked on the *Albemarle's* iron repairs for 26 days during April and from May 20 to September 9, 1864, on which day he was paid $527.00.

47. ORN, Ser. I, Vol. X, p. 720. Secretary Mallory's July 30, 1864, response to Secretary Seddon's request for consideration of views to revoke the *Albemarle's* orders.

NOTES for CHAPTER 14

1. ORN, Ser. I, Vol. X, p. 728.

2. *Ibid.*, pp. 339, 340.

3. Charles V. Peery, M. D., Collection, Charleston, S.C.

4. ORN, Ser. I, Vol. X, pp. 341, 342. Report of Lt. Cdr. William T. Truxtun, August 7-9, 1864, to Commander Macomb.

5. *Ibid.*, pp. 345, 346.

6. *Ibid.*, p. 369.

7. *Ibid.*, pp. 385, 386.

8. Micro Reel, M-1091, *Halifax Yard*, Confederate Subject File, Record Group 45, N. A.

9. *Ibid.*

10. Charles V. Peery, M. D., Collection, Charleston, S.C. Elliott's letter of August 18, 1864, to Captain Cooke.

11. *Ibid.,* Capt. J. S. Lee's notification of August 20, 1864, directed to Capt. James W. Cooke.

12. ORN, Ser. I, Vol. X, pp. 405, 406. Masters Mate John Woodman's August 28, 1864, reconnaissance report to Commander Macomb.

13. Contract dated August 29, 1864, between Gilbert Elliott & Co., and Confederate Navy Department. Subject File 'AD,' Record Group 45, N. A.

14. ORN, Ser. I, Vol. X, pp. 736, 737.

15. *Ibid.*, p. 738. Master James C. Long's September 5, 1864, letter to Commander Maffitt requesting expedition to Pamlico Sound.

16. *Ibid.,* p. 440.

17. *Ibid.,* p. 457. Admiral Lee's September 15, 1864, report to Secretary Welles of the search for the *Fawn's* captors;

    Frank P. O'Brien, extracts of memoirs in article, *The Story of A Flag.* Under Both Flags, (Philadelphia, Pa.: World Bible House, 1896), p. 260.

18. ORN, Ser. I, Vol. X, p. 739. Cdr. John N. Maffitt's September 9, 1864, orders from Capt. Sidney S. Lee to command blockade runner *Owl;*

    Maffitt papers 1761. Southern Historical Collection, University of North Carolina, Chapel Hill, N.C.

19. ORN, Ser. I, Vol. XV, p. 770. Flag Officer William W. Hunter's September 10, 1864, orders transferring Lt. Commanding Alexander F. Warley, C.S.N., to Plymouth.

20. ORN, Ser. I, Vol. X, p. 741. September 13, 1864, orders of Secretary Mallory transferring Captain Cooke to command Halifax Yard.

21. Micro Reel M-1091, *Halifax Yard*, Confederate Subject File, Record Group 45, National Archives.

22. Smithwick papers PC 257. N. C. Archives & History.

23. ORN, Ser. I, Vol. X, p. 557.

24. *Ibid.,* p. 569. Rear Adm. David D. Porter's dispatch of October 15, 1864 to Commander Macomb concerning Lt. William B. Cushing.

25. *Ibid.,* p. 571. Master's Mate John Woodman's October 17, 1864, report of *Albemarle* reconnaissance to Master Francis Josselyn of the *Commodore Hull.*

26. *Ibid.,* p. 569. Rear Adm. David D. Porter's dispatch of October 16, 1864, to Secretary Welles concerning Cushing's orders to proceed.

27. *Ibid.,* p. 594. Rear Adm. David D. Porter's October 22, 1864, instructions to Commander Macomb on how to capture the *Albemarle.*

NOTES for CHAPTER 15

1. Please note! These nine references support the narrative on pages 249 through 278.

   Clark, *N.C. Regiments, 1861-1865*, Vol. III, p. 707;

   ORN, Ser. I, Vol. X, pp. 611, 612. Lt. William B. Cushing's October 30, 1864, report of *Albemarle's* destruction to Adm. David D. Porter;

   Ibid., pp. 613, 614. Ensign Thomas S. Gay's March 7, 1865, report of his participation to Secretary Welles;

   Ibid., p. 624. Lt. Alexander F. Warley's October 28, 1864, report of *Albemarle's* sinking to Secretary Mallory, also <u>Century Magazine</u>, July, 1888, p. 440;

   Wright-Herring papers 3234-2, Southern Historical Collection, University of North Carolina, Chapel Hill, N.C. Letter from J. U. Edmundson, Confederate soldier at Williamston, N.C. to his lady Miss Bettie, November 5, 1864;

   Francis H. Swan, U.S.N. paymaster, narrative of his participation as crewman on Lt. Cushing's launch during *Albemarle's* destruction. Written circa 1865 after release from Libby Prison. Manuscripts Division, Library of Congress;

   Lt. Cushing's report of October 30, 1864. U.S. Navy Dept. papers, Southern Historical Collection, University of North Carolina, Chapel Hill, N.C.;

   ORN, Ser. I, Vol. X, p. 622. *Valley City* log report October 28, 1864;

   Whitmel Joyner, descendant, Hill family of Scotland Neck, personal collection. Seventeen-year old Acting Masters Mate James C. Hill was hurt by the explosion which caused the hatchway to fall upon him. When later asked why he wasn't at the dance that night, he said "he had taken a few julips too many and didn't feel inclined to shake a foot". New Hill, N.C.

2. ORN, Ser. I, Vol. X, p. 611. Cdr. Macomb's brief October 29, 1864, report to Adm. Porter confirming *Albemarle's* sinking;

   Naval Chronology, IV-127;

   U.S. Navy Department papers, Southern Historical Collection, University of North Carolina, Chapel Hill, N.C.

3. *Naval Chronology,* IV-127.

4. *Journal of a Secesh Lady*, p. 628. N.C. Archives & History.

5. ORN, Ser. I, Vol. X, p. 616. Cdr. Macomb appoints survey board on November 1, 1864;

   Ibid., p. 615. Cdr. Macomb's November 1, 1864, enhanced report to Adm. Porter;

   Ibid., pp. 616, 617. Survey board's damage report submitted on November 1, 1864. Board composed of Chief Engineer H. H. Stewart, 1st. Ass't Engineer Thomas Dukehart, and 2nd. Ass't Engineer William H. Harrison.

6. *Ibid.*, p. 610. Adm. Porter's brief report at 1:25 P.M. on November 1, 1864, to Secretary Welles advising of his promise to Lt. Cushing;

   Ibid., pp. 610, 611. Adm. Porter forwards October 27, 28 reports of Macomb and Cushing.

7. *Ibid.*, p. 615. Cdr. Macomb's expanded November 1, 1864, report to Adm. Porter.

8. *Ibid.*, pp. 12-15. Cdr. Macomb's November 1, 1864, report to Adm. Porter that Plymouth had been retaken.

9. ORN, Ser. II, Vol. II, p. 751. Secretary Mallory's November 1, 1864, periodic shipbuilding activity report.

10. *Journal of a Secesh Lady*, p. 632. N.C. Archives & History.

11. ORN, Ser. I, Vol. XI, pp. 64, 65. Cdr. Macomb's November 6, 1864, questions for Adm. Porter about raising *Albemarle;*

    Ibid., p. 26. Adm. Porter's November 8, 1864, response to Cdr. Macomb about raising *Albemarle.*

12. ORN, Ser. I, Vol. X, p. 617. Cdr. Macomb's November 10, 1864, report to Rear Adm. Porter correcting Brooke rifle bore measurement;

    ORN, Ser. I, Vol XI, pp. 60, 61. Cdr. Macomb's November 11, 1864, letter to Rear Adm. Porter enclosing Capt. Cooke's captured letter and requesting land forces attack the ironclad at Halifax.

13. ORN, Ser. I, Vol. XI, p. 64. Adm. Porter's November 14, 1864, endorsement to Secretary Welles that contract be let to raise the *Albemarle;*

    Ibid., pp. 64, 65. Cdr. Macomb's November 14, 1864, letter to Adm. Porter asking if the sunken schooners blockading the river could be considered prizes.

14. *Journal of a Secesh Lady*, p. 635. N.C. Archives & History.

15. ORN, Ser. I, Vol. XI, p. 79. Adm. Porter's November 20, 1864, repetition of orders previously sent Cdr. Macomb to dismount all Plymouth guns and send captured stores to Hampton Roads.

16. *Ibid.*, p. 93. Cdr. Macomb's November 24, 1864, report to Adm. Porter of escaped prisoners' statement of events upriver.

17. *Ibid.*, pp. 95, 96. Cdr. Macomb's November 25, 1864, hand-carried response to Adm. Porter.

18. *Ibid.*, pp. 103, 104. Adm. Porter's November 28, 1864, request to Maj. Gen. Benjamin F. Butler for an Army expedition to capture Rainbow Bluffs and Halifax.

19. *Ibid.*, p. 162. Lt. Henry N. T. Arnold's December 11, 1864, report as *Otsego's* commander to Cdr. Macomb regarding loss of his ship;

    Ibid., pp. 163, 164. Rear Adm. Porter's December 12, 1864, preliminary report of event at Jamesville, N.C. to Secretary Welles;

    Naval Chronology, IV-144.

20. ORN, Ser. I, Vol. XI, p. 164. Cdr. Macomb's December 13, 1864, report to Adm. Porter from 7 miles above Jamesville, N.C;

    Ibid. Cdr. Macomb's December 13, 1864, second report of the day from 9 miles above Jamesville, N.C.

21. Clark, *N.C. Regiments, 1861-1865*, Vol. I, p. 527;

    Clark, *N.C. Regiments, 1861-1865,* Vol. III, pp. 680, 681, 720-722.

22. ORN, Ser. I, Vol. XI, p. 165. Cdr. Macomb's December 15, 1864, report to Adm. Porter of his requesting the diver surveying the *Albemarle* to examine the *Otsego*, and receipt of Col. Frankle's message he was withdrawing from Fort Branch.

23. *Journal of a Secesh Lady*, p. 646. N.C. Archives & History.

24. ORN, Ser. I, Vol. XI, p. 755. Secretary Mallory's periodic activity report of November 5, 1864.

25. *Journal of a Secesh Lady*, pp. 646, 647. N.C. Archives & History.

26. ORA, Ser. I, Vol. XLVI, Pt. 2, pp. 251, 252. Brig. Gen. Innis N. Palmer's January 24, 1865, letter to Gen. Ulysses S. Grant.

27. *Ibid.*, p. 223. General Grant's January 24, 1865, message to Secretary Welles.

28. *Journal of a Secesh Lady*, p. 659. N.C. Archives & History.

29. *Ibid.*

30. ORN, Ser. I, Vol. XI, p. 722. Secretary Welles' January 31, 1865, letter to General Grant;

    Ibid., p. 721. Secretary Welles' message to Rear Adm. Porter the same day.

31. ORN, Ser. I, Vol. XII, p. 9. Adm. Porter's February 6, 1865, letter to Cdr. Macomb regarding *Albemarle* pumps.

32. *Ibid.*, p. 15. Adm. Porter's February 11, 1865, letter of assurance to General Grant that precautions had been taken.

33. *Ibid.*, p. 22. Cdr. Macomb's report of February 15, 1865, to Adm. Porter concerning progress in raising *Albemarle.*

34. *Journal of a Secesh Lady*, pp. 669, 670. Visit to Edwards Ferry Yard on February 20, 1865;

    Ibid., p. 670. Return visit to Yard on February 21 in company with Capt. & Mrs. Cooke and visiting young people from Scotland Neck. N.C. Archives & History.

35. ORN, Ser. I, Vol. XII, p. 75. Cdr. Macomb's report to Adm. Porter on March 20, 1865, advising the *Albemarle* had been raised.

36. *Ibid.*, p. 87. Cdr. Macomb's March 28, 1865, report to Adm. Porter with news of the Roanoke ironclad obtained from two escaped U.S. Army prisoners.

37. *Journal of a Secesh Lady*, p. 690. N.C. Archives & History.

38. Confederate Naval Museum, Columbus, Georgia.

39. ORN, Ser. I, Vol. XII, p. 108. Lt. Charles L. Franklin's April 9, 1865 report to Lt. Cdr. John C. Febiger of his reconnaissance trip to locate the floating battery;

    Ibid., pp. 107, 108. Lt. Cdr. John C. Febiger's April 9, 1865, report to Cdr. Macomb relating events of Franklin's expedition.

40. *Ibid.*, pp. 109, 110. Lt. Cdr. John C. Febiger's April 10, 1865, report to Cdr. Macomb of the *Albemarle's* departure for Norfolk.

41. New York Herald, April 15, 1865, Courtesy of the New York Public Library, Research Library Section.

42. ORN, Ser. I, Vol. XII, p. 128. Capt. J. M. Berrien, Commanding Naval Station Norfolk, reports on April 27, 1865, to Secretary Welles of the *Albemarle's* arrival in tow the *Ceres.*

43. Engineering survey of *Albemarle*, May 18, 1865. Record Group 21, Case 146, U.S. District Court, Washington, D.C. National Archives.

44. *Dictionary of American Naval Fighting Ships*, Vol. I, 1864. Marshall W. Butt Library, Portsmouth Naval Shipyard Museum, Portsmouth, Va. (Washington, D.C.: Government Printing Office, 1959);

    Donald L. Canney, *The Old Steam Navy: Vol. I, Frigates, Sloops, and Gunboats, 1815-1885*. (Annapolis, Md.: Naval Institute Press, 1990), p. 193.

45. Norfolk Journal, October 9, 10, 11, 1867. Courtesy of Sargeant Memorial Room, Norfolk Public Library.

NOTES for EPILOGUE

1. *Lucy Ann Hill*, unpublished biographical sketch, Hill Family Collection, David B. Gammon, Raleigh, N.C.

2. ORN, Ser. I, Vol. XII, p. 159. Cdr. Macomb's June 19, 1865, report to Commodore William Radford requesting instructions for seized property.

3. *Ibid.*, p. 163. Secretary Welles' June 23, 1865, order to Commodore William Radford expressing disapproval of seizures and ordering them ceased.

4. *Ibid.*, p. 166. Cdr. Macomb's July 8, 1865, statement to Secretary Welles pleading failure to receive orders terminating property seizures.

5. David B. Gammon, Hill Family Collection, Raleigh, N.C;

    Milton Courtright Elliott, *A Century of Elliotts*, 1905, p. 10.

6. Norfolk City Directory, 1867. Sargeant Memorial Room, Norfolk Public Library, Norfolk, Va.;

    Milton Courtright Elliott, *A Century of Elliotts*, 1905, pp. 8, 9.

7. Milton Courtright Elliott, *A Century of Elliotts*, 1905, p. 11;

    Norfolk City Directory, 1869, pp. xix, xx, xxi, xxvi, 28.

8. Norfolk City Directory, 1870, pp. xiv, xx, 23, 46.

9. Norfolk City Directory, 1872, p. 59.

10. Norfolk City Directory, 1872-1873, pp. 69, 319;

    Milton Courtright Elliott, *A Century of Elliotts*, 1905, p. 11.

11. Norfolk City Directory, 1874-1875, pp. 81, 82, 334, 366.

12. Norfolk City Directory, 1875-1876, pp. 93, 382, 410.

13. Missouri Circuit Court, Archives Department, St. Louis,Missouri;

    Gould's St. Louis Directory, 1877, pp. 294, 1151. Missouri Historical Society, St. Louis, Mo.

14. Gould's St. Louis Directory, 1878, pp. 286, 1118. Missouri Historical Society, St. Louis, Mo.

15. Gould's St. Louis Directory, 1879, pp. 316, 588. Missouri Historical Society.

16. Gilbert Elliott, *A Century of Elliotts*, 1908, p. 11;

    St. Louis Directory, 1880, p. 332. Missouri Historical Society.

17. St. Louis Directory, 1881, pp. 174, 350. Missouri Historical Society.

18. St. Louis Directory, 1882, pp. 358, 1386. Missouri Historical Society

19. St. Louis Directory, 1883, pp. 174, 342. Missouri Historical Society.

20. St. Louis Directory, 1884, pp. 348, 1340. Missouri Historical Society.

21. St. Louis Directory, 1886, pp. 363, 1433. Missouri Historical Society.

22. St. Louis Directory, 1887, pp. 364, 1369, 1444. Missouri Historical Society.

23. St. Louis Directory, 1888, pp. 383, 1453, 1527. Elliott's 1888 law firm address was changed to 317 Olive St. The Bradstreet affiliation continued, and his residence address remained unchanged. There was no mention of son Gilbert, who had passed the June Term Missouri Bar exam on the fourth.

24. St. Louis Directory, 1890, pp. 397, 1519. Missouri Historical Society;

    St. Louis Directory, 1892, p. 463.

25. St. Louis Directory, 1893, pp. 344, 436, 1630. Missouri Historical Society.

26. St. Louis Post Dispatch, p. 18, May 12, 1895;

    New York City Directory, 1894-1895, Micro Reel #18, p. 391, and Brooklyn Directory, 1894-1895, Micro Reel #41, p. 377, Local History & Genealogy Division, The New York Public Library;

    Gilbert Elliott Death Certificate # 4906, May 9, 1895, The City of New York, Municipal Archives;

    New York Daily Tribune, p. 7, Col. 4, May 10, 1895;

    Norfolk Virginian, Friday May 10, 1895;

    Erysipelas: Acute, febrile disease with localized skin swelling and inflammation becoming painful, burning and itching. Sometimes fatal. Taber's Cyclopedic Medical Dictionary, (Philadelphia, Pa.: F. A. Davis Company, 1949).

INDEX

Acquia Creek, Va., 27(n.45)
Agencies:
Sharp-Alleman Law & Collection, 284
St. Louis Commission, 283
Alabama Rivers in, 131
Albemarle, CS Ironclad Ram:
History;
Origination & planning (late 1862-early 1863);
Elliott's open-ended Tarboro contract, 62(n.7); specifications for, 62(n.7); he proposes second ironclad, 63(n.11); Edwards Ferry yard site selected, 89(n.3); receives advance payment for second ironclad, 78(n.7); Porter's specifications, 95
Edwards Ferry Yard personnel;
Officers, CSN & civilian;
Cooke, James W., Cdr., CSN, Navy Liaison, 65; Elliott, Gilbert, contractor, 88; Hadley, __, accounts & inventory, Appendix IV; Smith, Peter Evans, Chief of Construction, 90; Smith, William Henry, supplies, 90; Smith, William Ruffin, Jr., Head of Supply Department, 88; Tredwell, Adam, CSN Ass't Paymaster, 93
Blacksmiths;
Ha(o)tten, John, Appendix IV; Smith, Peter Evans, 112(n.61); Thomas, John A., Wilson, E. H., Appendix IV
Carpenters;
Ellison, Jim, Appendix IV; Schafer, William, 226; Hickason, __, 98(n.25); Thrower, John, Appendix IV
Couriers;
Smith, Charles Stuart, first courier, 90(n.7): Smith, Francis Johnston, second courier 90(n.7)

General hands;
Burroughs, W. A.; Daniel, D. R.; Dunn, Franklin; Harrell, John T.; Herrington, Joseph; Hogwood, Carter; Hopkins, A.; Lipscomb, O.; Long, __; Lynch, I. R.; Martin, H. W.; Patrick, C.; Peal, ___; Sikes, Edward; Smith, Henry (black of Peter E. Smith); Smith, Z.; Snell, James F.; Staton, __.; Swain, I. L.; Thrower, Lafayette; Treviathan, I. W.; Williams, N. P.; Winbum, G. L., Appendix IV
Security of;
enemy five miles north, 109,110; no heavy guns, 106, 107(n.48); at Fort Branch, 10th N.C. Regiment, 110(n.57); at Edwards Ferry, 17th N.C. Regiment, 106(n.47), 22nd N.C. Regiment, 97(n.23); at Edwards Ferry, 25th N.C. Regiment, 56th N.C. Regiment, 113(n.64); at Hamilton, 34th N.C. Regiment, 122
Timbermen:
Gibson, Henry & Halsey, Dr. __ & Simmons, Dennis, Appendix IV; Smith, Benjamin Gordon, 90(n.4)
Workmen build (April-October 1863);
keel laid, 92(n.11); second & third payments, 95(n.18); Elliott describes construction, 96(n.20); framing described, 98; of drilling machine, 98(n.25); Lynch promises iron components, 98(n.25); interior construction, 99; forgings from Charlotte Navy Yard, 99(n.26); hull prepared for machinery, 99; engines, boilers sought, 99; casemate construction, 101, 102(n.33); six gunports,